Commentary
on
Galatians

Martin
Luther

Commentary
on
Galatians

Introduction by D. Stuart Briscoe

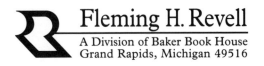

Fleming H. Revell
A Division of Baker Book House
Grand Rapids, Michigan 49516

© 1924, 1988 by Fleming H. Revell
Published by Fleming H. Revell
a division of Baker Book House Company
P.O. Box 6287, Grand Rapids, MI 49516-6287

ISBN 0-8007-1702-3

Printed in the United States of America

Scripture quotations are from the King James Version of the Bible.

Luther's Commentary on Galatians is based on lectures delivered by Martin Luther at the University of Wittenberg in 1531. It was first published in 1535. In 1577 it was translated and published in English, and in 1807 the Middleton edition was published, abridging the earlier text. The following text is modified and abridged from Middleton, drawing chiefly from the Philip S. Watson edition but from other editions and from the original Latin as well. We have attempted to retain the flavor of the original, but at the same time we have rendered the speech into modern English and have deleted references which were applicable more to sixteenth century problems than to contemporary life.

Contents

Introduction

Paul's evangelistic and apostolic ministry resulted in the founding of churches throughout a wide area. It would have been very easy for him, in the pressure of ministry, to have forgotten the churches he had helped to bring into being. But this was not the case; he showed repeatedly that these churches were deeply written on his heart and their concerns were his concerns. In fact, on one occasion he spoke of the "care of all the churches" as being an integral part of his life's burden.

The churches of Galatia were no exception, particularly as they began to experience severe problems after Paul had left the area. His epistle was a response to the situation and even a cursory reading suffices to show that Paul was deeply involved emotionally with what was going on in their midst.

There has been relatively little debate about the Galatian epistle coming from the heart and pen of Paul. In fact, it is known (along with Romans and the Corinthian epistles) as a "capital epistle," which means that its authenticity is so well established that other epistles are judged by it to determine their authenticity. It is, however, ironic that given such certainty about authenticity there is such uncertainty about the exact location of the churches addressed. There is no doubt that the churches were in Galatia but whether that means the Roman province of Galatia or the smaller and more ancient kingdom of Galatia, we are not sure. It is also important to note that this epistle could well have been the earliest of Paul's epistles and, if so, it holds a place of special significance as a statement of the primitive Christian faith and the issues confronting the fledgling church.

The problem Paul addressed was caused by certain people going into the churches he had founded and insisting that those who had trusted Christ now needed to go through the rite of circumcision so that their conversion could be validated. Whether or not they insisted on other aspects of Jewish ceremonial law being adhered to we cannot be sure, but Paul's response was swift and to the point. In effect, he told the Galatians that the extent to which anything needed to be added to the gospel of Christ to make it effective for salvation determined the extent to which Christ, Himself, was less than adequate for salvation. To suggest this to Paul was totally unacceptable and, in fact, he denounced this suggestion and its propagators as heresy and heretics respectively. Such was his resistance to their ideas that he used some of his most vehement and powerful language to get his point across. The epistle is also noteworthy in that it contains autobiographical material not available anywhere else detailing the early years of the apostle's Christian life. The people who were denigrating his message were using the oldest tricks in the book by attacking Paul himself, and his credentials as preacher and apostle. Paul's rebuttal of these slanderous charges was as challenging to them as it is informative to us.

The European Reformers of the sixteenth century saw clear similarities between the heretical attacks that Paul rebuffed and the specific theological battles they had been called upon to fight. In Paul's case, he was reminding the Galatians that they were justified freely by grace and that the flesh was incapable of producing meritorious works for salvation. The Reformers were speaking out against the accretion of rites and rituals in their church which were leading many to believe that their salvation was directly related to the way in which they adhered to the demanding dogma of the church, particularly in areas where the church spoke loudly on matters on which the Scriptures maintained a discreet silence.

Martin Luther was a sensitive youth who, because of the teaching to which he was exposed, developed a deep reverence for God's holiness and a correspondingly deep dismay for his own sinfulness. He was introduced at an early age to the terrors of hell and the possibilities of paradise, but the ways of gaining the one and escaping the other to which he was exposed led him from depression to despair. Things came to a head when he narrowly escaped death in a thunder and lightning storm and, in thankfulness to be alive, he became a monk of the Augustinian order. He soon discovered that in the monastery there were as many variations on the theme of devotion as there were over the wall in the outside world, but such was his intensity that he spared himself not at all in all manner of physical and ritualistic deprivations, the better to deal with his sinfulness, harness his desires, and find peace with God. Luther's intense introspection led him to his confessor, who admitted that he did not know how to help him but made a suggestion which was to change history. He directed Luther away from introspection and into Bible study and teaching. The rest, as they say, is history.

Some people may be more familiar with Luther the reformer than Luther the theologian and expositor. Without in any way detracting from the magnitude of his accomplishments in other fields of endeavor, it should be pointed out that the stimulus for his activities was found in the Scriptures, and that his love for and attention to them was in large part the secret of his passion and his accomplishments. Many modern would-be reformers would do well to remember this lest they be tempted in their revolutionary enthusiasm to overthrow a perceived evil only to replace it with another variety of human error. Luther was deeply concerned to impart the truth of the Scriptures to the people and then to lead them in the practical, political, and personal applications of the same.

His Commentary on Galatians provides us with an excellent insight into the timeless teachings of God's Word as they unequivocally state the principle of justification by faith, but it also demonstrates to us that the concerns of a particular era and environment can be addressed through the careful exegesis and exposition of the Scriptures. Luther's concern was with the errors which he perceived in his own church and the necessity for change and reform if God's will for His people in the community of believers was ever to be realized. He found it necessary to challenge the Pope, belabor the Papists and Anabaptists and speak often of the demons and devils which he saw as the emissaries of the archenemy, Satan. Some of this may sound strange and even, on occasion, offensive to modern ears but this should not deter us in our reading of this commentary. In an age that prizes tolerance there is always the danger of lapsing into mediocrity and in a church where confusion abounds about what it means to be soldier of Christ, the trenchant and militant tones of a Luther can serve to rouse us to the realities of defending the faith and propagating the truth. It has been suggested that the work of the minister is to comfort the afflicted and afflict the comfortable. Luther manages to do both in this Commentary and, accordingly, has something for everybody.

D. STUART BRISCOE

Luther's Preface

I myself can hardly believe I was as verbose when I lectured on St. Paul's Epistle to the Galatians, as this volume indicates. But since I recognize as mine all the thoughts which the brethren have taken such pains to set down in it, I am forced to admit that I said as much and perhaps even more. For the one doctrine which I have supremely at heart is that of faith in Christ, from whom, through whom and unto whom all my theological thinking flows back and forth day and night. Not that I find I have grasped anything of a wisdom so high, so broad and so profound, beyond a few meager rudiments and fragments; and I am ashamed that my poor, uninspired comments on so great an apostle and chosen instrument of God should be published. Yet I am compelled to forget my shame and be quite shameless in view of the horrible profanation and abomination which have always raged in the Church of God, and still rage today, against this one solid rock which we call the doctrine of justification. I mean the doctrine that we are redeemed from sin, death and the devil, and made partakers of eternal life, not by ourselves (and certainly not by our works, which are less than ourselves), but by the help of another, the only begotten Son of God, Jesus Christ.

This rock was shaken by Satan in Paradise, when he persuaded our first parents that they might by their own wisdom and power become like God, abandoning faith in God, who had given them life and promised its continuance. Shortly afterwards, that liar and murderer incited a brother to murder his brother, for no other reason than that the latter, a godly man, had offered by faith a more excellent sacrifice, while he himself, being ungodly, had offered his own works without faith and had not pleased God. After this there followed a ceaseless and intolerable persecution of this same faith by Satan through the sons of Cain, until God was compelled to purge the world and defend Noah, the preacher of righteousness, by means of the Flood. Thereafter the whole world acted like a madman against this faith, inventing innumerable idols and religions with which everyone went his own way, hoping to placate a god or goddess, gods or goddesses, by his own works; that is, hoping without the aid of Christ and by his own works to redeem himself from evils and sins.

Since, therefore, Cain kills Abel continually and the abomination of Satan now reigns supreme, it is necessary to pay the very closest heed to this doctrine, and to oppose Satan with it, whether we are eloquent or not, learned or not. Hence I am willing to do my duty and let this extremely verbose commentary be published in order to stir up my brethren in Christ against the wiles and malice of Satan, who in these last days has become so infuriated at the recovery of the sound knowledge of Christ, that it now seems as if the demons themselves are possessed by worse demons and raving with a more than demonic madness—which strongly suggests that the Enemy of truth and life feels the Day of Judgment to be imminent— a dreadful day of destruction for him, but a lovely day of redemption and the end of his tyranny for us. For he has reason to be alarmed, when all his members and his powers are so assailed, just as a thief or adulterer is alarmed when the dawn breaks upon him and he is caught in his act.

But these thoughts of mine on this epistle are being published not so much against these people as for our people, who will either thank me for my pains or pardon my weakness and temerity. I have certainly no wish that the impious should approve of them, but rather that they and their god should be irritated by them; for I produced them (with much toil) only for such as those to whom St. Paul himself wrote his epistle—the troubled, afflicted and tempted (who alone understand these things), wretched Galatians in the faith.

Let him who can, then, hold fast to this one article; and let the rest, who make shipwreck, be driven by the wind and waves until they either return to the ship or swim to the shore.

[*The foregoing formed the preface to the first edition (1535). In the second edition (1538) and subsequent editions, the following paragraphs were added after "swim to the shore."*]

One generation passes, another comes. If one heresy dies, another springs up, for the devil neither slumbers nor sleeps. I myself—although I am nothing—who have now been in the ministry of Christ for twenty years, can testify that I have been attacked by more than twenty sects, of which some have entirely perished, while others still show signs of life, like parts of dismembered insects.

Ministers of the Word, therefore, if they would be counted faithful and prudent on the Day of Christ, ought to be very sure that St. Paul did not speak empty words or prophesy of a thing of nought, when he said: "There must be heresies among you, that they which are approved may be made manifest among you." Let the minister of Christ know, I say, that as long as he preaches Christ purely, there will be no lack of perverse persons, even among our own people, who will make it their business to cause trouble in the Church. And he may comfort himself with the thought that there is no peace between Christ and Belial, or between the Seed of the woman and the seed of the Serpent. Indeed, he may rejoice in the trouble he is caused by sects and the constant succession of seditious spirits. For this is our glory, the testimony of our conscience that we are found standing and fighting on the side of the Seed of the woman against the seed of the Serpent. Let him bite our heel and never cease biting; we for our part will not cease to crush his head through Christ, the first to crush it, who is blessed forever. Amen.

Declaration

I have taken in hand, in the name of the Lord, once again to expound this Epistle of St. Paul to the Galatians: not because I desire to teach new things, or such as you have not heard before, but because we have to fear, as the greatest and nearest danger, that Satan take from us the pure doctrine of faith and bring into the Church again the doctrine of works and men's traditions.

The devil, our adversary, who continually seeks to devour us, is not dead; likewise our flesh and old man is yet alive. Besides this, all kinds of temptations vex and oppress us on every side. So this doctrine can never be taught, urged, and repeated enough. If this doctrine is lost, then is also the whole knowledge of truth, life and salvation lost. If this doctrine flourish, then all good things flourish.

The Argument of the Epistle to the Galatians

First of all, we speak of the argument of this epistle: in it Paul is seeking to establish the doctrine of faith, grace, forgiveness of sins, or Christian righteousness in order that we may know the difference between Christian righteousness and all other kinds of righteousness. There are many sorts of righteousness. There is a civil or political righteousness, which kings, princes of the world, magistrates and lawyers deal with. There is also a ceremonial righteousness, which the traditions of men teach. Besides these, there is another righteousness, called the righteousness of the law, or the Ten Commandments.

Above all these, there is yet another righteousness: the righteousness of faith or Christian righteousness, which we must diligently discern from the others. The others are quite contrary to this righteousness, both because they flow out of the laws of kings and rulers, religious traditions, and the commandments of God; and because they consist in our works, and may be wrought by us either by our natural strength, or else by the gift of God. These kinds of righteousness are also the gift of God, like all other good things which we enjoy.

But the most excellent righteousness of faith, which God through Christ, without any works, imputes to us, is neither political, nor ceremonial, nor the righteousness of God's law, nor consists of works, but is contrary to these; that is to say, it is a mere passive righteousness, as the others are active. For in the righteousness of faith, we work nothing, we render nothing unto God, but we only receive, and suffer another to work in us, that is to say, God. This is a righteousness hidden in a mystery, which the world does not know. Indeed, Christians themselves do not thoroughly understand it, and can hardly take hold of it in their temptations. Therefore it must be diligently taught, and continually practiced.

The troubled conscience, in view of God's judgment, has no remedy against desperation and eternal death, unless it takes hold of the forgiveness of sins by grace, freely offered in Christ Jesus, which if it can apprehend, it may then be at rest. Then it can boldly say: I seek not active or working righteousness, for if I had it, I could not trust it, neither dare I set it against the judgment of God. Then I abandon myself from all active righteousness, both of my own and of God's law, and embrace only that passive righteousness, which is the righteousness of grace, mercy, and forgiveness of sins. I rest only upon that righteousness, which is the righteousness of Christ and of the Holy Ghost. The highest wisdom of Christians is not to know the law and to be ignorant of works, especially when the conscience is wrestling with God. But among those who are not God's people, the greatest wisdom is to know the law and the active righteousness. Unless the Christian is ignorant of the law and is assuredly persuaded in his heart that there is now no law, nor wrath of

God, but only grace and mercy for Christ's sake, he cannot be saved; for by the law comes the knowledge of sin. Contrariwise, works and the keeping of the law is strictly required in the world, as if there were no promise, or grace.

A wise and faithful disposer of the Word of God must so moderate the law that it may be kept within its bounds. He that teaches that men are justified before God by the observation of the law, passes the bounds of the law, and confounds these two kinds of righteousness, active and passive. Contrariwise, he that sets forth the law and works to the old man, and the promise and forgiveness of sins and God's mercy to the new man, divides the Word well. For the flesh or the old man must be coupled with the law and works; the spirit or the new man must be joined with the promise of God and His mercy.

When I see a man oppressed with the law, terrified with sin, and thirsting for comfort, it is time that I remove out of his sight the law and active righteousness, and set before him, by the gospel, the Christian or passive righteousness, which offers the promise made in Christ, who came for the afflicted and sinners.

We teach the difference between these two kinds of righteousness, active and passive, to the end that manners and faith, works and grace, policy and religion, should not be confounded, or taken the one for the other. Both are necessary; but each must be kept within its bounds: Christian righteousness pertains to the new man, and the righteousness of the law pertains to the old man, which is born of flesh and blood. Upon this old man, as upon an ass, there must be laid a burden that may press him down, and he must not enjoy the freedom of the spirit of grace, except he first put upon him the new man, by faith in Christ. Then may he enjoy the kingdom and inestimable gift of grace. This I say, so that no man should think we reject or forbid good works.

We imagine two worlds, the one heavenly, the other earthly. In these we place these two kinds of righteousness, the one far separate from the other. The righteousness of the law is earthly and deals with earthly things. But Christian righteousness is heavenly, which we have not of ourselves, but receive from heaven; we work not for it, but by grace it is wrought in us, and is apprehended by faith.

Do we then do nothing? Do we do nothing at all for the obtaining of this righteousness? I answer, Nothing at all. For this is perfect righteousness, to do nothing, to hear nothing, to know nothing of the law, or of works, but to know and believe this only, that Christ is gone to the Father, and is not now seen; that He sits in heaven at the right hand of His Father, not as judge, but made unto us of God, wisdom, righteousness, holiness and redemption—briefly, that He is our high priest entreating for us, and reigning over us, and in us, by grace. In this heavenly righteousness sin can have no place, for there is no law; and where no law is, there can be no transgression (Romans 4:15). Seeing then that sin has here no place, there can be no anguish of conscience, no fear, no heaviness. Therefore John says (1 John 5:18): "He that is born of God cannot sin."

But if there is any fear, or grief of conscience, it is a token that this righteousness is withdrawn, that grace is hidden, and that Christ is darkened and out of sight. But where Christ is truly seen, there must be full and perfect joy in the Lord, with peace of conscience, which thinks this way: Although I am a sinner by the law and under condemnation of the law, yet I despair not, yet I die not, because Christ lives, who is both my righteousness and my everlasting life. In that righteousness and life I have no sin, no fear, no sting of conscience, no care of death. I am indeed a sinner as touching this present life, and the righteousness thereof, as a child of Adam. But I have another righteousness and life, above this life, which is Christ the Son of God, who knows no sin, no death, but is righteousness and life eternal; by whom this my body, being dead and brought to dust, shall be raised up again, and delivered from the bondage of the law and sin, and shall be sanctified together with my spirit.

So both these continue while we live here. The flesh is accused, exercised with temptations, oppressed with heaviness and sorrow, bruised by the active righteousness of the law; but the spirit reigns, rejoices, and is saved by this passive and Christian righteousness, because it knows that it has a Lord in Heaven, at the right hand of His Father, who has abolished the law, sin, death, and has trodden under His feet all evils, led them captive, and triumphed over them in Himself (Colossians 2:15).

St. Paul, in this epistle, goes about diligently to instruct us, to comfort us, to hold us in the perfect knowledge of this most Christian and excellent righteousness. For if the article of justification is lost, then all true Christian doctrine is lost. He who strays from Christian righteousness falls into the righteousness of the law; that is, when he loses Christ, he falls into the confidence of his own works. Therefore we also earnestly set forth, and so often repeat the doctrine of ''faith,'' or Christian righteousness, that by this means it may be kept in continual exercise, and may be plainly discerned from the active righteousness of the law.

Let us diligently learn to judge between these two kinds of righteousness. We have said before that, in a Christian, the law ought not to pass its bounds, but ought to have dominion only over the flesh, which is in subjection to it, and remains under it. But if it creeps into the conscience, play the cunning logician, and make the true division. Say: ''O law, you would climb up into the kingdom of my conscience, and there reprove it of sin, and take from me the joy of my heart, which I have by faith in Christ, and drive me to desperation that I may be without hope, and utterly perish. Keep within your bounds, and exercise your power upon the flesh: for by the gospel I am called to the partaking of righteousness and everlasting life.''

When I have Christian righteousness reigning in my heart, I descend from heaven as the rain makes fruitful the earth; that is to say, I do good works, how and wheresoever the occasion arises. If I am a minister of the Word, I preach, I comfort the brokenhearted, I administer the sacraments. If I am a householder, I govern my house and family well, and in the fear of God. If I am a servant, I do my master's business faithfully.

To conclude, whoever is assuredly persuaded that Christ alone is his righteousness, does not only cheerfully and gladly work well in his vocation, but also submits himself through love to the rulers and to their laws, yea, though they be severe, and, if necessity should require, to all manner of burdens, and to all dangers of the present life, because he knows that this is the will of God, and that this obedience pleases Him.

Commentary
on
Galatians

1

So Soon Removed

Galatians 1:1–10

1—Paul, an apostle (not of men, neither by man, but by Jesus Christ, and God the Father, who raised him from the dead).

Now that we have declared the argument of this Epistle to the Galatians, we need to show the occasion St. Paul wrote it. He had planted among the Gentiles the pure doctrine of the gospel, but after his departure, there crept in certain false teachers who overthrew all that he had planted and taught among them. For the devil must furiously impugn this doctrine with all his force; he will not rest as long as any spark of it remains. So as we preach the gospel we can expect to suffer of the world, the devil and his ministers all the mischief that they can work against us.

For the gospel teaches free remission of sins through Christ and that is a far higher matter than the wisdom, righteousness and religion of this world. The gospel leaves those matters to be as they are and commends them as the good creatures of God.

The world, however, prefers these matters; indeed it honors these creatures before the Creator, and in addition teaches that by them it can put away sin, be delivered from death, and be deserving of everlasting life. This is condemned by the gospel.

On the other hand, the world cannot allow those things to be condemned; so it charges that the gospel is a seditious doctrine that overthrows commonwealths, countries, dominions, kingdoms and empires and offends both God and the emperor. It also charges that the gospel abolishes laws, corrupts good manners and sets all men at liberty to do what they want. So, with great zeal and claiming high service to God, it persecutes this doctrine and abhors its teachers and professors, calling it the greatest plague that can be in the whole earth.

Yet, by the preaching of the gospel, the devil is overthrown, his kingdom is destroyed, and the law, sin and death are wrested out of his hand. Briefly, his prisoners are translated out of the kingdom of darkness into the kingdom of light and liberty.

Would you expect the devil to allow this? Wouldn't you expect the father of lies to employ all his force and subtle tactics to darken, to corrupt and to root out this doctrine of salvation and everlasting life? Indeed, Paul complains in this and all his epistles that even in his time the devil showed himself a cunning workman.

So Paul wrote this epistle because after his departure from Galatia false teachers had destroyed those things which he had built. Among these false apostles were men of great esteem and authority who bragged that they were of the holy and chosen stock of the Jews, that they were Israelites of the seed of Abraham, that they had the promises of the fathers and that they were not only the ministers of Christ but also scholars of the Apostles, whom they knew well. When men with such authority come into any city, the people soon come to admire them. And when they come under a cloak of godliness and religion, they deceive not only the simple but also the learned. Yes, they deceive even those who seem to be confirmed in the faith.

These false teachers also impugned the authority of Paul, saying, "Why do you esteem Paul? Why do you revere him? He was, after all, the last to be converted to Christ. On the other hand, we are the disciples of the Apostles; we have seen Christ working miracles and heard Him preach. Paul came after us and is inferior to us. Paul is only one man, who does not know the Apostles well and has not seen Christ. In fact, he persecuted the Church for a long time. Do you think that God would speak to Paul and not to us?"

Against this bragging and boasting, Paul sets forth his apostolic authority and defends his ministry. To abate their pharisaical pride and shameless boldness, he mentions his history in Antioch when he withstood the Apostle Peter. Besides this, he was bold to accuse and reprove Peter himself, the chief of the Apostles, who had seen Christ, and had been most familiarly conversant with Him. "I am an Apostle," Paul says, "and I was not afraid to chide the very pillar of all the rest of the Apostles."

So in the first two chapters of this epistle, Paul does nothing else but set out his calling, his office and his gospel, affirming that it was not of men, and that he had not received it by man, but by the revelation of Jesus Christ. He also declares that if he or an angel from heaven should bring any other gospel than that which he had preached, he should be accursed.

This is not boasting, but rather it indicates a certainty of his calling. Every minister of God's Word should be sure of his calling. Every minister should be able to preach the gospel as one who is called and sent, even as an ambassador of the king glories and takes pride not that he speaks as a private person, but that he speaks as the king's ambassador. As the king's ambassador, he is honored and set in a place he would not occupy as a private person. Thus, to glory is not vain, because he glories not in himself but in the king who sent him and whose authority he desires to be honored and magnified.

So, when Paul commends his calling, he seeks not his own praise, but with a necessary and a holy pride he magnifies his ministry. And this he does of necessity to maintain his authority that the people in hearing this might be more attentive and willing to give ear to him. For they hear not only Paul, but in Paul Christ Himself and God the Father, sending him out with the message. This manner of boasting, then, is necessary and pertains not to the glory of Paul, but to the glory of God, for by it, the name, the grace and the mercy of God are made known to the world.

Paul says, "My calling is not of men nor by man but by Jesus Christ and God the Father." When he says, "not of men," I take it to refer to those who run and speak for themselves. Neither God nor man has called them; they have called themselves. But when he says, "neither by man," I understand him to mean those who have a divine calling but yet by man as the means. God calls in two ways: by means and without means. Today He calls us to the ministry of His Word not immediately by Himself, but by other means; that is to say, by man. But the Apostles were called immediately by Christ Himself, as the prophets of the Old Testament were called by God Himself. Afterwards, the Apostles called their disciples, as Paul called Timothy and Titus. These men called bishops and the bishops their successors. This is a mediated calling, since it is done by man, even though it may be of God.

So Paul is saying, "As for me, my calling is like in all points the calling of the Apostles, and I am indeed an Apostle." This is the first assault that Paul makes against the false prophets, who ran when no man sent them. Therefore, calling is not to be despised; it is not enough for a man to have the Word and pure doctrine, but he must also be assured of his calling. He who enters without this assurance enters to no other purpose but to kill and destroy. God never prospers the labor of those who are not called. Though they teach some good and profitable matters, they edify not.

This is a comfort to us who are in the ministry of the Word that we have an office which is heavenly and holy, and in that office we will triumph over the gates of hell.

In times past when I was a young theologian, I thought Paul did unwisely in glorying so often in his calling. But I did not understand his purpose, for I knew not that the ministry of God's Word was so weighty a matter. I knew nothing of the doctrine of faith and a true conscience, for what I heard was no certainty, but the speculation and sophistry of the schoolmen, and therefore no man was able to understand the dignity and power of this holy and spiritual boasting. For by this boasting, we seek not estimation of the world, or praise of men, or money, or pleasure, or favor of the world; but so that people may know us to be in a divine calling, and in the work of God, therefore we vaunt and boast of it.

1b—And by God the Father, who raised him from the dead.

Paul here bursts out in the very title to utter what he has in his heart. His intent in this epistle is to treat of the righteousness that comes by faith and to defend the same; again, to beat down the law, and the righteousness that comes by works. This flame in his heart cannot be hid nor suffer him to hold his tongue. Therefore he thought it not enough to say that he was "an apostle sent by Jesus Christ," but also added, "and by God the Father, who raised him from the dead."

These words may seem unnecessary, but Paul speaking out of the abundance of his heart desires to set forth at the very beginning "the unsearchable riches of Christ," and to proclaim the righteousness of God which is called the resurrection of the dead—Christ who lives, and is risen, speaks out of him, and moves him thus to speak. Christ who was raised up by God the Father from the dead; by whom alone we are made righteous, and by whom also we shall be raised up at the last day from death to everlasting life.

But they who go about to overthrow the righteousness of Christ do resist the Father and the Son, and the work of both. So he mentions at once the resurrection of Christ, "who rose for our justification" to make us righteous; and in so doing He has overcome the law, sin, death, hell, and all evils. This victory He has given to us: "Thanks be to God, who has given us the victory by our Lord Jesus Christ."

2a—And all the brethren which are with me.

This he adds, as if to say: "Although it is enough that I am sent by divine calling, yet lest I should be alone, I name all the brethren who are not apostles, but fellow-soldiers; they write the epistle as well as I, and bear witness with me that my doctrine is true and godly."

2b—To the churches of Galatia.

Paul had preached the gospel throughout Galatia, and although he had not wholly converted it to Christ, yet he had started many churches. Into these churches the false apostles had crept. They brought their corrupt doctrine to no places of peril, nor to where the gospel was not preached before, as Paul and the other Apostles did, but they came to Galatia where the foundation of the gospel was already laid, and into Asia, Corinth, and other places where good men were suffering all things quietly. There might the enemies of Christ's Cross live in security, and without persecution.

And here we may learn how, to this day, it is the lot of godly ministers to suffer such contradiction of the true doctrine by fantastical spirits. This grieves godly ministers more than the persecution of tyrants. Therefore let him not be a minister of the gospel, who is not content to be thus condemned or despised, or is loath to bear this reproach. But this is our comfort and glory, that, being called of God, we have a promise of everlasting life, and look for that reward which "eye hath not seen, nor ear heard, neither has entered into the heart of man" (1 Corinthians 2:9). "For when the chief Shepherd shall appear, ye shall receive a crown of glory" (1 Peter 5:4); who here also in this world will not suffer us to perish for hunger.

Jerome asked a great question about this verse: "Why did Paul call those churches which were no churches?"

I answer that Paul called them the Churches of Galatia, by putting a part for the whole, which is a common thing in the Scriptures. To the Corinthians he wrote, "I thank my God always on your behalf, for the grace of God which is given you by Jesus Christ; That you are in all utterance enriched by him, and in all knowledge" (1 Corinthians 1:4, 5). And yet many of them were misled by false apostles, and believed not in the resurrection of the dead (1 Corinthians 15:12).

Although the Galatians were fallen away from the true doctrine, yet did baptism, the Word, and the name of Christ remain among them. There were also some good men that had not revolted, who had a right opinion of the Word, and sacraments, and used them well.

3—Grace be to you and peace from God the Father, and from our Lord Jesus Christ.

This greeting of the Apostle is strange unto the world, and was never heard of prior to the preaching of the gospel. These two words, *grace* and *peace,* comprehend in them whatever belongs to Christianity. Grace releases sin, and peace makes the conscience quiet. The two fiends that torment us are sin and conscience. But Christ has vanquished these two monsters, and trodden them underfoot, both in this world, and in that which is to come. This the world does not know, and therefore can teach no certainty of the overcoming of sin, conscience, and death. Only Christians have this kind of doctrine and are exercised and armed with it to get victory against sin, despair, and everlasting death. It is a kind of doctrine neither proceeding from free will, nor invented by the reason or wisdom of man, but given from above.

Moreover, these two words, *grace* and *peace,* contain in them the whole sum of Christianity. Grace contains the remission of sins; peace a quiet and joyful conscience. Peace of conscience can never be had, unless sin be first forgiven. But sin is not forgiven by the fulfilling of the law; for no man is able to satisfy the law. The law shows sin, accuses and terrifies the conscience, declares the wrath of God, and drives to desperation. Much less is sin taken away by the works and inventions of men, but sin is rather increased by works. So there is no means to take away sin, but grace alone. Therefore, Paul in all the greetings of his epistles sets grace and peace against sin and an evil conscience.

This thing must be diligently marked. The words are easy. But in temptation, it is the hardest thing that can be, to be certainly persuaded in our hearts, that by grace alone (all other means either in heaven or in earth set apart) we have remission of sins, and peace with God. The world understands not this doctrine; and therefore it neither will nor can abide it, but condemns it as heretical and wicked. It boasts of free will, of the light of reason, of the powers and qualities of nature, and of good works, as means whereby it can discern and attain grace and peace, that is to say, forgiveness of sins and a quiet conscience. But it is impossible that the conscience should be quiet and joyful, unless it have peace through grace, that is to say, through the forgiveness of sins promised in Christ.

The Apostle wishes for the Galatians grace and peace, not from emperors or kings, for these do commonly persecute the godly, nor from the world ("for in the world," said Christ, "you shall have tribulation");

but from God the Father and from our Lord Jesus Christ. So Christ said: "My peace I give unto you, not as the world gives." The peace of the world grants nothing but the peace of our goods and bodies. But in affliction, and in the hour of death, the grace and favor of the world cannot help us. The peace of God is not given to the world, because the world never longs after it, but to them that believe. And this comes to pass by no other means than by the grace of God.

Why does the Apostle add in the salutation, "And from our Lord Jesus Christ"? Was it not enough to say, "from God the Father"? It is a rule and principle in the Scriptures, diligently to be marked, that we must abstain from the curious searching of God's majesty, which is intolerable to man's body, and much more to the mind: "No man (saith the Lord) shall see me and live" (Exodus 33:20). Those who trust in their own merits regard not this rule, and therefore remove Christ the Mediator out of their sight. They speak only of God, and before Him only they pray, and do all that they do. They who know not justification take away Christ the mercy seat and seek to comprehend God in His majesty by the judgment of reason, and pacify Him with their own works.

But true Christian divinity commands us not to search out the nature of God, but to know His will set out to us in Christ, whom He willed to take upon Him flesh, to be born, and to die for our sins; and that this should be preached among all nations. "For after that in the wisdom of God the world by wisdom knew not God, it pleased God by the foolishness of preaching to save them that believe" (1 Corinthians 1:21). When your conscience stands in conflict, wrestling against the law, sin, and death in the presence of God, there is nothing more dangerous than to wander with curious speculations in heaven, and there to search out God in His incomprehensible power, wisdom, and majesty, how He created the world, and how He governs it.

If you seek thus to comprehend God, and would pacify Him without Christ the Mediator, making your works a means between Him and yourself, you will fall into despair and lose God all together. As God is in His own nature unmeasurable, incomprehensible, and infinite, so He is to man's nature intolerable.

So seek God as Paul teaches: "We preach Christ crucified, unto the Jews a stumbling block, and unto the Greeks foolishness; but unto them which are called, both Jews and Greeks, Christ the power of God, and the wisdom of God" (1 Corinthians 1:23, 24). For to this end Christ came down, was born, was conversant with men, suffered, was crucified, and died, that by all means He might set forth Himself plainly before our eyes, and fasten the eyes of our hearts upon Himself, that He might thereby keep us from climbing up into heaven and from the curious searching of the Divine Majesty.

Whenever you think about justification, and dispute with yourself how God is to be found, remember that Christ Himself said: "I am the way, the truth, and the life, no man cometh unto the Father but by me" (John 14:6). Therefore besides the way of Christ, you shall find no way to the Father. When any of us shall have to wrestle with the law, sin, and death, and all other evils, we must look upon no other God, but only this God incarnate and clothed with man's nature.

When you look at the man Jesus Christ, you perceive the love, goodness and sweetness of God, and you also see His wisdom, power, and majesty, according to that saying of Paul, "In Christ are hid all the treasures of wisdom and knowledge" (Colossians 2:3), and again, "For in Him dwelleth all the fullness of the Godhead bodily" (Colossians 2:9). The world is ignorant of this, and therefore it searches out the will of God, setting aside the promise in Christ to its destruction. "For no man knoweth the Father, save the Son, and he to whomsoever the Son will reveal Him" (Matthew 11:27).

This, then, is the cause why Paul so often couples Jesus Christ with God the Father, even to teach us what true Christian religion is, which begins not at the highest, as other religions do, but at the lowest. It will have us climb up by Jacob's ladder, whereupon God Himself leans, whose feet touch the very earth, hard by the head of Jacob (Genesis 28:12). Wherefore, whenever you are occupied in the matter of your salvation, set aside all curious speculations of God's unsearchable majesty, all cogitations of works, of traditions, of philosophy, and of God's law too, and run straight to the manger and embrace the Virgin's babe. Then behold Him born, growing in wisdom and stature, conversant among men, teaching, dying, risen, ascending up "far above all heavens," and having power above all things. By this means you shall be able to shake off all terrors and errors, as the sun drives away the clouds. And this sight and contemplation will keep you in the right way, that you may follow where Christ is gone. Therefore Paul, in wishing grace and peace not only from God the Father, but also from Jesus Christ, teaches first, that we should abstain from curious searching of the Divine Majesty and to hear Christ, who is in the bosom of the Father, and utters to us His will.

Christ Is God by Nature

The other thing that Paul teaches here is that Christ is very God. Such verses as this on the godhead of Christ, are to be gathered together and marked diligently, not only against the heretics, but also for the confirmation of our faith; for Satan will not fail to impugn in us all the articles of our faith. He is a most deadly enemy to faith, because he knows that it is the victory which overcomes the world (1 John 5:4).

Christ is very God. This is manifestly declared in that Paul attributes the same things equally to Him which he does to the Father, namely, the giving of grace, the forgiveness of sins, peace of conscience, life, and victory over sin, death, the devil and hell. It would be sacrilege to do this except Christ were very God, according to that saying: "My glory will I not give unto another" (Isaiah 42:8). Again: no man gives to others which he himself has not. But seeing Christ gives grace, peace and the Holy Ghost, delivers from the power of the devil, from sin and death, it is certain that He has an infinite and divine power, equal in all points to the power of the Father.

Neither does Christ give grace and peace as the Apostles gave, but He gives as the Author and Creator. The Father creates and gives life, grace, peace, and all other good things. The same things also the Son creates and gives. Now, to give grace, peace, everlasting life, to forgive sins, to make righteous, to quicken, to deliver from death and the devil, are not the works of any creature, but of the Divine Majesty alone. The angels can neither create nor give these things; therefore these works pertain only to the glory of the sovereign Majesty, the Maker of all things. Seeing Paul attributes the same power of creating and giving all these things unto Christ equally with the Father, it must follow that Christ is verily and naturally God.

Many such arguments are in John, where it is proved and concluded by the works which are attributed to the Son as well as to the Father that the divinity of the Father and of the Son is all one. Therefore the gifts which we receive of the Father, and which we receive of the Son, are all one. Otherwise, Paul would have spoken after this manner: Grace from God the Father, and peace from our Lord Jesus Christ. But in knitting them both together, he attributes them equally to the Son as to the Father.

4a—Who gave himself for our sins.

Paul has nothing in his mouth but Christ; and therefore in every word there is a fervency of spirit and life. He does not say that Christ has received our works from our hands, nor that He received the sacrifices of Moses' law. No, Paul says that Christ "has given." What? Not gold, nor silver, nor beasts, nor paschal lambs, nor an angel, but "Himself." For what? Not for a crown, not for a kingdom, not for our holiness or righteousness, but "for our sins." These words are very thunderclaps from heaven, as is also this sentence of John: "Behold the Lamb of God, who takes away the sin of the world."

But how may we obtain remission of our sins? Paul answers that the man Jesus Christ, the Son of God, has given Himself for them. Our sins are taken away by none other means than by the Son of God delivered unto death. With such gunshot and such artillery must all other notions be destroyed, and all the religions of the heathen, all works, all merits and superstitious ceremonies. For if our sins may be taken away by our own works, merits and satisfactions, what needed the Son of God to be given for them? But seeing He was given for them, it follows that we cannot put them away by our own works.

Again, by this verse it is declared that our sins are so great, so infinite and invincible, that it is impossible for the whole world to satisfy for one of them. And surely the greatness of the ransom (namely, Christ the Son of God, who gave Himself for our sins) declares sufficiently that we can neither satisfy for sin nor have dominion over it. The force and power of sin is set forth and amplified exceedingly by these words: "Who gave Himself for our sins." Therefore here is to be marked the infinite greatness of the price bestowed for it, and then it will appear evident that the power of it is so great, that by no means it could be put away, but that the Son of God must be given for it. He that considers these things well, understands that this one word "sin" comprehends God's everlasting wrath and the whole kingdom of Satan, and that it is a thing more horrible than can be expressed; this ought to move us and make us afraid indeed. But we are careless, yea, we make light of sin; although it brings with it the sting and remorse of conscience, yet we think it not to be of such weight and force, but that by some little work or merit we may put it away.

This verse therefore witnesses that all men are servants and bondslaves to sin, and are "sold under sin" (Romans 7:14); and again that sin is a most cruel and mighty tyrant over all men, and cannot be vanquished by the power of any creatures, whether they be angels or men, but only by the sovereign and infinite power of Jesus Christ.

Furthermore, this verse sets out to the consciences of all men who are terrified with the greatness of their sins, a singular comfort. Forasmuch as Christ has overcome sin through His death, it cannot hurt them that believe in Him. Moreover, if we arm ourselves with this belief and cleave with all our hearts to Christ Jesus, then is there a light opened and a sound judgment given unto us.

But weigh diligently every word of Paul, and specially mark well this pronoun, "our." You may easily believe that Christ the Son of God was given for the sins of Peter, of Paul, and of other saints, whom we account to have been worthy of this grace; but it is a very hard thing that you who judge yourself unworthy of this grace should from your heart say and believe that Christ was given for your own invincible, infinite and horrible sins. Therefore generally and without the pronoun, it is an easy matter to magnify and amplify the benefit of Christ, namely, that Christ was given for sins, but for other men's sins. But when it comes to the putting of this pronoun "our," there our weak nature and reason starts back, and dares not come near to God, nor promise to herself that so great a treasure shall be freely given unto her. Wherefore, although she read or hear this sentence: "Who gave Himself for our sins," or such like, yet does she not apply this pronoun "our" to herself, but to others who are worthy and holy; and as for herself, she will tarry till she be made worthy by her own works.

Hypocrites, being ignorant of Christ, although they feel the remorse of sin, think that they shall be able easily to put it away by their good works and merits; and secretly in their hearts they wish that these words, "Who gave Himself for our sins," were but as words spoken in humility, and would have their sins not to be true and very sins indeed, but light and small matters. To be short, man's reason would like to bring and present to God a counterfeit sinner, which is not afraid nor has any feeling of sin. It would bring him that is whole, and not him that has need of a physician; and when it feels no sin, then would it believe that Christ was given for our sins.

The whole world is thus affected, and especially they that would be counted more holy and religious than others. These confess with their mouths that they are sinners, and they confess also that they commit sins daily, howbeit not so great and many, but that they are able to put them away by their own works; besides all this, they will bring their righteousness and deserts to Christ's judgment seat, and demand the recompense of eternal life for them at the judge's hand. In the meanwhile, because they will not vaunt themselves to be utterly void of sin, they feign certain sins, that for the forgiveness thereof they may with great devotion pray with the publican: "God be merciful to me a sinner" (Luke 18:13). These words of St. Paul, "for our sins," seem to them to be but light and trifling; therefore they neither understand them, nor in temptation, when they feel sin indeed, can they take any comfort of them, but are compelled flatly to despair.

This is then the chief knowledge and true wisdom of Christians, to count these words of Paul, that Christ was delivered to death, not for our righteousness or holiness, but for our sins, to be of great importance. Therefore, think them not to be small, and such as may be done away by your own works; neither yet despair for the greatness of them, if you feel oppressed therewith, but learn here of Paul to believe that Christ was given, not for counterfeit sins, nor yet for small sins, but for great and huge sins; not for one or two, but for all; not for vanquished sins, but for invincible sins. And except you be found in the number of those who say "our sins," there is no salvation for you.

Labor diligently, that not only out of the time of temptation, but also in the time and conflict of death, when your conscience is thoroughly afraid with the remembrance of your sins past, and the devil assails you with great violence, going about to overwhelm you with heaps, floods and whole seas of sins, to terrify you and to drive you to despair; that then I say, you may be able to say with sure confidence: Christ the Son of God was given, not for the righteous and holy, but for the unrighteous and sinners. If I were righteous and had no sin, I should have no need of Christ to be my reconciler.

Herein consists the effect of eternal salvation, namely, in taking these words to be true and of great importance. I have often proved by experience, and I still daily find, what a hard matter it is to believe (especially in the conflict of conscience) that Christ was given, not for the holy, righteous, worthy, and such as were His friends, but for the ungodly, for sinners, for the unworthy, and for His enemies, who have deserved God's wrath and everlasting death.

Let us therefore arm ourselves with these and like verses of the Holy Scripture, that we may be able to answer the devil (accusing us, and saying: You are a sinner, and therefore you are damned) in this sort: "Christ has given Himself for my sins; therefore, Satan, you shall not prevail against me when you go about to terrify me in setting forth the greatness of my sins, and so to bring me into heaviness, distrust, despair, hatred, contempt and blaspheming of God. As often as you object that I am a sinner, you call me to remembrance of the benefit of Christ my Redeemer, upon whose shoulders, and not upon mine, lie all my sins; for 'the Lord hath laid on him the iniquity of us all,' and 'for the transgression of people was he stricken' (Isaiah 53:6, 8). Wherefore, when you say I am a sinner, you do not terrify me, but comfort me above measure.''

Christ is the Son of God and of the Virgin, delivered and put to death for our sins. Wherefore if you are a sinner (as indeed we are all), set not Christ down upon the rainbow as a judge (for so shalt thou be terrified, and despair of His mercy), but take hold of His true definition, namely, that Christ the Son of God and of the Virgin is a person who has given Himself for our sins.

Learn this definition diligently, and especially so exercise this pronoun "our," that this one syllable being believed may swallow up all your sins; that is to say, that you may know assuredly, that Christ has taken away the sins, not of certain men only, but also of you. Believe that Christ was not only given for other men's sins, but also for yours.

Christ, according to the proper and true definition, is no Moses, no lawgiver, no tyrant, but a mediator for sins, a free giver of grace, righteousness, and life; who gave Himself, not for our merits, holiness, righteousness and godly life, but for our sins. If He gave Himself to death for our sins, then undoubtedly He is no tyrant or judge who will condemn us for our sins. He is no caster-down of the afflicted, but a raiser-up of those who are fallen, a merciful reliever and comforter of the heavy and brokenhearted. Otherwise Paul would be lying when he says: "Who gave Himself for our sins.''

If I define Christ thus, I define Him rightly, and take hold of the true Christ, and possess Him indeed. Here then is no fear, but sweetness, joy, and peace of conscience. And here is a light which shows me the true knowledge of God, of myself, of all creatures, and of all the iniquity of the devil's kingdom.

These things, as touching the words, we know well enough and can talk of them. But in practice and in the conflict, when the devil goes about to pluck the word of grace out of our hearts, we find that we do not yet know them as we should. He who at that time can define Christ truly, and can magnify Him and behold Him as his most sweet Savior and high priest, and not as a judge, this man will overcome all evils, and is already in the kingdom of heaven. But to do this in the conflict is of all things the most hard. I speak this by experience.

4b—That he might deliver us from the present evil world.

Here Paul calls the whole world the "present" world to put a difference between this and the everlasting world to come. Moreover, he calls it "evil" because whatever is in this world is subject to the malice of the devil reigning over the whole world. The world is the devil's kingdom. In it is nothing but ignorance, contempt, blasphemy, hatred of God, and disobedience against all the words and works of God. In and under this kingdom of the world are we. As many then as are in the world are the bondslaves of the devil, constrained to serve him and do his pleasure.

What does it avail then to set up so many orders of religion, for the abolishing of sin; to devise so many and painful works, as to wear shirts of hair, to beat the body with whips till the blood flows, to go on pilgrimages and such like?

When you do all these things, you are still in this present evil world and not in the Kingdom of Christ. And if you are not in the Kingdom of Christ, it is certain you belong to the kingdom of Satan, which is this evil world. Therefore all the gifts, either of the body, or of the mind, which you enjoy, as wisdom, righteousness, holiness, eloquence, power, beauty, and riches, are but the slavish instruments of the devil, and with all these you are compelled to serve him, and to advance his kingdom.

First with your wisdom you darken the wisdom and knowledge of Christ, and by your doctrine you lead men out of the way, so that they cannot come to the grace and knowledge of Christ. You praise your own righteousness and holiness; but the righteousness of Christ, by which only we are justified, and quickened, you hate and condemn. To be brief, by your power you destroy the Kingdom of Christ, and abuse the same to root out the gospel, to persecute and kill the ministers of Christ, and as many as hear them.

Therefore Paul rightly calls it the present evil world: for when it is at the best, then is it worst. In the religious, wise, and learned men, the world is at the best, and yet, in very deed in them it is double evil. This white devil, which forces men to commit spiritual sins that they may sell them for righteousness, is far more dangerous than the black devil which forces them to commit only fleshly sins, which the world acknowledges to be sins.

By these words then, ''That He might deliver us from this present world,'' Paul shows what is the argument of this epistle: to wit, that we have need of grace and of Christ, and that no creature, neither man nor angel, can deliver man out of the present evil world. For these works are belonging only to the Divine Majesty, and are not in the power of any, whether angel or man. Christ has put away sin and has delivered us from the tyranny and kingdom of the devil; that is to say, from this wicked world, which is an obedient servant, and a willing follower of the devil its god. The world is full of the ignorance of God, of hatred, lying, blasphemy, and of contempt of God—moreover of gross sins, as murders, adulteries, fornication, thefts, and such like—because it knows its father the devil, who is a murderer and a liar. And the more wise, righteous, and holy that men are without Christ, so much the more hurt they do to the gospel.

Let these words then of Paul remain true and effectual, namely, ''that this present world is evil.'' Let it not surprise you that in a great number of men there are many excellent virtues, and there is so great a show of holiness in hypocrites. But mark rather what Paul says, whose words boldly and freely pronounce this sentence against the world, that with all its wisdom, power, and righteousness, it is the kingdom of the devil, out of which God alone is able to deliver us by His only begotten Son.

Therefore let us praise God the Father, and give Him hearty thanks for this His immeasurable mercy, that He has delivered us out of the kingdom of the devil (in which we were held captives) by His own Son, when such was impossible to be done by our own strength. And let us acknowledge together with Paul that ''all our work and righteousness'' are but ''loss and dross.''

Also let us cast under our feet and utterly abhor all pharisaical wisdom and righteousness as a most filthy rotten rag, or as dung, and as the most dangerous poison of the devil. Contrariwise, let us extol and magnify the glory of Christ, who has delivered us by His death, not from this world only, but from "this present evil world."

Paul then, by this word, *evil,* shows that the kingdom of the world, or the devil's kingdom, is the kingdom of iniquity, ignorance, error, sin, death, blasphemy, desperation, and everlasting damnation.

On the other side, the Kingdom of Christ is the kingdom of equity, light, grace, remission of sins, peace, consolation, saving health, and everlasting life, into which we are translated by our Lord Jesus Christ, to whom be glory, world without end. Amen.

4c—According to the will of God, and our Father.

Christ has delivered us from this wicked world. And this He has done according to the will, good pleasure and commandment of the Father. So we are not delivered by our own will or cunning, our own wisdom or policy; but God has taken mercy upon us, and has loved us. As it is written in another place: "Herein is love, not that we loved God, but that He loved us, and sent His Son to be the propitiation for our sins" (1 John 4:10). Paul is so vehement in amplifying and extolling the grace of God, that he sharpens and directs every word against the false apostles.

There is another reason Paul mentions the Father's will. Christ came into this world, by the Father's will, and took our nature upon Himself that He might be made a sacrifice for the sins of the whole world, and so to reconcile the Father to us, that we by fastening our eyes on Christ might be drawn and carried straight to the Father.

6a—I marvel that so soon.

To fall in faith is an easy matter. Paul warns Christians in another place that he who stands should take heed that he fall not (1 Corinthians 10:12).

We also daily prove by experience with what great difficulty a perfect people is gotten to the Lord. A man may labor half a score years before he shall get some little church to be rightly and religiously ordered; and when it is so ordered, there creeps in some mad brain, yea and a very unlearned idiot, who can do nothing else but speak slanderously and spitefully against sincere preachers of the Word, and he in one moment overthrows all.

We by the grace of God have gotten here at Wittenberg the form of a Christian church. The Word among us is purely taught, the sacraments are rightly used, exhortations and prayers are made also for all estates, and to be brief, all things go forward prosperously. This most happy course of the gospel some mad head would soon stop, and in one moment would overturn all that we in many years with great labor have built. Even so it befell to Paul, the elect vessel of Christ. He had won the churches of Galatia with great care and travail, which the false apostles in a short time after his departure overthrew, as this and diverse other of his epistles do witness. So great is the weakness and wretchedness of this present life, and so walk we in the midst of Satan's snares, that one fantastical head may destroy and utterly overthrow, in a short space, all that which many true ministers, laboring night and day, have built up many years before. This we learn at this day by experience to our great grief, and yet we cannot remedy this enormity.

Seeing then that the Church is so soft and so tender a thing, and is so soon overthrown, men must watch carefully against these fantastical spirits who, when they have heard two sermons, or have read a few leaves in the Holy Scriptures, make themselves masters and controllers of all learners and teachers, contrary to the authority of all men. Many such you may find among craftsmen, bold fellows, who, because they have been tried by no temptations, never learned to fear God nor had any taste or feeling of grace. These teach whatever they like best, and such things as are plausible and pleasant to the common people. Then the unskillful multitude, longing to hear news, join themselves unto them. Yea, and many are seduced by them.

Since Paul by his own experience teaches us that congregations which are won by great labor are easily and soon overthrown, we ought with singular care to watch against the devil ranging everywhere, lest he come while we sleep, and sow tares among the wheat. For though the shepherds be ever so watchful and diligent, yet is the Christian flock in danger of Satan. For Paul (as I said) with singular study and diligence had planted churches in Galatia, and yet he had scarcely set his foot (as they say) out of the door, but the false apostles overthrew some, whose fall afterward was the cause of great ruin in the churches of Galatia. This so sudden and so great a loss, no doubt, was more bitter to the Apostle than death itself.

6b—You are removed away.

Here again he uses not a sharp, but a most gentle word. He says not: I marvel that you so suddenly fall away, that you are so disobedient, light, inconstant, unthankful; but, that you are so soon removed. As if he should say: You are altogether patients or sufferers; for you have done no harm, but you have suffered and received harm. To the intent therefore that he might call back again those backsliders, he rather accuses those that did remove, than those that were removed; and yet very modestly he blames them also. As if he would say: Although I embrace you with a fatherly affection and know that you are fallen, I would have wished that you had grown up a little more in the strength of sound doctrine. You took not hold enough upon the Word, you rooted not yourselves deep enough in it, and that is the cause that with so light a blast of wind you are carried and removed.

Jerome thinks that Paul meant to interpret this word "Galatians" by alluding to the Hebrew word *Galath,* which means "fallen or carried away." As though he would say: You are right Galatians, both in name and in deed, that is, fallen or removed away. Some think that the Germans are descended of the Galatians, neither is this divination perhaps untrue. For the Germans are not much unlike to them in nature. I myself also am constrained to wish for my countrymen more steadfastness and constancy; for we do, in all things, at the first be very hot, but when the heat of our affections is allayed, we become more slack, and with what rashness we begin things, with the same we give them over, and utterly reject them.

6c—From him that called you into the grace of Christ.

This place is somewhat doubtful, and therefore it has a double meaning. The first is: "From Christ who has called you in grace." The other is: "From Him," that is to say from God, "who has called you in the grace of Christ."

I embrace the former, for even as Paul, a little before, made Christ the Redeemer, also the giver of grace and peace, equally with God the Father, so we should make Him here also the caller in grace, for Paul's purpose is to beat into our minds the benefit of Christ, by whom we come to the Father.

There is in these words—"from Him that has called us in grace"—a contrary relation (or inference), as if he would say, how lightly do you suffer yourselves to be withdrawn and removed from Christ, who has called you, not as Moses did, to the law, works, sin, wrath and damnation but altogether to grace! So we also complain at this day with Paul, that the blindness and perverseness of men is horrible, in that so few will receive the doctrine of grace and salvation. Or, if any receive it, they quickly slide back again, and fall from it. The grace of Christ brings all good things, spiritually as well as bodily, namely, forgiveness of sins, true righteousness, peace of conscience, and everlasting life. They that are called of Christ, instead of the law which works sorrow, gain the glad tidings of the gospel, and are translated out of God's wrath into His favor, out of sin into righteousness, and out of death into life.

6d—Unto another gospel.

No false teacher comes under the title of errors, neither does the devil come in his own likeness, especially that white devil we spoke of before.

Even the black devil which forces men to manifest wickedness makes a cloak for men to excuse and cover that which they commit or purpose. The murderer has an excuse to cover his horrible deed. Adulterers, whoremongers, thieves, covetous persons, drunkards and such like, have excuses for their sins. So the black devil comes disguised and counterfeit in all his works and devices. But in spiritual sins, where Satan comes forth, not black but white in the likeness of an angel, he passes himself with most crafty dissimulation, and sets forth his most deadly poison for the doctrine of grace, for the Word of God, for the gospel of Christ. This is why Paul calls the doctrine of the false apostles a gospel, saying "another gospel," but in derision, as if he would say, "Ye Galatians have now other evangelists, and another gospel; my gospel is now despised of you; it is now no more in estimation among you."

Hereby it may easily be gathered that these false apostles had condemned the gospel of Paul, saying Paul has begun well, but there remain yet many higher matters, as certain Pharisees said in Acts 15:5, "that it was needful to circumcise them, and to command them to keep the law of Moses." This is as much as to say, Christ is a good workman who has indeed begun a building, but has not finished it; this must Moses do. The devil will not be ugly, but he sets forth all his words with the color of truth, and with the name of God. Herein is sprung that common proverb among the Germans: "In God's name begins all mischief." Wherefore let us learn, that this is a special point of the devil's cunning, that if he cannot hurt by persecuting and destroying, he does it under a color of correcting and building up.

So he stirs up wicked spirits and ungodly teachers, which at first allow our doctrine to be holy and heavenly, and teach the same with a common consent together with us; but afterwards they say, that further mysteries of the Scriptures are revealed to them from above, and they are called for this purpose, to open them to the world.

In this manner the devil hinders the course of the gospel, both on the right hand and on the left, but more on the right hand, by building and correcting, than on the left by persecuting and destroying. So we must pray without ceasing, read the Holy Scriptures, and cleave fast unto Christ, that we may overcome the devil's subtleties: "For we wrestle not against flesh and blood, but against principalities, against powers, against the rulers of the darkness of this world, against spiritual wickedness in high places" (Ephesians 6:12).

7a—Which is not another [gospel]; but there be some that trouble you.

Here again he excuses the Galatians, and most bitterly reproaches the false apostles, who had reported Paul to be an imperfect apostle and a weak, erroneous teacher. Therefore, he calls them here troublers of the Church and overthrowers of the gospel of Christ.

Thus they condemn each other. The false apostles condemn Paul, and Paul condemns the false apostles. Contending and condemning is always in the Church, especially when the gospel flourishes. Wicked teachers prosecute, condemn, and oppress the godly; and on the other side, the godly reprove and condemn the ungodly.

Mark here diligently, that every teacher of works, and of the righteousness of the law, is a troubler of the Church, and of the consciences of men. The more holy the heretics seem in outward show, the more mischief they do; for if the false apostles had not been endued with notable gifts, with great authority, and show of holiness, and had not vaunted themselves to be Christ's ministers, the Apostles' disciples, and sincere preachers of the gospel, they could not so easily have defaced Paul's authority and led the Galatians out of the way.

Now, the cause why he sets himself so sharply against them, calling them the troublers of the churches, is that besides faith in Christ, they taught that circumcision and the keeping of the law were necessary to salvation. The false apostles obstinately contended that the law ought to be observed, and easily persuaded such as were not established in the faith that Paul was not a sincere teacher, because he regarded not the law, but preached such a doctrine as did abolish and overthrow the law. It seemed to them a strange thing that the law of God should be utterly taken away, and the Jews, who, until that time, had been counted the people of God, to whom also the promises were made, should now be rejected. Also, it seemed more strange that the Gentiles, being wicked idolaters, should attain to this dignity and glory, to be the people of God without circumcision, and without the works of the law, by grace only and faith in Christ.

7b—And would pervert the gospel of Christ.

Because they mingled the law and the gospel, they perverted the gospel. For either Christ must remain and the law perish, or the law must remain and Christ perish. Christ and the law can by no means agree and reign together in the conscience. Where the righteousness of the law rules, the righteousness of grace cannot rule; one of them must give place to the other. If you cannot believe that God will forgive your sins for Christ's sake, how then will you believe that He will forgive you your sins for the works of the law, which you could never perform?

The doctrine of grace can by no means stand with the doctrine of law. Yet if it comes to debating, the greater part overthrows the better: for Christ with His side is weak, and the gospel is but a foolish preaching; contrariwise, the kingdom of the world and the devil, the prince thereof, are strong. But this is our comfort that the devil, with all his limbs, cannot do what he would. He may trouble many, but he cannot overthrow Christ's gospel. The truth may be assailed, but vanquished it cannot be; for "the Word of the Lord endureth forever."

It seems a light matter to mingle the law and the gospel, faith and works together, but it does more harm than a man's reason can conceive, for it takes away Christ with all His benefits, and overthrows the gospel, as Paul says. The cause of this great evil is our flesh, which being plunged in sins, sees no way how to get out, but by works. Therefore it would live in the righteousness of the law, and rest in the confidence of its own works. So the false apostles perverted the gospel of Christ.

*8—But though we, or an angel from heaven, preach any other gospel
unto you than that which we have preached unto you, let him be
accursed.*

Here Paul casts out very flames of fire, and his zeal is so fervent that
he begins almost to curse the angels and himself. I would rather that I
myself, and my brethren, yea, and the very angels from heaven should be
holden accursed, than that my gospel should be overthrown.

This is indeed a vehement zeal. The Greek word *anathema,* in Hebrew
herem, signifies a thing accursed, execrable, and detestable, which has
nothing to do, no participation, or communion with God. So Joshua said:
"Cursed be the man before the Lord that riseth up and buildeth this city
Jericho" (Joshua 6:26). So God had appointed that Amalek, and certain
other cities, accursed by God's own sentence, should be utterly destroyed.

As cunning artificers first find fault with themselves that they may the
more freely reprove others, so Paul first curses himself if he should fail
in the true gospel of Christ. He concludes and states that there is no other
gospel besides that which he himself had preached. For he preached not
a gospel of his own devising, but that which God had promised before by
His prophets in the Holy Scriptures. For the voice of the gospel, once sent
forth, shall not be called back again till the day of judgment.

*9—As we said before, so say I now again, If any man preach any
other gospel unto you than that ye have received, let him be
accursed.*

Paul repeats the same thing, only changing the persons. Before, he
cursed himself, his brethren, and an angel from heaven. Here it is any
besides us, any who preach "any other gospel than that ye have
received" of us, let him also be accursed. Therefore he plainly excom-
municates and curses all teachers in general that preach not the pure
gospel which he by revelation had preached.

Here with great fervency the Apostle dares curse all teachers throughout
the whole world, yes, in heaven also, which pervert his gospel, and teach

any other; for all men must either believe that gospel that Paul preached, or else they must be accursed and condemned. Would to God that this terrible sentence of the Apostle might strike terror into the hearts of those who seek to pervert the gospel of Paul.

The changing of the persons is to be noted. In the first curse it is of those who "preach any other than that we have preached"; in the second it is, "than that ye have received."

This he does intentionally, lest the Galatians should say: "We do not pervert the gospel, but the preachers that followed you have declared unto us the true meaning thereof."

This, Paul says, I will in no case admit. They ought to add nothing, to correct nothing, for that which you heard of me is the true Word of God; let only this remain.

The first chapters of the epistle contain nothing else but a defense of his doctrine and confutations of error, so that, until he comes to the end of the second chapter, he does not touch on the chief matter of the epistle, namely, the article of justification.

Here then is a plain text like a thunderbolt, wherein Paul subjects both himself and an angel from heaven, and all others, doctors, teachers, and masters, to be under the authority of the Scriptures: for they ought not to be masters, judges, or arbiters, but only witnesses, disciples, and confessors of the Church, whether it be the Pope, or Luther, or Augustine, or Paul, or an angel from heaven. Neither ought any doctrine to be taught or heard in the Church, besides the pure Word of God, that is to say, the Holy Scripture; otherwise accursed be both the teachers and hearers, together with their doctrine.

10a—For do I now persuade men, or God?

Do I preach a man's doctrine, or God's?

Is it not clear to you whether I serve man or serve God? I have not only stirred up persecution against me in every place, but have also procured the hatred of my own nation, and of all other men. I show plainly enough by this, that I seek not the favor or praise of men, but I strive to set forth the benefit and glory of God.

We seek not the favor of men by our doctrine, for we teach that all men are wicked by nature, and the children of wrath. We condemn man's free will, his strength, wisdom, and righteousness, and all religion of man's own devising, and, to be short, that there is nothing in us to deserve grace, and the forgiveness of sins; but we preach that we obtain this grace by the free mercy of God only, for Christ's sake. This is not to preach for the favor of men, and of the world; for the world does not like to have its wisdom, righteousness, religion, and power condemned. For if we speak against men, or anything that pertains to their glory, cruel hatred, persecutions, excommunications, murders and condemnations inevitably follow.

If then (says Paul) they see other matters, why do they not see this also, that I teach the things that are of God, and not of men? I seek no man's favor by my doctrine, but I set out God's mercy unto us in Christ. If I sought the favor of men, I would not condemn their works. It is because I condemn men's works—how that men are sinners, unrighteous, wicked, children of wrath, bondslaves of the devil, and that they are not made righteous by works, or by circumcision, but by grace only, and faith in Christ—that I procure for myself the deadly hatred of men.

10b—Or do I seek to please men?

Paul takes a glance at the false apostles. These, says he, seek to please men: for by this means they seek, that they may glory in their flesh. Because they will not bear the hatred and persecution of men, they teach circumcision, to avoid the reproach of the Cross.

So today, we find many who seek to please men so that they may live in peace and security of the flesh. We, because we endeavor to please God, and not men, stir up against us the malice of the devil and hell itself. So Paul says here: ''I seek not to please men,'' that they may praise my doctrine, and report me an excellent teacher: but I desire only that my doctrine may please God. Contrariwise, the false apostles teach the things that are of men, such things as are pleasant and plausible to man's reason, to the end that they may live at ease, and purchase the favor, good will, and praise of the people. Such men find what they seek, and as the Savior said: "They have their reward."

10c—For if I yet pleased men, I should not be the servant of Christ.

These things refer to the whole ministry of Paul, to show what a difference there was between his life before in the Jewish law, and his life now under the gospel. As if he would say, do ye think that I go about still to please men, as I did in times past? So afterwards in the fifth chapter, he says: "If I yet preach circumcision, why do I suffer persecution?" For if I should preach the law and circumcision, and commend the strength, the power, and the will of man, I should not be so odious to them, but should please them.

Preaching the Faith He Once Destroyed

Galatians 1:11–24

11, 12—But I certify you, brethren, that the gospel which was preached of me is not after man. For I neither received it of man, neither was I taught it, but by the revelation of Jesus Christ.

Here is the principal point of this matter: it contains a confutation of his adversaries, and a defense of his doctrine to the end of the second chapter. Upon this he stands, and with an oath confirms, that he learned not his gospel of man, but received it by the revelation of Jesus Christ. He is constrained to confirm it by an oath so that the Galatians may believe him and that they should give no ear to the false apostles, whom he calls liars, because they had said he received his gospel of the Apostles.

When he says that his gospel is not after men, he does not mean that it is not earthly. The false apostles had bragged that their doctrine was not earthly, but heavenly; but Paul means that he did not learn his gospel by the ministry of men or receive it by any earthly means, but he received it only by the revelation of Jesus Christ. Here the Apostle shows, by the way, that Jesus Christ is not only man, but that He is both man and very God, when he says that he received not his gospel of man.

Paul received his gospel on the way to Damascus, where Christ appeared to him, and talked with him. Afterwards He talked with him in the Temple at Jerusalem. "Arise," said Christ, "and go into the city (Damascus), and it shall be told thee what thou must do" (Acts 9:6).

He did not bid him go into the city that he might learn the gospel of Ananias; but Ananias was bid to go and baptize him, to lay his hands upon him, to commit the ministry of the Word unto him, and to commend him unto the Church, but not to teach him the gospel, which he had received before by the sole revelation of Jesus Christ. Ananias himself confessed this, saying: "Brother Saul, the Lord which appeared to thee in the way, hath sent me, that thou mightest receive thy sight." Therefore he received not his doctrine of Ananias, but being already called, enlightened, and taught of Christ on the way, he was sent to Ananias that he might also have the testimony of men, that he was called of God to preach the gospel of Christ.

This Paul was constrained to recite, because the false apostles had founded their argument upon the inferiority of his authority, in not being one of the twelve, from whom they themselves had received the gospel. On this plea they had deceived the Galatians, and got them to discredit Paul's doctrine of justification by faith alone.

O good Lord, what horrible and infinite mischief may one single argument bring! By this subtlety then did the false apostles deceive the Galatians, being, as yet, weak in faith.

Moreover, the matter of justification is slippery; not of itself, for of itself it is most sure and certain, but in respect of us. I myself have good experience in this matter. I know in what hours of darkness I sometimes wrestle. I know how often I suddenly lose the beams of the gospel, and grace, as being shadowed from me with thick and dark clouds. I know in what a slippery place even such as I who am well taught do stand, although I should have a sure footing in matters of faith.

We have good experience of this matter, and we are able to teach it to others, and this is a sure token that we understand it. But when in the conflict we should use the gospel, which is the word of grace, consolation, and life, the law, the word of heaviness, wrath, and death rises against the gospel, and begins to rage; and the terrors which it raises up in the conscience are no less than was that horrible show on Mount Sinai.

Again, we have against us one-half of ourselves: that is to say, the flesh, and all the powers thereof. The flesh resists the spirit and cannot believe that all the promises of God are assuredly true. It fights against the spirit, as Paul says in chapter 5:17 of this epistle: "The flesh lusteth against the spirit, and the spirit against the flesh, and these are contrary the one to the other."

So we teach continually, that the knowledge of Christ and of faith is no work of man, but simply the gift of God, who as He creates faith, so He keeps us in it. Even as He first gives faith unto us through the Word, so afterwards He exercises, increases, strengthens, and makes perfect the same in us by the Word.

Therefore the greatest service that a man can do for God is to exercise himself in true godliness, diligently to hear and to read the Word. Contrariwise, there is nothing more dangerous than to be weary of the Word. He therefore that is so cold, that he thinks himself to know enough, and begins little by little to loathe the Word, that man has lost Christ and the gospel, and that which he thinks himself to know, he attains only by bare speculation.

So let every faithful man labor and strive with all diligence to learn and to keep this doctrine: and to that end, let him use humble and hearty prayer, with continual study and meditation of the Word. Our enemies are not small, but they are strong and mighty, and such as are in continual war against us. These enemies include our own flesh, all the dangers of the world, the law, sin, death, the wrath and judgment of God, and the devil himself, who never ceases to tempt us inwardly by his fiery darts, and outwardly by his false apostles, so that he may overthrow, if not all, yet the greater part of us.

This argument of the false apostles seemed to be very strong, and it continues to prevail even to this day with very many:

Holy men, more ancient and learned than you are, have taught these things. Who are you who dare dissent from all these, and bring to us a contrary doctrine?

When Satan reasons thus, conspiring with the flesh and reason, then your conscience is terrified and utterly despairs, unless you constantly return to yourself again, and say, whether it be Cyprian, Ambrose, Augustine, or St. Peter, St. Paul or St. John, yea, or an angel from heaven that teaches otherwise, yet this I know assuredly, that I teach not the things of men, but of God; that is to say, I attribute all things to God alone, and nothing to man.

When I first took upon me the defense of the gospel, I remember that Dr. Staupitius, a worthy man and vicar of the Augustinian order, said to me: "This doctrine which you preach gives glory unto God alone, and nothing unto man; unto God there cannot be attributed too much glory, goodness and mercy." His words did greatly comfort and confirm me. And true it is that the doctrine of the gospel takes from men all glory, wisdom, righteousness, etc., and gives the same unto the Creator alone, who made all things of nothing. We may more safely attribute too much to God than unto man, and my doctrine is such that it sets forth and preaches the grace and glory of God alone, and in the matter of justification, and salvation, it condemns the righteousness and wisdom of all men. In this I cannot offend, because I give both to God and man that which properly belongs to them both.

But you will say, the Church is holy. It is true; nevertheless, although the Church is holy, yet is it compelled to pray: "Forgive us our trespasses." So, though the fathers be holy, yet are they saved by the forgiveness of sins. Therefore neither am I to be believed, nor the Church, nor the fathers, nor the Apostles, no, nor an angel from heaven, if we teach anything against the Word of God, but let the Word of God abide forever; for else this argument of the false apostles had mightily prevailed against Paul's doctrine.

For indeed it was a great matter, to set before the Galatians the whole Church, with all the company of the Apostles, against Paul alone, but lately sprung up and of small authority. For no man says willingly, the

Church errs, and yet it is necessary to say that it errs, if it teach anything besides or against the Word of God.

13—For ye have heard of my conversation in time past in the Jews' religion, how that beyond measure I persecuted the church of God, and wasted it.

Paul presents his own example, saying, I have defended the traditions of the Pharisees, and the Jewish religion more constantly than you and all your false teachers.

If the righteousness of the law had been worth anything, I had not turned back from it. In the keeping of it, before I knew Christ, I did so exercise myself, that I excelled my companions of my own nation. I was so zealous in defense of the law that I persecuted the Church of God and wasted it. Having received authority from the chief priests, I put many in prison. When they should be put to death I gave my voice against them and punished them throughout all the synagogues. I compelled them to blaspheme, and was so mad at them that I persecuted them even to strange cities.

14—And profited in the Jews' religion above many my equals in mine own nation, being more exceedingly zealous of the traditions of my fathers.

When he speaks here of the traditions of the fathers he refers not to pharisaical or human traditions, but to a far higher matter, and calls even that holy law of Moses, the traditions of the fathers: that is to say, received and left as an inheritance from the fathers. For these, says he, I was very zealous, when I was in the Jews' religion. After the same manner, to the Philippians (3:6): ''As concerning the law a Pharisee, concerning zeal, I persecuted the Church, and as concerning the righteousness of the law I was blameless.''

These things (O Galatians) ought to have persuaded you not to believe those deceivers who magnify the righteousness of the law as a matter of great importance. If there had been any cause to glory in the righteousness of the law, I would have had more cause to glory than any other.

In the same way I say of myself, that before I was enlightened with the knowledge of the gospel, I was as zealous for the law and traditions of the fathers as any were, maintaining and defending them as holy and necessary to salvation. Moreover, I endeavored to keep them myself, as much as was possible for me to do, punishing my poor body with fasting, watching, praying, and other exercises, more than all they which at this day do so bitterly hate and persecute me. I was so diligent and superstitious in the observation thereof, that I laid more upon my body than it was able to bear without danger to its health. Whatever I did, I did it with a single heart, of a good zeal, and for the glory of God. But those things which were then gain unto me, I now, with Paul, count to be but loss for the excellency of the knowledge of Jesus Christ my Lord. But our adversaries do not believe that I, and many others, have endured such things.

> *15, 16, 17—But when it pleased God, who separated me from my mother's womb, and called me by his grace, to reveal his Son in me, that I might preach him among the heathen; immediately I conferred not with flesh and blood: neither went I up to Jerusalem to them which were apostles before me; but I went into Arabia, and returned again to Damascus.*

This is the first journey of Paul. After he was called of God to preach Christ among the Gentiles, he went straightway into Arabia, without the advice of any man, to that work to which he was called.

This verse tells us by whom he was taught, and by what means he came to his apostleship: "When it had pleased God." As if he would say, I did not deserve it, for my zeal in the law led me to abominable and outrageous sins. I persecuted the Church of God, and was an enemy to Christ, I blasphemed His gospel, and was the author of shedding much innocent blood. In the midst of this cruel rage, I was called to such inestimable grace. What! because of his outrageous cruelty? No! but the abundant grace of God, who calls, and shows mercy to whom He will.

We also are come at this day, to the knowledge of grace by the same merits. I crucified Christ daily in my monkish life, and blasphemed God through my false faith, wherein I then lived continually. Outwardly, I was not as other men, extortioners, unjust, whoremongers; but I kept chastity, poverty, and obedience.

Moreover, I was free from the cares of this present life. Notwithstanding, I fostered under this cloaked holiness, and trust in mine own righteousness, continual mistrust, doubtfulness, fear, hatred, and blasphemy against God. And this my righteousness was nothing but a filthy puddle, and the very kingdom of the devil. For Satan loves such saints, and accounts them for his dear darlings, who destroy their own bodies and souls, and deprive themselves of all the blessings of God's gifts.

Such saints are the bondslaves of Satan, and therefore are driven to speak, think, and do whatever he will, although outwardly they seem to excel all others in good works, in holiness and strictness of life.

"Who separated me from my mother's womb" is a Hebrew phrase, meaning when I was born, I was an apostle in the sight of God, and when the time was come, I was declared an apostle before the whole world. Thus Paul cuts off all deserts, and gives God alone the glory, but to himself all shame and confusion.

It was as though he would say, all the gifts which God purposed to give me, God Himself had before appointed when I was as yet in my mother's womb, where I could neither wish, think, nor do any good thing. This gift came to me by the mere predestination and free mercy of God before I was yet born. And that He might the more manifestly declare the inestimable greatness of His mercy towards me, He of His mere grace forgave me my abominable and infinite sins, and furnished me with so much of His grace, that I did not only know what things are given to us in Christ, but preached the same also unto others.

"He called me," says Paul, but how? Was it for my pharisaical religion, or for my blameless and holy life? For my fastings, prayers, and works? No. How then? "He called me by His grace."

When he goes on, "To reveal His Son in me," Paul states that the purpose of the gospel is the revelation of the Son of God. This is a doctrine quite contrary to the law, which reveals sin, death, the wrath and judgment of God. If the gospel is the revealing of the Son of God, then surely it accuses not, it threatens not death, nor brings to despair, as the law does; but it is a doctrine concerning Christ, which is neither law nor works, but our righteousness, wisdom, sanctification, and redemption (1 Corinthians 1:30). The gospel teaches that Christ came not to set forth a new law and to give commandments as touching manners, but He came that He might be made an oblation for the sins of the whole world, and that our sins might be forgiven, and everlasting life given unto us for His sake, and not for the works of the law, or for our own righteousness.

So it is not a kind of doctrine that can be gotten by any study, diligence, or wisdom of man, but it is revealed by God Himself, as Paul says in this place: first by the external Word, then by the working of God's Spirit inwardly. The gospel therefore is a divine Word that came down from heaven, and is revealed by the Holy Ghost, who was also sent for the same purpose: yet in such sort that the outward Word must go before.

For Paul himself had no inward revelation, until he had heard the outward Word from heaven, which was this: "Saul, Saul, why persecuteth thou me?" (Acts 9:4). First therefore he heard the outward Word, then followed revelations, the knowledge of the Word, faith, and the gifts of the Holy Ghost.

"It pleased God to reveal His Son in me," not only that I should believe in the Son of God myself, but "that I should preach Him among the Gentiles." And why not among the Jews? Here we see that Paul is properly the Apostle to the Gentiles, although he also preached Christ among the Jews.

Paul comprehends here, in a few words, his whole purpose, which is to preach Christ among the Gentiles.

As if he would say, I will not burden the Gentiles with the law, because I am the Apostle and evangelist to the Gentiles, and not their lawgiver. My office and ministry is to bring the gospel unto you, and to show you the same revelation which I myself have had. Therefore you ought to hear no teacher that teaches the law. For among the Gentiles, the law ought not to be preached, but the gospel: not Moses, but the Son of God; not the righteousness of works, but the righteousness of faith. This is the gospel that properly belongs to the Gentiles.

When Paul states the fact that after his conversion, he went into Arabia, without consulting those who were Apostles before him, it is a confutation of the false apostles' argument that he was but a scholar of the Apostles who lived after the law, and therefore it was necessary that the Gentiles should keep the law, and be circumcised.

18, 19—Then after three years I went up to Jerusalem to see Peter, and abode with him fifteen days. But other of the apostles saw I none, save James, the Lord's brother.

He grants that he was at Jerusalem, but that of the Apostles he saw only Peter and James the Lord's brother. He grants moreover that he had lived after the manner of the Jews, but yet only among the Jews. So he also says in 1 Corinthians 9:20: "To the Jews I became as a Jew that I might gain the Jews, and I was made all things to all men that I might by all means save some." The whole effect of the matter lies in the word "to see": to see Peter is not to learn of him, for Peter is not my master, nor James, and as for the other Apostles I saw none of them.

Why does Paul repeat this so often, that he learned not his gospel of men, nor of the Apostles themselves? His purpose is to persuade the churches of Galatia, which were led away by the false apostles, and to put them out of all doubt that his gospel was the true Word of God. He desires to retain the churches in true and sound doctrine; to show by this history, that he received the gospel of no man; and that he preached for a certain time, the space of three or four years, both in Damascus and in Arabia, by revelation from God, before he had seen any of the Apostles.

> *20—Now the things which I write unto you, behold, before God, I lie not.*

Why did he need to add an oath? Because he reports history, he is constrained to swear, so that the churches might believe him, and that the false apostles could not say, who knows whether Paul speaks the truth, or no?

You see that Paul, the elect vessel of God, was held in such great contempt among his own converts of Galatia, that it was necessary for him to swear that he spoke the truth. If this happened then to the Apostles, to have so mighty adversaries, what marvel is it if the like at this day happen unto us, who are not worthy to be compared to the Apostles?

> *21, 22—Afterwards I came into the region of Syria and Cilicia; and was unknown by face unto the churches of Judea which were in Christ.*

Syria and Cilicia are countries near together. He still goes about to persuade, that before he had seen the Apostles, as well as after, he was always a teacher of the gospel he had received by the revelation of Jesus Christ, and was never a disciple of the Apostles.

> *23, 24—But they had heard only, That he which persecuted us in times past now preacheth the faith which once he destroyed. And they glorified God in me.*

As though he would say, I appeal to the testimony of all the churches, not only in Damascus, Arabia, Syria, and Cilicia, but also Judea that I have preached the same faith which once I withstood and persecuted. And they glorified God in me; not that I taught that circumcision and the law of Moses ought to be kept, but for the preaching of faith, and for the edifying of the churches by my ministry in the gospel.

3

Withstanding Peter

Galatians 2:1–14

1a—Then fourteen years after I went up again to Jerusalem.

Paul taught that the Gentiles were justified by faith alone without the works of the law. After he had published this doctrine among the Gentiles, he went to Antioch, and declared to the disciples what he had done. Those who had been brought up in the old customs of the law rose against Paul with great indignation.

There followed great dissension. Paul and Barnabas stood for the truth, declaring, wherever they preached among the Gentiles "the Holy Ghost fell upon those which heard the word. But we preached not circumcision, neither did we require the keeping of the law, but we preached only faith in Jesus Christ, and at this preaching of faith God gave to the hearers the Holy Ghost." The Holy Ghost therefore, approved the faith of the Gentiles, without the law and circumcision. If the preaching of the gospel and faith of the Gentiles in Christ had not pleased Him, He would not have come down upon the uncircumcised which heard the Word. Seeing then by the hearing only of faith, He came down upon them, it is certain that the Holy Ghost approved the faith of the Gentiles. It is apparent that this was never done before at the preaching of the law.

Then the Jews and many of the Pharisees who believed, but yet did bear a great zeal for the law, striving to maintain the glory thereof, set themselves fiercely against Paul, contending that the law ought to be kept, and that the Gentiles ought to be circumcised, for otherwise they could not be saved.

It is little wonder that the Jews did strive so zealously for the maintenance of their law which they had received from God. Custom is of such force, that whereas nature is of itself inclined to the observations of the law, by long continuance, it so confirms nature, that now it becomes a double nature. So it was not possible for the Jews who were newly converted to Christ suddenly to forsake the law. And with this weakness God did bear for a while, until the doctrine of the gospel might be plainly discerned from the law. Paul, therefore, seeing this contention and these clamors increase daily, and being warned of God by revelation, after fourteen years (besides those years he had preached at Damascus and in Arabia) goes up again to Jerusalem to confer with the other Apostles; yet not for his own cause, but for the people's sake.

1b—With Barnabas, and took Titus with me also.

Paul joins two witnesses with himself. Barnabas was Paul's companion in preaching to the Gentiles freedom from the servitude of the law. He also had seen the Holy Ghost given unto the Gentiles, who were uncircumcised and free from Moses' law, only by faith in Jesus Christ. He stuck to Paul in this point, that it was not necessary that the Gentiles should be burdened with the law, but that it was enough for them to believe in Christ. So, with Paul, he testifies of his own experience, that the Gentiles were made the children of God and saved by faith alone in Jesus Christ, without the law of circumcision.

Titus was not only a Christian, but also a Gentile, and the chief overseer in Crete. To him Paul had committed the charge of the churches there.

2a—And I went up by revelation.

For unless Paul had been admonished by revelation, he had not gone up to Jerusalem; but God warned him, and commanded him to go. So he went.

2b—And communicated unto them that gospel which I preach among
the Gentiles.

Among the Jews Paul had suffered the law and circumcision for a time, as the other Apostles did; yet ever holding the true doctrine of the gospel, which he preferred above the law, circumcision, the Apostles, yes, and even an angel from heaven. For thus he said to the Jews: "Through this man is preached unto you forgiveness of sins, and by Him all that believe are justified from all things, from which ye could not be justified by the law of Moses" (Acts 13:38, 39). Notwithstanding he did not break away at first, but had regard for the weak. In order that the weak should not be offended, he probably spoke to the Jews after this manner: if that unprofitable service of Moses' law, which avails nothing for righteousness, pleases you so highly, you may keep it still, as long as the Gentiles, which know not the law, are not charged with it.

The question whereupon the Apostles conferred together on this occasion was this, whether the keeping of the law was necessary to justification or not. To this Paul argued: I have preached unto the Gentiles that gospel I received from God, that is, faith in Christ, and not the law; at this preaching of faith, they received the Holy Ghost, whereunto Barnabas is also a witness. Wherefore I conclude that the Gentiles ought not to be burdened with the law, nor to be circumcised. Yet I give no restraint to the Jews herein, who if they must keep the law and be circumcised, I am not against it, as long as they do it with freedom of conscience. Thus have I taught and lived among the Jews, being made a Jew unto the Jews, yet holding the truth of the gospel.

2c—But privately to them which were of reputation, lest by any
means I should run, or had run, in vain.

That is to say, I did not confer only with the brethren, but with those who were chiefest among them.

Not that Paul thought that he ran or had run in vain, forasmuch as he had now preached the gospel eighteen years. But many Jews did think that he had preached in vain, because he had set the Gentiles at liberty from the observation of the law.

3—But neither Titus, who was with me, being a Greek, was compelled to be circumcised.

This word "compelled" indicates what conclusion was reached at the conference: that the Gentiles should not be constrained or compelled to be circumcised. Otherwise, Titus would have been compelled. But it was permitted for a time, not as necessary to righteousness, but for a reverence to the fathers, and for charity towards the weak; for it might seem a strange thing to forsake immediately all the law and traditions of the fathers which had been given to this people from God with so great glory.

Paul then did not reject circumcision as a damnable thing, neither did he by word or deed enforce the Jews to forsake it. For in 1 Corinthians 7 he says: "If any man be called, being circumcised, let him not become uncircumcised." But Paul rejected it as necessary to righteousness, seeing the fathers themselves were not justified thereby (Romans 4:11); it was to them a sign only, or a seal of righteousness, whereby they testified their faith.

So we at this day do not reject fasting and other good exercises as damnable things; but we teach that by these exercises we do not obtain remission of sins.

When the people hear this, they judge us to speak against good works. But they lie and do us great wrong. For many years past, there was never any that taught more sound and godly doctrine as touching good works than we do at this day.

At this conference then it was decided that circumcision was not necessary to justification, and therefore not to be forced upon the Gentiles. Briefly, none should be constrained to be circumcised, or any constrained from circumcision.

But the false apostles would not consider the observation of the law and circumcision as optional, but saw it as necessary to salvation. So at this day, our adversaries contend that men's traditions cannot be omitted without peril of salvation; thus of an example of charity they make an example of faith, when yet there is but one example of faith, which is to believe in Jesus Christ.

This triumph of Paul, therefore, was very glorious, that Titus, who was a Gentile, though in the midst of the Apostles at Jerusalem where this very question was debated, was not compelled to be circumcised.

Thus were the false apostles confounded.

4, 5—And that because of false brethren unawares brought in, who came in privily to spy out our liberty which we have in Christ Jesus, that they might bring us into bondage: to whom we gave place by subjection, no, not for an hour; that the truth of the gospel might continue with you.

Here Paul shows why he went to Jerusalem and there conferred with the other Apostles, and why he would not circumcise Titus. It was not that he might be more confirmed in his gospel by the Apostles, for he doubted nothing thereof, but that the truth of the gospel might continue in the churches of Galatia, and in all the churches of the Gentiles.

When he speaks of the truth of the gospel, he shows that there are two gospels, a true one and a false one. Indeed the gospel of itself is simple, true, and sincere; but by the malice of Satan's ministry, it is corrupt and defaced. Therefore, when he says "the truth of the gospel," he would have us understand also the contrary. As if he would say: the false apostles do also preach a faith and a gospel, but they are both false; therefore have I set myself so constantly against them.

Even today heretics pretend the name of God, of Christ, and of the Church, and teach their doctrine as the pure gospel of Christ.

The truth of the gospel is that our righteousness comes by faith alone, without the works of the law. The corruption or falsehood of the gospel is that we are justified by faith but not without the works of the law.

That is the gospel the false apostles preached. For they say that we must believe in Christ, and that faith is the foundation of our salvation, but it justifies not, except it be furnished with something else. This is not the truth of the gospel, but falsehood and dissimulation. The true gospel is that the works of charity are not the ornament or perfection of faith: but that faith itself is God's gift and God's work in our hearts, which therefore justifies us, because it apprehends Christ our Redeemer. Man's reason has the law for its object, thus thinking with itself: this have I done, this I have not done. But faith being in her own proper office, has no other object but Jesus Christ the Son of God, delivered to death for the sins of the whole world. It looks not to charity: it says not, what have I done? what have I offended? what have I deserved? but what has Christ done? What has He deserved? Here the truth of the gospel answers you: He has redeemed you from your sin, from the devil, and from eternal death. Faith therefore acknowledges that in this one person, Jesus Christ, it has forgiveness of sins and eternal life. He that turns his eyes from this object has no true faith, but a fantasy and a vain opinion, and turns his eyes from the promise to the law, which terrifies and drives to desperation.

So those things which are taught concerning the justifying faith being furnished with charity are nothing else but dreams. For that faith which apprehends Christ the Son of God and is furnished with Him is the same faith which justifies, and not the faith which includes charity. For a true and steadfast faith must lay hold on nothing but Christ alone, and in the terrors of conscience it has nothing else to lean upon, but this diamond Christ Jesus. So he who apprehends Christ by faith, although he be ever so much terrified with the law, and with the weight of his sins, yet may he be bold to glory that he is righteous. How, or by what means? Even by that precious pearl, Christ Jesus, whom he possesses by faith. This our adversaries understand not, and therefore they cast away this precious pearl Christ, and in His place they set charity. Now when they cannot tell what faith is, it is impossible that they should have faith, much less can they teach it to others. And as for that which they seem to have, it is nothing but natural reason, an opinion, a very dream and no faith.

This I say, to the end you may receive and note that by these words, "the truth of the gospel," Paul vehemently reproves the contrary. He reprehends the false apostles because they had taught a false gospel, requiring circumcision and the observation of the law as necessary to salvation. Moreover, they went about by craft and subtlety to entrap Paul, for they watched him to see whether he would circumcise Titus or not; also, whether he would dare withstand them in the presence of the Apostles, and for this cause he reprehends them bitterly. "They went about to spy out our liberty which we have in Christ Jesus, to bring us into bondage." We did not suffer our liberty to come in danger, but we overcame them even by the judgment of the Apostles themselves, and we would not yield to them, no, not for one hour, since we saw they required the observation of the law as necessary to salvation.

In like manner we will not suffer our consciences to be bound to any work, so that by doing this thing or that, we should be righteous, or leaving the same undone, we should be damned.

As our adversaries will not leave this free unto us, that only faith in Christ justifieth, so on the other side neither will we, nor can we, give place to them, that faith furnished with charity justifies. For the matter which we have in hand is weighty and of great importance, even touching the death of the Son of God, who by the will and commandment of the Father was made flesh, was crucified, and died for the sins of the world. If faith in Him here give place, then is this death and resurrection of the Son of God in vain; then it is but a fable that Christ is the Savior of the world. Our stoutness then in this matter is godly and holy, for by it we seek to keep our liberty which we have in Christ Jesus, and thereby to retain the truth of the gospel; which if we lose, then do we also lose God, Christ, all the promises, faith, righteousness, and everlasting life.

> 6—But of these who seemed to be somewhat (whatsoever they were,
> it maketh no matter to me: God accepteth no man's person): for they
> who seemed to be somewhat in conference added nothing to me.

Paul does not give to the true Apostles any glorious title; but, as it were, abasing their dignity, he says: "these who seemed to be somewhat''; that is, who were in authority and upon whom the determination of matters depended. But he spoke so because the false apostles set the dignity and authority of the Apostles against Paul to weaken his authority and bring his ministry into contempt. This Paul would not suffer. He admits the Apostles are indeed somewhat and their authority to be reverenced. Yet his gospel and ministry ought not to be overthrown for the name or title of any, whatsoever he be, an apostle, or an angel from heaven.

He adds a reason for this: ''God accepteth no man's person.'' This he alleges out of Moses: ''Thou shalt not respect the person of the poor, nor honour the dignity of the mighty'' (Leviticus 19:15). It is a principle of divinity: God is no respecter of person, so King Jehoshaphat said in 2 Chronicles 19:7; Peter in Acts 10:34; and Paul himself in Romans 2:11, Ephesians 6:9, Colossians 3:25. It is not the dignity or authority of men that God regards. He suffered Judas to fall away, and Saul, the first King, He rejected, and you will find throughout the Scriptures that God oftentimes rejected those who in outward show were good and holy men.

If in these examples God seemed to be cruel, it was necessary that such fearful examples should be given and also written. For this vice is naturally grafted in us, to highly esteem the persons and outward state of men, and regard them more than the Word of God. Contrariwise God will have us fix our eyes, and to rest wholly upon the Word itself; He will not have us reverence the apostleship in the persons of Peter or Paul, but Christ speaking in them, and the Word that they bring, and preach unto us.

This the natural man cannot see: but the spiritual man only discerns the person from the Word, the veil of God from God Himself. Now this veil of God is every creature.

Moreover, God here in this life deals not with us face to face, but covered and shadowed from us; that is, as Paul says in another place: ''Now we see through a glass, darkly, but then face to face'' (1 Corinthians 13:12). Therefore we cannot be without veils in this life. And here wisdom is required, which can discern the veil from God Himself; and this wisdom the world does not have. The covetous man hears, "Man doth not live by bread alone, but by every word that proceedeth out of the mouth of God" (Deuteronomy 8:3; Matthew 4:4). He eats the bread, but sees not God in the bread, for he beholds the veil only. So he does with gold and other creatures, trusting in them so long as he has them; but when they leave him, he despairs. So he honors not the Creator, but the creatures; not God, but his own belly.

This I speak, lest any man should think that Paul utterly condemns these outward veils or persons. For he says not that there ought to be no persons, but that there is no respect of persons with God. There must be persons, and outward veils: God has given them, and they are His good creatures; but we must not trust in them.

So the prince, the magistrate, the preacher, the schoolmaster, the scholar, the father, the mother, the children, the master, the servant, are persons, and outward veils, which God will have us acknowledge, love, and reverence, as His creatures. This is necessary in this life, but He will not have us so reverence them and put our trust in them that we forget Him. To this end we should not too much magnify the outward persons, or put too great trust in them; God leaves in them offenses and sins, yea, great and foul sins, to teach us what difference there is between persons and God Himself. David, that good King, because he should not seem to be a person upon whom men should trust, fell into horrible sins, adultery and murder. Peter, that excellent Apostle, denied Christ. These and such examples of which the Scriptures are full, ought to warn us, that we must not put our trust in persons and outward veils, nor think that when we have the outward show, we have all things. Those who judge things according to the outward veil are guilty of a mere respecting of persons and outward shows.

Let us then use bread, wine, apparel, possessions, gold, silver, and all other creatures; but let us not trust or glory in them. We must trust and glory in God alone. He only is to be loved; He only is to be feared and honored. Paul here calls the apostleship, or office of the Apostles (which wrought miracles, converted many to the faith, and were also familiar with Christ) the person of man. The word *person* includes the whole outward behavior of the Apostles which was holy, and their authority great. Yet, Paul says, God esteems not these things; not that He esteems them not at all, but in the matter of justification He regards them not, no matter how great and glorious they seem. For we must mark this distinction, that in matters of divinity we must speak far otherwise than in matters of policy. In matters of policy, God will have us honor and reverence these outward veils, or persons, as His instruments by whom He governs the world. But when the question touches religion, conscience, the fear of God, faith, and the service of God, we must not fear these outward persons, we must put no trust in them, look for no comfort from them, or hope of deliverance by them. For this cause God will have no respect of persons in judgment: for judgment is a divine thing.

By this rule, I would honor the Pope and love his person, if he would leave my conscience free and not compel me to sin against God. But he will be so feared and adored as cannot be done without offense to the majesty of God.

If we must lose one, let us lose the person and stick to God. For it is written: "That we must obey God rather than man" (Acts 5:29).

Apart from religion, we must have regard to the person; for otherwise there would follow confusion and an end of all reverence and order. In this world God will have an order, a reverence, and a difference of persons. Or else the child, the scholar, the servant, the subject would say: I am a Christian as well as my father, my schoolmaster, my master, my prince; why then should I reverence him? Before God, then, there is no respect of persons, neither of Grecian nor of Jew, but all are one in Christ; although not so before the world.

The question is not concerning respect of persons, but there is a far weightier matter in hand, that is to say, a divine matter concerning God and His Word, and whether this Word ought to be preferred before the apostleship or no. Paul answers: So that the truth of the gospel may continue, so that the Word of God and the righteousness of faith may be kept pure and uncorrupt, let the apostleship go, let an angel from heaven, let Peter, let Paul altogether perish.

As though he would say: I did not so confer with the Apostles, that they taught me anything. For what should they teach me, since Christ by His revelation had taught me all things, and since I have now preached the gospel for eighteen years among the Gentiles? Wherefore it was but a conference and no disputation. I learned nothing, neither did I recant, nor yet defend my cause, but only declared what things I had done: to wit, that I had preached to the Gentiles faith only in Christ, without the law, and that by this preaching of faith the Holy Ghost came down upon the Gentiles. When the Apostles heard it, they witnessed that I had taught the truth.

Now this pride of Paul, whereby he said that the other Apostles communicated nothing unto him, is not a fault, but most necessary; for had he yielded here, the truth of the gospel had perished. But if Paul would give no place to the false apostles, which set the authority of the true Apostles against him, much less ought we to give place to our adversaries. I know that the godly ought to be humble, but against the Pope I ought to be proud with a holy pride. We do not then disregard the authority of the Pope because we would bear rule over him, neither would we go about to exalt ourselves above all sovereign power, since it is evident that we teach all men to humble and submit themselves to the higher powers ordained of God; but this is it that we only seek, that the glory of God may be maintained, and the righteousness of faith may be kept pure and sound.

If the Pope will grant unto us that God alone by His mere grace through Christ does justify sinners, we will not only carry him in our hands, but will also kiss his feet. But since we cannot obtain this, we in God will give no place, no, not one hair's breadth, to all the angels in heaven, not to Peter, not to Paul, not to a hundred emperors, nor to a thousand popes, nor to the whole world. Let this be then the conclusion: that we will suffer our goods to be taken away, our name, our life, and all that we have; but the gospel, our faith, Jesus Christ, we will never suffer to be wrested from us.

Wherefore, God assisting me, my forehead shall be more hard than all men's foreheads. Here I take upon me this title, according to the proverb: *cedo nulli,* I give place to none. Yea, I am glad even with all my heart, in this point to seem rebellious and obstinate. And here I confess that I will not one inch give place to any creature. Charity gives place, for it "beareth all things, believeth all things, hopeth all things, endureth all things" (1 Corinthians 13:7), but faith gives no place.

7, 8—But contrariwise, when they saw that the gospel of the uncircumcision was committed unto me, as the gospel of the circumcision was unto Peter; (for he that wrought effectually in Peter to the apostleship of the circumcision, the same was mighty in me towards the Gentiles).

With these words Paul mightily refutes the false apostles, for here he takes to himself the same authority which the false apostles attributed to the true Apostles; and he uses here a figure which is called an inversion, returning their argument against themselves. The false apostles, says he, use against me the authority of the great Apostles to maintain their cause; but I, contrariwise, use the same against them for my defense, for the Apostles are on my side. Wherefore, O Galatians, believe not these counterfeit apostles. For the Apostles, when they saw the gospel of the uncircumcision to be committed to me, and knew of the grace that to me was given, gave to me and Barnabas the right hand of fellowship, approving my ministry and giving thanks unto God for the gifts which I had received. Thus he returns the argument of the false apostles upon themselves.

Paul says that the gospel of the uncircumcision was committed unto him, and of the circumcision unto Peter, although Paul almost everywhere preached to the Jews in their synagogues, and Peter likewise to the Gentiles. There are examples and testimonies of both in the Acts. Peter converted the centurion with his family, who was a Gentile (Acts 10:1 ff.). He wrote also to the Gentiles, as his first epistle testifies. Paul, preaching Christ among the Gentiles, entered into the synagogues of the Jews, and there preached the gospel (Acts 9:20). And our Savior Christ, in Matthew and Mark, commanded His Apostles to go throughout the whole world, and preach the gospel to every creature. Paul likewise says: ''the Gospel preached to every creature which is under heaven'' (Colossians 1:23). Why then does he call himself the Apostle of the Gentiles, and Peter the Apostle of the circumcision?

Paul is referring to the fact that the other Apostles remained specially in Judea and Jerusalem, until God called them unto other places. While the political state of the Jews continued, the Apostles remained in Judea; but when the destruction of Jerusalem approached, they were dispersed throughout the whole world. But Paul, as it is written in the Acts (13:2), by a singular vocation was chosen to be the Apostle of the Gentiles, and being sent out of Judea, he traveled through the countries of the Gentiles. Now were the Jews dispersed almost throughout the whole world, and dwelt here and there in cities and other places among the Gentiles. Paul coming thither, made it his custom to go into the synagogues of the Jews, and by this occasion he first brought unto them, as the children of the kingdom, this glad tidings, that the promises made to the fathers were accomplished by Jesus Christ. When they would not hear this, he turned to the Gentiles, as Luke witnesses, Acts 13:46—''It was necessary that we should first preach the word of God unto you; but seeing ye reject it, and judge yourselves unworthy of everlasting life, lo! we turn to the Gentiles'' and Acts 28:28—''Be it known therefore unto you, that this salvation of God is sent unto the Gentiles, and they shall hear it.'' Wherefore Paul was sent specially unto the Gentiles. But because he was a debtor unto all, and became all things unto all men, therefore he went into the synagogues of the Jews, where not only the Jews, but also the Gentiles, heard him preaching Christ. At other times he preached publicly in the marketplace, in houses, and by the rivers' sides. He was specially then the Apostle of the Gentiles, as Peter was of the Jews.

And here he calls uncircumcision the Gentiles, and circumcision the Jews, by a figure named *synecdoche,* by which a part comprehends the whole. The gospel then of the uncircumcision is that which was appointed to be sent unto the Gentiles. This gospel, says he, was committed unto him, as the gospel of the circumcision was unto Peter; for as Peter preached the gospel among the Jews, so did he among the Gentiles.

This he often repeats, that Peter, James, and John, which seemed to be the pillars of the Church, taught him nothing, nor committed unto him the office of preaching the gospel, as having authority and rule over him. But they themselves, says he, did see that the gospel was committed unto me, for as I did not receive or learn the gospel of man, so did I receive no commandment by man to preach the same, but both the knowledge and the commandment to preach it among the Gentiles, I received immediately from Christ.

This place witnesses very plainly that the Apostles had like calling, like charge, and all one gospel. Peter preached no other gospel than the rest of the Apostles did, neither did he appoint to others their charge and office; but there was an equality among them all, for they were all taught and called of God. There was none, therefore, greater than other, none that had any prerogative above other.

To conclude, Paul will be counted in no point inferior to the rest of the Apostles; and herein he glories with a godly and a holy pride. Necessity constrained him stoutly to withstand Peter, and the burning zeal he had for the glory of God moved him so to do. Certain profane spirits, as Julian and Porphyrius, thought it to be but a carnal pride that caused Paul thus to do. But Paul had not here his own business in hand, but a matter of faith. Now, as concerning faith we ought to be invincible, and more hard, if it might be, than the adamant stone; but as touching charity, we ought to be soft, and more flexible than a leaf shaken in the wind. Therefore, the controversy was not concerning the glory of Paul, but the glory of God, the Word of God, the true worship of God, and the righteousness of faith, to the end that these things might remain pure and uncorrupt.

9—And when James, Cephas, and John, who seemed to be pillars, perceived the grace that was given unto me, they gave to me and Barnabas the right hands of fellowship: that we should go unto the heathen, and they unto the circumcision.

Paul is saying, when they heard that I had received my calling and charge from God, to preach the gospel among the Gentiles, and that God had wrought so many miracles by me, and that so great a number of the Gentiles had received the Holy Ghost, without the law and circumcision, by the preaching of faith only, they glorified God for His grace which was given unto me. He calls grace here whatsoever he had received of God: to wit, that from a persecutor and waster of the Church, he was made an Apostle, was taught by Jesus Christ, and enriched with spiritual gifts. And he shows that when Peter, John, and James became aware of all this, they approved him, gave to him the right hands of fellowship, and were wholly with him, not against him.

"The right hands of fellowship" expressed agreement between the chief Apostles and Paul, as if to say, in doctrine we are companions and have fellowship together therein, for we preach one gospel, one baptism, one Christ, one faith. And we conclude that neither uncircumcision nor circumcision ought to hinder our society and fellowship, since it is but one gospel which we preach.

> *10—Only they would that we should remember the poor; the same which I also was forward to do.*

After the preaching of the gospel, the office and charge of a true and faithful pastor is to be mindful of the poor.

Where the Church is, there must needs be poor, for Christ said we should have the poor with us always: and "the poor have the gospel preached to them" (Matthew 11:5). For the world and the devil do persecute the Church and bring many to poverty. A true and faithful pastor must have a care of the poor; and this care Paul here confesses that he had.

> *11—But when Peter was come to Antioch, I withstood him to the face, because he was to be blamed.*

Going on with his confutation, Paul says that having got the testimony of Peter and the other Apostles to his ministry, he was forced to withstand Peter when he came to Antioch, in the presence of the whole Church.

Here he has no trifling matter in hand, but the chiefest article of all Christian doctrine. When you understand the utility and majesty of this doctrine, all other things seem worth nothing. What is Peter? What is Paul? What is an angel from heaven? What are all creatures together, compared to the article of justification, which Paul here saw in danger by the conduct of Peter. Wherefore he was obliged to put aside the dignity of Peter for the truth's sake.

Wherefore we are not ashamed for the defense of the truth, to be counted and called hypocrites, proud and obstinate, such as will be only wise, will hear none, will give place to none. For here we must needs be obstinate and inflexible. For the cause why we offend man is so great that the sins which the world judges to be most heinous are counted singular virtues before God. In that we love our parents, honor the magistrates, show reverence to Peter and other ministers of the Word, we do well. But here we have in hand the cause neither of Peter, nor parents, nor magistrates, nor of the world, nor of any other creatures, but of God Himself. Here if I give no place to these or to an angel from heaven, I do well. For what is the creature in respect of the Creator? Yes, what are all creatures compared to Him? This I say so that you should diligently weigh and consider the matter which Paul treats: for he treats of the Word of God which can never be magnified enough.

And when Paul says he withstood Peter "to his face," he makes a point specially against those apostles of Satan, which slander those who are absent, and in their presence dare not open their mouths, as the false apostles did. So did not I (says he) speak evil of Peter, but frankly and openly I withstood him to his face, not for any ambition or other carnal affection, but because he was to be blamed.

Here let other men debate whether an Apostle may sin or no; this say I, that we ought not to make Peter's fault less than it was indeed. The prophets themselves have sometimes erred, and been deceived. Nathan said unto David that he should build a house unto the Lord (2 Samuel 7:3). But this prophecy was later corrected by a revelation from God. So did the Apostles err also, for they imagined that the Kingdom of Christ should be carnal and of this world, saying, "Lord, wilt Thou at this time restore again the Kingdom to Israel?" (Acts 1:6).

And Peter, although he heard the command of Christ, "Go into all the world, and preach the gospel to every creature" (Mark 16:15), would not have gone to Cornelius if he had not been admonished and compelled by a vision. And in this matter of Paul's rebuke, he did not only err in judgment, but committed a great sin. If Paul had not resisted him, all the Gentiles which did believe would have been constrained to receive circumcision and to keep the law. The believing Jews also had been confirmed in their opinion, to wit, that the observation of these things was necessary to salvation, and by this means they had received again the law instead of the gospel, Moses instead of Christ. And of all this great enormity, Peter, by his dissimulation, had been the occasion. Therefore, we may not attribute to the saints such perfection, as though they could not sin.

Luke witnesses that there was "sharp contention" between Paul and Barnabas, those long and close companions, over John Mark (Acts 15:39), that led to their separation. We must needs say there was some fault either in Paul or Barnabas. Such examples are written for our consolation.

For it is a comfort to us, when we hear, that even the saints, which have the Spirit of God, do sin.

Samson, David, and many other excellent men, fell into great sins (Judges 16; 2 Samuel 11). Job and Jeremiah cursed the day of their birth (Job 3:1; Jeremiah 20:14). Elijah and Jonah are weary of their life and desire death. No man takes so fast footing but that he may fall. If Peter fell, I may fall too. If he rose again, I, too, may rise again. We have the selfsame spirit of grace and prayer which the Apostles and all the saints had; neither had they any prerogative above us.

12—For before that certain came from James, he did eat with the Gentiles: but when they were come, he withdrew and separated himself, fearing them which were of the circumcision.

The newly converted Gentiles ate meats forbidden by the law, and Peter ate and drank with them, and therefore transgressed the law with the Gentiles. Paul confesses that he did the like. Peter, in eating and drinking with the Gentiles, sinned not, but did well, and knew that it was lawful for him so to do. For he showed by this transgression of the law, that the law was not necessary to righteousness, and also delivered the Gentiles from the observation of the law. And Paul does not here reprove Peter for breaking the law, but for his dissimulation that followed.

Paul accuses him not of malice or ignorance, but of dissimulation and infirmity, fearing lest the Jews which came from James should be offended to see him eat with Gentiles. Hereby he gave occasion, as much as in him was, to overthrow the Christian liberty and truth of the gospel.

Note that the end and inference of this fact was evil, and not the fact itself; for the fact itself was not evil.

To eat and drink, or not to eat and drink, is nothing; but the end, that is, if you eat, you sin, if you abstain, you are righteous, is evil. So circumcision of itself is good, but the end evil: if you are not circumcised after the law of Moses, you cannot be saved.

Also to eat meats not sanctioned in the law is not evil. But this shrinking and dissimulation of Peter is evil. Thereafter Peter abstained from meats forbidden in the law, wherefore if you do not likewise abstain, you cannot be saved. This Paul might in no wise dissemble: for the truth of the gospel was in danger. To the end that the truth might continue sound and uncorrupt, he resisted Peter to his face.

Here we must make a distinction. Meats may be refused two manner of ways. First, for Christian charity's sake. And herein is no danger, for to bear with the infirmity of my brother is good. Second, by abstaining from meat to obtain righteousness, and this is to deny Christ through whom alone we obtain righteousness.

Jerome, who understood neither this place nor this epistle, thinks this but a feigned reprehension of Paul and excuses Peter's fall, saying it was done by ignorance.

But Peter offended through dissimulation, and thereby had established the necessity of the law. He had constrained both Gentiles and Jews to revolt from the truth of the gospel, had given them great occasion to forsake Christ, to despise grace, to return to the Jewish religion, and to bear all the burdens of the law, if Paul had not reproved him, and by that means recalled the Gentiles and Jews which were offended through this example of Peter, to the liberty which is in Christ Jesus, and to the truth of the gospel. So we may not trifle with this article of justification: neither is it without good cause that we do so often and so diligently put you in mind thereof.

It is much to be marveled that Peter, being so excellent an Apostle, should fall into this error, for at the council in Jerusalem, he was very bold in defense of this very article, when the Pharisees which believed, held that it was necessary to circumcise the Gentile converts, and command them to keep the law of Moses. Peter then protested vehemently against putting a yoke upon the Gentiles "which neither our fathers nor we were able to bear" (Acts 15:5–11).

"Let him that thinketh he standeth take heed lest he fall" (1 Corinthians 10:12). No one would think what danger there is in traditions and ceremonies. Of the law comes a trust in works, and where that is, there can be no proper trust in Christ.

Peter knew the article of justification better than we do, and yet how easily he gave great occasion of offense, if Paul had not withstood him.

13—And the other Jews dissembled likewise with him; insomuch that Barnabas also was carried away with their dissimulation.

Here you see plainly that Paul charges Peter with dissimulation. If Peter dissembled, then did he certainly know what was the truth, and what was not. He that dissembles sins not of ignorance, but deceives by a color which he knows to be false.

That Barnabas, Paul's companion and witness of Gentile conversion to faith in Christ without the law, should now be brought into their dissimulation, shows the great seriousness of this occasion.

It is a wonderful matter to consider that God preserved the Church being yet young, and the gospel itself by one person only, Paul alone standing for the truth. Peter was against him, and Barnabas was wavering. So sometimes one man is able to do more in a council than the whole council itself.

Paul then reproved Peter for no light matter, but for the chief article of all Christian doctrine, which by Peter's dissimulation was in great danger. Certainly it is much to be marveled that such excellent men as Peter, Barnabas, and others, should so suddenly and so lightly fall, especially in that thing which they had before held, and taught to others. It is a perilous thing to trust to our own strength, for in that we think ourselves most sure, we may err and fall, and bring ourselves and others into great danger.

Thus we see that we are nothing with all our gifts be they ever so great, except God assist us. When He leaves us to ourselves, our wisdom and knowledge are nothing. For in the hour of temptation it may suddenly come to pass, that, by the subtlety of the devil, all the comfortable places of the Scriptures shall be taken away out of our sight, and such places only as contain threatenings shall be set before our eyes. These places shall oppress us and utterly confound us. Let us learn therefore that if God withdraws His hand, we may soon be overthrown; and let no man glory of his own righteousness, wisdom, and other gifts; but let him humble himself, and pray with the Apostles, "Lord, increase our faith" (Luke 17:5).

14—*But when I saw that they walked not uprightly according to the truth of the gospel, I said unto Peter before them all, If thou, being a Jew, livest after the manner of Gentiles, and not as do the Jews, why compellest thou the Gentiles to live as do the Jews?*

There is none but Paul that has his eyes open, and sees the offense of Peter, of Barnabas, and the other Jews that dissembled. They do not see their offense, but rather think they do well in bearing with the infirmity of the weak Jews. Wherefore it was very necessary that Paul should reprove their offense, that is, that they swerved from the truth of the gospel.

It is a great matter that Peter should be accused by Paul as one that had fallen from the truth of the gospel. He could not be more grievously reprehended. Yet he suffered it patiently; and, no doubt, acknowledged his offense. I said before, that many have the gospel, but not the truth of the gospel.

So Paul says here of Peter, Barnabas, and other Jews, they ''went not the right way of the gospel,'' that is to say, they had the gospel, but they walked not uprightly according to the gospel. They preached the gospel, but through their dissimulation, they established the law. The establishing of the law, however, is the abolishing of the gospel.

Whoso then can rightly judge between the law and the gospel, let him thank God, and know he is a good minister. In the time of temptation, I confess that I myself do not know how to do it as I ought. Now the way to discern the one from the other is to place the gospel in heaven, and the law on the earth. Call the righteousness of the gospel heavenly, and the righteousness of the law earthly, and put as great difference between the righteousness of the gospel and of the law, as God hath made between heaven and earth, light and darkness, between day and night.

If your conscience be terrified with the sense and feeling of sin, think this within yourself: You are now remaining upon earth; there let the ass labor; there let him serve and carry the burden that is laid upon him; that is, let the body, with its members, be subject to the law. But when you mount up into heaven, then leave the ass with his burden upon earth, for the conscience has nothing to do with the law or works or with the earthly righteousness. So does the ass remain in the valley, but the conscience ascends with Isaac into the mount, knowing nothing at all of the law or works thereof, but only looking to the remission of sins and pure righteousness offered and freely given to us in Christ.

Contrariwise, in civil policy, obedience to the law must be severely required. There nothing must be known as concerning the gospel, conscience, grace, remission of sins, heavenly righteousness, or Christ Himself, but Moses only, with the law and the works thereof. If we mark well this distinction, neither the one nor the other shall pass its bounds, but the law shall abide without heaven, that is, without the heart and conscience, and the liberty of the gospel should abide without the earth, that is, without the body and the members thereof.

Therefore, as soon as the law and sin come into heaven (that is, into the conscience), let them be cast out. For the conscience ought to know nothing of the law and sin, but of Christ only. On the other side, when grace and liberty come into earth (that is, into the body) then say: you ought not to dwell in the dregs and dunghill of this corporal life, but you belong in heaven.

This distinction between the law and the gospel Peter confounds through his dissimulation, and therefore he persuades the believing Jews that they must be justified by the gospel and the law together. This, Paul could not accept and therefore he reproves Peter, not to put him to any reproach, but to the end that he might again establish a plain distinction between these two, namely, that the gospel justifies in heaven, and the law on earth.

This place, touching the difference between the law and the gospel, is very necessary to be known, for it contains the sum of all Christian doctrine. Wherefore let all who love and fear God, diligently learn to discern the one from the other, not only in words, but in deed and in practice; that is to say, in heart and conscience.

Paul's rebuke of Peter contains this: You are a Jew and therefore are bound to live as a Jew; that is, to abstain from meats forbidden in the law. Yet you live like a Gentile: that is, you do things contrary to the law. For, as a Gentile, which is free from the law, you eat common and unclean meats, and therein you do well, for in Christ we have liberty in these things. But in that you, being afraid at the presence of brethren converted from the Jewish religion, abstained from meats forbidden in the law, you compel the Jews likewise to keep the law.

For, in that you abstain from profane meats, you give occasion to the Gentiles thus to think: Peter abstains from those meats the Gentiles eat, which also he himself before did eat. Therefore we ought also to avoid the same and live after the manner of the Jews; otherwise we cannot be justified or saved. We see then that Paul reproves not ignorance in Peter (for he knew that he might freely eat with the Gentiles all manner of meats) but dissimulation, whereby he deceived the Gentiles, and gave them occasion to live like the Jews. Here I say again, that to live as the Jew is not evil of itself, for it is a thing indifferent either to eat swine's flesh, or other meats. But so to play the Jew, that for conscience' sake you abstain from certain meats, is to deny Christ and to overthrow the gospel. Therefore when Paul saw that Peter's act tended to this end, he withstood him, and said: You know that the keeping of the law is not necessary to righteousness, but that we are justified only through faith in Christ, and therefore you keep not the law, but transgress the law and eat all manner of meats. Yet by your example, now that the Jews are come, you constrain the Gentiles to forsake Christ and turn to the law. For you give them occasion thus to think: faith only is not sufficient to righteousness, but the law and works are also required; and this Peter teaches us by his example. Therefore the observation of the law must needs be joined with faith in Christ, if we are to be saved.

Wherefore Peter, by his example, is not only prejudicial to the purity of doctrine, but also to the truth of faith and Christian righteousness. For if the Gentiles received of him that the keeping of the law was necessary to righteousness, in case that be admitted, and not contradicted, then Christ profits us not at all.

Paul does nothing by dissimulation, but deals sincerely; Peter had dissembled, but Paul reproved him. The controversy was for the maintenance of pure doctrine, and the truth of the gospel, and in this dispute Paul did not care for the offense of any. In this, and such cases, all people and nations, all kings and princes, all judges and magistrates ought to give place. Since then it is so dangerous a thing to have to do with the law, and that this fall was so sudden and great, as it had been from heaven above, even down into hell, let every Christian learn diligently to discern between the law and the gospel. Let him suffer the law to rule over the body, and the members thereof, but not over the conscience. For that queen and spouse may not be defiled with the law, but must be kept without spot for her only husband Christ, as Paul says (2 Corinthians 11:2): "I have espoused you to one husband, that I may present you as a chaste virgin to Christ."

4

The Way of Justification

Galatians 2:15–21

> *15, 16—We who are Jews by nature, and not sinners of the Gentiles, knowing that a man is not justified by the works of the law, but by the faith of Jesus Christ, even we have believed in Jesus Christ, that we might be justified by the faith of Christ, and not by the works of the law: for by the works of the law shall no flesh be justified.*

That is to say, we are born unto the righteousness of the law, to Moses, and to circumcision, and even in our birth we bring the law with us. We have the righteousness of the law by nature. If we are compared to the Gentiles, we are not sinners; we are not without the law and works as the Gentiles are; but we are Jews born, born righteous, and brought up in righteousness. The law of circumcision was received from the fathers and confirmed by Moses. It is a great matter that we are Jews by nature. Yet, although we have this prerogative, that we are righteous by nature, born to the law, and the works thereof, and are not sinners of the Gentiles, we are not thereby righteous before God.

It is evident that Paul speaks not of the ceremonial law, as some affirm, but of a far weightier matter, namely, of the nativity of the Jews, whom he deems to be righteous. They are born holy, are circumcised, keep the law, have the adoption, the glory, the covenant, the fathers, the true worship, God; as they say: "We be Abraham's seed" (John 8:33); also:

"We have one Father, which is God"; and in Romans (2:17): "Behold, thou art called a Jew, and restest in the law." Yet Christian righteousness comes not thereby, for none of these is faith in Christ which alone justifies, and not the law. Not that the law is evil, for the law, circumcision, and such like, are not therefore condemned because they do not justify. Paul takes from them the office of justification because the false apostles contended that by them, without faith, men are justified and saved. This was not to be allowed by Paul, for without faith all things are deadly; the law, circumcision, the adoption, the temple, worship of God, the promises, all without faith profit nothing.

> *16a—Knowing that a man is not justified by the works of the law, but by the faith of Jesus Christ.*

This word "works of the law" reaches far; it extends to all that is contrary to grace. Whatever is not grace is the law, whether it be judicial, ceremonial, or the Ten Commandments. Wherefore if you could do the works of the law according to this commandment, "Thou shalt love the Lord thy God with all thy heart," etc. (which no man yet ever did nor could do), yet you should not be justified before God, for a man is not justified by the works of the law.

The works of the law, then, according to Paul, signify the works of the whole law, judicial, ceremonial, or moral. Now if the moral law does not justify, much less does the ceremonial law justify, and that includes circumcision.

When Paul says that a man is not justified by the law, or by the works of the law (which are the same), he speaks generally of the whole law, setting against it the righteousness of faith.

Wherefore any opinion which attributes merit of grace and remission of sins to work wrought is utterly to be condemned. Some say that a good work before grace is able to obtain grace because it is right that God should reward such a work. But when grace is obtained, the work following deserves everlasting life of due debt and worthiness. For example, if a man who is in deadly sin without grace, does a good work of his own natural inclination; that is, if he say or hear mass or give alms, and such like, this man deserves grace, they say. When he has thus obtained grace, he does now a work which of worthiness deserves everlasting life. For the first, God is no debtor; but because He is just and good, it behooves Him to approve such a good work, though it be done in deadly sin, and to give grace for such a service. But when grace has been obtained, God is become a debtor, and is constrained of right and duty to give eternal life.

You can see how far from the truth these blind guides have wandered, and how by this wicked and blasphemous doctrine they have not only darkened the gospel but have taken it clean away, and buried Christ utterly. For if I being in deadly sin, can do any little work which is not only acceptable in God's sight of itself, but also is able to deserve grace, and if when I have received grace, I may do works according to grace, that is to say, according to charity, and get eternal life; what need have I now of the grace of God, forgiveness of sins, and of the death and victory of Christ? According to this argument Christ is now to me unprofitable, and His benefit of no effect: for I have free will and power to do good works, whereby I deserve grace, and afterwards, by the worthiness of my work, eternal life.

By deadly sin they understood only the external work committed against the law, as murder, theft, and such like. They could not see that ignorance, hatred and contempt of God in the heart, ingratitude, murmuring against God, are also deadly sins, and that the flesh cannot think, speak, or do anything but that which is devilish and altogether against God. If they had seen these mischiefs fast rooted in the nature of man, they would never have dared to devise such execrable and impudent dreams.

So we must plainly define what a deadly sinner is. He is such a holy and bloody hypocrite as Paul was, when he was on the way to Damascus, to persecute Jesus of Nazareth, to stamp out the doctrine of the gospel, to murder the faithful, and utterly to overthrow the Church of Christ. And who will not say, but that these were horrible sins? Yet Paul could not see them. He was blinded by a perverse zeal for God, so that he thought these things perfect righteousness and high service unto God.

So with Paul, we affirm that these speculations are nothing else but mere deceits of Satan. These disputations of the schoolmen are nothing else but vain toys and dreams of idle brains, to no other end and purpose but to draw men from the true worship of God.

The True Way to Christianity

The true way to Christianity is this, that a man first acknowledges himself by the law to be a sinner, and that it is impossible for him to do any good work. For the law says: You are an evil tree, and therefore all that you think, speak, or do, is against God. You cannot therefore deserve grace by your works: which if you go about to do, you double your offense; for since you are an evil tree, you cannot but bring forth evil fruits, that is to say, sins. "For whatsoever is not of faith, is sin" (Romans 14:23). So he who would merit grace by works going before faith, goes about to please God with sins, which is nothing else but to heap sin upon sin, to mock God, and to provoke His wrath. When a man is thus taught and instructed by the law, then is he terrified and humbled, then he sees indeed the greatness of his sin, and cannot find in himself one spark of the love of God; therefore, he justifies God in His Word, and confesses that he is guilty of death and eternal damnation. The first part then of Christianity is the preaching of repentance and the knowledge of ourselves.

The second part is: if you will be saved, you may not seek salvation by works; for God has sent His only begotten Son into the world, that we might live through Him. He was crucified and died for you, and bore your sins in His own body. Wherefore the law does nothing else but utter sin, terrify and humble, and by this means prepares us to justification, and drives us to Christ. For God has revealed to us by His Word that He will be to us a merciful Father, and without our deserts (seeing we can deserve nothing) will freely give to us remission of sins, righteousness and life everlasting, for Christ His Son's sake. For God gives His gifts freely to all men, and that is the praise and glory of His divinity. This briefly is our doctrine of Christian righteousness.

This doctrine is contrary to the teaching of the schoolmen who imagine that when a man does any good work, God accepts it, and for that work He pours into him charity, which they call charity infused. This they call formal righteousness, and they can abide nothing less than to hear that this quality adorning the soul, as whiteness does the wall, should not be counted righteousness. They can climb no higher than to this notion that man is righteous by his own formal righteousness, which is grace making him acceptable unto God. So to this quality cleaving to the soul they attribute formal righteousness and they say that this righteousness is worthy of everlasting life.

But instead of charity we place faith, and we say that faith apprehends Jesus Christ, who is the form which adorns faith, as the color adorns and beautifies the wall. Christian faith therefore is not an idle quality or empty husk in the heart, which may be in deadly sin until charity comes and quickens it. If it is true faith, it is a sure trust and confidence of the heart, and a firm consent whereby Christ is apprehended, so that Christ is the object of faith, yea rather in the faith itself Christ is present. Faith therefore is a certain obscure knowledge, or rather darkness which sees nothing, and yet Christ apprehended by faith sits in this darkness, as God in Sinai and in the Temple sat in the midst of darkness. Wherefore our formal righteousness is not charity furnishing and beautifying faith, but it is faith itself, which is, as it were, a certain cloud in our hearts; that is to say, a steadfast trust in the thing which we see not, which is Christ who, although He is not seen at all, yet is present.

Faith therefore justifies because it apprehends and possesses this treasure, even Christ present.

As the schoolmen say that charity adorns faith, so do we say that it is Christ who adorns faith. Wherefore Christ apprehended by faith, and dwelling in the heart, is the true Christian righteousness, for which God counts us righteous and gives us eternal life. Here is no work of the law, no charity, but a far other manner of righteousness, and a certain new world beyond and above the law.

The True Rule of Christianity

Contrary to these vain trifles and doting dreams we teach faith, and give a true rule of Christianity in this sort: first, that a man must be taught by the law to know himself, so he may learn to say: "All have sinned, and come short of the glory of God" (Romans 3:23); also, "There is none righteous, no, not one: there is none that understandeth, that seeketh after God; they are all gone out of the way" (Romans 3:10 ff.); also: "Against thee, thee only, have I sinned" (Psalms 51:4).

When a man is humbled by the law, and brought to the knowledge of himself, then follows true repentance (for true repentance begins at the fear and judgment of God), and he sees himself to be so great a sinner that he can find no means how he may be delivered from his sin by his own strength, endeavor and works. Then he perceives well what Paul means when he says that man is the servant and bondslave of sin (Romans 7:14); also that God has shut up all under sin (Romans 11:52; Galatians 3:22) and that the whole world is guilty before God (Romans 3:19). Then he sees that all the teaching of the schoolmen is nothing else but mere foolishness.

Now the sinner begins to sigh, and say: who then can help me? Terrified by the law and utterly despairing of his own strength, he looks about and sighs for the help of another, of a mediator and savior. Then comes in good time the healthful word of the gospel, which says, "Son, thy sins be forgiven thee" (Matthew 9:2). Believe in Jesus Christ, crucified for your sins. If you feel your sins and their burden, look not upon them in yourself, but remember that they are translated and laid upon Christ, whose stripes have made you whole (Isaiah 53:5). This is the beginning of health and salvation. By this means we are delivered from sin, justified and made inheritors of everlasting life, not for our own works and deserts, but for our faith, whereby we lay hold upon Christ.

Here it is necessary that you know the true definition of Christ. The schoolmen, being utterly ignorant thereof, have made Christ a Judge and a tormentor. But Christ, according to His true definition, is no lawgiver, but a forgiver of sins, and a Savior. Faith sees this and believes that He has wrought works and merit before and after grace abundantly. For He might have satisfied for all the sins of the world by only one drop of His blood; but now He has shed it plentifully, and has satisfied abundantly (Hebrews 9:12–14): "By His own blood He entered in once into the holy place, having obtained eternal redemption for us." And we are "justified freely by His grace, through the redemption that is in Christ Jesus" (Romans 3:24). So it is a great matter to lay hold upon Christ by faith, bearing the sins of the world. And this faith alone is counted for righteousness.

Here it should be noted that these three things—faith, Christ, acceptation, or imputation—must be joined together. Faith takes hold of Christ, and has Him present, and holds Him enclosed, as the ring does the precious stone. And whoever shall be found having this confidence in Christ in his heart, him will God accept for righteous. This is the mean and this is the merit whereby we attain the remission of sins and righteousness.

Because you believe in Me, says the Lord, and your faith lays hold upon Christ, whom I have freely given unto you, that He might be your mediator and high priest, therefore you are justified and righteous. So God accepts or accounts us as righteous for our faith in Christ only.

And this acceptation or imputation is very necessary: first, because we are not yet perfectly righteous, "but while we remain in this life, sin dwelleth still in our flesh"; and this remnant of sin God purges in us. Moreover, we sometimes fall into grievous sins, as did David, Peter and others. Yet have we always recourse to this article of faith, "That our sins are covered, and that God will not lay them to our charge" (Psalms 32:1; Romans 4:7). Not that sin is not in us; yea, sin is indeed always in us, and the godly do feel it, but it is covered, and is not imputed to us by God, for Christ's sake. Because we apprehend Christ by faith, all our sins are now no sins. But where Christ and faith are not, there is no remission or covering of sins, but imputation of sins and condemnation. Thus will God glorify His Son, and will be glorified Himself in us through Him.

When we have thus taught faith in Christ, then do we also teach good works. Because you have laid hold of Christ by faith, through whom you are made righteous, begin now to work well. Love God and your neighbors, call upon God, give thanks unto Him, praise Him, confess Him. These are good works indeed, which flow out of this faith, and this cheerfulness conceived in the heart, for that we have remission of sins freely by Christ.

Now the cross or affliction that follows is easily borne and cheerfully suffered, for Christ's yoke is easy and His burden is light (Matthew 11:30). But when a man walks in his own righteousness, whatever he does is grievous and tedious to him, because he does it unwillingly.

We therefore make this definition of a Christian: a Christian is not one who has no sin, but one to whom God imputes not his sin, through faith in Christ. That is why we so often repeat and beat into your minds, the forgiveness of sins and imputation of righteousness for Christ's sake. Therefore, when the law accuses him and sin terrifies him, he looks up to Christ, and when he has apprehended Him by faith, he has present with him the Conqueror of the law, sin, death, and the devil: and Christ reigns and rules over them, so that they cannot hurt the Christian. So that he has indeed a great and inestimable treasure, or as Paul said: "the unspeakable gift" (2 Corinthians 9:15), which cannot be magnified enough, for it makes us the children and heirs of God. This gift may be said to be greater than heaven and earth, because Christ, who is this gift, is greater.

While this doctrine remains pure and uncorrupt, Christians are made judges over all kinds of doctrine. This, says the Christian, is not the right way to justify us, neither does this way lead to heaven. Not by work going before grace, shall I deserve grace, nor by my work following grace shall I deserve eternal life; but to him that believes, sin is pardoned, and righteousness imputed. This truth and this confidence makes him the child of God, and heir of His Kingdom; for in hope he possesses everlasting life already, assured unto him by promise. Through faith in Christ therefore all things are given to us: grace, peace, forgiveness of sins, salvation, and everlasting life.

So these doctrines of the schoolmen are most abominable blasphemies against God, sacrileges and plain denials of Christ, as Peter has foretold in these words: "There shall be false teachers among you, who privily shall bring in damnable heresies" (2 Peter 2:1).

They take that privilege to themselves which belongs unto Christ alone. Only He forgives sins, only He gives righteousness and everlasting life. And they most impudently and wickedly do vaunt that they are able to obtain these things by their own merits and worthiness before and after grace. This, say Peter and the other Apostles, is to bring in damnable heresies, and sects of perdition.

When we are in the matter of justification, that is not the time or place to speak of the law: but the question is, what Christ is, and what benefit He has brought to us. Christ is not the law; He is not my work or the work of the law; He is not my charity, my obedience, my poverty; but He is the Lord of life and death, a mediator, a Savior, a Redeemer of those that are under the law and sin. In Him we are by faith, and He in us. The bridegroom must be alone with the bride, all the family and servants being put apart. But afterwards, when the door of their chamber is open, and he comes forth, then let the servants and handmaidens return to minister unto them: then let charity do her office, and let good works be done.

We must learn to discern all laws, yea, even the law of God, and all works, from the promise of the gospel, and from faith, that we may define Christ rightly. For Christ is no law, and therefore He is no exactor of the law and works, but "He is the Lamb of God, which taketh away the sin of the world" (John 1:29). So victory over sin and death, salvation and everlasting life, came not by the law, nor by the works of the law, nor yet by the power of free will, but by Jesus Christ only and alone.

So far we have heard the words of Paul which he spoke to Peter; now he turns to the Gentiles, to whom he writes, and thus concludes: "Because by the works of the law, no flesh shall be justified." Flesh does not signify here manifest and gross sins, for these Paul calls by their proper names, as adultery, fornication, uncleanness and such like; but by flesh, he means here, as Christ does in the third chapter of John, "That which is born of the flesh is flesh." Flesh therefore signifies the whole nature of man, with reason and all other powers which belong to man. This flesh is not justified by works, no, not of the law. Flesh, therefore, according to Paul, signifies all the righteousness, wisdom, devotion, religion, understanding and will that is possible to be in a natural man; so that if a man be ever so righteous according to reason, and the law of God, yet with all this righteousness, works, merits, devotion, and religion, he is not justified.

Wherefore I have often marveled that with sects of perdition reigning so many years in so great darkness and errors, the Church could endure and continue as it has done. Some there were whom God called by the test of the gospel and by baptism. These walked in simplicity and humbleness of heart, thinking the monks and friars, and such as were anointed by the bishops, to be religious and holy, and themselves to be profane and secular, and not worthy to be compared to them. Wherefore they, finding in themselves no good works to set against the wrath and judgment of God, did fly to the death and passion of Christ and were saved in this simplicity.

"Them that honour me," says God, "I will honour" (1 Samuel 2:30). Now God is honored in His Son. Whoever then believes that the Son is our mediator and Savior, he honors the Father, and him again does God honor; that is to say, adorns him with gifts, forgiveness of sins, righteousness, the Holy Ghost, and everlasting life. Contrariwise, "They that despise Me shall be lightly esteemed."

This then is a general conclusion, "By the deeds of the law no flesh shall be justified"; therefore, "only faith justifies."

> 17—But if, while we seek to be justified by Christ, we ourselves also
> are found sinners, is therefore Christ the minister of sin? God forbid.

If it is true, he says, that we are justified by Christ, then is it impossible that we should be justified by the law. On the contrary, if this be not true, but that we must be justified by the law, it is then impossible that we should be justified by Christ. One of these two must be false. Either we are not justified by Christ, or we are not justified by the law.

But the truth is that we are justified by Christ; therefore, we are not justified by the law. He reasons after this manner: If we have need, I say, of the observation of the law to justify us, so that they which are righteous in Christ are not righteous, but yet have need of the law to justify them; or if he that is justified by Christ must yet further be justified by the law, then Christ is nothing else but a lawgiver and a minister of sin.

But we are indeed justified and made righteous in Christ; for the gospel teaches us that a man is not justified in the law, but in Christ. Now, if they who are justified in Christ are yet found sinners, and are under the law (as the false apostles teach), then are they not yet justified. For the law accuses them, and shows them to be yet sinners, and requires of them the works of the law as necessary to their justification. Therefore, they that are justified in Christ are not justified; and so it follows that Christ is not a justifier, but a minister of sin.

The false apostles teach that besides Christ and all the righteousness of Christ, the observation of the law is necessary to justification. Thus by their intolerable perverseness, they make the law Christ, for they attribute to the law that which properly belongs to Christ. If you do the works of the law, say they, you shall be justified; but if you do them not, you shall not be justified, although you believe in Christ ever so much.

Christ, according to His true definition, is a justifier and a Redeemer from sins. If I attribute this to the law, then is the law my justifier, delivering me from my sins, and so now the law is Christ, and Christ utterly loses His name, His office and glory, and is nothing else but a minister of the law, reproving, terrifying, presenting and sending the sinner to another that may justify him, which is the proper office of the law.

Who would ever believe that these things could so easily be confounded and mingled together? There is no man so unsensible who does not perceive this distinction between the law and grace to be most plain and manifest. For the very nature and meaning of the words makes this distinction and difference.

Paul therefore grounds his argument upon an impossibility and a sufficient division. If we being justified in Christ are yet found sinners, and cannot be justified but by another means than Christ, that is, by the law, then Christ cannot justify us, but He only accuses and condemns us; and so consequently it follows that Christ died in vain, and these with other like phrases are false: "Behold the Lamb of God, which taketh away the sin of the world" (John 1:29); also: "He that believeth on the Son hath everlasting life" (John 3:36). Yea, the whole Scripture is false, which bears witness that Christ is the justifier and Savior of the world. For if we are found sinners after we are justified by Christ, it follows that they who fulfill the law without Christ are justified. But if the adversaries must defend this doctrine, why do they not then reject faith in Christ altogether; why do they not say in plain words, that works justify and not faith? Yea, why do they not generally deny, not only Paul, but also the whole gospel, which attributes righteousness to faith alone and not to works? For if faith and works together justify, then is the disputation of Paul altogether false, which plainly pronounces that a man is not justified by the deeds of the law, but by faith alone in Jesus Christ?

17b—Is therefore Christ the minister of sin?

This is a kind of speech used by the Hebrews, which Paul also uses in 2 Corinthians 3, where he most plainly speaks of these two ministries: to wit, of the letter and the spirit, of the law and grace, or of death and life. And he says that Moses has the ministry of the law, which he calls the ministry of sin, of wrath, death, and condemnation.

Now a minister of sin is nothing else but a lawgiver, or a schoolmaster of the law, who teaches good works and charity, and that a man must suffer the cross and afflictions, and follow the example of Christ and of the saints. By this doctrine he does nothing else but terrify and afflict men's consciences, and shut them under sin. For it is impossible for the nature of man to accomplish the law: yea, in those who are justified and have the Holy Ghost, the law of the flesh fights against the law of the mind, as is plainly shown in Romans 7:23. If the justified cannot do this, how shall the wicked who have not the Holy Ghost do it? So he that teaches that righteousness comes by the law does not understand what he says, much less does he keep the law himself, but lays upon others such a burden as they are not able to bear, requiring impossible things.

The right use and end of the law is to accuse and condemn as guilty such as live in security, that they may see themselves to be in danger of sin, wrath, and death, and be brought to trembling and desperation. For the law requires perfect obedience unto God, and condemns all those that do not accomplish the same. No man living is able to accomplish this obedience which God requires. The law therefore justifies not, but condemns, according to that saying, "Cursed be he that confirmeth not all the words which are written in the book of the law" (Deuteronomy 27:26; Galatians 3:10). Therefore, he that teaches the law is the minister of law.

So it is not without good cause that Paul in 2 Corinthians 3 calls the minister of the law, "the minister of sin"; for the law shows and utters sin, which without the law is dead. Now these schoolmasters of the law and works are in the Scripture oppressors and tyrants. For as the taskmasters of Egypt did oppress the children of Israel with corporal servitude, so do these lawgivers and taskmasters drive men into most heavy bondage of soul, and at length bring them to desperation and destruction.

When Paul answers the question: "Is Christ the minister of sin?" with a very vehement, "God forbid," it is as if to say Christ is not the minister of sin, but the giver of righteousness and eternal life. He separates Moses far from Christ. Let Moses then tarry on the earth, let him be the schoolmaster of the letter and exactor of law. But the believers have another schoolmaster in their conscience: not Moses but Christ, who has abolished the law and sin, overcome the wrath of God, and destroyed death. He bids us who labor and are oppressed with calamities to come unto Him. So when we fly to Him, Moses with his law vanishes away, so that his sepulchre can nowhere be found, sin and death can hurt us no more (Deuteronomy 34:5). For Christ our instructor is Lord over the law, sin, and death: so that they who believe in Him are delivered from the same. It is the proper office of Christ to deliver from sin and death; and this Paul teaches and repeats everywhere.

We are condemned and killed by the law, but by Christ we are justified and restored to life. The law astonishes us, and drives us from God; but Christ reconciles us to God, and makes for us an entrance, that we may boldly come unto Him. For "He hath taken away the sin of the world." Now, if the sin of the world be taken away, then is the wrath of God, death, and damnation also taken away. In the place of sin succeeds righteousness; in the place of wrath, reconciliation and grace; in the place of death, life; and in the place of damnation, salvation.

Let us learn to practice the distinction, not in words only, but in life and lively experience, and with an inward feeling. For where Christ is, there must be joy of heart and peace of conscience; for Christ is our reconciliation, righteousness, peace, life, and salvation. Whatever the afflicted conscience desires, it finds abundantly in Christ.

18—For if I build again the things which I destroyed, I make myself a transgressor.

Behold how I have destroyed the law by the preaching of the gospel, that the law should no longer reign in the conscience. For when the new guest Jesus Christ comes into the new house, there to dwell alone, then Moses the old inhabiter must give place to Him, and depart somewhere else. Also where Christ the new guest is come to dwell, there can sin, wrath, and death have no place; but there now dwell grace, righteousness, joy, life, and trust in the Father, now pacified and reconciled to us, gracious, longsuffering, and full of mercy for His Son Christ's sake. Should I then now begin to drive out Christ whom I have planted through the preaching of the gospel, and begin to build up again the law, and set up again the kingdom of Moses? This indeed I should do, if I teach circumcision, and the observation of the law as necessary to salvation, as the false apostles do; and by this means, in the stead of righteousness and life, I should restore again sin and death.

We, by the grace of Christ, holding the article of justification, do assuredly know that we are justified and reputed righteous before God only by faith in Christ. Therefore, we do not mingle the law and grace, faith and works together; but we separate them far asunder. And this distinction between law and grace, let every Christian mark diligently, so that when he hears that good works ought to be done and that the example of Christ is to be followed, he may be able to judge rightly, and say, All these things will I gladly do. What follows? Salvation and everlasting life obtained? No, not so, for though I do all these things which are good, yet am I not thereby justified, neither do I obtain salvation, but through faith only in Christ.

We must not draw good works into the article of justification as the monks have done, who say that not only good works, but also the punishment and torments which malefactors suffer for their wicked deeds do deserve everlasting life. For thus they comfort them when they are brought to the gallows, or place of execution: you must suffer patiently this shameful death; if you do, you shall deserve remission of your sins and everlasting life. What a horrible thing is this, that a wretched thief, murderer, robber, should be so miserably seduced in that extreme anguish, that even at the point of death, he should not be directed to the gospel and the sweet promises of Christ which are alone able to bring comfort and salvation, but should be commanded to hope for pardon of his sins, if he willingly and patiently endure the opprobrious death which he suffers for his mischievous deeds.

In their confessions the monks make no mention of faith or the merit of Christ, but they teach and set forth the satisfaction and merits of men, as it may plainly appear in the form of absolution which the monks used among themselves.

I myself also was once entangled with this monkish error. I thought Christ to be a judge (although I confessed with my mouth that He suffered and died for man's redemption) and ought to be pacified by the observation of my rule and order. So when I prayed or said mass, I used to add this at the end: ''O Lord Jesus, I come unto Thee, and I pray Thee that these burdens and this straitness of my rule and religion may be a full recompense for all my sins.'' But now I give thanks unto God the Father of all mercies, who has called me out of darkness unto the light of His glorious gospel, and has given unto me plentiful knowledge of Christ

Jesus my Lord; for whose sake I count all things to be but loss, yea, but as dung, that I may gain Christ, and be found in Him, not having mine own righteousness out of the rule of Augustine, but that righteousness which comes by faith in Christ, unto whom, with the Father, and the Holy Ghost, be praise and glory, world without end. Amen.

We conclude therefore with Paul that we are justified by faith only in Christ, without the works of the law. Now after a man is once justified, and possesses Christ by faith, and knows that He is his righteousness and life, doubtless he will not be idle, but as a good tree he will bring forth good fruit. For the believing man has the Holy Ghost, and where the Holy Ghost dwells He will not suffer a man to be idle, but stirs him up to all exercises of piety and godliness, of true religion, to the love of God, to the patient suffering of afflictions, to prayer, to thanksgiving, to the exercise of charity towards all men.

19—For I through the law am dead to the law, that I might live unto God.

These are marvelous words which man's reason cannot understand. As though he were moved through indignation of the Holy Ghost, Paul calls grace itself the law, giving a new name to the effect and working of grace, in contempt of the law of Moses and the false apostles who contended that the law was necessary to justification; and so he sets the law against the law. And this is a sweet kind of speech, full of consolation, when in the Scriptures, and especially in Paul, the law is set against the law, sin against sin, death against death, captivity against captivity, hell against hell, the altar against the altar, the lamb against the lamb, the passover against the passover.

In the eighth chapter of Romans it is said: "For sin He condemned sin"; in Ephesians (4): "He led captivity captive"; in Hosea (13): "O death, I will be thy plagues; O grave, I will be thy destruction." So he says here, that through the law he is dead to the law. It is as if he said: the law of Moses accuses and condemns me; but against that accusing and condemning law, I have another law, which is grace and liberty. James

(1:25) also calls grace "the law of liberty." This law accuses the accusing law, and condemns the condemning law. So death kills death, but the killing death is life itself. But it is called the death of death, by a vehement indignation of spirit against death. So righteousness takes the name of sin, because it condemns sin, and this condemning of sin is true righteousness.

Here Paul seems to be a heretic; yea, of all heretics the greatest, and his heresy is strange and monstrous. For he says: "That he being dead to the law, liveth unto God." The false apostles said, "Except thou live to the law, thou art dead to God, that is, unless thou live after the law, thou art dead before God." But Paul says quite the contrary, "Except thou be dead to the law, thou canst not live unto God." The doctrine of our adversaries at this day is like the doctrine of the false apostles of that time. They say, if you will live to God, live to the law, or after the law. But contrariwise we say: if you will live to God, you must be utterly dead to the law. Man's reason and wisdom understands not this doctrine; therefore it teaches always the contrary, for is it not written, "Do this and thou shalt live"?

So we must mount up to this heavenly altitude, that we may be assured that we are far above the law, yea, that we are utterly dead to the law. If we are dead to the law, then the law has no power over us, even as it has no power over Christ, who has delivered us from the same, that we might live unto God.

Here Paul speaks not of the ceremonial law only, but of the whole law, whether ceremonial or moral, which to a Christian is utterly abrogated, for he is dead to it; not that the law is utterly taken away: no, it remains, lives, and reigns still in the wicked. But a godly man is dead to the law, even as he is dead to sin, the devil, death, and hell, which notwithstanding do still remain; and the world with all the wicked still abide in them.

Christ rising from death is free from the grave, and yet the grave remains still. Peter is delivered from his prison, the sick of the palsy from his bed, the young man from his coffin, the maiden from her couch; and yet the prison, the bed, the coffin, the couch still remain. Even so the law is abolished when I am not subject to it, and yet it remains. Because I am dead unto it by another law, therefore it is dead also unto me: as the grave of Christ, the prison of Peter, etc., do still remain; and yet Christ by His resurrection is dead unto the grave, Peter by his deliverance is freed from the prison, and the maid through life is delivered from the couch.

So these words, ''I am dead to the law,'' are very effectual. For he does not say: I am free from the law for a time, or I am Lord over the law; but simply, I am dead to the law, I have nothing more to do with it. Paul could have uttered no words more effectual and conclusive.

Therefore let him that will live unto God endeavor that he may be found without the law, and let him come out of the grave with Christ. For we know that when we apprehend Christ by faith inwardly in conscience, we enter into a new law which swallows up the old law that held us captive.

It is necessary that we be well instructed to understand the difference between the righteousness of the law and grace. The righteousness of grace does not pertain to the flesh. For the flesh may not be at liberty, but must remain in the grave, the prison, the couch: it must be in subjection to the law. But the Christian conscience must be dead to the law, that is, free from the law, and must have nothing at all to do with it.

This seems a strange and wonderful definition, that to live to the law is to die to God, and to die to the law is to live to God. These propositions are contrary to reason.

To live unto God is to be justified by grace or by faith for Christ's sake, without the works of the law.

This then is the proper and true definition of a Christian: that he is the child of grace and remission of sins, because he is under no law, but is above the law, sin, death, and hell. Even as Christ is free from the grave, and Peter from the prison, so is a Christian free from the law; the conscience by grace is delivered from the law. So is everyone that is born of the Spirit. But the flesh knows not from whence this comes, nor whither it goes, for it cannot judge but after the law.

The Christian says: let the law accuse me, let sin and death terrify me ever so much, yet I do not therefore despair; for I have the law against the law, sin against sin, and death against death. In like manner I find death in my flesh, which afflicts me and kills me; but I have in me a contrary death, which is the death of death, for this death crucifies and swallows up my death. We must receive the benefit of Christ with a sure faith: nothing is required of us but faith alone, by which we apprehend Christ and believe that our sins and our death are condemned and abolished in the death of Christ.

This the blind sophisters do not understand, and therefore they dream that faith justifies not, except it do the works of charity. But let us now set apart the law and charity until another time, and let us rest upon the principal point of this present matter: which is this, that Jesus Christ the Son of God died upon the Cross, did bear in His body my sins, the law, death, the devil and hell. These invincible enemies and tyrants do oppress, vex, and trouble me, and therefore I am careful how I may be delivered out of their hands, be justified and saved. Here I find neither law, work, nor charity which is able to deliver me. There is none but the Lord Jesus only and alone, who takes away the law, kills and destroys my death in His body, and by this means spoils hell, judges and crucifies the devil, and throws him down into hell. To be brief, all the enemies which before tormented and oppressed me, Christ Jesus has brought to nought: He has spoiled them, and made a show of them openly, triumphing over them by His cross (Colossians 2:15), in such sort that they can now rule and reign no more over me, but are constrained to obey me.

By this we plainly see that there is nothing here for us to do, it only belongs to us to hear that these things have been wrought and done in this sort, and by faith to apprehend the same. Now when I have thus apprehended Christ by faith, and through Him am dead to the law, justified from sin, delivered from death, the devil and hell, then I do good works, I love God, I give thanks to Him, I exercise charity towards my neighbors. But this charity or works following neither forms nor adorns my faith, but rather my faith forms and adorns charity. This is our teaching which seems strange and foolish to carnal reason: to wit, that I am not only blind and deaf to the law, yea, delivered and freed from the law, but also wholly dead unto the same.

Christ, with most sweet names, is called my law, my sin, my death, against the law, sin, and death: whereas, in very deed He is nothing else but liberty, righteousness, life, and everlasting salvation. And for this cause He is made the law of the law, the sin of sin, the death of death, that He might redeem from the curse of the law, justify me, and quicken me. So then, while Christ is the law, He is also liberty; while He is sin (for "He was made sin for us"), He is righteousness; and while He is death, He is life. For in that He suffered the law to accuse Him, sin to condemn Him, and death to devour Him, He abolished the law, He condemned sin, He destroyed death, He justified and saved me. So Christ is the poison of the law, sin, and death, and the remedy for the obtaining of liberty, righteousness, and everlasting life.

So Paul goes about to draw us wholly from the beholding of the law, sin, death, and all other evils, and to bring us to Christ, that there we might behold this joyful conflict: to wit, the law fighting against the law, that it may be to me liberty; sin against sin, that it may be to me righteousness; death against death, that I may obtain life; Christ fighting against the devil, that I may be the child of God, and destroying hell that I may enjoy the Kingdom of heaven.

> 20—*I am crucified with Christ: nevertheless I live; yet not I, but Christ liveth in me: and the life which I now live in the flesh I live by the faith of the Son of God, who loved me and gave himself for me.*

Paul speaks here not of crucifying by imitation or example (for to follow the example of Christ is also to be crucified with Him) which crucifying belongs to the flesh. Whereof Peter speaks in his first epistle, chapter 2: "Christ also suffered for us, leaving us an example, that ye should follow His steps." But Paul speaks of that high crucifying, whereby sin, the devil, and death are crucified in Christ and not in me. Here Christ Jesus does all Himself alone. But I believing in Christ, am by faith crucified also with Christ, so that all these things are crucified and dead unto me.

"Nevertheless I live"—I speak not so, says Paul, of my death and crucifying, as though I did not live. Indeed, I live, for I am quickened by this death and crucifying, through the which I die: that is, forasmuch as

I am delivered from the law, sin, and death, I now live indeed. Wherefore that crucifying, and that death, whereby I am crucified and dead to the law, sin, death, and all evils, is to me resurrection and life. For Christ crucified the devil, He killed death, condemned sin, and bound the law; and I believing this, am delivered from the law, sin, death, and the devil.

Here (as I have said before) we must observe Paul's manner of speaking. He says that we are dead and crucified to the law, whereas in very deed the law itself is dead and crucified unto us. But this manner of speech he uses here intentionally, that it may be more sweet and comfortable for us. For the law is crucified and dead only to those who believe in Christ; and to them alone belongs this glory, that they are dead to sin, hell, death, and the devil.

"Yet not I"—that is to say, not in my own person, nor in my own substance. Here he plainly shows by what means he lives; and he teaches what true Christian righteousness is, namely, that righteousness whereby Christ lives in us, and not that which is in our own person. And here Christ and my conscience must become one body, so that nothing remains in my sight but Christ crucified, and raised from the dead. If I behold myself only and set Christ aside, I am gone. For Christ being lost, there is no counsel nor succor, but certain desperation and destruction must follow.

Where Paul says, "I live, yet not I, but Christ liveth in me," he speaks, as it were, in his own person. Therefore he corrects himself in the second part of the sentence, saying: "Yet not I." That is, I live not now in my own person, but Christ lives in me. Indeed, the person lives, but not in himself, nor for anything that is in him. But who is that *I*, of whom he says, "yet not I"? This I is he who has the law and is bound to do the works thereof, who also is a person separate from Christ. This person Paul rejects. For he is separate from Christ, he belongs to death and hell. Therefore he says: "Not I, but Christ liveth in me." He is my form, my furniture and perfection, adorning and beautifying my faith, as the color, the clear light or the whiteness garnish and beautify the wall. Thus are we constrained grossly to set forth this matter. For we cannot spiritually conceive that Christ is so nearly joined and united to us as the color or whiteness are to the wall. Christ therefore, says he, thus joined and united to me, and abiding in me, lives this life in me which now I live: yes, Christ Himself is this life, which now I live. Wherefore Christ and I in this behalf are both one. This union or conjunction, then, is the cause that I am delivered from the terror of the law and sin, am separate from myself, and translated unto Christ and His Kingdom, which is a kingdom of grace, righteousness, peace, joy, life, salvation, and eternal glory. While I dwell in Him, what evil is there that can hurt me?

Meanwhile the old man abides without and is subject to the law; but as concerning justification, Christ and I must be entirely conjoined and united together, so that He may live in me, and I in Him. And this is a wonderful manner of speech. Because Christ lives in me, look now what grace, righteousness, life, peace, and salvation is in me; it is His, and yet it is mine also, by that inseparable union and conjunction which is through faith, by which Christ and I are made as it were one body in spirit.

Paul has his peculiar kind of speech, which is not after the manner of men, but divine and heavenly, nor used by the other Apostles, except John. If Paul had not first used this phrase and set forth the same in plain words, the saints themselves would not have dared to use it. For it seems a very strange manner of speaking to say: I live, I live not; I am dead, I am not dead; I am a sinner, I am not a sinner; I have the law, I have not the law. This phrase is sweet and comfortable to all those who believe in Christ. As they behold themselves, they have both the law and sin; but as they look unto Christ, they are dead to the law and have no sin. If therefore in the matter of justification you separate the person of Christ from your person, then you are in the law, you live in the law, and not in Christ, and so you are condemned of the law and dead before God. For you have only that faith which is furnished with charity. This I speak for example's sake. There was never anyone found that was saved by this faith. But let us grant that some have this faith. Yet they are not justified. For they have but a historical faith concerning Christ which the devil also has.

Faith therefore must be purely taught: namely, that you are so entirely joined to Christ, that He and you are made as it were one person; so that you may boldly say, I am now one with Christ, that is to say, Christ's righteousness, victory, and life are mine. Again, Christ may say, I am that sinner, that is, his sins and his death are Mine, because he is united and joined to Me, and I to him. For by faith we are so joined together that we are become "members of his body, of his flesh, and of his bones" (Ephesians 5:30).

We have declared the first argument of Paul, that Christ must either be the minister of sin, or else the law does not justify. He then sets forth himself for an example, saying: "I am dead unto the law." Now he answers two objections which might have been made against him. His first answer is against the cavillings of the proud, and the offense of the weak. For when remission of sins is freely preached, then do the malicious slander this preaching: "Let us do evil, that good may come" (Romans 3:8). For these, as soon as they hear that we are not justified by the law, do maliciously conclude and say, let us then reject the law. Again, if grace abounds where sin abounds, let us then abound in sin that we may become righteous, and that grace may the more abound. These malicious spirits do slander the Scriptures and sayings of the Holy Ghost, even as they slandered Paul while the Apostle lived, to their own confusion and condemnation. As Peter said, they wrest the words of Paul to their own destruction (2 Peter 3:16).

Moreover, the weak, who are not malicious, are offended when they hear that the law and good works are not to be done as necessary to justification. These must be helped; they must be instructed how good works do not justify, how they ought to be done and how not to be done. These ought to be done not as the cause, but as the fruits of righteousness. When we are made righteous, we ought to do them, but not contrariwise, to the end that when we are unrighteous, we may, by these, be made righteous. The tree makes the apple, but not the apple the tree.

Paul said before: "I am dead to the law." Here some might question: What are you saying? Are you dead? Then how do you speak or write? The weak might be offended and say to him: Do we not see that you are living, and do such things as are of this life? To these he answers: "I live indeed, and yet now not I, but Christ liveth in me." There is then a double life. The first is mine, which is natural; the second is the life of another, that is, the life of Christ in me. As touching my natural life I am dead, and now I live another life, I live not now as Paul, for Paul is dead. Who is it then who lives? The Christian. Paul is wholly dead through the law, and now lives, but as Christ lives in him, he lives by another's life, even Christ. If I lived by my own life, the law would have dominion over me and hold me in captivity. To the end therefore that it should not hold me captive, I am dead to it, and this death purchases for me the life of another, even the life of Christ. This life is not mine by nature but is given to me by Christ through faith in Him.

Secondly, this objection might have been made: How can this be? We see your flesh, but we see not Christ. Would you be fooling us? He answers: "The life which I now live in the flesh, I live by the faith of the Son of God." As Christ says: "Thou hearest the sound of the wind, but canst not tell whence it cometh, and whither it goeth" (John 3:8); even so you see me speaking, eating, laboring, sleeping, and yet you do not see my life. I live indeed in the flesh, but not through the flesh, or according to the flesh, but through faith, and according to faith. This new life "I live by the faith of the Son of God." For the word which I now speak corporally, and in human nature, is the word not of flesh, but of the Holy Ghost, and of Christ. A Christian speaks none other but chaste, sober and holy words, which pertain to Christ, to the glory of God, and the profit of his neighbor. These things come not of the flesh, nor are they done according to the flesh, and yet they are done in the flesh. For I cannot teach, write, pray, or give thanks, but with these instruments of the flesh, yet these works proceed not of the flesh, but are given by God from above. In like manner I behold a woman but with a chaste eye, not lusting after her. This comes not of the flesh, although it is in the flesh, because the eyes are the carnal instruments of this sight: but the chasteness of this sight comes from heaven.

Thus a Christian uses the world and all creatures so that there is no difference between him and the infidel. For in their apparel, feeding, hearing, speaking, gestures, countenances, and such other things, they are alike, and seem to be all one (as Paul speaks of Christ: "He being found in fashion of a man"—Philippians 2:8), yet indeed there is a great difference. Paul before his conversion spoke with the same voice and tongue wherewith he spoke afterwards; but his voice and tongue were then blasphemous and spoke against Christ and His Church. After he was converted, he had the same flesh, voice and tongue, nothing outward was changed; but his voice and his tongue now uttered spiritual and heavenly words, thanksgiving and the praise of God—these came of faith and the Holy Ghost.

So then I live in the flesh, but not of or after the flesh, but by the faith of the Son of God. In this way we see whence this spiritual life comes. For this life is in the heart by faith, where the flesh is killed, and Christ reigns with His Holy Spirit, who now sees, hears, speaks, works, suffers, and does all other things in him, although the flesh resists. To conclude, this is not the life of the flesh, although it is in the flesh; but it is the life of Christ the Son of God, whom the Christian possesses by faith.

Happy is he who can say with Paul: "I live by the faith of the Son of God, who loved me and gave Himself for me." Here we have the true manner of justification, and a perfect example of the assurance of faith.

We must diligently consider these words, "Who loved me, and gave Himself for me." It was not I that first loved the Son of God and delivered myself for Him. Some teach that a man *ex puris naturalibus*, that is, of his own pure natural strength, is able to do meritorious works before grace, and love God and Christ above all things. These fellows pervert the love of God and Christ, for they say they do not only fulfill the commandments, but also they observe the counsels, they do the works of supererogation, and sell their superfluous works to laymen, and so they dream that they give themselves for Christ, and thereby save both themselves and others, contrary to the words of Paul: "Who loved me, and gave Himself for me." These schoolmen teach that if a man does what he can, God will give him His grace. And hereof comes this verse:

Ultra posse viri non vult Deus ulla requiri.

That is:

> *God will no more require of man,*
> *Than of himself perform he can.*

This is a good saying, if it be rightly applied: that is, in the government of nations or families. If I am a magistrate, and in the kingdom of reason execute the office of a magistrate, as far as I can, with justice and equity, I am excused. This kingdom has its bounds and limits, to which this saying pertains, to do as much as we are able. But it is wrong to apply this saying to the spiritual kingdom, because a man can do nothing else but sin; for he is "sold under sin" (Romans 7:14). So they have done wickedly in applying this saying to the Church. For the kingdom of man's reason and the spiritual kingdom must be kept separate and far asunder. In addition, they say that nature is corrupt, but the qualities of nature are still sound and uncorrupt. Upon this ground they reason like this: if the natural qualities be sound and uncorrupt, then is a man's understanding and will sound and uncorrupt, and so consequently all other qualities of nature are pure and perfect in him.

I grant that the qualities of nature are uncorrupt. But what qualities are they? That a man drowned in sin and iniquity, and a bondslave of Satan, has will, reason and power to execute the office of a magistrate, govern a family, guide a ship, build a house, and do such things as are subject to man: for these qualities are not taken from him. In the corporal realm therefore we do not deny this sentence; but if they are wrested to apply to the spiritual kingdom, I utterly deny them, for there we are clean overwhelmed and drowned in sin. Whatever is in our will is evil; whatever is in our understanding is error.

How then shall a man work well, fulfill the law, and love God?

Wherefore Paul says here that Christ first began and not we: "He loved me, and gave Himself for me." As if he said, although He found in me no good will, or right understanding, this good Lord had mercy on me. He saw me to be nothing else but wicked, going astray, condemning God, and flying from Him more and more, carried away and led captive of the devil. Thus of His mere mercy, preventing my reason, my will, and my understanding, He loved me, and so loved me that He gave Himself for me, to the end that I might be freed from the law, sin, the devil and death.

Again, these words, "the Son of God loved me, and gave Himself for me," are mighty thunderings and lightnings from heaven against the righteousness of the law and all the works thereof. So great and horrible wickedness, error, and darkness was in my will and understanding that it was impossible for me to be ransomed by any other means than by such an inestimable price.

Let us consider well this price, and let us behold the captive, delivered, as Paul says, for me: the Son of God, I mean, and we shall see Him, without all comparison, to exceed and excel all creatures. What will you do when you hear the Apostle say that such an inestimable price was given for you? What shall the law of Moses avail? What shall the works of all men, and all the sufferings of the martyrs profit you? What is the obedience of all the holy angels in comparison to the Son of God delivered, and that most shamefully, even to the death of the Cross, so that there was no drop of His most precious blood, but it washed, and that for your sins. If you could rightly consider this incomparable price, you should hold as accursed all those ceremonies, vows, works, and merits before grace and after, and throw them all down to hell. For it is a horrible blasphemy to imagine that there is any work by which you should presume to pacify God, since you see that there is nothing which is able to pacify Him but this inestimable price, even the death and the blood of the Son of God, one drop of which is more precious than the whole world.

"Who gave Himself for me"—who is this *me?* Even I, wretched and damnable sinner, but loved so dearly by the Son of God that He gave Himself for me. If I through any works, efforts, or merits could have come to Him, what need was there that He should give Himself for me? Therefore I say again, as I have often said, that there is no remedy against sects, or power to resist them, but only this article of Christian righteousness. For because there was no other price either in heaven or upon earth, but Christ the Son of God, it was therefore most necessary that He should be delivered for me. Moreover, this He did of inestimable love; for Paul says: "Who loved me."

Wherefore these words, "Who loved me," are full of faith. And he that can utter this little word "me," and apply it to himself with a true and a constant faith as Paul did, shall be a good disputer with Paul against the law.

These words Paul sets against the righteousness of the law. The law loved me not nor gave itself for me; yea, it accused me, terrified me, and drove me to desperation. But I have now another who has delivered me from the terrors of the law, sin, and death, and has brought me into liberty, the righteousness of God, and eternal life. He is called the Son of God, who loved me and gave Himself for me; to whom be praise and glory forever.

Faith therefore embraces and wraps in itself Christ Jesus the Son of God, delivered to death for us, as Paul here teaches, who being apprehended by faith, gives to us righteousness and life. Let us learn therefore to give a true definition of Christ; let us define Him as Paul does: namely, that He is the Son of God, who not for any righteousness of ours, but of His own free mercy and love, offered up Himself as a sacrifice for us sinners, that He might sanctify us forever.

Christ then is no Moses, no exactor, no giver of laws, but a giver of grace, a Savior, and one that is full of mercy: briefly, He is nothing else but infinite mercy and goodness, freely given and bountifully giving to us. And thus shall you paint Christ in His right colors. If you suffer Him to be painted otherwise, when temptation and trouble come you shall soon be overthrown. Now, as it is the greatest knowledge that Christians can have, thus to define Christ, so it is the hardest. For I myself have difficulty in holding this definition of Christ which Paul here gives: so deeply has the doctrine that Christ is a lawgiver entered like oil into my bones.

Young men are in this case much more happy than we that are old. For you are not infected with these pernicious errors, wherein I have been so drenched even from my youth, that at the very hearing of the name of Christ my heart trembled and quaked for fear; for I was persuaded that He was a severe judge. Wherefore it is to me double trouble to correct and reform this evil: first to forget, and to resist this old grounded error, that Christ is a lawgiver and a judge; for it always returns and plucks me back; then to plant in my heart a new and a true persuasion of Christ, that He is a justifier and a Savior. You that are young may learn with much less difficulty to know Christ purely and sincerely. Wherefore if any man feel himself oppressed with heaviness and anguish of heart, he must not impute it unto Christ, but unto the devil, who often comes under the color of Christ, and transforms himself into an angel of light.

Let us learn therefore to put a difference between Christ and a lawgiver, not only in word but also in deed and in practice; that when the devil comes under the shadow of Christ, and goes about to trouble us under His name, we may know him not to be Christ, but a very fiend indeed. For Christ when He comes is nothing else but joy and sweetness to a trembling and broken heart, as here Paul witnesses. Christ therefore in very deed is a lover of those which are in trouble or anguish, in sin and death, and such a lover as gave Himself for us: who is also our High Priest, that is to say, a mediator between God and us miserable and wretched sinners. What could be said, I pray you, more sweet and comfortable than this? Now, if these things be true (as they are indeed most true, or else the gospel must be nothing but a fable), then we are not justified by the righteousness of the law; but much less by our own righteousness.

Read therefore with great vehemence these words *"ME"* and *"FOR ME,"* and so inwardly practice with yourself that you with a sure faith may conceive and print this *"ME"* in your heart, and apply it to yourself, not doubting that you are of the number of those to whom this *"ME"* belongs; also that Christ has not only loved Peter and Paul and given Himself for them, but that the same grace also which is comprehended in this *"ME"* pertains as well to us as to them. For as we cannot deny that we are all sinners, and are constrained to say that through the sin of Adam we are all lost, were made the enemies of God, subject to the wrath and judgment of God, and guilty of eternal death; so can we not deny that Christ died for our sins, that He might make us righteous. For He died not to justify the righteous, but the unrighteous, and to make them the friends and children of God, and inheritors of all heavenly gifts. Therefore, when I feel and confess myself to be a sinner through Adam's transgression, why should I not say that I am made righteous through the righteousness of Christ, especially when I hear that He loved me, and gave Himself for me?

21a—I do not frustrate the grace of God:

To seek to be justified by the works of the law is to reject the grace of God. What can be more horrible than to reject the grace of God, and to refuse to be justified by faith in Christ? It is enough that we are ungodly and transgressors of all the commandments of God; and yet we commit moreover the very sin of sins, in that we do so confidently refuse the grace of God and remission of sins offered us by Christ. This blasphemy is more horrible than can be expressed. There is no sin which Paul and the other Apostles did so much detest as the contempt of grace and denial of Christ; and yet there is no sin more common.

Thus to deny Christ, what else is it but to spit in His face, to tread Him underfoot, to set yourself in His place?

Do we then sin in keeping the law? No. But we despise grace when we observe the law that we may be justified through it. The law is good, holy, and profitable, and yet it justifies not. He then that keeps the law to be justified thereby, rejects grace, denies Christ, despises His sacrifice, and will not be saved by this inestimable price, but will satisfy for his sins through the righteousness of the law, or deserve grace by his own righteousness. And this man blasphemes and despises the grace of God. Now, what a horrible thing is it to say that any man should be so devilish as to despise the grace and mercy of God! And yet all the world does so.

21b—For if righteousness come by the law, then Christ is dead in vain.

These words of Paul ought to be weighed and considered in this manner: Is it true that Christ suffered death or not? Again, did He suffer in vain or not? Here we are constrained to answer, except we be stark mad, that He suffered in very deed, and that He suffered not in vain, not for Himself, but for us. If then He suffered not in vain, it follows of necessity that righteousness comes not by the law.

Take now therefore both laws, the ceremonial law and the moral, or the Ten Commandments, and show me any man that has been justified thereby. But if a man could be justified by the law or the Ten Commandments, then that man would have power in himself to obtain righteousness. This being granted, it must follow that Christ died in vain. For what need of Christ to give Himself for him, if he without Christ was able to be justified by his keeping of the law? Then let Christ be taken away with all His benefits, for He is utterly unprofitable. But why was He born? Why was He crucified? Why did He suffer? Why was He made my High Priest, loving me and giving "Himself" an inestimable sacrifice for me? In vain, no doubt, and to no purpose at all, if righteousness comes by other means, for then I find righteousness in the law or in myself, apart from grace and Christ.

Is this horrible blasphemy to be suffered or dissembled, that the Divine Majesty, not sparing His own dear Son, but delivering Him up to death for us all, should not do all these things seriously and earnestly, but as it were in sport? Before I would admit this blasphemy, I would not only that the holiness of all the meritmongers, but also of all the saints and holy angels should be thrown into the bottom of hell, and condemned with the devil. My eyes shall behold nothing else but Christ the Son of God. He ought to be such a treasure unto me, that all other things should be but dung in comparison to Him. He ought to be such a light unto me, that when I have apprehended Him by faith, I should not know whether there be any law, any sin, any righteousness, or any unrighteousness in the world. For what are all things in heaven and in earth in comparison to the Son of God, Jesus Christ my Lord, who loved me and gave Himself for me?

In their blind and obstinate following of these traditions against the great light of the gospel, the meritmongers continue in their wicked opinions and doting dreams, saying that the qualities of nature remain sound and uncorrupt, and that men are able to prepare themselves for grace, or to deserve grace by their own works and merits. And so far off are they from acknowledging their impiety and error, that they still obstinately defend the same, even against their own conscience. But we do constantly affirm with Paul, that either Christ died in vain or else the law does not justify.

But Christ died not in vain; therefore, the law does not justify. Christ, the Son of God, of His own free grace and mercy, has justified us;

therefore, the law could not justify us, for if it could, Christ had done unwisely in that He gave Himself for our sins, that we might thereby be justified. If my salvation was so costly and dear a price to Christ that He was constrained to die for my sins, then all my works, with all the righteousness of the law, are but vile and worth nothing in comparison with this inestimable price.

How can I buy for a farthing that which cost many thousand talents of gold? The law, with all the works and righteousness thereof, is but as a farthing, if we compare it to Christ, who by His death has vanquished my death and has purchased righteousness and everlasting life. Should I then despise and reject this incomparable price, and by the law, or by the works and merit of men (vile dross and dung, for so Paul calls them, if they be compared unto Christ), seek that righteousness which Christ freely and of mere love has given unto me already, and has cost Him so great a price, that He was constrained to give Himself, and even His own heart-blood for me!

Paul here has no civil matter in hand, which yet God allows and requires. Here Paul is discussing the righteousness that avails before God, whereby we are delivered from the law, sin, death, and all evils, and are made partakers of grace, righteousness and everlasting life, and finally are now become lords of heaven and earth, and of all other creatures. This righteousness neither man's law nor the law of God is able to perform.

These words therefore are very effectual and full of power when he says: "If righteousness come by the law, then Christ is dead in vain." Set therefore the death of Jesus Christ alone against all laws, and with Paul, "know nothing among you, save Jesus Christ, and him crucified" (1 Corinthians 2:2). Then you shall be learned indeed, righteous and holy, and shall receive the Holy Ghost, who shall preserve you in the purity of the Word and faith; but set Christ aside, and all things are vain. It is a small matter to say that any man died in vain; but to say that Christ died in vain is to take Him quite away. Now to make the death of Christ unprofitable is to make the resurrection, His victory, His glory, His Kingdom, heavens, earth, God Himself, the Majesty of God, and briefly all things else unprofitable and of no effect.

5

Who Has Bewitched You?

Galatians 3:1–5

1—O foolish Galatians, who hath bewitched you, that ye should not obey the truth, before whose eyes Jesus Christ hath been evidently set forth, crucified among you?

Paul here shows his apostolic care and burning zeal. In disputing and confuting, he intermingles sometimes gentle exhortation and sharp reproof, according to his own rule given to Timothy: "Preach the word; be instant in season, out of season; reprove, rebuke, exhort" (2 Timothy 4:2). Here the reader may think, if he is not careful, that Paul in teaching keeps no order at all. Indeed, after the manner of the rhetoricians, he observes none; but as concerning the spirit he uses a goodly order.

Now after he has proved with strong arguments that Christian righteousness comes not by keeping the law, but by faith in Christ, and has confuted the doctrine of the false apostles, he turns his talk to the Galatians themselves, and reproves them, saying: "O foolish Galatians," as if he would say, alas, from whence are you fallen, O miserable Galatians? I have most carefully taught you the truth of the gospel, and you received it of me with fervent zeal and great diligence. How then has it come to pass that you are so suddenly fallen away from it? "Who hath bewitched you?"

He reproves very sharply when he calls them fools, bewitched, and disobedient to the truth. Whether he did this of zeal or compassion, I will not argue; both may be true. A carnal man would interpret this to be a reviling, rather than a godly reprehension. Did Paul then give an evil example or was he spiteful against the churches of Galatia, because he called them foolish and bewitched? No, not so. For with a Christian zeal it is lawful for an apostle, a pastor, or preacher, sharply to reprove the people committed to his care, and such reprovings are both fatherly and godly. So parents, of affection, do sharply rebuke their children, which they would not bear if another should do it. The schoolmaster is angry with his scholar, he rebukes him and beats him; the student takes it in good part, but would not bear it at the hands of an equal. The magistrate likewise reproves and punishes some that are brought before him. And this discipline is not only good, but very necessary; without which nothing can be well done. Unless the magistrate, the schoolmaster and the parent are angry and reprove when the case requires, they are unprofitable and do not discharge their offices rightly.

Chidings and bitter words are as necessary in every kind of life, as any other virtue. Yet must this anger be so tempered, that it proceed not of any malice, but only of fatherly concern and affection. These kinds of anger are good, and are called in the Scripture zeals or jealousies. In chastising my child, my scholar, or subject in this manner, I seek not his hurt, but his profit and welfare.

It may be then that Paul here rebukes the Galatians out of zeal (not to destroy but to amend them), or else out of pity and compassion, by way of complaint, for it grieves him that they should be so miserably reduced, as if he would say, I am sorry and ashamed to hear this of you. Even so, we reprehend the miserable; not that we tread them down, but as having compassion on them and seeking their amendment. This I say, lest any man should cavil and say that Paul railed upon the churches, contrary to the rule of the gospel.

In like manner Christ rebukes the Pharisees, calling them serpents, the generation of vipers, the children of the devil. But these are the rebukings of the Holy Ghost. They are fatherly and motherly, and as the chidings of a faithful friend; as it is said in the Book of Proverbs: "Better are the wounds of a friend than the kisses of an enemy" (Proverbs 27:6). The same rebuke, if it come out of the mouth of a father, may be of great benefit; but if it proceed from an equal or an enemy, it is a spiteful reproach. But when Christ and Paul reprove, it is done with singular virtue and commendation; but when a private man should do it, it is in him a great vice.

There is a certain vehemency to be noted in this word, *Galatians,* for he calls them not his brethren, as elsewhere he is wont to do; but he calls them by the name that was proper to their country. And it seems that it was the natural vice of that nation to be foolish; as it was the fault of the Cretans to be liars. As if he would say: As ye are called, even so are ye indeed, and so ye continue; that is to say, "foolish Galatians"; and so you show yourselves now in the business of the gospel (wherein you ought to have been most wise), yet you continue in your own nature. Thus Paul, by way of correction, reminds the Galatians of their corrupt nature.

We are here admonished, that, according to the flesh, natural vices remain in the churches and in the godly. Grace does not so change the faithful that by-and-by they become perfect in all things; but certain dregs of their old and natural corruption remain. If a man who is naturally prone to anger is converted to Christ, although he is mollified by grace (the Holy Ghost so framing his heart, that he is now more meek and gentle), yet this natural vice is not utterly quenched in his flesh. So it is with such as are by nature severe and sharp, although they be converted to the faith, yet they cannot entirely forsake this vice. Even so, the Holy Scriptures are diversely handled by the various writers. One in teaching is mild and gentle; another more rough and rigorous. Thus the Spirit of God, being poured into diverse vessels, does not quench at once the vices of nature; but little by little during this life, He purges that sin which is rooted, not only in the Galatians, but also in all men of all nations.

Though the Galatians were enlightened and did believe and had now received the Holy Ghost by the preaching of faith, this remnant of vice (this foolishness I mean) and the original corruption, which afterwards did easily burst out into a flame of false doctrine, remained in them still.

So let no man trust so much in himself, as to think that when he has received grace, he is thoroughly purged from his old vices. Indeed many things are purged in us, and principally the head of the serpent; that is to say, infidelity and ignorance of God is cut off and bruised, but the slimy body and the remnants of sin remain in us. For we are not yet dead, but still we live in the flesh, which, because it is not yet pure, continually lusts against the Spirit. "I am carnal," says Paul, "sold under sin." "I see another law in my members warring against the law of my mind" (Romans 7:14, 21, 23). So the natural vices that were in us before we received faith still remain in us after we have received faith, except that now they are subdued by the Spirit, who has the upper hand to keep them under, and yet not without great conflict. This glory is due to Christ alone; and this title He bears, that He is without spot and blemish "who did no sin, neither was guile found in his mouth" (1 Peter 2:22).

When Paul asks: "Who hath bewitched you, that ye should not believe the truth?" he has another fling at the righteousness of the law and of our own righteousness, namely, that it makes us despise the truth; it bewitches us so that we do not believe, or obey, the truth but rebel against it.

Of the Bodily and Spiritual Witchcraft

Later, in the fifth chapter, Paul discusses sorcery among the works of the flesh, and sorcery is a kind of witchcraft. It cannot be denied that the devil lives and indeed reigns throughout the whole world. Witchcraft and sorcery are the works of the devil. Through them he not only hurts men, but also, by the permission of God, he sometimes destroys them. Furthermore, we are all subject to the devil both in body and goods, and we are strangers in this world, of which he is the prince and god. So, the bread we eat, the liquids we drink, the garments we wear, and whatever we live by in the flesh is under his dominion.

But he not only bewitches men after this gross manner, but also after a more subtle and much more dangerous way, wherein he is a marvelous cunning workman. And here Paul applies the bewitching of the senses to the bewitching of the spirit. For by this spiritual witchcraft that old serpent bewitches not men's senses but their minds with false and wicked opinions, which are taken to be true and godly. Briefly, so great is the malice of this sorcerer the devil and his desire to hurt, that he not only deceives those secure and proud spirits with his enchantments, but even those who are professors of true Christianity and well established in religion; to tell the truth, he sometimes assails me so mightily and oppresses me with such heavy cogitations, that he utterly shadows my Savior Christ from me and, in a manner, takes Him out of my sight. There is not one of us who is not often bewitched by false persuasions; that is, who does not fear, trust, or rejoice when he ought not, or does not sometimes think otherwise of God, of Christ, of faith, of his vocation, etc., than he should do.

Indeed, we have many times been cast down in this conflict, but we perish not; for Christ has always triumphed, and does triumph through us. Therefore we hope assuredly that we shall also hereafter by Jesus Christ obtain the victory against the devil. And this hope brings us sure consolation, so that in the midst of our temptations we take courage, and say: "Greater is He that is in us, than he that is in the world" (1 John 4:4). Christ is stronger, who has overcome that strong one and shall overcome him forever. But the devil sometimes overcomes us in the flesh, that we may have experience of the power of a stronger against that strong one, and may say with Paul: "When I am weak, then am I strong" (2 Corinthians 13:9). Let no man think that the Galatians only were bewitched by the devil; but let every man think that he himself might have been, and yet may be bewitched by him.

When Paul asks, "Who hath bewitched you?" he excuses the Galatians, and lays the blame upon the false apostles. It is as though he would say, I see that you are not fallen through willfulness or malice, but the devil has sent the enchanting false apostles, his children, among you, and they bewitched you in teaching that you are justified by the law. But we labor, both by preaching and writing unto you, to uncharm that sorcery by which you have been bewitched and to set at liberty those who have been ensnared.

So we also labor by the Word of God that we may set at liberty those that are entangled, and bring them to the pure doctrine of faith, and hold them there. Yet such there are as will not allow themselves to be taught, especially the chief sorcerers and authors of this witchery. They will hear no reason, nor admit the Scriptures. In fact, they abuse and corrupt the Scriptures with their false glosses and devilish dreams, which is a sure sign that they are bewitched by the devil. Surely I could never have believed that the power of the devil is so great, that he is able to make falsehood so like the truth. When he goes about to overwhelm sorrowful consciences with much heaviness, he can so cunningly change himself into the likeness of Christ that it is impossible for the poor tempted soul to perceive it. By this, many are deceived and driven down to desperation.

Such a thing happened to one man who said: "I have denied Christ, and therefore He stands now before His Father and accuses me." And he so strongly conceived this imagination in his mind that by no consolation, no promise of God, could he be brought from it. Finally, he despaired and miserably destroyed himself. But the Scripture does not set forth Christ as an accuser, a judge, or a tempter, but as a reconciler, a mediator, a comforter, and a throne of grace.

But this poor man could not see this, and therefore against all Scripture, he thought this to be an undoubted truth: "Christ accuses you before His Father." This temptation is not of man, but of the devil, which that enchanter strongly imprints upon the heart of the tempted. But to us who are led and taught by another Spirit, it is a cursed lie and a bewitching of the devil. Seeing then that the devil is able to print in our heart so manifest a lie, we must not be proud, but walk in fear and humility, calling upon the Lord Jesus, that we be not led into temptation.

Worldly and secure men, who having heard the gospel once or twice preached imagine that they have received abundance of the Spirit, eventually fall because they do not fear God, nor are thankful unto Him, but persuade themselves that they are able not only to hold and defend the doctrines of true religion, but also to stand against the devil in any assault or conflict. Such are easy prey for the devil to bewitch and to throw down to desperation.

Do not say then, I am perfect; I cannot fall. But humble yourself and fear, lest, if you stand today, tomorrow you might be overthrown.

I myself, although I am a doctor of divinity and have now preached Christ a great while, by my own experience have found how hard a matter this is. But thanks be to God who keeps us in the Word, in faith, and in prayer, that we may walk before Him in humility and fear, and not presume of our own righteousness and strength. Our trust is in the power of Christ, who is strong when we are weak and feeble creatures. He it is who continually overcomes and triumphs; to whom be glory forever.

The Galatians at first gladly heard and obeyed the truth. Therefore when Paul says: "Who hath bewitched you, that ye should not obey the truth?" as if he would say, you are so deluded and bewitched that now you cannot obey the truth. I fear lest many of you are utterly lost, and so fallen away that you will never return to the truth again.

It is written in the Epistle to the Hebrews that the law brings none to perfection. In this epistle, Paul confirms the same, reasoning thus: Tell me, you that would be justified by the law, did you receive the Spirit of God by hearing the law, or by the gospel of faith preached? By their own experience, it was not the law, but the gospel that raises a man being fallen, and quickens him to true repentance.

More vehemently he now says: "To whom Jesus Christ hath been evidently set forth, crucified among you."

It was bitterly spoken where he said before that they were so bewitched, that they could not obey the truth; but it is more bitterly said that Christ was so lively described before them that they might handle

Him with their hands. Yet they would not obey the truth. Thus he convinced them even by their own experience. I have with great pains and diligence set forth Christ plainly before your eyes, yet does this profit not at all.

In these words he refers to his former argument, in which he proved that to those who will be justified by the law Christ is but the minister of sin; such reject the grace of God; to them Christ died in vain. Now he reminds them of the same things, saying: "Before whose eyes Jesus Christ hath been evidently set forth, crucified among you." As if he said, no painter with his colors can so lively set out Christ unto you as I have painted Him by my preaching; yet you remain most miserably bewitched. What did I then paint? Even Christ Himself. How was that done? In this way, that He is crucified in you or among you. Here are sharp words. Before he had said, that they sought righteousness by the law, rejected the grace of God, and that to them Christ died in vain. Now he adds that they even crucify Christ, who before lived and reigned in them. In the same way he speaks in Hebrews 6: "Crucifying to themselves the Son of God afresh, and putting Him to an open shame."

Those who seek to be justified by the law of God are not only deniers and murderers of Christ, but also they most wickedly crucify Him again. If they are crucifiers of Christ who seek to be justified by the righteousness of the law of God, what are they, I pray you, who seek salvation and eternal life, by the dregs and dung of man's righteousness?

This is undoubtedly a horrible delusion of the devil, by which he has bewitched almost the whole world. And this was the cause that we could not know that Jesus Christ is our Savior and mediator, but we thought He is a severe judge, who should be pacified by our works.

It is not without cause that Paul adds these words "among you," or in you. For Christ is no more crucified, nor can be. He dies no more in His own Person, as is said in Romans 6, but He dies in us, when we rejecting true doctrine, grace, faith, free remission of sins, seek to be justified by our own works, or those commanded by the law. Whoever then has any fear of God or love of Christ and His true religion, let him fly quickly out of this Babylon.

2—This only would I learn of you, Received ye the Spirit by the works of the law, or by the hearing of faith?

Paul presses the Galatians with an argument about which they themselves had good experience and which they could not deny. As if he would say, Go to, now; answer me, who am your scholar, for you are so suddenly become doctors, that you are now my masters and teachers: "Received ye the Holy Ghost by the works of the law, or by the hearing of faith?" With this argument he so convinces them that they have nothing to reply. Their own experience was altogether against them; they had received the Holy Ghost by the preaching of the gospel, and not by the works of the law.

Here again, Paul is speaking not only of the ceremonial law but of the whole law. It is an argument standing upon two parts: one must be true, and the other false; that is, either you received the Holy Ghost by the law or by the hearing of faith. If by the law, then not by the preaching of faith; if by the preaching of faith, then not by the law. All that is not of the Holy Ghost or the preaching of faith is the law. Here are we in the matter of justification. But to attain justification, there is no other way; it is either by the voice of the gospel or by the voice of the law. So the law is here taken generally as wholly separate from the gospel. But it is not the ceremonial law only that is separate from the gospel, but also the moral law or the law of the Ten Commandments. Thus Paul speaks here of the whole law.

As long as you were under the law and did the works thereof, you never received the Holy Ghost. You taught and heard the law of Moses every Sabbath, but the Holy Ghost was not given to any through the preaching of the law. But as soon as the hearing of faith or the gospel came to you, you received the Holy Ghost, before you had done any work or showed any fruit of the gospel. For as Luke witnesses in the Acts, at the preaching of Peter and Paul, "the Holy Ghost came upon those which heard the word, through whom also they received divers gifts, so that they spake with new tongues" (Acts 10:44; 11:15; 19:6).

For they who are ignorant of the righteousness of God, and "going about to establish their own righteousness, have not submitted themselves unto the righteousness of God," as Paul says in another place (Romans 10:3). Again, "Israel, which followed the law of righteousness, hath not attained to the law of righteousness. Wherefore? Because they sought it not by faith" (Romans 9:31, 32). Now Paul speaks here of the manifestation of the Holy Ghost in the primitive Church. For by this sign He plainly witnesses that He was present at the preaching of the Apostles; also that those who heard the word of faith preached were accepted as righteous before God; or else the Holy Ghost would not have come upon them.

The Argument of the Acts of the Apostles

It may be seen from the quotation above that the Book of the Acts is written to confirm and establish this argument; for it teaches nothing else but that the Holy Ghost is not given by the law, but by the hearing of the gospel. For when Peter preached, the Holy Ghost fell on all those which heard him, "and in one day three thousand believed and received the Holy Ghost" (Acts 2). To Cornelius and those with him, while Peter was yet speaking, the Holy Ghost fell upon them (Acts 10:44). These are arguments, experiences, and divine works which cannot deceive us.

Luke also writes of Paul in the fifteenth chapter, that when he and Barnabas had preached the gospel among the Gentiles and were returned to Jerusalem, he set himself against the Pharisees and disciples of the Apostles who urged circumcision and the keeping of the law; the whole Church was amazed at his report, and had nothing to reply. By the same preaching of faith did Sergius Paulus, the lieutenant, and all those cities, regions, kingdoms, and countries, which the Apostles visited, believe, and receive the Holy Ghost, without the law and works.

These things are to be marked, because of the adversaries who do not consider what is handled in the Acts of the Apostles.

I myself, in times past, read Acts, when indeed I understood nothing at all in it. When you read in it the word "Gentiles," you must think that it is not to be understood literally of the common nature of the Gentiles, but it carries with it a spiritual meaning and is to be taken, not for those who are under the law, as were the Jews (as it is said before: "We who are Jews by nature"), but for those who are without the law. To say that the Gentiles are justified by faith is nothing else, but that they who do not observe the law, nor do its works, are justified and receive the Holy Ghost. By what means? Not by the law, but freely, and without any other means than the hearing of the gospel.

So Cornelius and his friends do nothing, neither do they look upon any works going before, and yet as many as were present receive the Holy Ghost. No man speaks but Peter. Sitting by, they do nothing: they do not think of the law, much less do they keep it; they sacrifice not; they do not care for circumcision, but are only bent to hear Peter. Yet by his preaching the Holy Ghost is brought into their hearts, "for they spake with tongues and glorified God." When they at Jerusalem heard of it, they complained to Peter, that he went in to men uncircumcised "and didst eat with them" (Acts 11:3). But when they heard the matter declared in order by Peter, they marveled, and glorified God, saying: "Then hath God also to the Gentiles granted repentance unto life."

This report and this fame, that God had given salvation also to the Gentiles, was at first a great offense even to the believing Jews, which they could not easily shake off; for they had this prerogative above all other nations, "that they were the people of God." The adoption, the glory, the worship, etc., belonged to them (Romans 9). Moreover, they exercised themselves in the righteousness of the law, they labored all the day long, they bore the burden and heat of the day, as in Matthew 20. Yet, the Gentiles received without labor the same gift of righteousness and the Holy Ghost, which they by labor could not obtain. So it was that some murmured, and said: "For we who are the people of God have been vexed all the day long; but they who are not the people of God, neither have any law, nor have done any good at all, are made equal with us."

As a result, the council of Apostles was assembled at Jerusalem to satisfy and pacify those Jews who, though they believed in Christ, yet had the opinion deeply rooted in their hearts that the law of Moses ought to be observed. There Peter, upon his own experience, set himself against them, saying: "As God gave them the like gift as he did unto us, who believed on the Lord Jesus Christ; what was I, that I could withstand God?" (Acts 11:17). Again, "God, which knoweth the hearts, bare them witness, giving them the Holy Ghost, even as He did unto us; and put no difference between us and them, purifying their hearts by faith" (Acts 15:8, 9). With these words Peter at once overthrows the whole law.

This position the believing Jews little by little accepted; but the wicked rejected it, and at length were altogether hardened.

The Commendation of the Acts of the Apostles

We ought to love and diligently read the Book of the Acts because it contains substantial testimonies to comfort and confirm us against false doctrine. Those who teach error can find in this book that the Holy Ghost is given only by the hearing of faith, at the preaching of the gospel, and not at the preaching of the law, or by the works of the law.

Wherefore we teach that although you fast, give alms, honor your parents, obey the magistrate, etc., yet you are not justified thereby. What then? Hear the word of faith; this word being heard does justify. Wherefore? Because it brings the Holy Ghost, who justifies a man and makes him righteous before God.

The law never brings the Holy Ghost, but only teaches what we ought to do; therefore, it justifies not. But the gospel brings the Holy Ghost, because it teaches what we ought to receive. Therefore, the law and the gospel are two contrary doctrines. To put righteousness in the law is nothing else but to fight against the gospel. For Moses with his law is a severe exactor, requiring of us that we should work and that we should give. Contrariwise, the gospel gives freely and requires of us nothing else, but to hold out our hands and to take that which is offered. Now to exact and to give, to take and to offer, cannot stand together. For that which is given I take; but that which I give, I do not take, but I offer it unto another. Therefore, if the gospel be a gift, it requires nothing. On the other hand, the law gives nothing, but it requires and exacts of us even impossible things.

Cornelius

Our adversaries set against us the example of Cornelius.

He, they say, was (as Luke witnesses) a good man, just and fearing God, who gave alms to the people and prayed to God continually; therefore he merited forgiveness of sins and the sending of the Holy Ghost. I answer: Cornelius was a Gentile, and this the adversaries cannot deny; for Peter witnesses to the fact (Acts 10:28). He was therefore not circumcised and did not keep the law. In fact, he did not even think of it, for it did not pertain to him. Nevertheless, he was justified and received the Holy Ghost.

Let this suffice for the defense of justification, that Cornelius was a Gentile, uncircumcised, not keeping the law; therefore, he was not justified by the law, but by the hearing of faith. God justifies therefore without the law. Otherwise, God would have given the Holy Ghost to the Jews only, who had kept the law, and not to the Gentiles, who had not the law.

Here again the adversaries object and say: we admit that Cornelius was a Gentile, and did not receive the Holy Ghost by the law, yet the text plainly states: "that he was a just man, fearing God, giving alms," etc. By such works he deserved to have the Holy Ghost given unto him. I answer that Cornelius was a just and holy man because of his faith in Christ who was to come, as all the fathers, prophets and godly kings were righteous, and received secretly the Holy Ghost through faith in Christ to come. If Cornelius had died before Christ was revealed, he would not have been damned, because he had the faith of the fathers, who were saved by faith only in Christ to come. He remained always a Gentile, uncircumcised and without law, and yet he worshiped the selfsame God, whom the fathers worshiped by faith in the Messiah to come. But now, because Messiah was already come, it was necessary that it should be shown to him by the Apostle Peter that He was not now to be looked for, but that He had already come.

This teaching concerning Christ believed in before His coming, and in Christ come, is very necessary to be known. For seeing that Christ is now revealed, we cannot be saved by faith in Christ to come, but we must believe that He is already come, has fulfilled all things and abolished the law. Therefore it was necessary that Cornelius should be brought to another belief, not that Christ was yet to come, as he believed before, but that He was already come. So faith gives place to faith: "from faith to faith" (Romans 1:17).

The adversaries are deceived when they say that Cornelius, by the natural and moral work of reason, deserved grace and the sending of the Holy Ghost. For to be a "just man and one that feareth God" are the properties not of a Gentile or of a natural man, but of a spiritual man who has faith already. For unless he did believe in God and fear God, he could not hope to obtain anything from Him by prayer. The first commendation, therefore, that Luke gives unto Cornelius, is that he was "a just man and one that feareth God"; afterwards Luke commends him for his works and alms deeds. This our adversaries do not consider, but emphasize this sentence, that "he gave much alms to the people," for that seems to support their teaching. But first it is said that Cornelius was "a devout man, and one that feared God with all his house." First the person, or the tree, must be commended, and then the works or the fruit. Cornelius is a good tree, for he is a just man and fears God; therefore he brings forth good fruit, he gives alms, he calls upon God, and these fruits please God, because of his faith.

So the angel praises Cornelius for his faith in Christ to come and brings him from that faith to another faith in Christ who was already come, when he says, "Call for one Simon, whose surname is Peter—he shall tell thee what thou oughtest to do" (Acts 10:5, 6). Cornelius was without the law before Christ was revealed; but after Christ was revealed, he received neither the law nor circumcision. Cornelius was justified without the law, therefore the law does not justify.

Much earlier, when the kingdom of Moses was standing and flourishing, God showed that He justified men without the law. Nineveh, that great city, was justified and received the promise of God that it should not be destroyed. By what means? Not because it heard and fulfilled the law, but because it believed the Word of God which the prophet Jonah preached. For it is written: "The people of Nineveh believed God, and proclaimed a fast, and put on sackcloth, from the greatest of them even to the least of them" (Jonah 3:5). That is to say, they repented. Our adversaries pass over this word "believed," and yet everything rests on it. Believing the Word of God, they repented.

"Received ye the Spirit by the works of the law, or by the hearing of faith?" asks Paul, and the Galatians were compelled to grant that they had heard nothing of the Holy Ghost before the preaching of Paul; but when he preached the gospel to them, they received the Holy Ghost. Now many in our day have gone about with great labor to keep the law and the decrees of the fathers. Some with painful and continued exercises in fasting, watching, and praying, so weakened their bodies, that afterwards they were able to do nothing. Yet they gained nothing else, but they miserably afflicted and tormented themselves. They could not attain to a quiet conscience and peace in Christ, but continually doubted the good will of God towards them. Since the gospel teaches that the law and works do not justify, but faith alone in Jesus Christ, there follows a most certain knowledge and understanding, a most joyful conscience, and a true judgment of every kind of life, and of all things else whatever. Since the clear light of the gospel has appeared, all kinds of life in the world are under our judgment. We may boldly pronounce out of the Word of God that the condition of servants, which before the world is most vile, is far more acceptable to God than all the religious orders. For by this Word He commends, approves, and adorns the state of servants, but not the orders of monks, friars, and such others.

It is not without cause that I take so much time in writing of these things. It seems to reason but a small matter that the Holy Ghost is received only by the hearing of faith and that there is nothing else required of us, but we, setting apart all our works, should give ourselves only to the hearing of the gospel.

Man's heart does not understand or believe that so great a treasure, namely, the Holy Ghost, is given by only the hearing of faith. Instead, we reason this way: forgiveness of sins, deliverance, the giving of the Holy Ghost, of righteousness, and everlasting life, are great things; therefore, if you will obtain these inestimable benefits, you must perform some other great and weighty matter. The devil likes and approves that idea and increases it in the heart. Therefore when your reason hears this: you can do nothing for obtaining forgiveness of sins but only hear the Word of God, eventually it cries out, and says, "You are making too small account of the remission of sins," etc. So the inestimable greatness of the gift is the reason we cannot believe it; because this incomparable treasure is offered freely, therefore it is despised.

But this we must learn, that forgiveness of sins, Christ, and the Holy Ghost are freely given unto us, only at the hearing of faith preached, in spite of our horrible sins and demerits. And we must not weigh our unworth with the greatness of the thing given, but we must think that it pleases God to freely give this unspeakable gift unto us, I say, who are unworthy. As Christ said in Luke: "Fear not, little flock; for it is your Father's good pleasure to give you the kingdom" (12:32). To whom? To you unworthy, which are His little flock. If I then be little, and the thing great (yes, the greatest) which God has given me, I must think that He is great who gives it—and I receive the greatness of the gift with joy and gladness—to me, I say, unworthy, by the hearing of faith.

Hear also what Christ Himself says, and answers to Martha, who hardly bears it that her sister Mary, sitting at the feet of Jesus and hearing His Word, should leave her to minister alone: "Martha, Martha, thou art careful and troubled about many things: but one thing is needful: and Mary hath chosen that good part, which shall not be taken away from her" (Luke 10:41, 42). A man therefore is made a Christian not by working, but by hearing: "but one thing is needful"; wherefore he who will exercise himself to righteousness must first exercise himself in hearing the gospel.

When he has heard and received the gospel, let him give thanks to God with a joyful and a glad heart, and afterwards let him exercise himself in those good works which are commanded in the law, so that the law and works may follow the hearing of faith. So may he quietly walk in the light which is Christ and boldly choose and do works not hypocritical, but good works indeed, such as he knows will please God and are commanded by Him.

Our adversaries think that faith, whereby we receive the Holy Ghost, is but a light matter; but how high and hard a matter it is, I myself do find by experience, and so do all they who with me embrace it. It is soon said that by the hearing of faith the Holy Ghost is received, but not so easily laid hold of, believed, and retained. Wherefore if you hear from me that Christ is that lamb of God sacrificed for your sins, see also that you hear it effectually. Paul, very aptly, calls it "the hearing of faith," and not the word of faith. The Word must be heard. The Word is not God's voice only; it must be heard by you: then it is truly and indeed the hearing of faith, through which you receive the Holy Ghost, and by whom, after you have once received, you shall also mortify your flesh.

> *3—Are ye so foolish? having begun in the Spirit, are ye now made perfect by the flesh?*

Now Paul begins to exhort and terrify the Galatians regarding a double danger. The first is: "Are ye so foolish, that after ye have begun in the Spirit, ye would now end in the flesh?" In other words, you began in the Spirit, that is, your religion was excellently well begun, but what have you gotten thereby? It seems as if you will now end in the flesh.

Here Paul sets the Spirit against the flesh. He does not call the flesh, fleshly lust, beastly passions, or sensual appetites; for he does not talk here of lust and other fleshly desires. He is talking instead of forgiveness of sins, of justifying the conscience, of obtaining righteousness before God, of deliverance from the law, sin, and death. Yet he says that they, forsaking the Spirit, do now end in the flesh. Flesh therefore is taken for the very righteousness and wisdom of the flesh, and the judgment of reason, which seeks to be justified by the law. Whatever therefore is most excellent in man, the same Paul calls here flesh. The Spirit is whatever is done in us according to the Spirit; the flesh is whatever is done in us according to the flesh, without the Spirit. Wherefore all the duties of a Christian man, such as to love his wife, to bring up his children, to govern his family, and such like (which unto them are worldly and carnal) are the fruits of the Spirit.

Here is also to be noted the manner of speech which the Apostle uses when he says, "Yea, rather ye are ended in the flesh." For the righteousness of the law, which Paul here calls the flesh, is so far from justifying, that they who after receiving the Holy Ghost through the hearing of faith, fall back again into it, are ended in it; that is to say, are utterly destroyed.

Paul always has a glance at the false apostles; for they still urged the law, saying faith in Christ takes not away sin, pacifies not the wrath of God, justifies not; you must not only believe in Christ but you must also keep the law, and be circumcised. If you do these things, then you shall be free from sin, from the wrath of God, and everlasting death. Rather, says Paul, by those things you establish unrighteousness, you provoke the wrath of God, you add sin to sin, you quench the Spirit, you fall away from grace, and you end in the flesh. This is the first danger, with which he terrifies the Galatians.

4—Have ye suffered so many things in vain? if it be yet in vain.

The other danger is this: "Have ye suffered so many things in vain?" Paul says, Consider how well you began, and how miserably you have forsaken your good beginning, having fallen again into the ministry of sin and death, and a miserable bondage to the law. Consider this also, that you have suffered much for the gospel's sake, and for the name of Christ. You have suffered the spoiling of your goods, railings and reproaches, dangers of bodies and lives, etc. You taught purely, you lived holily, and you endured many evils constantly, for the name of Christ. But now all is lost, doctrine as well as faith, doing as well as suffering, the Spirit as well as the fruits thereof.

So you see the danger of following the righteousness of the law. They who trust in it lose unspeakable benefits. What a miserable thing it is to lose such glory and assurance of conscience towards God! Also to endure so many great afflictions, such as loss of goods, wife, children, body and life, and yet to sustain all these things in vain. No eloquence can sufficiently set forth these matters, for they are inestimable things: the glory of God, victory over the world, the flesh, and the devil, righteousness and everlasting life; and on the other hand, sin, desperation, eternal death, and hell. In a moment we lose all these incomparable gifts and procure to ourselves these horrible and endless miseries, and all by false teachers, when they lead us away from the truth of the gospel.

"If it be yet in vain." This he adds as a correction, whereby he eases the previous rebuke which was somewhat sharp. This he does as an Apostle, lest he should terrify the Galatians too much. Although he chides them, yet he always does it in such a way that he pours in sweet oil, lest he should drive them to desperation.

It is as if he would say, I do not take away all hope from you. But if you will so end in the flesh, then know that all your afflictions are unprofitable. Yet I will not utterly discourage you, so that you repent and amend. Sickly children must not be cast away, but cherished the more carefully than they who are in health.

5—He therefore that ministereth to you the Spirit, and worketh miracles among you, doeth he it by the works of the law, or by the hearing of faith?

When a preacher so preaches that the Word is not fruitless, but effectual in the hearts of the hearers, that is to say, when faith, hope, love, and patience follow, then God gives the Spirit, and works miracles in the hearers. In like manner Paul says here, that God has given His Spirit to the Galatians and has worked miracles among them.

He is saying: God has not only brought to pass that through my preaching you should believe, but also that you should live holily, bringing forth many fruits of faith, and suffer many afflictions.

By the same power of the Holy Ghost you have become chaste, gentle, patient, and lovers of your neighbors. Afterwards Paul testifies of them in the fourth chapter that they had received him as an angel of God, yes, rather as Christ Jesus, and that they had loved him so entirely that they were ready to have plucked out their own eyes for him.

To love your neighbor so heartily, that you are ready to give your money, your goods, your eyes, and all that you have for his salvation, and moreover to suffer patiently all adversities and afflictions, these, no doubt, are the effects and fruits of the Spirit, and these, says he, you received and enjoyed before these false teachers came among you. But you received these things not by the law, but from God, who so ministered unto you and daily increased in you His Holy Spirit that the gospel had a most happy course among you, in teaching, believing, working and suffering. Now, seeing you know these things, how did it happen that you are not showing the same fruits that you did before? Who has corrupted you, that you bear not so loving affection toward me as before? Why do you not receive me now as an angel of God? Why has your once fervent zeal waxed so cold towards me?

The same thing has happened to me. When we first preached the gospel, there were many who favored our doctrine and had a good and reverend opinion of us. After our preaching followed the fruits and effects of faith. But what ensued? Some light and brain-sick heads sprang up and soon destroyed all that we had planted, and also made us so odious to them who before had loved us, and thankfully received our doctrine, that they now hate nothing more than our name. But of this mischief the devil is the author, working in his members contrary works, which wholly fight against the Holy Ghost.

True it is, that at the beginning of our preaching, the doctrine of faith had a most happy course. No man could justly condemn us, for our doctrine was pure, raising up and comforting many poor consciences, which had been long oppressed with men's traditions. Many therefore gave thanks to God that through the gospel they were so mightily delivered out of these snares. But when these newfound heads sprang up (who went about by all means to work our discredit), then began our doctrine to be evil thought of. Many being greatly offended fell from the truth.

If we all had, with a common consent, taught and urged the article of justification, doubtless this one article, little by little, as it began, would have overthrown all. But they, leaving off the preaching of faith and true Christian righteousness, have gone another way to work, to the great hindrance both of sound doctrine and of the churches.

6

The Example of Abraham

Galatians 3:6–10

6—Even as Abraham believed God, and it was accounted to him for
righteousness.

Now Paul adds the example of Abraham and rehearses the testimony of
the Scriptures. The first is out of Genesis 15:6: "Abraham believed in the
Lord; and He counted it to him for righteousness." The Apostle deals
with this verse in Galatians in a similar way that he treated it in his epistle
to Romans: "For if Abraham were justified by works, he hath whereof to
glory; but not before God" (4:2). That is, he might glory before men, but
before God there is nothing but sin and wrath. "Now it was not written
for his sake alone, that his faith was imputed to him for righteousness; but
for us also, to whom it shall be imputed, if we believe on him that raised
up Jesus our Lord from the dead" (Romans 4:23, 24).

By these words, "Abraham believed," Paul makes faith in God our
chief worship, our chief duty, our chief obedience, and our chief
sacrifice. Let him that is a rhetorician amplify this verse, and he shall see
that faith is an almighty thing, and that the power thereof is infinite and
inestimable for it gives glory to God, which is the highest service that can
be given Him. To give glory to God is to believe in Him, to count Him
true, wise, righteous, merciful, almighty, briefly to be the author and
giver of all goodness. This comes not of reason, but of faith. This is it

which makes us divine people, and (as a man would say) it is the creator of a certain divinity, not in the substance of God, but in us. For without faith God loses in us His glory, wisdom, righteousness, truth, and mercy. To conclude, no majesty or divinity remains unto God where faith is not. And the chief thing that God requires of man is that he give unto Him His glory and His divinity; that is, that he take Him not for an idol, but for his God, who regards him, hears him, shows mercy to him, and helps him. This being done, God has His full and perfect divinity, that is, He has whatever a faithful heart can attribute to Him. To be able therefore to give that glory to God is the wisdom of wisdoms, the righteousness of righteousness, the religion of religions, and the sacrifice of sacrifices. In this we can see what a high and an excellent righteousness faith is, and so, by the contrary, what a horrible and grievous sin infidelity is.

Whoever then believes the Word of God as Abraham did is righteous before God, because he has faith, which gives glory to God; that is, he gives to God that which is due Him. Faith says, ''I believe Thee, O God, when Thou speakest.'' And what does God say? Impossible things, foolish, weak, absurd, heretical things, if you believe reason. To reason, what is more absurd, foolish, improbable, yes, impossible, than when God said to Abraham that he should have a son by the barren and dead body of his wife Sarah?

So, if we will follow the judgment of reason, God sets forth absurd and impossible things, when He sets out to us the articles of the Christian faith. Indeed, it seems to reason an absurd and a foolish thing that the dead shall rise again at the last day, that Christ the Son of God was conceived and carried in the womb of the Virgin Mary, that He was born, that He suffered the most reproachful death of the Cross, that He was raised up again, that He now sits at the right hand of God the Father, and that He has all power in heaven and earth. For this reason Paul calls the gospel of Christ crucified, foolishness (1 Corinthians 1:18), which to the Jews was offensive, and to the Gentiles foolish doctrine. Wherefore reason does not understand that to hear the Word of God and to believe it is the chief service that God requires of us, but it thinks that those things which it chooses, and does of a good intent and of its own devotion, please God. Therefore, when God speaks, reason judges His Word to be heresy, for it seems foolish and absurd.

But faith kills reason and slays the beast which the whole world and all creatures cannot kill. So Abraham killed it by faith in the Word of God, by which seed was promised to him through Sarah, who was barren and now past childbearing. Reason did not yield immediately, but it fought against faith in him, judging it an absurd and impossible thing that Sarah, now ninety years of age, should bear a son. Thus faith wrestled with reason in Abraham, but faith got the victory and finally killed and crucified reason, that most cruel and pestilent enemy of God. So all the godly, entering like Abraham into the darkness of faith, can kill reason, saying: "Reason, you are foolish; you do not savor those things that be of God. Therefore, speak not against me, but hold your peace; judge not, but hear the Word of God and believe it." So the godly by faith kill such a beast as is greater than the whole world and offer to God a most acceptable sacrifice and service.

In comparison to this sacrifice of the faithful, all the religions of all nations are nothing at all. For by this sacrifice, first, as I said, they kill reason, a great and mighty enemy of God. For reason despises God and denies His wisdom, justice, power, truth, majesty and divinity. Moreover, by the same sacrifice, they yield glory unto God; they believe Him to be just, good, faithful, true, etc. They believe that He can do all things, that all His words are holy, true, lively, and effectual, etc., which is a most acceptable obedience unto God. So there can be no greater or more holy religion in the world than faith, nor can there be a more acceptable service to God than faith.

On the other hand, those who seek righteousness by their own works, lacking faith, do many things. They fast, they pray, they watch, they lay crosses upon themselves. But because they think to appease the wrath of God and deserve grace by these things, they give no glory to God. In other words, they do not judge Him to be merciful, true, and keeping promise, etc., but to be an angry judge, who must be pacified by works.

In this way they despise God, they deny Christ and all His benefits. In effect, they thrust God out of His seat and set themselves in His place. Only faith gives glory to God, as Paul witnesses of Abraham who "was strong in faith, giving glory to God; and being fully persuaded that, what he had promised, he was able also to perform, and therefore it was imputed to him for righteousness" (Romans 4:20–22).

It is not without cause that he adds this sentence from the fifteenth chapter of Genesis, "and it was imputed to him for righteousness." For Christian righteousness consists in two things: faith in the heart, and in God's imputation. Faith is indeed a formal righteousness, and yet this righteousness is not enough. After faith, certain remnants of sin in our flesh remain. This sacrifice of faith began in Abraham, but, at the last, it was finished in his death.

So the other part of righteousness must be added also: God's imputation. For faith gives not enough to God, because it is imperfect. Rather, our faith is but a little spark which only begins to render unto God His true divinity. We have received the firstfruits of the Spirit, but not yet the tenths. Besides this, reason is not utterly killed in this life; it may still appear by our concupiscence, wrath, impatience, and other fruits of the flesh, and of infidelity, yet remaining in us. Even the holiest that live have not yet a full and continual joy in God, but have their various passions, as the Scriptures witness of the prophets and apostles. But such faults are not laid to their charge, because of their faith in Christ; otherwise, no flesh would be saved.

We conclude, therefore, that righteousness indeed begins through faith, and by it we also have the firstfruits of the Spirit. But because faith is weak, it is not made perfect without God's imputation. So faith begins righteousness, but imputation makes it perfect unto the day of Christ. When reason hears this, it is offended; it rages, and utters all its malice against God, saying, Are then my good works nothing? Have I labored and borne the burden and heat of the day in vain? (Matthew 20:11). Here rise those uproars of nations, kings, and princes, against the Lord and His Christ (Psalms 2:2). For the world neither will nor can allow her wisdom, righteousness, religions, and worshipings to be reproved and condemned.

So let those who give themselves to the study of Holy Scripture learn from this saying, ''Abraham believed God, and it was counted to him for righteousness,'' to set forth truly and rightly this true Christian righteousness after this manner: that it is a faith and confidence in the Son of God, or rather a confidence of the heart in God through Jesus Christ; and let them add this clause as a difference: which faith and confidence is accounted righteousness for Christ's sake. For these two things (as I said before) work Christian righteousness: namely, faith in the heart, which is a gift of God, and assured belief in Christ; and also that God accepts this imperfect faith for perfect righteousness for Christ's sake, in whom I have begun to believe. Because of this faith in Christ, God sees not my doubting of His good will towards me, my distrust, heaviness of spirit, and other sins which are yet in me. For as long as I live in the flesh, sin is truly in me. But because I am covered under the shadow of Christ's wings, as is the chicken under the wing of the hen, and dwell without any fear under that most ample and large heaven of the forgiveness of sins, which is spread over me, God covers and pardons the remnant of sin in me. In other words, because of that faith wherewith I began to lay hold upon Christ, He accepts my imperfect righteousness even for perfect righteousness, and counts my sin for no sin.

So we shroud ourselves under the covering of Christ's flesh, who is our ''pillar of a cloud for the day, and our pillar of fire for the night'' (Exodus 13:21), lest God should see our sin. And although we see it and feel the terrors of conscience, yet flying unto Christ, our mediator and reconciler (through whom we are made perfect) we are sure and safe. As all things are in Him, so through Him we have all things, who also does supply whatever is wanting in us. When we believe this, God winks at the sins and remnants of sin yet sticking to our flesh, and so covers them, as if they were no sin. Because, says He, you believe in My Son, although you have many sins, yet they shall be forgiven you, until you are delivered from them by death.

Let Christians learn that Christian righteousness consists of these two things: faith, which gives glory to God, and in God's imputation. For faith is weak, and God's imputation must be joined to it. Thus a Christian man is both righteous and a sinner, holy and profane, an enemy of God, and yet a child of God. The schoolmen will not accept these seeming contradictions for they do not know the true manner of justification. And this was why they constrained men to work so long, until they should feel in themselves no sin at all. So they gave occasion to many (striving with all their endeavor to be perfectly righteous) to become stark mad; an infinite number of those who were the authors of this devilish opinion, at the hour of death were driven to desperation. This would have happened to me also, if Christ had not mercifully looked upon me and delivered me out of this error.

On the other hand, we teach and comfort the afflicted sinner after this manner: Brother, it is not possible for you to become so righteous in this life that you should feel no sin at all, that your body should be clean like the sun, without spot or blemish. You still have wrinkles and spots, and yet are you holy. But you say: How can I be holy when I have and feel sin in me? I answer: In that you feel and acknowledge your sin, it is a good token; give thanks to God, and do not despair. It is one step to health when the sick man acknowledges and confesses his infirmity. But how shall I be delivered from sin? Run to Christ, the physician, who heals them that are broken in heart and saves sinners. If you believe, you are righteous, because you give glory to God, that He is almighty, merciful, and true. You justify and praise God. You yield unto Him His divinity, and whatever else belongs to Him; and the sin which remains in you is not laid to your charge, but is pardoned for Christ's sake, in whom you believe. His righteousness is your righteousness, and your sin He took upon Himself.

Here we see that every Christian is a high priest: for first he offers up and kills his own reason, and the wisdom of the flesh; then he gives glory to God, that He is righteous, true, patient, pitiful, and merciful. And this is that daily sacrifice of the New Testament, which must be offered evening and morning. The evening sacrifice is to kill reason; the morning sacrifice is to glorify God. This is therefore a strange and wonderful definition of Christian righteousness, that it is the imputation of God for righteousness, or unto righteousness, because of our faith in Christ, or for Christ's sake. When the schoolmen hear this definition, they laugh at it; for they imagine that righteousness is a certain quality poured into the soul and afterwards spread into all the parts of a man. They cannot put away the vain imaginations of reason, which teaches that a right judgment and a good will is true righteousness. This unspeakable gift therefore excels all reason, that God accounts and acknowledges him for righteous, without works, who embraces His Son by faith alone, who was sent into the world, was born, suffered, and was crucified for us.

This matter, as touching the words, is easy, but in very deed it is no small or light matter, but very weighty and of great importance. For Christ who was given for us, and whom we apprehend by faith, has done no small thing for us, but as Paul said before: "He loved me and gave Himself for me"; "He was made a curse for us" (Galatians 3:13). And this is no vain speculation, that Christ was delivered for my sins, and was made accursed for me, that I might be delivered from everlasting death. Therefore, to apprehend the Son of God by faith, and with the heart to believe in Him given to us and for us by God, causes God to account that faith, though it be imperfect, as perfect righteousness.

Here we are altogether in another world, far from reason, where we dispute not what we ought to do, or with what works we may deserve grace and forgiveness of sins. We are in a matter of most high and heavenly divinity, where we hear this gospel or glad tidings, that Christ died for us, and that we, believing this, are counted righteous, although sins remain in us.

So our Savior Christ also defines the righteousness of faith: "The Father," said He, "loveth you." Why does He love you? Not because you were Pharisees, unreprovable in the righteousness of the law, circumcised, doing good works, fasting, etc., but because I have chosen you out of the world, and you have done nothing but love Me, and believe that I came out from the Father. Because you have apprehended and embraced Me, therefore the Father loves you, and therefore you please Him. Yet in another place He calls them evil, and commands them to ask forgiveness of their sins. These two things are contrary: that a Christian is righteous and beloved of God, and yet he is a sinner. God cannot deny His own nature; He must hate sin and sinners; and this He does of necessity, for otherwise He would be unrighteous and love sin. How then can these two contradictions stand together: I am a sinner, and most worthy of God's wrath and indignation; and yet the Father loves me? Here nothing comes between, but only Christ the mediator. The Father, says He, does not therefore love you because you are worthy of love, but because you have loved Me, and have believed that I came out from God (John 16:27; 17:8).

Thus a Christian man abides in true humility, feeling sin in him effectually, and confessing himself to be worthy of wrath, the judgment of God, and everlasting death. Yet he continually turns to Christ, and in Him he lifts up himself against this feeling of God's wrath and judgment, and believes that not only the remnants of sin are not imputed to him, but also that he is loved by the Father, not for his own sake, but for Christ's sake, whom the Father loves.

Now we can see how faith justifies without works, and yet how imputation of righteousness is also necessary. Sins remain in us, and God utterly hates sin. Therefore it is necessary that we should have imputation of righteousness, which we obtain through Christ and for Christ's sake, who is given to us and received of us by faith. Meanwhile, as long as we live here, we are carried and nourished in the bosom of the mercy of God, until the body of sin be abolished, and we are raised up as new creatures in that great day. Then shall there be new heavens and a new earth, in which righteousness shall dwell. Meanwhile, under this heaven, sin and wicked men dwell, and the godly also have sin dwelling in them. For this cause, Paul in Romans (7) complains of sin which remains in the saints; yet he says in the eighth chapter: "There is no condemnation to them which are in Christ Jesus." How shall these things, so contrary and repugnant, be reconciled together: that sin in us is no sin? That he who is damnable shall not be condemned? That he who is rejected shall not be rejected? That he who is worthy of the wrath of God, and everlasting damnation, shall not be punished? The only reconciler is the Mediator between God and man, even the man Christ Jesus: "There is therefore no condemnation to them which are in Christ Jesus."

7—Know ye therefore that they which are of faith, the same are the children of Abraham.

This is the general argument of Paul against the Jews, that they who believe are the children of Abraham, and not they who are born of his flesh and blood (Romans 9:7, 8). Paul vehemently presents his position here and in the fourth and ninth chapters of the Epistle to the Romans. This was the greatest confidence and glory of the Jews: "Abraham is our father" (John 8:39); "We are the seed and children of Abraham." He was circumcised and kept the law: therefore, if you will be the true children of Abraham, you must follow our father, etc. It was, no doubt, an excellent glory and dignity to be the seed of Abraham; for no man could deny but that God spoke to the seed, and of the seed of Abraham. But this prerogative did not profit the unbelieving Jews. So Paul, especially in this place, mightily fought against this argument, and this could he do above all others, as the elect vessel of Christ (Acts 9:15). If we had disputed with the Jews without Paul, we would have prevailed very little against them.

But let us come to the patriarch Abraham himself, and let us see by what means he was justified and saved. Doubtless, not for his excellent virtues and holy works; not because he forsook his country, kindred, and father's house; not because he was circumcised, and observed the law; not because he was about to offer up in sacrifice, at the commandment of God, his son Isaac, in whom he had the promise of posterity: but because he believed (Genesis 12:1; 17:22; 17:24; 22:1, 3). He was not justified by any other means than by faith alone. If you then will be justified by the law, much more ought Abraham your father to have been justified by the law. But Abraham could not otherwise be justified nor receive forgiveness of sins and the Holy Ghost, than by faith alone. Since this is true by the testimony of the Scriptures, why do you stand so much upon circumcision and the law, contending that you have righteousness and salvation by them, whereas Abraham himself your father, your fountainhead, of whom you do boast so much, was justified and saved without these, by faith alone. What can be said against this argument?

Paul therefore concludes with this sentence: "They which are of faith, they are the children of Abraham." Corporal birth or carnal seed does not make the children of Abraham before God. There is none before God accounted as the child of this Abraham (whom God has chosen, and made righteous by faith) through carnal generation; such children must be given him before God, as he was a father. But he was a father of faith, was justified and pleased God, not because he could beget children after the flesh, not because he had circumcision and the law, but because he believed God. He therefore that will be a child of the believing Abraham, must also himself believe, or else he is not a child of the elect and justified Abraham, but only of the begetting Abraham, which is nothing else but a man conceived, born, and wrapped in sin, without faith, and therefore condemned. This boasting then, "we are the seed of Abraham," is to no purpose.

This argument Paul sets out plainly in the ninth chapter of Romans by two examples from the Old Testament. The first is of Ishmael and Isaac, who were both the seed and natural children of Abraham; yet Ishmael, though the elder, is shut out, for the Scripture says: "In Isaac shall thy seed be called." The second is of Esau and Jacob, of whom, when yet in their mother's womb and had done neither good nor evil, it was said: "the elder shall serve the younger"; "Jacob have I loved, but Esau have I hated." Therefore it is plain that they who are of faith are the children of Abraham.

But some will object, saying that this word *faith* in the Hebrew signifies truth, and therefore we do not rightly apply it. We will briefly answer their objections.

Faith is nothing else but the truth of the heart; that is to say, a true and right opinion of the heart as touching God. Now, only faith thinks and judges rightly of God, and not reason. And a man thinks rightly of God when he believes His Word. And when he will measure God without the Word, and believe Him according to the wisdom of reason, he has no right opinion of God in his heart, and therefore he cannot think or judge of Him as he should do. Truth therefore is faith itself, which judges rightly of God, namely that God regards not our works and righteousness, because we are unclean, but that He will have mercy upon us if we believe in His Son, whom He hath sent to be a sacrifice for the sins of the whole world (1 John 2:2). This is a true opinion of God, and in fact nothing else but faith itself.

Paul rightly alleges in the fifteenth chapter of Genesis (verse 6): "And he believed in the Lord; and he counted it to him for righteousness," applying it to faith in Christ. Faith always must be joined to a certain assurance of God's mercy. Now this assurance comprehends a faithful trust of remission of sins for Christ's sake. It was impossible that your conscience should look for anything at God's hand, except first it is assured that God is merciful to you for Christ's sake. Therefore all the promises are to be referred to that first promise concerning Christ: "The seed of the woman shall bruise the serpent's head" (Genesis 3:15). So did all the prophets both understand it and teach it. By this we may see that the faith of our fathers in the Old Testament, and ours now in the New is all one, although they differ in their outward objects. Peter witnesses to this in Acts, when he says, "which neither our fathers nor we were able to bear. But we believe that through the grace of our Lord Jesus Christ we shall be saved, even as they" (Acts 15:10, 11). And Paul says: "Our fathers did all drink of that spiritual Rock that followed them: and that Rock was Christ" (1 Corinthians 10:4). And Christ Himself says: "Abraham rejoiced to see my day: and he saw it, and was glad" (John 8:56). So the faith of the fathers was grounded on Christ who was to come, as ours is on Christ who is now come. It is as I have said before of Cornelius, who at first believed in Christ to come, but being instructed by Peter he believed that Christ was already come. The diversity of times does not change faith nor the Holy Ghost nor the gifts thereof. For there has been, is, and ever shall be, one mind, one judgment and understanding concerning Christ, as well in the ancient fathers, as in the faithful of this day, and those that shall come hereafter. For we also look for Christ to come again with glory, to judge both the quick and the dead, whom we believe to have come already for our salvation.

At this day also Christ is present to some, to others He is to come. To all believers He is present; to the unbelievers He is not yet come, neither does He profit them anything at all; but if they hear the gospel, and believe that He is present unto them, He justifies and saves them.

Paul is saying, you know by this example of Abraham, that they are the children of Abraham who are of faith, whether they are Jews or Gentiles, without respect either to the law, to works, or to the carnal generation of his posterity. For not by works or by the law, but by the righteousness of faith, the promise was made to Abraham that he should be the heir of the world; that is to say, that in his seed all the nations of the earth should be blessed, and that he should be called the father of nations. Lest the Jews should falsely interpret this word *nations,* applying it to themselves alone, the Scripture prevents this, and says not only, "a father of nations," but "a father of many nations have I made thee" (Genesis 17:4; Romans 4:17). Therefore, Abraham is not only the father of the Jews, but also of believing Gentiles.

So Paul makes two Abrahams, a begetting and a believing Abraham. Abraham has children and is a father of many nations. Where? Before God, where he believes; not before the world where he begets. For in the world he is a child of Adam and a sinner, or, which is more, he is a worker of righteousness of the law, living after the rule of reason, that is, after the manner of men; but this pertains not to the believing Abraham.

8—And the scripture, foreseeing that God would justify the heathen through faith, preached before the gospel unto Abraham, saying, In thee shall all nations be blessed.

This argument, founded upon the certainty of time, is very strong. The promise of blessing is given to Abraham 430 years before the people of Israel received the law. It is said to Abraham: because you have believed God and have given glory to Him, therefore you shall be a "father of many nations" (Genesis 17:4). So the inheritance of the world for his posterity is given to him before the law was published. Why then do you brag, O Galatians, that you obtain forgiveness of sins and are become children, and receive the inheritance through the law, which followed a long time after the promise, that is to say, 430 years.

Afterward, when he was now accounted righteous because of his faith, the Scripture makes mention of circumcision, "This is my covenant, which ye shall keep, between me and you" (Genesis 17:10). This argument Paul handles in the fourth chapter of Romans: to wit, that righteousness was imputed to Abraham before circumcision; much more then was he righteous before the giving of the law. Therefore, righteousness comes by faith only, and not by the law.

The Jews pass over these years and do not see that they treat of faith towards God, and of righteousness before God. After this manner, the Jew, say they, which is born of the seed of Abraham, is blessed; and the proselyte, or stranger, which worships the God of the Jews, and joins himself unto them, is also blessed. Therefore, they think that blessing is nothing else but praise and glory in the world; in that a man may glory and vaunt, that he is of the stock and family of Abraham.

But this is to pervert the Scriptures, and not to expound them. Paul defines, by the words "Abraham believed," a spiritual Abraham, faithful, righteous, and having the promise of God, not of the old flesh, which is of Adam, but of the Holy Ghost. And of this Abraham, renewed by faith, and regenerated, by the Holy Ghost, speaks the Scripture, and pronounces that he should be a father of many nations; that all the

Gentiles should be given unto him for an inheritance, when it says: "In thee shall all the nations of the earth be blessed."

It follows that the blessing and faith of Abraham is the same that ours is; that Abraham's Christ is our Christ who died for the sins of Abraham as he did for us. "Abraham saw my day and was glad" (John 8:56). Therefore, all found the same thing. The Jews look but through a veil into the Scriptures, and therefore they do not understand what or whereof the promise is which was made to the fathers, which we ought to consider above all things, and we see that God spoke to Abraham, not of the law, or of things to be done, but of things to be believed, that is, of promises which are apprehended by faith.

"So then they which are of faith are blessed with faithful Abraham." All the weight and force of these words lies in "faithful." For he puts a plain difference between Abraham and Abraham, making two of one and the same person. It is as if he said: There is a working, and there is a believing, Abraham. With the working Abraham we have nothing to do. For if he were justified by works, he has to rejoice, but not before God. Let the Jews rejoice as much as they will over that working, begetting Abraham; but we glory of the faithful Abraham, of whom the Scripture says that he received the blessing of righteousness through his faith, not only for himself, but also for all those who believe as he did, and so the world was promised to Abraham because he believed. And all the Gentile world receives imputation of righteousness if it believes as Abraham did.

So the blessing is nothing else but the blessing of the gospel. And that all nations are blessed is to say all nations shall hear the blessing; that is, the promise of God shall be preached and published by the gospel among all nations. And out of this place the prophets have drawn many prophecies by spiritual understanding: "Ask of me and I will give thee the heathen for thine inheritance, and the uttermost parts of the earth for thy possession" (Psalms 2:8). And again: "Their line is gone out through all the earth" (Psalms 19:4). To say that the nations are blessed is nothing else but that righteousness is freely given unto them; or that they are counted righteous before God, not by the law, but by the hearing of faith.

Here we see that to bless signifies to preach and teach the gospel, to confess Christ, and to spread abroad the knowledge of Him among all the Gentiles. And this is the priestly office and continual sacrifice of the New Testament Church, which distributes this blessing of preaching, administering the sacraments, comforting the brokenhearted, and distributing the Word of grace which Abraham had, and which was also his blessing when he believed. So we also believing the same are blessed. And this blessing is a great glory, not before the world, but before God. For we have heard that our sins are forgiven us, and that we are accepted by God; that God is our Father, and we are His children, with whom He will not be angry, but will deliver us from sin, from death, and all evils, and will give unto us righteousness, life, and eternal salvation.

So the prophecy of Hosea (13:14): "I will ransom them from the power of the grave; I will redeem them from death: O death, I will be thy plagues; O grave, I will be thy destruction," and such verses from the prophets all spring out of these promises, in which God promised to the fathers the bruising of the serpent's head and the blessing of all nations.

If the nations are blessed, that is to say, if they are accounted righteous before God, it follows that they are free from sin and death and are made partakers of righteousness, salvation and everlasting life, not for their works, but for their faith in Christ. So that verse in Genesis, "In thee shall all nations be blessed," speaks not of the blessing of the mouth, but of such blessing as belongs to the imputation of righteousness, which is available before God and redeems from the curse of sin, and from all those evils which accompany sin. This blessing is received only by faith, for the text says plainly: "Abraham believed God, and it was counted unto him for righteousness." So it is a spiritual blessing, and there is no blessing indeed but this; although it is accursed in the world (as indeed it is), yet it is available before God.

Even as the Jews glory only of a working Abraham, even so many today set forth only a working Christ, or rather an example of Christ. He that will live godly (they say) must walk as Christ walked, according to

His own saying in John 13:15: "I have given you an example, that ye should do as I have done to you." We do not deny that the faithful ought to follow the example of Christ, and to work well, but we say that they are not justified thereby before God. And Paul does not here reason what we ought to do, but by what means we are made righteous. In this matter we must set nothing else before our eyes but Jesus Christ dying for our sins, and rising again for our righteousness; and Him must we apprehend by faith, as a gift, not as an example. As the Jews who were saved follow the believing Abraham, so we also, if we will be delivered from our sins and be saved, must take hold of the justifying and saving Christ, whom Abraham himself also by faith did apprehend, and through Him was blessed.

It was indeed a great glory that Abraham received circumcision at the command of God, that he was endued with excellent virtues, that he obeyed God in all things; as it is also a great praise and felicity to follow the example of Christ working, to love your neighbor, to do good to them that hurt you, to pray for your enemies, patiently to bear the ingratitude of those who render evil for good: but all this avails not to righteousness before God. To make us righteous before God, there is a far more excellent price required, which is neither the righteousness of man, nor yet of the law. Here we must have Christ to bless us and save us, as Abraham had Him for his Blesser and Savior. How? Not by works, but by faith. Therefore he adds with great vehemence: "They which be of faith are blessed with faithful Abraham." A man, believing in Christ, is altogether the child of God, the inheritor of the world, a conqueror of sin, death, the world, and the devil; therefore, he cannot be praised or magnified enough.

By these words, "shall be blessed," Paul gathers an argument of the contrary: for the Scripture is full of oppositions, as when two contraries are compared together. And it is a point of cunning to mark well these oppositions. When the Scripture says that all nations which are of faith are blessed with faithful Abraham, it follows necessarily that all, Jews as well as Gentiles, are accursed without faith. Therefore, whatever is without that blessing is accursed. And this Paul shows plainly when he says:

10—For as many as are of the works of the law are under the curse:
for it is written, Cursed is every one that continueth not in all things
which are written in the book of the law to do them.

Here we see that the curse is as it were a flood, swallowing up whatever is without Abraham; that is to say, without faith, and the promise of the blessing of Abraham. Now if the law itself given by Moses at the command of God makes them subject to the curse who are under it, much more shall the laws and traditions do so, which are devised by men. He who will avoid the curse must lay hold upon the promise of blessing, or upon the faith of Abraham, or else he shall remain under the curse.

To know these things is very necessary, for they help greatly to comfort troubled consciences, and they teach us to separate the righteousness of the flesh, or civil righteousness, from the righteousness of faith. We must note that Paul has here in hand, not a matter of policy, but a divine and spiritual matter, lest any mad brain should cavil, and say that he curses and condemns polite law and magistrates. Here all the schoolmen are dumb and can say nothing. So readers must be admonished that in this verse there is nothing handled as touching civil laws, manners, or matters political, but of a spiritual righteousness by which we are justified before God, and are called the children of God in the Kingdom of heaven. To be brief, what is handled here does not concern the bodily life but everlasting life.

For good reason I diligently teach and repeat this distinction, for there are few who mark it or understand it. In civil righteousness we must regard laws and works; but in the spiritual righteousness, divine and heavenly, we must utterly reject all laws and works, and set before our eyes only the promise and blessing which lays hold on Christ, our only Savior, the giver of this blessing and grace.

This argument is invincible. For if we must hope to receive the blessing by Christ alone, then it must follow that it is not received by the law. For the blessing was given to faithful Abraham before the law, and without the law.

When our adversaries hear this, they pervert and slander our words, as though we taught that the magistrates should not be honored, but that we raise up sedition against the emperor, that we condemn all laws, that we overthrow and destroy governments. But they do us great wrong. For we put a difference between corporal and spiritual blessing, and we say that the emperor is blessed with a corporal blessing. To have a kingdom, laws, and civil ordinances, to have a wife, children, house, and lands, is a blessing. For all these things are the good creatures and gifts of God. But we are not delivered from the everlasting curse by this corporal blessing, which is but temporal and must have an end. Therefore, we condemn not laws, neither do we stir up sedition against the emperor; we teach that he must be obeyed, that he must be feared, reverenced, and honored, but yet civilly. But when we speak of the blessing after the manner of divines, then we say boldly, with Paul, that all things that are without faith, and the promise of Abraham, are accursed, and abide under that everlasting curse of God. For there we must look for another life after this, and another blessing after our corporal blessing. And as touching life everlasting it is not enough to have corporal blessings; for the very wicked do sometimes abound therein most of all. These things God distributes in the world freely, and bestows them upon good and bad, as He makes the sun to rise both on the evil and on the good, and sends rain upon the just and upon the unjust.

Paul might have said, as a general proposition, whatever is without faith is under the curse. He does not say it that way, but he takes that which, besides faith, is the best, the greatest, and most excellent among all corporal blessings of the world: to wit, the law of God. The law, says he, is indeed holy and given of God. Nevertheless it does nothing else but make men subject to the curse and keep them under the curse. If the law of God brings men under the curse, much more may the same be said of inferior laws and blessings. And that it may be plainly understood what Paul means to be under the curse, he declares by this testimony of the Scripture: "Cursed be he that confirmeth not all the words of this law to do them" (Deuteronomy 27:26).

Paul goes about to prove, by this testimony from Deuteronomy, that all men who are under the law, or under the works of the law, are accursed or under the curse, that is to say, under sin, the wrath of God, and everlasting death. For he speaks not (as I said before) of a corporal, but of a spiritual curse, which must be of everlasting death. Paul proves this affirmative sentence, which he takes from Moses, by this negative, "Cursed be he that confirmeth not the words of the law to do them."

These two sentences of Moses and Paul seem contrary. Paul says: "Whosoever shall do the works of the law are accursed." Moses says: "Whosoever shall not do the works of the law are accursed."

How shall these sayings be reconciled? Or else how shall the one be proved by the other? Indeed no man can understand this verse, unless he knows and understands justification.

These two sentences are not repugnant, but do very well agree. We also teach in the same way: that "not the hearers of the law are just before God, but the doers of the law shall be justified" (Romans 2:13). And, contrary, they that are of the works of the law are under the curse. For justification teaches that whatever is without the faith of Abraham is accursed. Yet, the righteousness of the law must be fulfilled in us (Romans 8:4). To a man that is ignorant of the doctrine of faith, these two sentences seem to be quite contrary.

First of all we must note that Paul here is treating a spiritual matter, separated from policy and from all laws, and he looks into Moses with other eyes than the hypocrites and false apostles do, and expounds the law spiritually. So the whole effect of the matter consists in this word *do*. To do the law is not only to do it outwardly, but to do it truly and perfectly. There are two sorts of doers of the law: the first are they who do the works of the law, against whom Paul inveighs throughout this epistle. The other sort are they who are of the faith, of whom we will speak hereafter. Now to be of the law, or of the works of the law, and to be of faith, are quite contrary: yea, even as contrary as God and the devil, sin and righteousness, death and life. For they are of the law who would be justified by the law. They are of faith who trust assuredly that they are justified through mercy alone for Christ's sake. He who says that righteousness is of faith condemns the righteousness of works. He who says that righteousness is of the law condemns the righteousness of faith. Therefore, they are altogether contrary the one to the other.

To do the law is not to do it in outward show only, but in spirit, that is truly and perfectly. But where shall we find him, who so will accomplish the law? Let us see him, and we will praise him. Here our adversaries have their answer, saying: "The doers of the law shall be justified" (Romans 2:13). Very well. They call him a doer of the law who does the works of the law, and so by these works going before, he is made righteous. This is not to do the law according to Paul: for, to be of the works of the law, and to be of faith, are contrary things. To seek to be justified by the works of the law is to deny the righteousness of faith. Those who do the law deny the righteousness of faith, and sin against the first, the second, and the third commandments, yes, even against the whole law. For God commands that we should worship Him in faith, and in the fear of His name. Therefore, we must say that in doing of the law, they sin and deny the Divine Majesty in all His promises. To this end the law was not given.

Not understanding the law, they abuse the law and, as Paul says: "They being ignorant of God's righteousness, and going about to establish their own righteousness, have not submitted themselves unto the righteousness of God" (Romans 10:3). Thus they rush into the Scripture, taking hold of one part, to wit the law, and this they imagine they are able to fulfill by works. But this is a dream, a bewitching and illusion of the heart.

There is no blessing but in the promise of Abraham: "In thee shall all the nations of the earth be blessed," and if you are without that promise, you are under the curse. So when God saw that we could not fulfill the law, He provided for this long before the law and promised the blessing to Abraham and by him to all nations. To do is first of all to believe, and so through faith to perform the law. We must first receive the Holy Ghost, through whom we, being enlightened and made new creatures, begin to do the law, that is to say, to love God and our neighbor. Before all things we must hear and receive the promise which sets out Christ, and offers Him to all believers; when we have taken hold on Him by faith, the Holy Ghost is given to us for His sake. Then do we love God and our neighbor, then we do good works, then do we carry the Cross patiently. If you will truly define what it is to do the law, it is nothing else but to believe in Jesus Christ, at which time the Holy Ghost is received through faith in Christ to work those things which are commanded in the law; otherwise, we are not able to perform the law. For the Scripture says there is no blessing without the promise; no, not in the law.

The apples make not the tree, but the tree makes the apples. So faith first makes the person who afterwards brings forth works. Therefore, to do the law without faith is to make the apples of wood and earth, without the tree, which is not to make apples, but is a mere fantasy. So, if the tree be made, that is to say, the person or doer which is made through faith in Christ, works will follow. For the doer must be before the things done, and not the things which are done before the doer.

Christians are not made righteous by doing righteous things, but being made righteous by faith in Christ, they do righteous things. In earthly matters the doer or the worker is made of the things that are wrought, as a man in playing the carpenter becomes a carpenter; but in divine matters the workers are not made of the works going before, but the persons made and framed already by faith, which is in Christ, are now become doers and workers. Of such Paul speaks when he says: ''The doers of the law shall be justified'' (Romans 2:13), that is, shall be counted righteous.

The schoolmen are compelled to admit that a moral work outwardly done, if it is not done with a pure heart, a good will, and true intent, is but hypocrisy. The wickedest knave in the world may counterfeit the same works that a godly man works by faith. Judas did the same works that the other Apostles did. What fault was there in the works of Judas, seeing he did the same works the other Apostles did? Note what the schoolmen answer out of their moral philosophy. Although he did the same works, because the person was reprobate and his judgment of reason perverse, therefore his works were hypocritical and not true as were the works of the other Apostles, however alike they seemed in outward show. So they are constrained to grant that in external matters works do not justify, unless they be joined to an upright heart, will, and judgment. How much more are they compelled to confess the same in spiritual matters where, before all things, there must be knowledge of God, and faith to purify the heart. They walk therefore in works and in the righteousness of the law, no matter what they say or what they affirm. And although Paul says plainly that the law justifies not, but causes wrath, utters sin, and reveals the judgment and indignation of God, yet, reading these things, they do not see them, much less do they understand them.

So when Paul proves this verse, "Whosoever are of the works of the law are under the curse," by this sentence of Moses, "Cursed is every one that continueth not in all things that are written in this book," he proves not one contrary by another, as at first sight it may appear, but he proves it rightly and in due order. For Moses means and teaches the same thing that Paul does. For no man keeps all things that are written in the book of the law. And if he keeps them not, he is under the curse. But there are two sorts of men that are doers of the law: true doers, and hypocrites; the true doers must be separated from the hypocrites. The true doers are they who, through faith, are the good tree before the fruit, doers and workers before the works. But the hypocrites are not of this sort; for they think they can obtain righteousness by works, and by them to make the person just and acceptable. For they dream: we who are sinners and unrighteous will be made righteous. How? By good works. Therefore, they do even as a foolish builder, who goes about the roof to make the foundation, about the fruit to make the tree. And this is plainly to renounce God, and to set themselves in the place of God. For to make righteous is the work of the Divine Majesty alone, and not of any creature either in heaven or on earth.

Here Paul was able to show, out of the first commandment, the abominations which Antichrist should bring into the Church. For all who teach that any other worship is necessary to salvation than that which God requires of us in the first commandment, which is the faith, fear, and love of God, are plain antichrists and set themselves in the place of God. That such should come, Christ Himself foretold when He said in Matthew 24:5: "Many shall come in My Name, saying, I am Christ." So we at this day may boldly pronounce that whoever seeks righteousness by works without faith, denies God, and makes himself God. Upon the same ground Peter also prophesies when he says: "There shall be false teachers among you, who privily shall bring in damnable heresies, even denying the Lord that bought them" (2 Peter 2:1).

And in the Old Testament all the prophecies against idolatry sprang out of the first commandment. For all the wicked kings and prophets, with all unfaithful people, did the same. Despising the first commandment and the worship appointed of God, and despising the promise of Abraham's seed, in which all nations should be blessed, they ordained a wicked worship contrary to the Word of God and said: "With this worship will we serve God and set forth His praise, who hath brought us out of the land of Egypt." So Jeroboam made the calves, and said: "Behold thy gods, O Israel, which brought thee up out of the land of Egypt" (1 Kings 12:28). This he said of the true God, and yet both he and his people were idolaters, for they worshiped contrary to the first commandment. They only regarded the work; and having done the work, they counted themselves righteous before God. Paul speaks of such idolaters when he says: "They profess that they know God; but in works they deny Him" (Titus 1:16).

He who knows all these things rightly may certainly judge that he is an antichrist who teaches another manner of worship than that the first tablet sets out. He may know and understand what it is to deny God and Christ, and what Christ meant when He said: "Many shall come in My name, saying, I am Christ" (Matthew 24:5); what it is to be against God, and lifted up above all that is called God, and worshipful; what it signifies that Antichrist sits in the temple of God, showing himself that he is God; what it is to see the abomination of desolation standing in the holy place, etc. (2 Thessalonians 2:4; Mark 13:14; Daniel 9:27, 12:11).

Therefore we, being justified by faith, do good works, through which, as is said in 2 Peter 1:10, our calling and election is made sure or confirmed. But because we only have the firstfruits of the Spirit, as have not as yet the tenths, and the remnants of sin do remain in us, therefore we do not the law perfectly.

But this imperfection is not imputed unto us who believe in Christ, who was promised to Abraham, and has blessed us. For we are nourished and tenderly cherished in the mean season for Christ's sake, in the lap of God's long-sufferance. We are that wounded man who fell among thieves, whose wounds the Samaritan bound up, pouring in oil and wine, and afterwards laying him upon his beast, brought him to the inn and made provision for him, and departing, commended him to the host, saying, "Take care of him . . ." (Luke 10:30–35). And so in the meantime, we are cherished as it were in an inn, until the Lord put to His hand the second time, as Isaiah said, to deliver us (Isaiah 11:11).

So the sentence of Moses, "Cursed is everyone that continueth not in the things that are written in this book," is not contrary to Paul, who pronounces all them to be accursed who are of the works of the law. For Moses requires such a doer to do the law perfectly. But where shall we find him? For Moses himself confesses that he is not such a one, for he says that none is innocent before God (Exodus 34:9). And David says, "Enter not into judgment with thy servant, O Lord, for in thy sight shall no man living be justified" (Psalms 143:2). And Paul says, "For what I would, that do I not; but what I hate, that do I" (Romans 7:15). So Moses, together with Paul, drives us to Christ, through whom we are made doers of the law, and are not accounted guilty of any transgression.

How so? First, by forgiveness of sins, and imputation of righteousness, because of our faith in Christ. Secondly, by the gift of God and the Holy Ghost, who brings forth a new life and motions in us, so that we may also do the law effectually. For that which is not done is pardoned for Christ's sake; and moreover, what sin is left in us, is not imputed to us. So Moses agrees with Paul. Moses spoke negatively, and Paul affirmatively, and both verses are true: all are accursed who abide not in all that is written in this book, and also they are accursed who are of the works of the law.

An Answer to These Arguments Which the Adversaries Allege Against the Doctrine and Righteousness of Faith

We must here say something about the arguments against the doctrine of faith, which is, that we are justified by faith alone. The schoolmen, and such as do not understand the article of justification, know no other righteousness than civil righteousness and the righteousness of the law. Therefore they borrow certain words out of the law and moral philosophy, as "to do," "to work," and such like, and they apply the same to spiritual matters most perversely and wickedly. We must make a difference between philosophy and divinity. The schoolmen grant and teach that in the order of nature, being goes before working; for naturally the tree is before the fruit. Again, in philosophy they grant that a work morally wrought is not good, except there is first a right judgment of reason, and a good will or intent; so then they will have a right judgment of reason, and a good intent to go before the work; that is, they make the person morally righteous before the work. Contrariwise, in divinity and in spiritual matters, where they ought most of all to do so, such dull and senseless asses they are, that they pervert and turn all quite contrary, placing the work before right judgment of reason and good intent.

So, doing is one thing in nature, another thing in moral philosophy, and another thing in divinity. In nature the tree must be first, then the fruit. In moral philosophy, doing requires a good intent, and a sound judgment of reason to work well. And here all the philosophers go no further. Therefore, the divines say that moral philosophy takes not God for the object, and final cause. For Aristotle, or a Sadducee, or a man of any civil honesty, calls this a right reason, and a good intent, if he seek the public commodity of the commonwealth, and the quietness and honesty of it. A philosopher or law-worker ascends no higher. He thinks not through a right judgment of reason and good intent to obtain remission of sins and everlasting life. He abides within his bounds, not mingling earthly and heavenly things together. Contrariwise, the blind schoolman imagines that God regards his good intent and works. Therefore, he mingles earthly and heavenly things together, and pollutes the name of God. And this imagination he learns out of moral philosophy, except that he abuses it much worse than the heathen man does.

So we must ascend higher in divinity with this word "doing" than in natural things and in philosophy, so that now it must have a new meaning and be made altogether new, joined with a right judgment of reason and a good will, not morally but divinely; which is, that I know and believe by the Word of the gospel, that God has sent His Son into the world to redeem us from sin and death. Here, doing is a new thing, unknown to reason, to philosophers, to law-workers, and unto all men: for it is a wisdom hidden in a mystery. Therefore, in divinity the work necessarily requires faith going before. So, when we speak of doing, we must speak of that faithful doing; for in divinity we have no other right judgment of reason, no good will or intent besides faith.

This rule is well observed in the eleventh chapter to the Hebrews where many works of the saints are recited. It is said of Abel that he through faith offered up a better sacrifice than Cain. If the schoolmen happen upon this place, as it is read in Genesis 4:5 (where it is simply set out that both Cain and Abel offered up their gifts, and that the Lord had respect unto Abel and his offering), they soon take hold of these words, and cry out, "Here we see that God had respect to offerings; therefore works do justify." So they think that righteousness is but a moral thing, only beholding the outward show of the work, and not the heart of him who does the work; whereas, even in philosophy, they are constrained not to look upon the bare work, but the good will of the worker. But here they stand altogether upon those words: "They offered gifts; the Lord had respect unto Abel and to his offering," and see not that the text says plainly in Genesis, that the Lord had respect first to the person of Abel, who pleased the Lord because of his faith, and afterwards to his offering. Therefore in divinity we speak of faithful works, sacrifices, oblations, and gifts, which are offered up and done in faith, as the Epistle to the Hebrews declares, saying: "Through faith Abel offered up a better sacrifice; through faith Enoch was taken away; through faith Abraham obeyed God,'' etc. We have here then a rule, set forth in Hebrews 11, how we should simply answer the arguments of the adversaries as touching the law and works, that is to say: this or that man did this or that work in faith; and by this means you give a solution to all their objections, and so stop their mouths that they can have nothing to reply.

It is manifest that in divine matters, the work is nothing without faith, but you must have faith before you begin to work: ''For without faith it is impossible to please God'' (Hebrews 11:6). He that will come to God must believe that He is. Wherefore it is said in Hebrews 11 that the sacrifice of Abel was better than the sacrifice of Cain, because he believed. Contrariwise in Cain, because he was wicked and a hypocrite, there was no faith or trust of God's grace or favor, but mere presumption of his own righteousness, and therefore his work was rejected. Wherefore the adversaries themselves are bound to admit that in all the works of the saints, faith is presupposed, or goes before. Because of their faith, their works please God and are accepted by Him. Therefore in divinity there is a new doing completely contrary to the moral doing.

So, when you read in the Scriptures of the fathers, prophets, and kings, how they wrought righteousness, raised up the dead, overcame kingdoms, you must remember that these sayings are to be expounded as the Epistle to the Hebrews expounds them: ''By faith they wrought righteousness, by faith they raised up the dead, by faith they subdued kingdoms,'' etc. (Hebrews 11:33, 34, 35). So faith incorporates the work and gives it perfection. Reason must be enlightened by faith before it can work. And when it has a true opinion and knowledge of God, then is the work incarnate and incorporated into it; so that whatever is attributed to faith is afterwards attributed to works also, but yet because of faith only and alone.

Therefore in reading the Scriptures we must learn to put a difference between the true and the hypocritical, the moral and the spiritual doing of law. So shall we be able to declare the true meaning of all those places which seem to maintain the righteousness of works. The true doing of the law is a faithful and a spiritual thing, which he does not who seeks righteousness by works. Therefore, every such doer of the law is accursed. For he walks in the presumption of his own righteousness against God, while he will be justified by man's free will and reason, and so in doing of the law, he does it not. And this, according to Paul, is to be under the works of the law, that is to say, that hypocrites do the law, and yet in doing it, they do it not.

All objectors against this doctrine of justification by faith alone must be answered after this manner: Here is Christ, there are the testimonies of the Scriptures touching the law and works. Now Christ is the Lord of the Scriptures and of all works. He also is Lord of heaven, the earth, the sabbath, the Temple, righteousness, life, wrath, sin, death, and all things whatever. And Paul His Apostle shows that "He was made a curse for us" (Galatians 3:13). I hear then that I could by no other means be delivered from my sin, my death, my malediction, but by His blood-shedding and death. So I conclude that it properly belongs to Christ Himself to overcome my sin, death, and malediction in His own body, and that these cannot be overcome by my own works or the works of the law. Therefore, if He is the price of my redemption, if He was made sin that He might justify and bless me, I care not if you bring a thousand places of Scripture for the righteousness of works against the righteousness of faith. I have the Author and Lord of the Scripture with me. On His side I will rather stand than believe all the rabble of law-workers and meritmongers. As for me, I will stick to the Author and Lord of the Scripture.

Therefore, if any man thinks himself not able to reconcile such places of Scripture or answer the same sufficiently, and yet is constrained to hear the objections of the adversaries, let him answer simply after this sort: You set against me the servant, that is to say, the Scripture, and that not wholly, neither the principal part thereof, but only certain verses touching the law and works. But I come with the Lord Himself who is above the Scripture, and is made unto me the merit and price of righteousness and everlasting life. On Him I lay hold, Him I stick to, and leave works unto you. This solution, neither the devil, nor any justiciary can ever wrest from you, or overthrow. Moreover, you are in safety before God: for your heart abides fixed in the object which is called Christ who, being nailed to the Cross, was accursed not for Himself, but for us, as the text says: "was made a curse for us." Hold fast to this, and lay it against all the sentences of the law, and works whatever, and say: Do you hear this, Satan? Here he must give place, for he knows that Christ is his Lord and Master.

7

Christ Made a Curse

Galatians 3:11–14

> *11—But that no man is justified by the law in the sight of God, it is evident: for, The just shall live by faith (Habakkuk 2:4; Romans 1:17).*

This argument is grounded upon the testimony of the prophet Habakkuk. And it is a verse of great weight and authority, which Paul sets against all the verses touching the law and works. It is as if he would say: Why do we need a long argument? Here I bring forth a most evident testimony of the prophet, against which no man can quarrel: "The just shall live by faith." If he lives by faith, then he lives not by the law; for the law is not of faith. And here Paul excludes works and the law as things contrary to faith.

The schoolmen pervert this verse after this manner: "The just man doth live by faith"; that is to say, by a working faith, or formed and made perfect with charity, but if it is not formed with charity, it does not justify. This gloss they themselves have added, and by it they do injury to the words of the prophet. If they called this formed or furnished faith, the true faith which the Scripture teaches, their gloss would not offend me, for then faith should not be separated from charity, but from the vain opinion of faith. We also put a difference between a counterfeit faith and a true faith. The counterfeit faith is that which hears of God, of Christ, and of all the mysteries of His incarnation, and our redemption; it also apprehends those things and can talk well of them, and yet there remains nothing else in the heart but a naked opinion, and a sound of the gospel. For it neither renews nor changes the heart; it makes not a new man, but leaves him in the vanity of his former opinions and conversation. This is a very pernicious faith. The moral philosopher is much better than the hypocrite having such a faith.

So if they would make a distinction between faith formed and a false or counterfeit faith, their distinction would not offend me. But they speak of faith formed and made perfect with charity, and make a double faith, formed and unformed. This pestilent and devilish gloss I utterly detest. Although, say they, we have faith infused, called *fides infusa,* which is the gift of the Holy Ghost, and also faith gotten by our own industry, called *fides acquisita;* yet both of them are formed with charity. This is to prefer charity before faith, and to attribute righteousness not to faith but to charity. So, when they do not attribute righteousness to faith, but only in respect of charity, they attribute to faith nothing at all.

Moreover, these perverters of the gospel of Christ do teach, that even that faith which they call infused, and not received by hearing, nor gotten by any working, but created in man by the Holy Ghost, may stand with deadly sin, and that the worst men may have this faith. Therefore, they say, if it is alone, it is utterly idle and unprofitable. Thus they take from faith her office and give it unto charity, so that faith is nothing unless charity, which they call the form and perfection thereof, is joined to it. This is a devilish and blasphemous kind of doctrine, which utterly overthrows the doctrine of faith, and carries a man away from Christ the mediator and from faith, which is the hand and only means by which we apprehend Him. If charity is the form and perfection of faith, as they dream, then am I constrained to say that charity is the principal part of the Christian religion, and so I lose Christ, His blood, and all His benefits, and rest in a moral doing.

But the Holy Ghost, who gives to all men both mouth and tongue, knows how to speak. He could have said (as the schoolmen imagine) the righteous man shall live by faith formed, beautified and made perfect by charity. But this He omitted on purpose and says plainly: "The righteous man shall live by faith." We therefore will still hold and extol this faith, which God Himself has called faith; that is to say, a true and certain faith, which doubts not God, nor His promise, nor the forgiveness of sins through Christ, that we may dwell safe and sure in this our object Christ, and may keep still before our eyes the passion and blood of the Mediator and all His benefits.

12—And the law is not of faith: but, The man that doeth them shall live in them.

Paul says: "The law is not of faith." But what is the law? Is it not also a commandment touching charity? Yes, the law commands charity, as we may see by the text: "Thou shalt love the Lord thy God, with all thy soul . . ." (Deuteronomy 6:5; Matthew 22:37). Again, "showing mercy unto thousands of them that love Him, and keep His commandments." If the law that commands charity is contrary to faith, it must follow that charity is not of faith. Paul plainly confutes the gloss which the schoolmen have forged touching their formed faith, and speaks only of faith, as it is separate from the law. Now the law being separate and set apart, charity is also set apart with all that belongs to the law, and faith only is left, which justifies and quickens to everlasting life.

Paul therefore reasons here, out of a plain testimony of the prophet, that there is none which obtains justification and life before God but the believing man who obtains righteousness and everlasting life without the law, and without charity, by faith alone. The reason is because the law is not of faith, or anything belonging to faith, for it believes not; neither are the works of the law faith, nor yet of faith. Therefore, faith is a thing much different from the law. For the promise is not apprehended by working, but by believing. Yes, there is as great a difference between the promise and the law, and consequently between faith and works, as there is between heaven and earth.

It is impossible therefore that faith should be of the law. For faith only rests in the promise, it only apprehends and knows God, and stands only in receiving good things from God. Contrariwise, the law and works consist in exacting, in doing, and giving unto God. As Abel, offering his sacrifice, gives unto God; but he believing, receives of God. Paul, therefore, concludes from this verse in Habakkuk that the just man lives by faith alone. For the law in no way belongs to faith, because the law is not the promise. But faith rests upon the promise. That gloss of the schoolmen is false and wicked, which joins the law and faith together. Yes, rather it quenches faith, and sets law in the place of faith. And here note that Paul always speaks of such as would do the law morally, and not according to the Scripture. But whatever is said of such good works as the Scripture requires, the same is attributed to faith alone.

When Paul says, "The man that doeth them, shall live in them," it is to show the true righteousness of the law and the gospel. The righteousness of the law is to fulfill the law, according to that saying: "He that doeth these things shall live in them." The righteousness of faith is to believe, according to that saying: "The just shall live by faith." The law therefore requires that we should give something to God. But faith requires no works of us, or that we should give anything unto God, but that we, believing the promise of God, should receive of Him. Therefore, the office of the law is to work, as the office of faith is to assent unto the promises. For faith is the faith of the promise, and the work is the work of the law. He says that of the law there comes nothing but only doing; but faith is a totally contrary thing, namely, that which assents to the promise, and lays hold upon it.

These four things must be perfectly distinguished. For as the law has its proper office, so has the promise. To the law pertains doing, and to the promise believing. By this distinction Paul separates charity from faith and teaches that charity justifies not, because the law helps nothing to justification. Faith alone justifies and quickens; and yet it stands not alone, that is to say, it is not idle. Works must follow faith, but faith must not be works, or works faith. The bounds must be rightly distinguished one from the other. When we believe therefore, we live only by faith in Christ, who is without sin, who is also our mercy-seat. Conversely, when we observe the law, we work indeed, but we have no righteousness nor life. For the office of the law is not to justify and give life, but to show forth sin and to destroy. But faith works not, but believes in Christ the justifier. And a faithful man performs the law, and that which he does not is forgiven him through the remission of sins for Christ's sake; that which remains is not imputed to him.

Paul therefore in this verse, and in the tenth chapter to the Romans, compares the righteousness of the law and of faith, and says: "He that doeth these things shall live in them." It is as though he would say, it were indeed a goodly matter if we could accomplish the law; but because no man does, we must fly unto Christ "who is the end of the law for righteousness to every one that believeth"; "He was made under the law that He might redeem us who were under the law" (Romans 10:4; Galatians 4:4). Believing in Him, we receive the Holy Ghost and we begin to do the law, and that which we do not is not imputed to us because of our faith in Christ.

But in the life to come we shall no more have need of faith (1 Corinthians 13:12). For then we shall not see darkly through a mirror (as we do now), but we shall see face-to-face. There shall be a most glorious brightness of the eternal Majesty, in which we shall see God even as He is. There shall be a true and perfect knowledge and love of God, a perfect light of reason, and a good will, not a moral and philosophical will, but a heavenly, divine, and eternal will. In the meantime, inspirited by faith, we look for the hope of righteousness. Conversely, they who seek forgiveness of sins by work and the law, and not by Christ, never perform the law, but abide under the curse.

Paul therefore calls only them righteous who are justified through the promise, or through faith in the promise without the law. They who are of the works of the law and seem to do the law, do it not. The Apostle generally concludes that all they who are of the works of the law are under the curse, under which they would not be, if they fulfilled the law. Indeed it is true, that a man doing the works of the law shall live in them, that is, shall be blessed, but such a man cannot be found.

There is a double use of the law, the one politic, and the other spiritual. He who understands this sentence civilly, may do it after this sort: "He that shall do these things shall live in them''; that is, if a man obey the magistrate outwardly, and in the public government, he shall avoid punishment and death, for then the civil magistrate has no power over him. This is the public use of the law, which serves to bridle those that are rude and intractable. But Paul here speaks not of this use, but treats the matter like a theologian. It is as if he said, if men could keep the law, they would be happy. But where are they? They are not therefore doers of the law, unless they are justified before and without the law, through faith. So, when Paul curses and condemns those who are of the works of the law, he speaks not of such as are justified through faith, but of such as go about to be justified by works, without faith in Christ. This I say, lest any man should follow the fond imagination of Jerome who, being deceived by Origen, understood nothing at all in Paul, but took him as a mere civil lawyer. He reasoned after this manner: the holy patriarchs, prophets, kings, were circumcised and offered sacrifice; therefore, they observed the law. But it were a wicked thing to say, they are under the curse; therefore, all they that are of the works of the law are not under the curse. Thus he sets himself against Paul, making no difference between the true doers of the law justified by faith, and those workers who seek to be justified by the law without faith.

We also who are justified by faith, as were the patriarchs, prophets, and all the saints, are not of the works of the law as concerning justification; but in that we are in the flesh, and have the remnants of sin in us, we are under the law, and yet not under the curse, because the remnants of sin are not imputed unto us for Christ's sake, in whom we believe. For the flesh is an enemy to God, and that concupiscence which yet remains in us not only fulfills not the law, but also sins against it, rebelling, and leading us captive into bondage (Romans 7:23). Now if the law is not fulfilled in the saints, but that many things are done by them contrary to the law, much more is this true in a man who is not yet justified by faith, but is an enemy of God, and with all his heart despises and hates the Word and work of God. You see then that Paul speaks here of such as will fulfill the law, and be justified thereby, although they have not yet received faith.

*13—Christ hath redeemed us from the curse of the law, being made
a curse for us: for it is written, Cursed is every one that hangeth on
a tree (Deuteronomy 21:23).*

Here again Jerome is much troubled, seeking, as it would seem, with
a godly zeal, to turn away this reproach from Christ, that He should be
called a curse. The schoolmen say that the verse from Moses which Paul
here quotes speaks not of Christ. Moreover, this general clause *every one*
which Paul quotes is not in Moses. Again, Paul omits the words *of God*
which are in Moses. To conclude, it is evident enough that Moses speaks
of a thief or a malefactor who by his evil deeds has deserved the gallows,
as the Scripture plainly witnesses in the twenty-first chapter of Deuteronomy. Therefore, they ask this question, How can this sentence be applied
to Christ, that He is accursed of God, and hanged upon a tree, seeing He
is no malefactor or thief but righteous and holy? This may convince not
only the simple and ignorant, but also the very godly, who wish to defend
the honor and glory of Christ. Let us see therefore what is the meaning
and purpose of Paul.

Here we must make a distinction, as the words of Paul plainly show.
For he says not that Christ was made a curse for Himself, but for us.
Therefore, all the weight of the matter stands on this word, ''for us.'' For
Christ is innocent as concerning His own person, and therefore He ought
not to have been hanged on a tree; but because, according to the law of
Moses, every thief and malefactor ought to be hanged, therefore Christ
also, according to the law, ought to be hanged, for He sustained the
person of a sinner and a thief, not of one, but of all sinners and thieves.
For we are sinners and thieves, and therefore guilty of death and
everlasting damnation. But Christ took our sins upon Himself, and for
them died upon the Cross; therefore, it is right that He should become a
transgressor, and (as Isaiah says, chapter 53) be ''numbered with the
transgressors.''

This, no doubt, all the prophets foresaw in spirit, that Christ should
be accounted the greatest transgressor that could be, having all sins
imputed to Him. For He being made a sacrifice for sin, yes, for the sins

of the whole world, is not as such an innocent person and without sin, but a sinner who has and carries the sin of Paul, who was a blasphemer and a persecutor; of Peter who denied Him; of David who was an adulterer and a murderer; and who bears all the sins of all men in His body—not that He is Himself guilty of any, but that He received them, being committed or done by us, and laid them upon His own body, that He might make satisfaction for them with His own blood (Isaiah 53:5). Therefore, this general sentence of Moses includes Him also (though Himself innocent) because He was found and reckoned among sinners and transgressors; as a magistrate takes him for a thief and punishes him whom he finds among thieves, though he never committed any deed worthy of death. So Christ was not only found among sinners, but of His own accord, and by the will of His Father, He would also be a companion of sinners, taking upon Him the flesh and blood of those who were sinners, and plunged into all kinds of sin. When the law therefore found Him among thieves it condemned and killed Him as a thief. The schoolmen spoil us of this knowledge of Christ, namely, that Christ was made a curse that He might deliver us from the curse of the law, when they separate Him from sins and sinners, and only set Him out to us as an example to be followed. By this means they make Christ not only unprofitable to us, but also a judge and a tyrant who is angry with our sins, and condemns sinners. But we must wrap Christ, and know Him to be wrapped in our sins, in our malediction, in our death, and in all our evils, as He is wrapped in our flesh and blood.

But some man will say, it is absurd and slanderous to call the Son of God a cursed sinner. I answer, if you will deny Him to be a sinner and accursed, deny also that He was crucified and dead. For it is no less absurd to say that the Son of God (as our faith confesses and believes) was crucified and suffered the pains of sin and death, than to say that He is a sinner and accursed. But if it is not absurd to confess and believe that Christ was crucified between two thieves, then it is not absurd to say also that He was accursed and of all sinners the greatest. These words of Paul are not spoken in vain, "Christ was made a curse for us: God made

Christ, who knew no sin, to be sin for us; that we might be made the righteousness of God in Him'' (2 Corinthians 5:21).

After the same manner, John the Baptist calls Him ''the Lamb of God, which taketh away the sin of the world'' (John 1:29). He is innocent because He is the unspotted and undefiled Lamb of God. But because He bears the sins of the world, His innocence is burdened with the sins and guilt of the whole world. Whatever sins I, you, or we all have done, or shall do hereafter, they are Christ's own sins, or else we should perish forever. This true knowledge of Christ which Paul and the prophets have most plainly delivered unto us, the sophisters have darkened and defaced.

Isaiah speaks thus of Christ: ''The Lord hath laid on Him the iniquity of us all'' (Isaiah 53:6). We must not make these words less than they are, but leave them in their own proper signification. For God dallies not in the words of the prophet, but speaks earnestly and in great love, to wit, that this Lamb of God should bear the sins of us all. But what is it to bear? The sophisters answer, to be punished. Very well; but why is Christ punished? Is it not because He has sin and bears sin? Now that Christ has sin the Holy Ghost witnesses in the fortieth Psalm: ''Mine iniquities have taken hold upon me, so that I am not able to look up; they are more than the hairs of mine head.'' In this Psalm and certain others, the Holy Ghost speaks of the Person of Christ, and in plain words witnesses that He had sins. For this testimony is not the voice of an innocent, but of a suffering Christ, who took upon Him to bear the person of all sinners, and therefore was made guilty of the sins of the whole world.

So Christ was not only crucified and died, but sin also (through the love of the Divine Majesty) was laid upon Him. When sin was laid upon Him, then comes the law and says: ''Every sinner must die.'' Therefore, O Christ, if You will answer, become guilty, and suffer punishment for sinners, You must also bear sin and malediction. Paul therefore quotes this general sentence out of Moses as concerning Christ: ''Cursed is every one that hangeth on a tree.'' Christ has hanged upon a tree; therefore, Christ was accursed of God.

And this is a singular consolation for all Christians, so to clothe Christ with our sins, and to wrap Him in my sins, your sins, and the sins of the whole world, and so to behold Him bearing all our iniquities. For the beholding of Him after this manner shall easily vanquish all the fantastical opinions of the schoolmen concerning the justification of works. For they imagine (as I have said) a certain faith formed and adorned with charity. By this (they say) sins are taken away and men are justified before God. And what else is this, I pray you, but to unwrap Christ, and to strip Him of our sins, to make Him innocent, and to charge and overwhelm ourselves with our own sins, and to look upon them not in Christ, but in ourselves? And what is this but to take Christ entirely away, and to make Him utterly unprofitable to us? For if it is true that we put away our sins by the works of the law and charity, then Christ takes them not away. But if He is the Lamb of God, ordained from everlasting to take away the sins of the world, and if He is so wrapped in our sins that He became accursed for us, it must follow that we cannot be justified by works. For God has laid our sins not upon us, but upon Christ His Son, that He, bearing our punishment, might be our peace and that by His stripes we might be healed (Isaiah 53). To all this the Scripture bears witness; and we also confess the same in the articles of the Christian belief when we say, ''I believe in Jesus Christ . . . that He suffered, was crucified, and died for us.''

Hereby it appears that the doctrine of the gospel (which of all others is most sweet and full of most singular consolation) speaks nothing of our works or of the works of the law, but of the inscrutable mercy and love of God towards most wretched and miserable sinners. Our most merciful Father, seeing us to be oppressed and overwhelmed with the curse of the law, and that we could never be delivered from it of our own power, sent His only Son into the world and laid upon Him all the sins of all men, saying, be Thou Peter that denier; Paul that persecuter and cruel oppressor; David that adulterer; that sinner who did eat the fruit in Eden; that thief who hanged upon the cross, and be Thou that person who has committed the sins of all men: see therefore, that Thou pay and satisfy for them. Here comes the law and says, I find Him a sinner, and such a one as has taken upon Himself the sins of all men, and I see no sins else but in Him: therefore, let Him die upon the Cross; and so it sets upon and kills

Him. By this means the whole world is purged and cleansed from sin, and so delivered from death and all evils. Now sin being vanquished and death abolished by this one man, God would see nothing else in the whole world, if it did believe it, but a perfect cleansing and righteousness. And if any remnants of sin should remain, yet for the great glory that is in Christ, God would not see them.

Thus we must magnify the article of Christian righteousness against the righteousness of the law and works, although no eloquence is able to sufficiently set forth the inestimable greatness thereof. So the argument that Paul handles in this place is the most mighty against all the righteousness of the law. For it contains this invincible opposition: that is, if the sins of the whole world be in the one man Jesus Christ, then they are not in the world; but if they be not in Him, then they are yet in the world. Also, if Christ be made guilty of all the sins which we all have committed, then are we delivered from all sins, but not by ourselves, not by our own works and merits, but by Him. But if He be innocent, and bear not our sins, then we do bear them, and in them we shall die and be condemned. "But thanks be to God, which giveth us the victory through our Lord Jesus Christ" (1 Corinthians 15:57).

But now let us see by what means these two things, so contrary and repugnant, may be reconciled in this one person Christ. Not only my sins and yours, but the sins of the whole world, past, present, or to come, take hold upon Him, go about to condemn Him, and do indeed condemn Him. But because in the same Person, who is the highest, the greatest, and the only sinner, there is also an invincible and everlasting righteousness, therefore these two do encounter together, the highest, the greatest, and the only sin, and the highest, the greatest, and the only righteousness. Here one of them must be overcome and give place to the other, seeing they fight together with so great force and power. The sins therefore of the whole world come upon righteousness with all might and main. In this combat what is done? Righteousness is everlasting, immortal, and invincible. Sin also is a most mighty and cruel tyrant ruling and reigning over the whole world, subduing and bringing all men into bondage. To conclude, sin is a mighty and strong god, which deceives and devours all mankind, learned, unlearned, holy, mighty, and wise men. This tyrant, I say, flies upon Christ, and would swallow Him up as he does all others. But he sees not that He is a person of invincible and everlasting righteousness. Therefore, in this combat, sin must be vanquished and killed and righteousness must overcome, live, and reign. So in Christ all sin is vanquished, killed, and buried, and righteousness remains a conqueror and reigns forever.

In like manner death, which is an omnipotent queen and empress of the whole world, killing kings, princes, and all men generally, enters into combat with life, thinking utterly to overcome it and to swallow it up; and that which it intended to do, it brings to pass indeed. But because life was immortal, therefore when it was overcome, yet did it overcome and get the victory, vanquishing and killing death. Death therefore through Christ is vanquished and abolished throughout the whole world, so that now it is but a painted death which, losing its sting can no more hurt those who believe in Christ, who is become the death of death, as Hosea the prophet says: "O death, I will be thy death" (Hosea 13:14).

So the curse, which is the wrath of God upon the whole world, has a conflict with the blessing: that is to say, with grace and the eternal mercy of God in Christ. The curse therefore fights against the blessing, and would condemn it and bring it to nought; but it cannot do so. For the blessing is divine and everlasting, and therefore the curse must give place. For if the blessing in Christ could be overcome, then should God Himself also be overcome. But this is impossible; therefore Christ the power of God, righteousness, blessing, grace and life, overcomes these monsters and destroys them, even sin, death, and the curse, without war or weapons, in His own body, and in Himself, as Paul delights to speak: "Having spoiled principalities and powers, triumphing over them in the Cross" (Colossians 2:15), so that they cannot hurt any more those that believe.

And this circumstance makes that combat much more wonderful and glorious. For it shows that it was necessary that these inestimable things should be accomplished in that one Person, and the whole creature should be renewed through this one Person. Therefore, if you look upon this person Christ, you shall see sin, death, the wrath of God, hell, the devil, and all evils vanquished and mortified by Him. As Christ reigns by His grace in the hearts of the faithful, there is no sin, no death, no curse; but where Christ is not known, there all these things do still remain. Therefore, all they who believe not lack this inestimable benefit and glorious victory. For (as John says), ''This is the victory that overcometh the world, even our faith'' (1 John 5:4).

This is the principal article of all Christian doctrine. And here you see how necessary a thing it is to believe and confess the article of the divinity of Christ, which, when Arius denied, he must also deny the article of our redemption. For to overcome the sin of the world, death, the curse, and the wrath of God *in Himself* is not the work of any creature, but of the divine power. Therefore, He who in Himself should overcome these must be truly and naturally God. Against this mighty power of sin, death, and the curse (which of itself reigns throughout the world, and in the whole creature), it was necessary to set a more high and mighty power. But besides the sovereign and divine power, no such power can be found. So to abolish sin, to destroy death, to take away the curse, and again, to give righteousness, to bring life to light, and to give the blessing—all in Himself—are the works of the divine power only and alone. Now, because the Scripture attributes all these to Christ, He in Himself is life, righteousness, and blessing, which is naturally and substantially God. So they who deny the divinity of Christ lose all Christianity. We must learn diligently the article of justification, for all other articles of the faith are comprehended in it; and if that remain sound, then all the rest are sound. When we teach that men are justified by Christ, that Christ is the conqueror of sin, death, and the everlasting curse, we witness that He is naturally and substantially God.

Hereby we may plainly see how horrible was the wickedness and blindness of those who taught that these cruel and mighty tyrants, sin, death, and the curse, could be vanquished by a man's own works, such as fasting, vows, pilgrimages, masses, and such other like paltry things. But I pray you, was there ever any found, that being furnished with this armor, overcame sin, death, and the devil? Paul in the sixth chapter to the

Ephesians describes a far different armor which we must use against these most cruel and raging beasts.

Let us receive this most sweet doctrine, so full of comfort, with thanksgiving and with an assured faith, which teaches that Christ being made a curse for us (that is, a sinner under the wrath of God), put upon Himself our person, and laid our sins upon His own shoulders, saying, I have committed the sins which all men have committed. Therefore, He was made a curse indeed according to the law, not for Himself, but, as Paul says, for us. For unless He had taken upon Himself my sins and yours, and the sins of the whole world, the law would have had no right over Him, for it condemns none but sinners only, and holds them under the curse. So He could neither have been made a curse nor die, since the only cause of the curse and of death is sin, from which He was free. But because He had taken upon Himself our sins, not by constraint, but of His own good will, it behooved Him to bear the punishment and wrath of God not for His own Person, but for our person.

So, making a happy change with us, He took upon Himself our sinful person, and gave unto us His innocent and victorious Person; wherewith we being now clothed are freed from the curse of the law. Christ was willingly made a curse for us, saying, "I am blessed and need nothing. But I will abase Myself, and will put upon Me your person''—that is to say, our human nature (Philippians 2:7)—''and I will walk among you, and will suffer death, to deliver you from death.'' So He, bearing the sin of the whole world, was taken, suffered, was crucified and put to death, and became a curse for us. But because He was a Person divine and everlasting, it was impossible that death should hold Him. Wherefore He arose again the third day from the dead, and now lives forever; and there is neither sin nor death found in Him anymore, but only righteousness, life, and everlasting blessedness.

This image and this mirror we must have continually before us, and behold the same with a steadfast eye of faith. He that does so has the innocence and victory of Christ, although he may be ever so great a sinner. By faith only therefore we are made righteous, for faith lays hold of this innocence and victory of Christ. If you believe, sin, death, and the curse are abolished. For Christ has overcome and taken away these in Himself and will have us to believe that, as in His own Person there is now no sin or death, even so there is none in ours, seeing He has performed and accomplished all things for us.

So if sin vex you, and death terrify you, think that it is (as indeed it is) but an imagination and a false illusion of the devil. For there is now no sin, no curse, no death, no devil, to hurt us anymore, for Christ has vanquished and abolished all these things. The victory of Christ is most certain, and there is no defect in the thing itself, but in our incredulity; for it is a hard matter to believe these inestimable good things and unspeakable riches. Moreover, Satan with his fiery darts, and his ministers with their wicked and false doctrine, go about to wrest from us and utterly to deface this doctrine; and especially for this article which we so diligently teach, we sustain the hatred and cruel persecution of Satan and the world, for Satan feels the power and fruit of this article.

Therefore, where sins are seen and felt, then are they indeed no sins; for according to Paul's teaching, there is no sin, no death, no malediction anymore in the world, but in Christ, who is the Lamb of God that has taken away the sin of the world. Christ was made a curse, to deliver us from the curse. Contrariwise, according to reason and philosophy, sin, death, and the curse are nowhere else but in the world in the flesh, and in sinners. For a sophisticated teacher speaks of sin in the same way as the heathen philosopher. As color, says he, cleaves to the wall, so does sin in the world, in the flesh, or in conscience; therefore, it is to be purged by contrary operations, to wit, by charity. But true doctrine teaches that there is no sin in the world anymore; for Christ, upon whom the Father has cast the sins of the whole world, has vanquished and killed it in His own body (Isaiah 53:6). He once dying for sin and raised up again, dies no more. Therefore, wherever is a true faith in Christ, there sin is abolished, dead, and buried. But where no faith in Christ is, there sin still remains. And though the remnants of sin are still in the saints because they believe not perfectly, yet are they dead in that they are not imputed to them because of their faith in Christ.

This text then is plain, that all men, yes, apostles, prophets, and patriarchs, had remained under the curse, if Christ had not set Himself against sin, death, the curse of the law, the wrath and judgment of God, and overcome them in His own body; for no power of flesh and blood could overcome these huge and hideous monsters. But Christ is not the law, but a divine and human Person who took upon Him sin, the condemnation of the law, and death, not for Himself, but for us. Therefore, all the weight and force of this verse consists in these words, "for us."

We must not then imagine Christ to be innocent and a private person who is holy and righteous for Himself alone, as do the schoolmen. True it is that Christ is a Person most pure and unspotted, but you must not stay there; for you do not yet have Christ, although you know Him to be God and man. But you have Him indeed when you believe that this most pure and innocent Person is freely given to you by the Father to be your high priest and Savior, yes, your servant, that He, putting off His innocence and holiness and taking your sinful person upon Him, might bear your sin, your death, and your curse, and might be made a sacrifice and a curse for you, that by this means He might deliver you from the curse of the law.

You see then with what an apostolic spirit Paul handles this argument of the blessing and the curse. He not only makes Christ subject to the curse, but says also that He is made a curse. So in 2 Corinthians 5 he calls Him sin when he says: "He hath made Him to be sin for us, who knew no sin; that we might be made the righteousness of God in him." And although these verses may be well expounded after this manner: Christ is made a curse, that is to say, a sacrifice for the curse; and sin, that is, a sacrifice for sin; yet, in my judgment, it is better to keep the proper meaning of the words, because there is a greater force and vehemence in them. When a sinner comes to the knowledge of himself indeed, he feels not only that he is miserable, but misery itself; not only that he is a sinner, and is accursed, but even sin and malediction itself. For it is a terrible thing to bear sin, the wrath of God, malediction and death. So that man who has a true feeling of these things (as Christ did truly and effectually feel them for all mankind) is made even sin, death, malediction, etc.

To conclude, all evils should have overwhelmed us, as they shall overwhelm the wicked forever; but Christ being made for us a transgressor of all laws, guilty of all our malediction, our sins, and all our evils, comes between as a mediator, embracing us wicked and damnable sinners. He took upon Him and bore all our evils, which should have oppressed us and tormented us forever; and these cast Him down for a little while and ran over His head like water, as the Spirit of Christ complains in the prophetic words of the Psalmist: "Thy wrath lieth hard upon me, and thou hast afflicted me with all thy waves" (Psalms 88:7).

By this means we are delivered from these everlasting terrors and anguish through Christ, and so shall enjoy everlasting and inestimable peace through believing in Him.

These are the sacred mysteries of the Scripture, which Moses also somewhat darkly in some places did foreshadow; which the prophets and apostles did know, and delivered to their posterity. For this knowledge and benefit of Christ to come, the saints of the Old Testament rejoiced more than we now do, when He is so comfortably revealed and exhibited to us.

14—That the blessing of Abraham might come on the Gentiles through Jesus Christ; that we might receive the promise of the Spirit through faith.

Paul always has this verse before his eyes: "In thy seed shall all the nations of the earth be blessed" (Genesis 22:18). For the blessing promised to Abraham could come upon the Gentiles only through Christ the seed of Abraham, and it behooved Him to be made a curse, that by this means the promise made unto Abraham might be fulfilled. Therefore, He became accursed and joined Himself to them that were accursed, that He might take away the curse from them, and through His blessing might bring unto them righteousness and life. And here note that this word *blessing* is not in vain. But Paul talks here of sin and righteousness, of death and life, before God. He speaks therefore of inestimable and incomprehensible things when he says, "That the blessing of Abraham might come upon the Gentiles through Jesus Christ."

For we were enemies of God, dead in sin, and accursed. What do we deserve then? What can he deserve that is dead in sin, accursed, ignorant of God? We must say that he is accursed before God who does nothing else but accursed things. Wherefore there is no other way to avoid the curse, but to believe, and with assured confidence to say, Thou Christ art my sin and my curse, or rather, I am Thy sin, Thy curse, Thy death, Thy wrath of God, Thy hell; and contrariwise, Thou art my righteousness, my blessing, my life, my grace of God, my heaven. Therefore, we are the cause that He was made a curse; no, rather we are His curse.

This is an excellent verse and full of spiritual consolation; and it satisfies us who have received this doctrine and who have concluded that we are blessed through the curse, the sin-bearing, and the death of Christ; that is to say, we are justified and quickened into life. So long as sin, death, and the curse abide in us, sin terrifies, death kills, and the curse condemns us. But when these are laid upon Christ, then are all these evils made His own, and His benefits are made ours. For God the Father "laid upon Him the iniquities of us all," as the prophet Isaiah says, and He has taken them upon Himself, though not guilty. And this He did, that He might fulfill the will of His Father, by which we are sanctified forever.

This is that infinite and immeasurable mercy of God, which Paul would amplify with all eloquence, but the slender capacity of man's heart cannot comprehend, much less utter that unsearchable and burning zeal of God's love towards us. And truthfully, the inestimable greatness of God's mercy not only engenders in us a hardness to believe, but also incredulity itself. For I not only hear that this Almighty God, the Creator and Maker of all things, is good and merciful, but also that the same high sovereign Majesty was so careful for me, a damnable sinner, a child of wrath, that He spared not His own dear Son, but delivered Him up to a most shameful death, that He hanging between two thieves, might be made a curse and bear sins for me a cursed sinner, that I might be made blessed, that is to say, the child and heir of God. Who can enough praise and magnify this exceeding great goodness of God? Not all the angels in heaven. Therefore, the doctrine of the gospel speaks of far different matters than any book of policy or philosophy, yes, or the books of Moses himself—to wit, of the unspeakable and most divine gift of God—which far passes the capacity and understanding of both angels and men.

"That we might receive the promise of the Spirit through faith" is a Hebrew phrase, that is to say, the promised Spirit. Now the Spirit is freedom from the law, sin, death, the curse, hell, and from the judgment and wrath of God. Here is no worth or merit of ours, but a free promise, and a gift given through the seed of Abraham, that we may be free from all evils, and obtain all good things. And this liberty and gift of the Spirit we receive not by any merit other than by faith alone. For only that takes hold of the promises of God, as Paul plainly says in this place, "That we might receive the promise of the Spirit through faith."

This is indeed a sweet and apostolic doctrine, which shows that those things are fulfilled in us which many prophets and kings desired to see and hear. And such verses as this one were gathered together out of various sayings of the prophets, who foresaw long before, in spirit, that all things should be changed, repaired, and governed by this man Christ. The Jews, therefore, although they had the law, nevertheless still looked for Christ. None of the prophets or governors of the people of God, made any new law, but Eli, Samuel, David, and all the other prophets continued to abide under the law of Moses. They did not appoint any new tables or a new kingdom and priesthood of the law, and the worship was referred and kept to Him only, of whom Moses had prophesied long before: "The Lord thy God will raise up unto thee a Prophet from the midst of thee, of thy brethren, like unto me; unto him ye shall hearken" (Deuteronomy 18:15). As if he would say: thou shall hear Him only, and none besides Him.

This the fathers well understood, for none could teach greater and higher points than Moses, who received from God the Ten Commandments, especially that first commandment: "Thou shalt have no other gods before me"; and that word: "Thou shalt love the Lord thy God with all thine heart" (Exodus 20:2). This law concerning the love of God is the headspring of all divine wisdom. And yet was it necessary that another teacher should come, even Christ, who should bring and teach another thing far passing the excellent law given before: to wit, grace and remission of sins. This text therefore is full of power, for in this short sentence: "That we might receive the promise of the Spirit through faith," Paul pours out at once whatever he was able to say. Therefore, when he can go no further (for he could not utter any greater or more excellent thing) he breaks off, and here he stays.

Why the Law?

Galatians 3:15–29

> *15—Brethren, I speak after the manner of men; Though it be but a man's covenant, yet if it be confirmed, no man disannulleth, or addeth thereto.*

After this principal and invincible argument, Paul adds another, grounded upon the similitude of a man's will and testament, which seems to be very weak, and such as the Apostle ought not to use for the confirmation of so great importance. For in high and weighty matters, we ought to confirm earthly things by divine things, and not heavenly and divine things by earthly and worldly things. And indeed it is true that those arguments of all other are most weak when we go about to prove and confirm heavenly matters by earthly and corruptible things as Scotus is wont to do. A man, says he, is able to love God above all things, for he loves himself above all things; for a good thing, the greater it is, the more it is to be loved. And from this he infers that a man is able *ex puris naturalibus* that is, of his own pure natural strength, easily to fulfill that high commandment, "Thou shalt love the Lord thy God with all thy heart. . . ." For, says he, a man is able to love the least good thing above all things: yes, he sets at nought his life (of all other things most dear to him) for a little vile money; therefore, he can much more do it for God's cause.

You have often heard me say that civil laws and ordinances are of God; for God has ordained them, and allowed them, as He has ordained the sun, the moon, and other creatures. Therefore, an argument taken of the ordinance of the creatures of God is good, if we use it rightly. So the prophets have often used metaphors and comparisons taken from creatures, calling Christ the sun, the Church the moon, the teachers and preachers of the Word the stars. Also, there are many similitudes in the New Testament. Therefore, where God's ordinance is in the creature, there an argument may be well borrowed and applied to heavenly and divine things.

So our Savior Christ, in Matthew 7, arguing from earthly things to heavenly things, says: "If ye then, being evil, know how to give good gifts unto your children, how much more shall your Father which is in heaven give good things to them that ask Him?"

Likewise Peter: "We ought to obey God rather than men" (Acts 5:29). Jeremiah (35:18) also: "The Rechabites obeyed their father, how much more ought ye to have obeyed me?" Now these things are appointed by God and are His ordinances, that men should give unto their children, and that children should obey their parents; therefore, such manner of arguments are good when they are grounded on the ordinances of God. But if they are taken from men's corrupt affections, they are useless. Such is the argument of Scotus: I love the lesser good thing; therefore, I love the greater more. I deny the consequence. For my loving is not God's ordinance, but a devilish corruption. Indeed it should be so, that I, loving myself, or another creature, should much more love God the Creator. But it is not so. For the love with which I love myself is corrupt and against God.

This I say, lest any man should cavil that an argument taken of corruptible things and applied to divine and spiritual matters is worth nothing. For this argument is strong enough, as long as we ground the same upon the ordinance of God. For the civil law, which is an ordinance of God, says that it is not lawful to break, or to change, the testament of a man. Yes, it commands that the last will and testament of a man be strictly kept; for it is one of the most laudable customs that are among men. Now therefore, upon this custom of man's testament, Paul argues after this manner: How does it happen that man is obeyed and not God? Politic and civil ordinances, as concerning testaments and other things, are diligently kept. There nothing is changed, nothing is added or taken away. But the testament of God is changed; that is to say, His promise concerning the spiritual blessing, about heavenly and everlasting things, which the whole world ought to receive with zeal and affection, and most religiously to reverence and honor. Therefore, Paul says, I speak after the manner of men; that is to say, I bring unto you a metaphor taken from the customs and manner of men. The testaments of men and such other corruptible things are strictly executed, and that which the law commands is diligently observed and kept. For when a man makes his last will, bequeathing his lands and goods to his heirs, and thereupon dies, his last will is confirmed and ratified by the death of the testator, so that nothing may now be added to it, or taken from it, according to all law and equity.

Now, if a man's will is kept with so great fidelity, how much more ought the last will of God to be faithfully kept, which He promised and gave to Abraham and his seed after him? For when Christ died, then was it confirmed in Him, and after His death the writing of His last testament was opened; that is to say, the promised blessing of Abraham was preached among all nations dispersed throughout the whole world. This was the last will and testament of God, the great testator, confirmed by the death of Christ. Therefore, no man ought to change it or add anything to it, as they that teach the law and man's traditions do; for they say, unless you are circumcised and keep the law, and do works and suffer many things, you cannot be saved. This is not the last will and testament of God. For He said not to Abraham, If you do this or that, you shall obtain the blessing, but He said, "In thy seed shall all the nations of the earth be blessed." As if He should say, I, of pure mercy, promise you that Christ shall come of your seed, who shall bring the blessing upon all nations oppressed with sin and death. This argument grounded upon the ordinance of God is strong enough.

16—Now to Abraham and his seed were the promises made. He saith
not, And to seeds, as of many; but as of one, And to thy seed, which
is Christ.

Here he calls the promises of God by a new name: a testament. And
indeed the promise is nothing else but a testament, not yet revealed but
sealed up. A testament is not a law, but a donation or free gift. Heirs look
not for law, exactions, or any burdens to be laid upon them by a
testament, but they look for the inheritance.

First of all therefore Paul expounds the words. Afterwards he applies
the metaphor and stands upon this word, ''seed.'' No laws were given to
Abraham, but a testament was delivered to him. If then the testament of
a man is kept, why should not rather the testament of God be kept? The
testament of man is but a sign. Again, if we will keep the signs, why do
we not rather keep the things which they signify?

The promises are made to Abraham, not in all his descendants or in
many seeds, but in one seed, which is Christ. The Jews say that the
singular number is put here for the plural, one for many. But we gladly
receive this meaning and interpretation of Paul, who often repeats this
word ''seed'' and expounds it of Christ; and this he does with an apostolic
spirit. Now, Paul proceeds to expound and amplify the same.

17—And this I say, that the covenant, that was confirmed before of
God in Christ, the law, which was four hundred and thirty years
after, cannot disannul, that it should make the promise of none
effect.

Here the Jews might object, that God was not only content to give
promises to Abraham, but also after four hundred and thirty years He
made the law. God, therefore, mistrusting His own promises as insuffi-
cient to justify, adds a better thing: that is to say, the law, to the end that
when a better successor was come, not the idlers, but the doers of the law
might be made righteous thereby. The law therefore which followed the
promise abrogated the promise.

To this cavilling Paul answers very well and strongly refutes it. The law, says he, was given four hundred and thirty years after this promise was made, and it could not make the promise void and unprofitable; for the promise is the testament of God, confirmed by God Himself in Christ, so many years before the law. That which God once promised and confirmed He calls not back again, but it remains ratified and sure forever.

Why then was the law added? Indeed it was delivered, so many years after, to the posterity of Abraham, not to the end that he might through it obtain the blessing (for it is the office of the law to bring under the curse, and not to bless), but that there might be in the world a certain people who might have the Word and testimony of Christ; out of whom Christ also, according to the flesh, might be born; and that men being kept and shut up under the law might sigh and groan for their deliverance through the seed of Abraham, which is Christ, who only could and should bless, that is to say, deliver all nations from sin and everlasting death. Moreover, the ceremonies commanded in the law foreshadowed Christ. So the promise was not abolished either by the law or the ceremonies of the law; but rather it was confirmed until the writing of the testament (to wit, the promise) might be opened, and by the preaching of the gospel might be spread among all nations.

So the law does not abolish the promise, but faith in the promise destroys the law, so that it cannot increase sin any more, terrify sinners, or bring them into desperation. And it is to be noted that Paul, with a certain vehemence, sets down the express number four hundred and thirty years. Consider how long a time it was, Paul says, between the promise and the law. Moreover, Paul says that the law cannot abolish the promise; therefore, that promise made to Abraham, four hundred and thirty years before the law, remains firm and constant. To make the matter better understood, I will declare the same by a comparison. If a rich man, of his own good will, should adopt one to be his son, whom he knows not, and to whom he owes nothing, and should appoint him to be the heir of all his lands and goods; and certain years after he had bestowed this benefit upon him, he should lay upon him a law to do this or that; he cannot now say that he has deserved this benefit by his own works, seeing that many years before, he asking nothing, had received the same freely and of mere favor. So God could not respect our works and deserts going before righteousness; for the promise and the gift of the Holy Ghost was four hundred and thirty years before the law.

Here it appears that Abraham did not obtain righteousness before God through the law. For there was as yet no law. If there were yet no law, then was there neither work nor merit. What then? Nothing else but the mere promise. This promise Abraham believed, and it was counted to him for righteousness. By the same means then that the father obtained this promise, the children also obtain it and retain it. So say we at this day: our sins were purged by the death of Christ, years ago, when there were yet no religious orders, no canon or rule of penance. We cannot then now begin to abolish the same by our own works and merits.

These two things, the promise and the law, must be diligently distinguished. When you have appointed these things their proper place, then you walk safely between them both, in the heaven of the promise, and in the earth of the law. In spirit you walk in the paradise of grace and peace; in the flesh you walk in the earth of works and suffering. And now troubles, which the flesh is compelled to bear, shall not be hard for you because of the sweetness of the promise, which comforts and rejoices your heart. But if you confuse and mingle these two together, and place the law in the conscience and the promise of liberty in the flesh, you will not know what the law, what the promise, what sin, or what righteousness is.

Paul prosecutes this argument so diligently because he foresaw in spirit that this mischief should creep into the Church, that the promise should be mingled with the law, and so the promise should be utterly lost. Therefore, separate the promise far from the law, that when the law comes and accuses your conscience, you may say: "Law, you come too soon; wait four hundred and thirty years, and then come back. But if you come then, you shall come too late. Therefore, I have nothing to do with you; I hear you not. For now I live with the believing Abraham, or rather, since Christ is now revealed and given to me, I live in Him who is my righteousness, who also has abolished you, O law.'' And thus let Christ be always before your eyes as a sure summary of all arguments for the defense of the faith against the righteousness of the flesh, against the law, and against all works and merits whatever.

Paul thus fortifies the doctrine of Christian righteousness with strong and mighty arguments. At the same time, he overthrows the arguments of the false apostles who contended that righteousness and life are obtained by the law.

Paul points them to the saying, ''He that doeth these things shall live in them'' (Leviticus 18:5). Now, who is he that does and accomplishes them? No man living. Therefore, ''As many as are of the works of the law are under the curse'' (Galatians 3:10). And again in another place, ''The sting of death is sin, and the strength of sin is the law'' (1 Corinthians 15:56). Now follows the conclusion of these arguments.

18—For if the inheritance be of the law, it is no more of promise: but God gave it to Abraham by promise.

So he says in Romans 4:14: ''For if they which are of the law be heirs, faith is made void, and the promise made of none effect.'' And it cannot be otherwise. For this distinction is plain, that the law is a thing far differing from the promise. Even natural reason is compelled to confess that it is one thing to promise, and another thing to require: one thing to give, and another thing to take. The law requires and exacts of us our works, the promise of the seed offers us the spiritual and everlasting benefits of God, and that freely for Christ's sake. Therefore, we obtain the inheritance or blessing through the promise, and not through the law. Therefore, he that has the law does not have enough, because he does not yet have the blessing. It cannot be denied that God, before the law was, gave unto Abraham the inheritance or blessing by the promise: that is to say, remission of sins, righteousness, salvation, and everlasting life, that we should be sons and heirs of God, and fellow-heirs with Christ.

19—Wherefore then serveth the law? It was added because of transgressions, till the seed should come to whom the promise was made; and it was ordained by angels in the hand of a mediator.

When we teach that a man is justified without the law and works, the question necessarily follows: why then was the law given? Also, why does God charge us and burden us with the law, if it does not justify? The Jews had the opinion that if they kept the law they would be justified by it. Therefore, when they heard that the gospel was preached concerning Christ, who came into the world to save, not the righteous, but sinners, which also should go before them into the Kingdom of God (Matthew 20:12–16), they were offended, complaining that they had borne the burden and heat of the day, that is, the heavy yoke of the law so many years, and that they were vexed and oppressed with the tyranny of the law without any profit, yes, rather, to their great hurt, for that the Gentiles, who were idolaters, obtained grace without labor or travail.

This is therefore a hard question that reason cannot answer. When it hears this sentence of Paul (which is so strange to the world) that "the law was added because of transgressions," it thinks: Paul abolishes the law, for he says we are not justified through it. He must be a blasphemer against God who gave the law, when he says the law was given because of transgressions. Let us live as Gentiles who have no law; let us sin and live in sin "that grace may abound." This happened to the Apostle Paul, and it happens to us today. When common people hear that righteousness comes by the sole grace of God through faith only, without the law, and without works, they think: If the law does not justify, then let us work nothing; and this do they truly perform.

This impiety vexes us very much, but we cannot remedy it. For when Christ preached, He too heard that He was a blasphemer and a seditious person, that is to say, that by His doctrine He deceived men and made them rebels against Caesar. The same thing happened to Paul and all the other Apostles. So what marvel is it if the world similarly accuse us this day? Let it accuse us, let it slander us, let it persecute us and spare not; yet we must not hold our peace, but speak freely, that afflicted consciences may be delivered out of the snares of the devil. And we must not regard the foolish people, in that they abuse our doctrine; for whether they have the law, or no law, they cannot be reformed. We must consider how afflicted consciences may be comforted, that they perish not with the multitude.

Paul therefore, when he saw that some resisted his doctrine, and others sought the liberty of the flesh and thereby became worse, comforted himself after this sort: that he was an Apostle of Jesus Christ, sent to preach the faith of God's elect; and that he must suffer all things for the elect's sake, that they might obtain salvation. So we at this day do all things for the elect's sake, whom we know to be edified and comforted by our doctrine.

But in so saying, we do not teach that the law is unprofitable. No, not so. It has a proper office and use, but not which our adversaries imagine. We say with Paul that the law is good, if a man rightly use it, that is, if he uses the law as the law.

Therefore, Paul fights here against those hypocrites who could not abide this verse: "The law was added because of transgressions," for they think the office of the law is to justify. And this is the general opinion throughout the whole world that righteousness is gotten through the works of the law. To conclude, they that trust in their own righteousness think to pacify the wrath of God by their worship and voluntary religion. Therefore, this opinion of the righteousness of the law is the sink of all evils, and the sin of sins of the whole world.

As things are distinct, so are their uses distinct. Let every man do that which his office and vocation requires. Let pastors preach the Word of God purely. Let magistrates execute their office justly, let the people obey their rulers. Let everything serve in due place and order. Let the sun shine by day, and the moon by night. Let the sea give fishes, the earth grain, the woods wild animals and trees. In like manner let not the law usurp the office and use of another, that is to say, of justification, but let it leave this only to grace, to the promise, and to faith. What then is the office of the law? Transgressions, or else, as Paul says in another place, "the law entered in that sin should abound'' (Romans 5:20). A goodly office indeed!

Of the Double Use of the Law

Here you must understand that there is a double use of the law. One is civil: for God has ordained civil law to punish transgressions. Every law therefore is given to restrain sin. If it restrains sin, then it makes men righteous. No, nothing less. For in that I do not kill, or commit adultery, or steal, or in that I abstain from other sins, I do it not willingly, or for the love of virtue, but I fear the prison, the sword, and the hangman. These restrain me that I sin not, as bonds and chains do restrain a lion, or a bear, that he tear and devour not all that he meets. Therefore, the restraining from sin is not righteousness, but rather a sign of unrighteousness. For as a mad or a wild beast is bound lest he should destroy, even so the law bridles a mad and furious man, that he sin not after his own lust. This restraint shows plainly enough that they which have need of the law (as all have who are without Christ) are not righteous, but rather wicked and mad men, whom it is necessary so to bridle, that they sin not. Therefore, the law does not justify.

The first use of the law then is to bridle wickedness. God has ordained magistrates, parents, ministers, and all civil ordinances, that if they do no more, yet, at least, they may bind the devil's hands, that he rage not in his bondslaves after his own lust.

Paul is not talking here of the civil use of the law, but of another use of the law, moral and spiritual, which is to increase transgressions, that is to say, to reveal unto a man his sin, his blindness, his misery, his iniquity, his ignorance, hatred and contempt of God, death, hell, judgment, and the deserved wrath of God. This use the Apostle discusses notably in the seventh chapter to the Romans. This is unknown to schoolmen and to all who walk in the opinion of the righteousness of the law or their own righteousness. But in order that God might bridle and beat down this monster (I mean the human presumption of self-righteousness), it behooved Him to send some Hercules who might set upon him with all force and courage, to overthrow him and utterly destroy him. So He was constrained to give the law in Mount Sinai, with so great majesty and with such terrors that the whole multitude was astounded (Exodus 19 and 20).

This, as it is a proper and the principal use of the law, so is it profitable and most necessary. If anyone is not a murderer, an adulterer or a thief, and outwardly refrains from sins, as the Pharisees did, he would swear that he was righteous, and therefore he conceives an opinion of righteousness, and presumes on his good works and merits. Such a one God cannot otherwise mollify and humble but by the law, for that is the hammer of death, the thundering of hell, and the lightning of God's wrath, that beats to powder the obstinate and senseless hypocrites. Therefore, says God by the prophet Jeremiah (23:29): "My word is a hammer, breaking rocks." As long as the opinion of righteousness remains in a man, there abides also in him incomprehensible pride, presumption, security, hatred of God, contempt for His grace and mercy, ignorance of the promises and of Christ. The preaching of free remission of sins, through Christ, cannot enter into the heart of such a one, neither can he feel any taste or savor thereof; for that adamant wall of the presumption of righteousness resists it.

This then is a great and terrible monster, and for the overthrowing of it, God needed a mighty hammer, that is, the law, which is in its proper office when it accuses and reveals sin after this sort: "Behold, you have transgressed all the commandments of God." And so it strikes terror into the conscience, so that it feels God to be offended indeed, and itself to be guilty of eternal death. Here the sinner feels the intolerable burden of the law and is quite beaten down, so that being in anguish and terror, he desires death. The law is God's hammer, His fire, His mighty strong wind, and that terrible earthquake rending the mountains and breaking the rocks (1 Kings 19:11, 13); that is to say, the proud and obstinate hypocrites. Elijah, not being able to abide these terrors of the law, covered his face with his mantle. But when the tempest ceased there came a soft and gracious wind, in the which the Lord was. After the tempest passed, the Lord revealed Himself. The terrible show and majesty wherein God gave His law in Mount Sinai represented the use of the law.

There was in the people of Israel, who came out of Egypt, a singular holiness. They gloried and said, "We are the people of God. We will do all those things which the Lord our God hath commanded" (Exodus 19:8). Moreover, Moses did sanctify the people, and bade them wash their garments, refrain from their wives, and prepare themselves against the third day. The third day Moses brought the people out of their tents to the mountain, into the sight of the Lord, that they might hear His voice. What followed? When the people beheld the terrible sight of the mount smoking and burning, with black clouds and flashing lightning in the darkness, and heard the sound of the trumpet blowing and waxing louder and louder, they were afraid, and standing afar off, they said to Moses: "We will do all these things willingly, if only the Lord speak not unto us, lest we die, and this great fire consume us. Teach thou us, and we will hearken unto thee" (Exodus 20:19; Deuteronomy 5:24; and 18:16). What did their washing and purifying profit them? Nothing at all. Not one of them could abide the presence of the Lord in His majesty and glory; but all being amazed and shaken with terror fled back from the awful sight. "For the Lord thy God is a consuming fire," in whose sight no flesh is able to stand (Deuteronomy 4:24).

The law of God, therefore, has properly and peculiarly that office which it had then in Mount Sinai, when it was first heard of them that were washed, purified, and chaste. Yet it brought that holy people into such a knowledge of their own misery that they were cast down even to desperation and the fear of death. No purifying could then help them, but theirs was such a feeling of their own uncleanness and sin, and of the judgment and wrath of God, that they fled from the sight of the Lord's majesty, and could not endure to hear His voice. "What flesh," said they, "was there ever, that heard the voice of the living God, speaking out of the midst of the fire, and lived?" (Deuteronomy 5:26).

Here I warn all such as fear God, and especially such as shall become teachers of others, that they learn out of Paul to understand the true and proper use of the law, which I fear, after our time, will be trodden underfoot, and abolished by the enemies of the truth. For even now there are few, even among those who make a profession of the gospel with us, who understand these things rightly.

It is no small matter to understand rightly what the law is, and what is its true use and office, which is first to bridle civil transgressions and then to reveal and to increase spiritual transgressions. Wherefore the law is also a light which shows and reveals, not the grace of God, not righteousness and life, but sin, death, the wrath and judgment of God. For the terrors of Sinai did not rejoice and comfort the children of Israel, but appalled and astonished them, and showed them how unable they were, with all their purifyings, to abide the majesty of God, speaking to them out of the clouds; even so the law, when in its true office, does nothing else but reveal sin, accuse and terrify men so that it brings them to the very brink of desperation. This is the use of the law and here it has an end, and ought to go no further.

Contrariwise, the gospel is a light which lightens, quickens, comforts, and raises up fearful consciences. For it shows that God, for Christ's sake, is merciful to sinners if they believe that by His death they are delivered from the curse, that is to say, from sin and everlasting death; and that through His victory, the blessing is freely given to them, that is to say, grace, forgiveness of sins, righteousness, and everlasting life. Thus, putting a difference between the law and the gospel, we give to them both their own proper use and office. Of this difference between the law and the gospel, there is nothing to be found in the books of the schoolmen; no, nor in the books of the ancient fathers. Augustine understood this difference and showed it. Jerome and others knew it not. There was a strange silence for many years about this difference, and this brought men's consciences into great danger. For unless the gospel is plainly discerned from the law, the true Christian doctrine cannot be kept sound and uncorrupt. But if this difference is well known, then is the true manner of justification also known, and then it is an easy matter to discern faith from works and Christ from Moses. For all things without Christ are the ministers of death for the punishing of the wicked.

"The law was added because of transgressions," that is, that transgressions might increase and be more seen and known. And so it has come to pass. For when sin, death, the wrath and judgment of God, and hell are revealed to a man through the law, it is impossible that he should not become impatient, murmur against God, and despise His will. For he cannot bear the judgment of God, his own death and damnation, and yet he cannot escape them. Here he must fall into hatred of God, and blasphemy against God. Before, when he was out of temptation, he was a holy man: he worshiped and praised God, he bowed his knees to God, and gave Him thanks, as did the Pharisee in Luke (18:11). But now when sin and death are revealed to him, he wishes that there were no God. Thus sin is not only known and revealed by the law, it is also stirred up and increased by the law. Therefore, Paul says, "Sin, that it might appear sin, working death in me by that which is good; that sin by the commandment might become exceeding sinful" (Romans 7:13).

If the law does not justify, to what end does it serve? Although it justifies not, yet it is profitable and necessary. For first it civilly restrains such as are carnal, rebellious, and obstinate. Also, it is a mirror that shows a man he is a sinner, guilty of death, and worthy of God's indignation and wrath. To what end serves this humbling and bruising? To the end that we have an entrance into grace. So then the law is a minister that prepares the way to grace. For God is the God of the humble, the afflicted, the oppressed, and of those who are brought even to nothing; and His nature is to exalt the humble, to feed the hungry, to give sight to the blind, to comfort the brokenhearted, to justify sinners, to quicken the dead, and to save the lost. For He is an Almighty Creator, making all things of nothing.

Christ came into the world not to break the bruised reed nor to quench the smoking flax, but to preach the gospel to the poor, to heal the contrite and to preach forgiveness to the captives. But here lies the difficulty of this matter, that when a man is terrified and cast down, he may be able to raise himself up again, and say, Now I am bruised and afflicted enough; the law has tormented me sharply; now is the time of grace; now is the time to hear Christ, out of whose mouth proceed the words of grace and life; now is the time to see, not the smoking and burning Mount Sinai, but Mount Moriah where is the throne, the temple, and the mercy seat of God, that is to say, Christ, who is the King of righteousness and peace. There will I hearken to what the Lord speaks to me, who speaks nothing else but peace to His people.

The foolishness of man's heart is so great that when the law has done its office and terrified his conscience, he does not only not lay hold upon the doctrine of grace, but seeks more laws to satisfy and quiet his conscience. "If I live," says he, "I will amend my life. I will do this and that." But unless you send Moses away, with his law, and in these terrors lay hold upon Christ, who died for your sins, there is no salvation for you.

Therefore, after the law has humbled you and utterly beaten you down, see that you learn to use it rightly: for the office and use of it is not only to reveal sin and convict us of it, but also to drive men to Christ. This use of the law the Holy Ghost sets forth in the gospel, where He witnesses that God is present with the afflicted and brokenhearted, and we hear Christ's voice saying to us, "Come unto me all ye that labour and are heavy laden, and I will give you rest" (Matthew 11:28). This is the true and best use of the law, when it drives men to Christ.

When Paul adds, "Till the seed should come to whom the promise was made," he sets a limit to the law. For it ought to be known how long the power and tyranny of the law ought to endure, which reveals sin and the wrath of God. They whose hearts are touched with an inward feeling of these matters should perish, if they received not comfort and hope. Therefore, if the days of the law should not be shortened, no flesh should be saved. How long then ought the dominion of the law to endure? Until the seed come; to wit, that seed of which it is written: "In thy seed shall all the nations of the earth be blessed."

We may understand the continuance of the law both according to the letter and also spiritually; according to the letter thus, that the law continued until the time of grace. The law and the prophets, says Christ, prophesied until John. "From the days of John the Baptist until now the kingdom of heaven suffereth violence, and the violent take it by force" (Matthew 11:12, 13). In this time Christ was baptized, and began to preach; at which time also, after the letter, the law, and all the ceremonies of Moses, ceased.

Spiritually the law may be thus understood: that it ought not to reign in the conscience any longer than to the appointed time of this blessed seed. When the law shows me my sin, and reveals the law and judgment of God, so that I begin to fear and tremble, there has the law its bounds, its time, and its end limited. Here we must say: Now leave off, law, you have done enough. "All thy waves and thy billows are gone over me"; "Hide not thy face from thy servant: for I am in trouble, hear me speedily"; "O Lord, rebuke me not in thine anger, neither chasten me in thy hot displeasure" (Psalms 42:7; 69:17; 6:1).

Thus the law ends, when Christ that blessed seed is come, who has gracious lips, with which He accuses not, nor terrifies, but speaks of far better things than does the law; namely, of grace, peace, forgiveness of sins, victory over sin, death, the devil, and damnation, gotten by His death and passion for all believers.

Paul therefore shows by the words, "Until the seed should come," how long the law should last literally and spiritually. According to the letter, it ceased after the blessed seed came into the world, taking upon Him our flesh, giving the Holy Ghost, and writing a new law in our hearts. But the spiritual time of the law does not end at once, but continues rooted in the conscience. Therefore, it is hard for a man who is exercised with the spiritual use of the law, to see the end of the law. For in those terrors and feelings of sin, the mind cannot conceive this hope, that God is merciful, and that He will forgive sins for Christ's sake. It judges only that God is angry with sinners and that He accuses and condemns them. If faith does not come to raise up the troubled and afflicted conscience, and there is no faithful brother at hand who may comfort him by the Word of God, desperation and death will follow. Therefore, it is a perilous thing for a man to be alone. For the wise man says, "Woe to him that is alone when he falleth; for he hath not another to help him up" (Ecclesiastes 4:10). Wherefore they that ordained the solitary life gave occasion for many thousands to despair. If a man should separate himself from the company of others for a day or two, to be occupied in prayer (as we read of Christ that He went apart alone), there is no danger, but when men are persuaded to live continually a solitary life, it is a device of the devil himself. For when a man is tempted and is alone, he is not able to raise up himself.

When Paul says, "And it was ordained by angels in the hands of a mediator," he makes a digression, and then returns again to his purpose when he says: "Is the law then against the promises of God?" Now this was the occasion of his digression. He fell into this difference between the law and the gospel: that the law, added to the promise, did differ from the gospel, not only in respect of time, but also as to the author and its efficient cause. The law was delivered by angels, but the gospel by the Lord Himself. So the gospel is far more excellent than the law, for the law is the voice of the servants, but the gospel is the voice of the Lord Himself. Therefore, to abase and to diminish the authority of the law and to exalt and magnify the gospel, he says that the law was given to last but a short time, but the gospel was forever. For all the faithful have had one and the same gospel from the beginning of the world, and were saved by that which was promised before all worlds (Titus 1:2).

Moreover, the law was not only ordained by the angels, being servants, but also by another servant far inferior to the angels, being a man, that is, by the hand of a mediator, Moses. Now Christ is not a servant, but the Lord Himself. He is not a mediator between God and man according to the law, as Moses was; but He is a mediator of a better testament. Moses and the people heard God speaking in Mount Sinai; that is, they heard angels speaking as the person of God. Therefore Stephen, in the seventh chapter of the Acts, said: "Ye have received the law by the ministry of angels, and ye have not regarded it." Also the text in the third chapter of Exodus shows plainly that the angel appeared to Moses in a flame of fire and spoke to him from the midst of the bush.

Paul therefore signifies that Christ is a mediator of a far better testament than Moses, and here he alludes to the giving of the law at Mount Sinai. Moses led the people out of their tents to meet with God and placed them at the foot of Mount Sinai. The whole mount was aflame with fire. It was a horrible sight. The people began to tremble, thinking that they would be destroyed. They pleaded with Moses: "Speak thou with us and we will hear; but let not God speak with us." It is plain from this that Moses stood between the people and God, and so was their mediator.

But what righteousness is this, not to be able to hear the law, but to be afraid and to fly from it, and so to hate it. So when sin is discovered, by certain bright beams which the law strikes into the heart, there is nothing more odious to a man than the law. He would rather choose death than be constrained to bear those terrors, proof that the law justifies not, or else men would love it, delight and take pleasure in it.

Paul sets out in the few words, "In the hands of a mediator," as if he would say, Do ye not remember that your fathers were so unable to hear the law, that they had need of Moses to be their mediator? And when he was appointed to that office, they were so far from loving the law, that they, by a fearful flight, showed themselves to hate the same, as the Epistle to the Hebrews witnesses. But they were enclosed round about, and escape was impossible; therefore they cried to Moses, "Speak thou with us; for if we hear the voice of the Lord our God any more, we shall die" (Exodus 20:19; Deuteronomy 5:25). Therefore, if they were not able to hear the law, how should they be able to accomplish it?

What then did the law? "The law was added that sin might abound" (Romans 5:20). The history of the giving of the law witnesses that all men, no matter how holy and purified, hate and abhor the law, and wish it were not. Therefore, it is impossible that men should be justified by the law; no, it has a contrary effect. Although Paul only touches upon this matter, he that shall diligently read it may easily understand that he speaks of both mediators, Moses and Christ, comparing one with the other.

If all men in the world had stood at the mount, as the people of Israel did, they would all have fled from it, as Israel did. The whole world, therefore, is an enemy to the law, and hates it. But the law is holy, righteous and good, and is the perfect rule of the will of God. How then can he be righteous who does not only abhor the law and fly from it, but, moreover, is an enemy of God, the author of the law? And true it is that flesh cannot do otherwise, for "The carnal mind is enmity against God: for it is not subject to the law of God, neither indeed can be," as Paul says (Romans 8:7). Therefore, it is extreme madness so to hate God and His law that you cannot stand to hear it and yet affirm that we are made righteous thereby.

Wherefore the schoolmen are stark blind, and understand nothing of this doctrine. Being ignorant of this, they conclude that a man has a good will and a right judgment of reason to do the will of God. But ask the people of the law, with their mediator, who heard the voice of the law at Mount Sinai. Ask David, who so often complained in the Psalms that he was cast from the face of God, that he was "in the lowest pit," that he was oppressed and terrified with the greatness of his sin. From these he was raised up and comforted not by sacrifices nor by the law itself, but only by the free mercy of God.

In that verse in the third chapter of second Corinthians, concerning the covered face of Moses, Paul shows that the children of Israel not only did not know, but also could not stand the true and spiritual use of the law: first, because they could not look unto the end of the law, because of the veil which Moses put upon his face. Again, they could not look upon the face of Moses, bare and uncovered, for the glory of his countenance. When Moses talked with them, he covered his face, without which veil they could not bear his talk. They could not hear Moses their mediator unless he had set another mediator between, that is to say, the veil. How then should they hear the voice of God, or of an angel, when they could not hear the voice of Moses, being but a man, yes, and also their mediator, except his face was covered? Therefore, except the blessed Seed come to raise up and comfort him who has heard the law, he perishes through desperation, in detesting of the law, in hating and blaspheming God, and daily more and more offending against God. The deeper the law pierces and the longer it continues, the more it increases hatred and blasphemy against God.

This history teaches the power of free will. The people are stricken with fear, they tremble, and they fly back. Where now is free will? Where now is the good intent, that right judgment of reason? What good is free will in these purified men? It can say nothing. It blinds their reason; it perverts their will. It receives not, salutes not, embraces not with joy, the Lord coming with thundering, lightning, and fire unto Mount Sinai. It cannot hear the voice of the Lord, but rather says, "Let not the Lord speak unto us, lest we die."

20—Now a mediator is not a mediator of one, but God is one.

Here Paul compares two mediators, and that with marvelous brevity. "A mediator," says he, "is not a mediator of one only." This word necessarily implies two, that is to say, him that is offended, and him that is the offender, of whom the one needs intercession, and the other needs none. So a mediator is not of one, but of two, and two at variance between themselves. So Moses, by a general definition, is a mediator, because he mediates between the law and the people. The law therefore must have a new face, and its voice must be changed; that is, the law must put on a veil that it may become more tolerable, and that the people may be able to hear it by the voice of Moses.

Now, the law, being thus covered, speaks no more in its majesty, but by the voice of Moses. After this manner, it no longer terrifies the conscience. And so the people do not understand or regard it; instead they become secure, negligent, and presumptuous hypocrites. Yet one of these two must be done: either the law must be without its use, and covered with a veil, or else it must be in its true use without a veil, and then it kills. For man's heart cannot abide the law in its true use without the veil. It is necessary, then, if you look at the end of the law without the veil, to lay hold of that blessed Seed by faith: that is, look beyond the end of the law, to Christ, who is the accomplishment of the law, who may say to you: "The law has terrified you enough; be of good comfort, your sins are forgiven you." Otherwise, you must surely have Moses with his veil as your mediator.

For this cause Paul says: "A mediator is not a mediator of one." It could not be that Moses should be a mediator of God alone, for God needs no mediator. And again he is not a mediator of the people only, but he mediates between God and the people which were at variance with God. For it is the office of a mediator to reconcile the party that is offended to the party that is the offender. To conclude, Moses is a mediator of the veil, and therefore he gives no power to perform the law, but only in the veil.

But what would have come to pass, if the law had been given without Moses, and there had been no mediator? Here the people being beaten down with intolerable fear would either have perished forthwith, or if they had escaped, there must have come some other mediator, who should have set himself between the law and the people so that both the people might be preserved and the law remain in force, and also an atonement be made between the law and the people. Therefore, when the poor sinner, at the hour of death, feels the wrath and judgment of God for sin, which the law reveals, he must have a mediator who may say to him, Although you are a sinner, you shall not perish, although the law, with its wrath, still remains.

That mediator is Jesus Christ, who sets Himself against the wrath of the law, takes it away, and satisfies in His own body by Himself. He says to you, "Be not afraid. The law indeed threatens you with the wrath of God and eternal death, but I supply all things for you and I satisfy the law for you." This is a mediator who sets Himself between God being offended and the offender. The intercession of Moses profits nothing. He has done his office, and he with his veil has now vanished away. Here the sinner, now approaching death, and God being offended by his sins, encounter each other. Therefore, there must come a mediator other than Moses, one who may satisfy the law, take away the wrath thereof, and reconcile him unto God who is angry, in order that the poor sinner, miserable and guilty of eternal death, may yet be saved.

Of this mediator Paul speaks briefly when he says, "A mediator is not a mediator of one." We are the offenders; God with His law is the offended. And the offense is such that God cannot pardon it, neither can we satisfy it. Therefore, between God and us, there is terrible discord. God cannot revoke His law. We who have transgressed the law cannot fly from the presence of God. Christ therefore has set Himself as a mediator between two that are quite contrary, and separate with an infinite and everlasting separation, and has reconciled them together. And how has He done this? By "blotting out the handwriting of ordinances that was against us, which was contrary to us"; He "took it out of the way, nailing it to his cross" (Colossians 2:14). Therefore, He is not a mediator of one, but of two utterly disagreeing between themselves.

This is a place full of power and efficacy to confound the righteousness of the law, and to teach us that, in the matter of justification, it ought to be utterly removed out of our sight. Also this word, *mediator,* proves that the law justifies not; or why should we need a mediator? This doctrine, which I so often repeat, and not without tediousness beat into your heads, is the true doctrine of the law.

The history of the giving of the law plainly witnesses that the people refused to hear that excellent law and those gracious words, "I am the Lord thy God, which brought thee out of the land of Egypt . . . thou shalt have no other gods before me . . . showing mercy unto thousands . . . Honour thy father and thy mother . . ." (Exodus 20:2ff.; Deuteronomy 4:13). They could not stand this most excellent and divine wisdom, this most comfortable, sweet, and gracious doctrine. "Let not the Lord speak unto us, lest we die. Speak thou unto us," they say to Moses. Doubtless, it is a strange thing that a man cannot hear that which is his for his greatest good, namely, that he has a God, yes, and a merciful God. And moreover, that he cannot abide that which is his chief safety and defense, namely, "Thou shalt not kill; thou shalt not commit adultery; thou shalt not steal." For by these words the Lord has defended and fortified the life of man, his wife, his children, and his goods, as it were, with a wall against the force and violence of the wicked.

The law then can do nothing, except that by its light, the conscience may know sin, death, the judgment and wrath of God. Before the law came, I am secure; I feel no sin. But when the law comes, sin, death, and hell are revealed to me. This is not to be made righteous, but guilty and condemned to death and hell fire. The principal point of the law in true Christian theology is to make men not better, but worse; that is, it shows them their sin, that by the knowledge thereof, they may be humbled, bruised and broken, and by this means driven to seek comfort, and so come to that blessed Seed, Christ.

When Paul adds, "but God is one," it may be taken to mean: God offends no man, and therefore needs no mediator. But we offend God, and therefore we have need of a mediator; not Moses, but Christ, who speaks far better things for us.

Until now Paul has continued in his digression; now he returns to his purpose.

21—Is the law then against the promises of God? God forbid: for if there had been a law given which could have given life, verily righteousness should have been by the law.

Paul said before that the law justifies not. Shall we then take away the law? No, not so. For it brings a certain commodity. What is that? It brings men into the knowledge of themselves. It discovers and increases sin. How can it be then that God should perform His promise unto those who not only refuse to receive His law, but also shun it and fly from it? Here rises the question: "Is the law against the promises of God?" This objection Paul touches and briefly answers, saying, "God forbid." Why so? First, because God makes no promise to us because of our worthiness, our merits or our good works; but for His own goodness' and mercy's sake in Christ. He says not to Abraham, "All nations shall be blessed in you because you have kept the law." But when he was uncircumcised, had no law, and was yet an idolater, He said unto him: "Get thee out of thy country—into a land that I will show thee: and I will make of thee a great nation, and I will bless thee, and make thy name great, and thou shalt be a blessing—and in thee shall all families of the earth be blessed" (Genesis 12:1, 3). These are absolute promises which God gave freely to Abraham, without any condition or respect of works, either going before or coming after.

God does not defer His promises because of our sins nor hasten them because of our righteousness. But although we become more sinful by the knowledge of the law, yet God is not moved thereby to defer His promise. For His promise does not stand upon our worthiness but upon His goodness and mercy. Therefore when the Jews say, "The Messiah is not yet come, because our sins do hinder His coming," it is a fantasy. As though God should become unrighteous because of our sins. He abides always just and true. His truth therefore is the only cause that He accomplishes and performs His promise. When the law constrains a man to acknowledge his own corruption, and to confess his sin from the bottom of his heart, then it has done its office truly, its task is accomplished and ended; now is the time of grace, that the blessed Seed may come to raise up and comfort him that is so cast down and humbled by the law.

After this manner the law is not against the promises of God. For, first, the promise hangs not upon the law, but upon the truth of God alone. Secondly, when the law is in its chief office, it humbles a man, and so makes him sigh and groan and seek the hand and aid of the Mediator, to find His mercy exceeding sweet and comfortable, as the Psalmist says, "Thy mercy is sweet" (Psalms 109:21) and His gift precious and inestimable. For, as the poet says,

> Whoso hath not tasted the things that are bitter,
> Is not worthy to taste the things that are sweeter.

There is a common proverb, that hunger is the best cook. As the dry earth covets the rain, even so the law makes afflicted souls thirst after Christ. To such, Christ savors sweetly; to them, He is nothing else but joy, consolation, and life.

And, indeed, Christ requires thirsty souls, whom He most lovingly and graciously allures and calls unto Him, when he says, "Come unto Me, all ye that labour and are heavy laden, and I will give you rest" (Matthew 11:28). He delights therefore to water these dry grounds. He pours not His waters upon fat and rank grounds, or such as are not dry and covet no water. His benefits are inestimable, and therefore He gives them to none but such as have need of them, and earnestly desire them. He preaches glad tidings to the poor: "If any man thirst, let him come unto me and drink"; "He healeth the broken in heart . . ." (John 7:37; Psalms 147:3). He comforts those that are bruised by the law. Therefore, the law is not against the promises of God.

When Paul says, "If there had been a law given which could have given life," he teaches plainly that the law of itself justifies not, but that it has a contrary effect.

These words are well known in all churches, and yet many teach and live quite against them. They affirm that many laws are given to quicken and bring life: works and merits before grace and after, and innumerable ceremonies and false worshipings which they have devised of their own heads, promising grace and remission of sins to all such as should keep and accomplish the same.

Contrariwise, we affirm with Paul that there is no law, whether man's or God's, that gives life. Therefore, we put as great a difference between the law and righteousness as between life and death. And the cause that moves us so to affirm is that verse of Paul that says that the law is not given to justify, to give life, and to save, but only to kill and destroy.

22—But the scripture hath concluded all under sin, that the promise
by faith of Jesus Christ might be given to them that believe.

Where? First, in the promises themselves about Christ, such as Genesis 3:15, "The seed of the woman shall bruise the serpent's head"; and Genesis 22:18, "In thy seed shall all nations of the earth be blessed." Wherever there is any promise in the Scriptures made to the fathers concerning Christ, there the blessing is pronounced, that is, righteousness, salvation, and eternal life. Therefore, by the contrary it is evident that they who must receive the blessing are subject to the curse, that is to say, sin and death: or else what need was there to promise the blessing?

Second, the Scripture shuts all men under sin and the curse, especially by the law: "Whosoever are of the works of the law are under the curse" (Galatians 3:10). The Apostle also refers to Deuteronomy 27:26, "Cursed is every one that abideth not in all the works of the law to do them.'' For these verses in plain words shut under sin and the curse not only those who sin manifestly against the law, or do not outwardly accomplish the law; but also those who are under the law, and with all endeavor go about to perform it.

Now he that says ''all under sin'' excludes nothing. Therefore we conclude with Paul that the policies and laws of nations, be they ever so good and necessary, with all ceremonies and religions, without faith in Christ are and abide under sin, death, and damnation, unless faith in Christ goes before.

Only faith justifies. The law does not give life; it was not given for that purpose. Much less do works justify. Paul has said in Romans 3:20, ''By the works of the law shall no flesh be justified,'' and again in this epistle, ''The law was not given to bring life.''

Paul also said that ''the Scripture hath concluded all under sin.'' Forever? No, until the promise should come.

The promise is the inheritance itself or the blessing promised to Abraham: to wit, deliverance from the law, sin, death, and the devil, and a free giving of grace, righteousness, salvation and eternal life. This promise, says he, is not obtained by any merit, by any law, or by any work, but it is given. To whom? To those who believe. In whom? In Jesus Christ, who is the blessed Seed who has redeemed all believers from the curse that they might receive the blessing.

Now what about those verses in Scripture that speak of the value of good works? When we are out of the matter of justification we cannot sufficiently praise and magnify those works that are commended by God. Who can sufficiently commend and set forth the profit and fruit of only one work which a Christian does through faith and in faith? Indeed, it is more precious than heaven and earth. The whole world is not able to give a worthy recompense to such a good work.

But works done without faith, although they have ever so goodly a show of holiness, are under sin and the curse. Wherefore, so far off is it that the doers thereof should deserve grace, righteousness, and eternal life, that rather they heap sin upon sin.

23—But before faith came, we were kept under the law, shut up unto
the faith which should afterwards be revealed.

Paul proceeds to declare the profit and necessity of the law. He had said
that the law was added for transgressions, not that it was the principal
purpose of God to make a law that should bring death and damnation. For
the law is a word that shows life and drives men to it. Therefore, it is not
only given as a minister of death, but its principal use and end is to reveal
death, that it might be seen and known how horrible sin is.

The office therefore of the law is to kill, but only so that God may
revive and quicken again. It is not given only to kill; but because man is
proud, and dreams that he is wise, righteous, and holy, it is necessary that
he should be humbled by the law so that this beast, the presumption of
righteousness, might be slain; otherwise, man cannot obtain life.

God, seeing that this universal plague of the whole world—that is,
man's opinion of his own righteousness, his hypocrisy, and confidence in
his own holiness—could not be beaten down by any other means, He
would that it should be slain by the law; not forever, but that when it is
once slain, man might be raised up again, above and beyond the law, and
there might hear this voice: "Fear not; I have not given the law and killed
thee by the law, that thou should abide in this death, but that thou should
fear Me and live." Where there is no fear of God, there can be no
thirsting for grace or life. God must therefore have a strong hammer to
break the rocks, and a hot burning fire in the midst of heaven to overthrow
the mountains, that is, to destroy this furious and obstinate beast, that
when a man by this breaking is brought to nothing, he should despair of
his own strength, and thus terrified, should thirst after mercy and
remission of sins.

When Paul says, "before faith came," he means before the time of the
gospel and grace came, we were shut up and kept as it were in prison. No
murderer, thief, adulterer, or other malefactor, loves the chains and
fetters or the dark prison where he lies bound; but rather, if he could he
would break out of that prison. While he is in prison, he refrains from
doing evil, not of a good will, or for righteousness' sake, but because he

is restrained. He hates not his theft and murder, but he hates the prison, and if he could escape he would pursue his crimes, and rob and murder as he did before.

The law shuts men under sin two ways, civilly and spiritually.

The law is a prison civilly and spiritually. First, it restrains and shuts up the wicked, that they run not headlong, according to their lust, into all kinds of mischief. Second, it shows us spiritually our sin, and humbles us, so that we may see and learn our own misery and condemnation. This is the true use of the law. This shutting up endures until faith comes, and when faith comes this spiritual prison must have its end.

Here we see, that though the law and the gospel be separate and far apart, yet concerning the inward affections they are very nearly joined together. This Paul shows when he says, "We were kept under the law, and shut up unto the faith which should be revealed unto us." But Paul adds that we are shut up and kept under a schoolmaster (which is the law) not forever, but to bring us to Christ, who is the end of the law.

All the wicked are ignorant of this knowledge. Cain knew it not, that is, he felt no terror when he had killed his brother, but tried to deny his crime, as though God could be in ignorance of it; so he says, "Am I my brother's keeper?" But when he heard the word of knowledge, "What hast thou done? The voice of thy brother's blood crieth unto me from the ground" (Genesis 4:10), then he began to feel his prison indeed, in which he remained shut up. He joined not the gospel with the law, but said, "My punishment is greater than I can bear." He only respected the prison, not considering that his sin was revealed to him to the end that he should fly to God for mercy and pardon.

These words "to be kept under, to be shut up," are not vain and unprofitable, but most true and of great importance. This keeping under, and this prison signifies the spiritual terrors whereby the conscience is so shut up that in the wide world it can find no place where it may be in safety. As long as these terrors endure, the conscience feels such anguish and sorrow that it thinks the whole earth is narrower than a mousehole. Here is a man utterly destitute of all wisdom, strength, righteousness, counsel, and succor. For the conscience is a tender thing, and so when it is shut up in the prison of the law, it sees no way out. It feels the wrath of God, which is infinite, whose hand it cannot escape, as Psalms 139:7 says, "Whither shall I flee from Thy presence?"

This poor conscience then must be raised up and comforted in this way: Brother, you are indeed shut up; but persuade yourself that this is not done so you should remain in prison, for it is written, "that we are shut up unto the faith which should afterwards be revealed." You are afflicted not to your destruction, but so you may be refreshed by the blessed Seed. You are killed by the law that through Christ you may be quickened and restored to life.

This holding in prison then must only continue to the coming or revealing of faith, as this sweet verse of the Psalms teaches us, "The Lord's delight is in them that fear Him," that is, those in prison under the law; after that he adds, "and in those that hope in His mercy" (147:11). Therefore, we must join two things together which are most contrary, to fear and to fly from the wrath of God, and again to trust to His mercy. The one is hell, the other heaven, and yet they must be joined together in the heart. By speculation a man may easily join them together, but in practice it is very hard. This I have myself often proved.

Seeing the law is a prison and a tormentor, we cannot love it. A thief should show himself to be stark mad to love the prison, the fetters, and chains. We love the law and the righteousness thereof as much as a murderer loves the dark prison, and the bonds and irons. How then should the law justify us?

When Paul says, "Shut up unto the faith which should afterwards be revealed," he speaks in respect of the fullness of the time wherein Christ came. But we must apply it not only at that time, but also to the inward man. That which is done according to the time wherein Christ came, abolishing the law, and bringing liberty and eternal life to light, is always done spiritually in every Christian, for in every Christian is found sometime the experience of the law and sometime the blessed experience of grace. The Christian man has a body, in whose members sin dwells and wars, as Paul says in Romans 7:23. I understand sin to be not only the deed or the work, but also the root and the tree. It is not only rooted in the flesh of every Christian, but also is at deadly war with it, and holds it captive. For although a Christian may not fall into outward and gross sin, such as murder, adultery, theft, and the like, yet he is not free from impatience, murmuring, doubting, which sins to the carnal man are not counted as sins. For as carnal lust is strong in a young man, love of glory in a man of middle age, and covetousness in an old man; even so in the faithful man impatience, murmuring, hatred and blasphemy are strong. Examples are many in the Psalms, in Job, in Jeremiah, and throughout the whole Scripture. Paul, therefore, describing and setting forth this spiritual warfare, uses vehement words, fit for the purpose, as *fighting, rebelling, holding* and *leading captive,* etc.

Here the law is in its true use, which a Christian often feels as long as he lives. So there was given to Paul a thorn in the flesh, that is, "the messenger of Satan, to buffet him" (2 Corinthians 12:7). He would gladly have felt every moment the joy of conscience, the laughter of the heart, and the sweet taste of eternal life. Again, he would gladly have been delivered from all trouble and anguish of spirit, and therefore he desired that this temptation be taken from him. But this was not done. Instead the Lord said to him: "My grace is sufficient for thee: for my strength is made perfect in weakness." This battle every Christian experiences. For myself, I often chide and contend with God and impatiently resist Him. The wrath and judgment of God displeases me, and my impatience, my murmuring and such sins displease Him. And this is the time of the law, under which a Christian lives, as touching the flesh. "For the flesh lusteth against the Spirit, and the Spirit against the flesh," but in some more and in some less (Galatians 5:17).

The time of grace is when the heart is raised up again by the promise of the free mercy of God, and says, "Why art thou so heavy, O my soul, and why art thou disquieted within me?" (Psalms 42:5). Do you see nothing but the law, sin, terror, death, hell and the devil? Is there not also grace, remission of sins, righteousness, consolation, joy, peace, life, heaven, Christ and God? Trouble me no more, O my soul. Trust in God, who has not spared His own Son, but has given Him to the death of the

Cross for your sins. This, then, is to be shut up under the law after the flesh; not forever, but till Christ be revealed.

When you are beaten down, tormented and afflicted by the law, you should say, "Lady Law, there are greater and better things than you, namely, grace, faith and God's blessing. These do not accuse me; instead, they comfort me, so there is no cause why I should despair."

I have scarcely learned the first principles. It is learned indeed; but so long as flesh and sin do endure, it is never perfectly learned, and as it should be. So then a Christian is divided into two times. In that he is flesh, he is under the law; in that he is spirit, he is under grace. Concupiscence, covetousness, ambition, and pride do always cleave to the flesh. Such types of sin are rooted in the flesh of the faithful. The law is not perpetual, but has an end, which is Jesus Christ. But the time of grace is eternal. For Christ "being once dead, dieth no more" (Romans 6:9). He is eternal; therefore, the time of grace is eternal.

Such notable sentences in Paul we may not pass over lightly, for they contain words of life which wonderfully comfort and confirm afflicted consciences, and they who know and understand them can judge of faith: they can discern a true fear from a false fear; they can distinguish all affections of the heart, and discern all spirits. The fear of God is a holy and a precious thing, but it must not be eternal. Indeed, it ought to be always in a Christian, because sin is always in him; but it must not be alone, for then it is the fear of Cain, Saul, and Judas, that is, a servile and desperate fear. A Christian therefore must vanquish fear by faith in the Word of grace; he must turn away his eyes from the time of the law, and look unto Christ, and to that faith which is to be revealed. Here fear begins to be sweet and makes us love God.

At this place, "Wherefore then serveth the law?" Paul refers to the disputation. For reason, hearing that the blessing, or righteousness, is obtained by grace and the promise, asks this question, and infers the law profits nothing. Wherefore the doctrine of the law must be well considered, that we may know what and how we ought to judge thereof, lest we either reject it altogether or else lest, on the other hand, we should attribute the force of justification to the law. For both sorts offend against the law; the one on the left hand, the other on the right. We must therefore keep to the highway, so that we neither reject the law, not attribute more to it than we ought to do.

In 1 Timothy 1:9 Paul declares that the law is not given for the righteous, but for the unrighteous and rebellious. Now of the unrighteous there are two sorts, they who are to be justified, and they who are not to be justified. They who are not to be justified must be bridled by the civil use of the law, they must be bound with bonds, as savage and untamed beasts. This use of the law has no end, and of it Paul here says nothing. But they who are to be justified are exercised with the spiritual use of the law for a time; for it does not always continue, as the civil use of the law does, but it looks to faith which is to be revealed, and when Christ comes it shall have its end. So, when Paul deals with the spiritual use of the law, he must be understood as referring to those who are to be justified, and not to those who are justified already. For they who are already justified, inasmuch as they abide in Christ, are far above all law. The law must be laid upon those who are to be justified, that when they are cast down and humbled by the law, they should fly to Christ. For Christ "is the end of the law, to every one that believeth" (Romans 10:4).

The true use of the law cannot be magnified enough: namely, that when the conscience finds itself shut up, it may yet not despair, but being instructed by the Holy Ghost, concludes after this sort: I am indeed a prisoner, shut up under the law, but not forever. Yes, this shutting up shall turn to my great profit, because I am hereby driven to sigh and seek for a helper. So the hungry soul is brought to Christ, who will satisfy him with good things. Therefore, the law not only kills, but it kills that we may live.

24—Wherefore the law was our schoolmaster to bring us unto Christ, that we might be justified by faith.

Here again Paul joins the law and the gospel together, regarding the affections and inward man, when he says, "the law was our schoolmaster to bring us to Christ." This similitude is worth noting. Although a schoolmaster is very profitable and necessary to instruct and bring up children, yet show me the child or scholar who loves his master. Such was the love and obedience the Jews showed to Moses that they would have stoned him to death (Exodus 17:4). It is not possible therefore that a scholar should love his master; for how can he love him who keeps him in prison, that is, who does not allow him to do that which he would gladly do? And if he do anything against his commandment, he is rebuked and chastised, yes, and is constrained, moreover, to kiss the rod when he is beaten. But does he do this willingly? As soon as his master has turned his back, he breaks the rod, or casts it into the fire. And if he had any power over his master, he would not allow himself to be beaten by him, but rather he would beat his master. Yet the schoolmaster is very necessary both to instruct and punish, for otherwise the child without discipline, instruction, and education would be utterly lost.

The schoolmaster therefore is appointed for the child, to teach him, to train him, to keep him, as it were, in a prison. And for what end and how long? To the end that this sharp dealing should always continue, or that the child should remain always in bondage? Not so, but only for a time, that this enforced obedience, this correction and bondage, may turn to the profit of the child, that when the time comes, he may be his father's heir; for it is not the father's will that his son should always be subject to the schoolmaster and always be beaten with the rod; but that, by discipline and instruction, he may be made meet and able to be his father's successor.

Even so, says Paul, the law is nothing else but a schoolmaster, not forever, but until it brings us to Christ; as he said before in other words: "The law was given because of transgression, until the blessed seed should come." Also: "We were shut up unto faith which should after be revealed." So the law is a schoolmaster to us till it brings us to Christ. For what schoolmaster would always punish and beat the child and teach him nothing at all? And yet such schoolmasters there were, in time past, when schools were nothing but a prison, and a very hell, and the schoolmasters cruel tyrants and very butchers. The children were always beaten; they learned, if they learned, with pain and travail. The law is not such a schoolmaster. For it does not always torment and terrify, but with its corrective rod it drives us to Christ; as a good schoolmaster exercises his scholars in reading and writing, to the end that they may come to the knowledge of good letters and other profitable things, that afterwards they may delight in doing that which once they did and learned against their will.

The law is not a schoolmaster to bring us to another lawgiver who requires of us works, but unto Christ our justifier and Savior, that by faith in Him we may be justified, and not by works. When a man feels the force of the law, he does not believe or understand this. Therefore, he says: "I have lived wickedly, for I have transgressed all the commandments of God. Therefore, I am guilty of death. If God would prolong my life, I would amend my ways and live holily." Here he abuses the law. Instead of looking for a Savior, he looks for another lawgiver.

Reason is bold to promise to God the fulfilling of all the works of the whole law. From this came into being so many sects, and swarms of monks, and religious hypocrites, so many ceremonies, so many works devised to deserve grace and remission of sins. And they who devised such things thought that the law was a schoolmaster to lead them not to Christ, but to a new law, or to Christ as a lawgiver, and not as one who has abolished the law.

Faith is neither law nor work, but an assured confidence which apprehends Christ, "who is the end of the law" (Romans 10:4). And how? Not that He has abolished the old law and given a new, or that He is a judge who must be pacified by works. He is the end of the law to all those who believe; that is, everyone who believes in Him is righteous, and the law shall never accuse him. The law then is holy, just, and good, if a man use it lawfully. Now they that abuse the law are, first, the hypocrites who attribute to the law the power to justify; and, secondly, they who despair, not knowing that the law is a schoolmaster to lead them to Christ, that the law humbles them, not to their destruction, but to their salvation. For God wounds that He may heal again; He kills that He may quicken again.

But what works the law in them who are already justified by Christ?

Paul answers by these words, which are, as it were, an addition to that which went before:

25—But after that faith is come, we are no longer under a schoolmaster.

We are free from the law, from the prison, and from the schoolmaster; for when faith is revealed, the law terrifies us no more. Paul here speaks of faith as it was preached and published to the world by Christ in the time before appointed. For Christ, taking upon Him our flesh, came once into the world: He abolished the law with all its effects, and delivered from eternal death all those who receive His benefit by faith. If therefore you look to Christ and that which He has done, there is now no law. For He, coming in the appointed time, took away the law. And since the law is gone, we are not under its tyranny anymore. Now we live in joy and safety under Christ, who sweetly reigns in us by His Spirit. Where the Lord reigns, there is liberty. But the law of the members, rebelling against the law of the mind, hinders us so that we cannot perfectly lay hold upon Christ. The lack is not in Christ, but in us, who have not yet put off this flesh to which sin continually cleaves as long as we live. According to the spirit, we serve, with Paul, "the law of God," but "with the flesh the law of sin" (Romans 7:25).

It follows that as far as the conscience, we are fully delivered from the law; therefore, a schoolmaster no longer rules over us. For the conscience now has Christ crucified before her eyes, who has removed all the offices of the law out of it, "blotting out the handwriting of ordinances that was against us . . ." (Colossians 2:14). As long, then, as the flesh remains the conscience is made heavy by revealing of sin, yet is it raised up again by the daily coming of Christ who, as He came once into the world, in the time appointed, to redeem us from the servitude of our schoolmaster, even so comes daily to us spiritually, to the end that we may increase in faith and in the knowledge of Him. For this is the exercise of the law in the saints, namely, the continual mortification of our corrupt affections, of reason, and our own strength, and the daily renewing of our inward man, as it is said in 2 Corinthians 4.

If I behold Christ, I am altogether pure and holy, knowing nothing of the law; but if I behold my own flesh, I feel in myself covetousness, lust, pride, anger, and arrogance; also the fear of death, heaviness, complaining. The more these sins are in me, the more Christ is absent from me; or if He be present, He is felt but little. For as Christ came once corporally, at the time appointed, abolished the whole law, vanquished sin, destroyed death and hell; even so He comes spiritually, without ceasing, and daily quenches and kills these sins in us.

This I say, that you may be able to answer, if any shall thus object: Christ came into the world, and at once took away all our sins, and cleansed us by His blood; then why need we hear the gospel continually? It is true, that as you behold Christ, the law and sin are quite abolished. But Christ has not yet come to you; or, if He has come, there are yet remnants of sin left in you, for where concupiscence, heaviness of spirit, and fear of death is, there is also the law and sin. But when He comes, He drives away fear and heaviness, and brings peace and quietness of conscience.

26—For ye are all the children of God by faith in Christ Jesus.

Paul, as a true and excellent teacher of faith, always has these words in his mouth, "by faith, in faith, of faith," which is in Christ Jesus. He says not, you are the children of God because you are circumcised, or because you have heard the law, and have done the works thereof (as the Jews imagine, and as the false apostles teach), but by faith in Christ Jesus. The law does not make us children of God, and much less do men's traditions. These cannot beget us into a new nature, or a new birth; but set before us the old birth, whereby we were born to be children of wrath; and so prepare us to a new birth, which is by faith in Jesus Christ. "For ye are all the sons of God by faith." Faith in whom? In Christ, who makes us the sons of God, and not the law. John also witnesses to the same, "To as many as received Him, to them gave He power to become the sons of God" (John 1:12).

What tongue, either of men or angels, can sufficiently extol and magnify the great mercy of God towards us, that we who are miserable sinners, and by nature the children of wrath, should be called to His grace and glory, to be made the children and heirs of God, fellow-heirs with the Son of God, and lords over heaven and earth, and that only by the means of our faith in Christ Jesus.

27—For as many of you as have been baptized into Christ have put on Christ.

To put on Christ is taken two ways: according to the law, and according to the gospel. According to the law, it is said in Romans 13: "Put ye on the Lord Jesus Christ"; that is, follow the example and virtues of Christ. Do that which He did, and suffer that which He suffered. And in 1 Peter 2: "Christ also suffered for us, leaving us an example that ye should follow his steps." Now, we see in Christ a singular patience, an inestimable mildness and love, and a wonderful modesty in all things. This goodly apparel we must put on, that is to say, we must follow these virtues.

But the putting on of Christ, according to the gospel, consists not in an imitation, but in a new birth and a new creation; that is to say, in putting on Christ's innocence, His righteousness, His wisdom, His power, His saving health, His life, and His Spirit. We are clothed with the leather coat of Adam, which is a mortal garment, and a garment of sin; that is, we are all subject unto sin, and sold under sin. This garment, this corrupt and sinful nature, we received from Adam, which Paul often calls "the old man." This old man must be put off, with all his works (Ephesians 4:22, 24), that from the children of Adam we may be made the children of God. This is not done by changing of a garment or by any law or works, but by a new birth, and by the renewing of the inward man, which is done in baptism, as Paul says, "As many of you as have been baptized into Christ, have put on Christ." Also, "According to his mercy he saved

us, by the washing of regeneration, and renewing of the Holy Ghost''
(Titus 3:5). They who are regenerate and renewed by the Holy Ghost to
a heavenly righteousness, and to eternal life, are given a new light, a new
flame, new and holy affections (as the fear of God), true faith and assured
hope. There begins in them also a new will. And this is to put on Christ
truly, according to the gospel.

The righteousness of the law is not given to us in our baptism, and our
own works count nothing; but Christ Himself is our garment. Now Christ
is no law, no lawgiver, no work, but a divine and inestimable gift, whom
God has given to us, that He might be our justifier, our Savior and our
Redeemer. Wherefore to be appareled with Christ, according to the
gospel, is not to be appareled with the law, nor with works, but with an
incomparable gift; that is to say, with remission of sins, righteousness,
peace, consolation, joy of spirit, salvation, life, and Christ Himself.

This is diligently to be noted, because of those who go about to deface
the majesty of baptism, and speak wickedly of it. Paul, contrariwise,
commends it, and sets it forth with honorable titles, calling it, ''the
washing of regeneration, and renewing of the Holy Ghost.'' And here
also he says, that ''all ye that are baptized into Christ, have put on
Christ.'' Wherefore baptism is a thing of great force and efficacy. Now,
when we are appareled with Christ as with the robe of righteousness and
our salvation, then we must put on Christ also by example and imitation.

*28—There is neither Jew nor Greek, there is neither bond nor free,
there is neither male nor female: for ye are all one in Christ Jesus.*

Here might be added many more names of persons and offices which
are ordained by God, as these: there is neither magistrate nor subject,
neither teacher nor hearer, neither schoolmaster nor scholar, neither
master nor servant, neither mistress nor maid, etc.: for in Christ Jesus all
states, yes, even such as are ordained by God, are nothing. Indeed, the
male and the female, the bond and the free, the Jew and the Gentile, the
prince and the subject, are the good creatures of God; but in Christ, that

is, in the matter of salvation, they are nothing, with all their wisdom, righteousness, religion and power.

Wherefore, with these words, "There is neither Jew nor Greek," etc., Paul mightily abolishes the law. For here, when a man has put on Christ, there is that distinction no more. The Apostle speaks here not of the Jew according to his nature and substance; but he calls him a Jew who is the disciple of Moses, is subject to the law, is circumcised, and with all his endeavor keeps the ceremonies commanded by the law. For Christ has abolished all the laws of Moses that ever were. Wherefore, the conscience believing in Christ must be so surely persuaded that the law is abolished, with its terrors and threatenings, that it should be utterly ignorant whether there were ever any Moses, any law, or any Jew. For Christ and Moses can in no way agree. Moses came with the law, with works, and with ceremonies; but Christ came without law, or works, or ceremonies, giving grace and righteousness, remission of sins and eternal life: "For the law was given by Moses, but grace and truth came by Jesus Christ" (John 1:17).

Therefore your false apostles do subtly seduce you (O ye Galatians), when they teach you that the law is necessary to salvation: by this means they spoil you of that excellent glory of your new birth and your adoption, and call you back to your old birth, and to the most miserable servitude of the law, making you, the free children of God, bond children again to the law. There is a difference of persons in the law, and in the world, and ought to be; but not before God: "All have sinned, and come short of the glory of God" (Romans 3:23).

Let the Jew, the Gentile, and the whole world keep silence in the presence of God. So many as are justified are justified, not by observation of God's law, or man's law, but by Christ alone, who has abolished all laws. Him alone does the Scripture set forth as the pacifier of God's wrath by the shedding of His own blood, thus becoming our Savior. Without faith in Him, neither shall the Jew be saved by the law, nor the monk by his order, nor the Greek by his wisdom, nor the magistrate by his good government, nor the master by his just management, nor the servant by his obedience.

28b—For ye are all one in Christ Jesus.

In the world, and according to the flesh, there is a great difference and inequality of persons, and the same must be observed. For if the woman would be the man, if the son would be the father, the servant would be the master, etc., there would be nothing but confusion of all estates and of all things. Contrariwise, in Christ there is no difference of persons, but all are one: "For there is one body, and one Spirit, and one hope of your calling; one Lord, one faith, one baptism, one God and Father of all, who is above all, and through all, and in you all" (Ephesians 4:4–6). We have the same Christ, I, you, and all the faithful, which Peter, Paul, and all the saints had. Therefore, Paul customarily adds this clause: "In Christ Jesus"; who, if He be taken out of our sight, then comes anguish and terror.

Christ should be set forth, that you should see nothing besides Him, and should think that nothing can be more near unto you, or more present within your heart than He is. For He sits not idly in heaven, but is present with us, working and living in us; as Paul says in the second chapter: "I live, yet not I, but Christ liveth in me." And here likewise, "Ye have put on Christ." Faith, therefore, is a certain steadfast beholding, which looks upon Christ alone, the conqueror of sin and death and the giver of righteousness, salvation, and eternal life. This is the cause why Paul names and sets forth Jesus Christ so often in his epistles.

This was notably represented by the brazen serpent, which is a figure of Christ. Moses commanded the Israelites who were stung by serpents in the desert to do nothing else but behold it steadfastly, and not to turn away their eyes. They that did so were healed by that steadfast and constant gaze (Numbers 21:6–8). But they which obeyed not Moses' command to behold the brazen serpent, but looked elsewhere upon their wounds, died.

So, if I would find comfort and life, when I am at the point of death, I must do nothing else but apprehend Christ by faith, and look at Him and say: I believe in Jesus Christ, the Son of God, who suffered, was crucified, and died for me; in whose wounds, and in whose death I see my sin, and in His resurrection victory over sin, death, and the devil, also righteousness and eternal life. Besides Him I see nothing, I hear nothing. This is true faith concerning Christ, and in Christ, whereby we are made "members of His body, of His flesh, and of His bones"; "In him, we live, and move, and have our being" (Ephesians 5:30; Acts 17:28). Christ and our faith must be thoroughly joined together.

29—And if ye be Christ's, then are ye Abraham's seed, and heirs according to the promise.

That is to say, if you believe and are baptized into Christ: if you believe, I say, that He is that promised seed of Abraham which brought blessing to all the Gentiles, then you are the children of Abraham, not by nature, but by adoption; for the Scripture attributes to him not only the children of the flesh, but also of adoption and of the promise, and shows that they shall receive the inheritance, and the other be cast out of the house. So Paul, in a few words, translates the whole glory of the Jews unto the Gentiles: to wit, that the Gentiles are the children of Abraham, and consequently the people of God. But they are the children of Abraham, not by carnal generation, but by the promise. The Kingdom of Heaven, then, life, and the eternal inheritance, belong to the Gentiles. And this the Scripture signified long before when it said: "I have made thee a father of many nations," and "In thy seed shall all nations be blessed" (Genesis 17:5; 22:18). Therefore, in this promise, Christ is become ours.

We are named in the promise: "In thy seed shall all nations be blessed." For the promise shows that Abraham should be the father not only of the Jewish nation, but of many nations. So the glory of the whole Kingdom of Christ is translated unto us.

9

The Adoption of Sons

Galatians 4:1–7

1, 2—Now I say, That the heir, as long as he is a child, differeth nothing from a servant, though he be lord of all; but is under tutors and governors until the time appointed of the father.

You see with what strong affection Paul goes about to call back the Galatians, and what vigorous arguments he uses in debating the matter, gathering similitudes of experience of the example of Abraham, of the testimonies of Scripture, and of the time, so that often he seems to renew the whole matter again. So now Paul, having previously used the comparison of a man's will and testament, of a prison, and of a schoolmaster, uses the comparison of an heir to move and persuade them.

You see, says he, that it is ordained by the civil law that an heir, though he is the lord of all his father's goods, differs not from a servant. Indeed, he has an assured hope of the inheritance, but before he comes of age, his tutors hold him in subjection, as the schoolmaster does his scholar. They commit not to him the ordering of his own goods, but constrain him to serve, so that he is kept with his own goods like a servant. This subjection is profitable for him; otherwise, through folly, he might soon waste all his goods. This captivity continues not always, but has a time limit appointed by the father.

3—Even so we, when we were children, were in bondage under the elements of the world:

In like manner, when we were little children, we were heirs, having the promise of the inheritance to come which should be given to us by the Seed of Abraham, that is, by Christ, in whom all nations should be blessed. But because the fullness of time was not yet come, Moses, our tutor, governor, and schoolmaster, came, holding us in captivity, with our hands bound, so that we could bear no rule nor possess our inheritance. In the meantime, as an heir is nourished in hope of liberty to come, even so Moses nourished us with the hope of the promise to be revealed at the time appointed: to wit, when Christ should come, who by His coming should put an end to the time of the law and begin the time of grace.

The time of the law ended in two ways: first, (as I have said) by the coming of Christ in the flesh, at the time appointed by the Father: "But when the fullness of time was come, God sent forth his Son, made of a woman, made under the law, to redeem them that were under the law" (Galatians 4:4, 5); "He entered into the holy place once by his own blood, having obtained eternal redemption for us" (Hebrews 9:12). Moreover, the same Christ, who came once at the time appointed, comes also to us daily and hourly in Spirit. Indeed, once with His own blood He redeemed and sanctified us; but because we are not yet perfectly pure (for the remnants of sin yet cleave to our flesh, which strives against the Spirit), therefore daily He comes to us spiritually, and continually more and more accomplishes the appointed time of the Father, abrogating and abolishing the law.

So He came also to the fathers of the Old Testament before He appeared in the flesh. They had Christ in Spirit. They believed in Christ who should be revealed, as we believe in Christ who is revealed, and were saved by Him, as we are, according to that saying: "Jesus Christ the same yesterday, and today, and forever." Yesterday, before His coming in the flesh; today now revealed in the time appointed; and to eternity one and the same Christ. In like manner, "we also," says he, "when we were children, served under the rudiments of the world''; that is, the law had dominion over us and kept us in bondage, as captives and servants. For first it restrained carnal and rebellious persons, that they should not run headlong into all kinds of vice. For the law threatens punishment to transgressors; if they feared not the law, there is no mischief they would not commit. Over those whom the law bridles, it rules and reigns. Again, it accused us, terrified us, killed us, and condemned us spiritually and before God. This was the chief dominion that the law had over us. Therefore, as an heir is subject to his tutors and governors and is compelled to obey their rules, even so men's consciences, before Christ comes, are oppressed by the servitude of the law. But this oppression is not continual, but must only endure until the time of grace: ''For the law is a schoolmaster to bring us to Christ.''

Contrariwise, the coming of Christ profits not the careless, the hypocrites, the wicked condemners of God. His coming only profits those who with a sure trust come to Christ the throne of grace, who has redeemed them from the curse of the law, being made a curse for them, and so obtain mercy, and find grace (Hebrews 4:16).

Some have thought that when Paul speaks of our being under the elements or rudiments of the world, that he refers to the corporal elements, the earth, the air, the water, and the fire. But in his peculiar manner of speech he refers here to the law of God; and his words seem to be very heretical. So, in other places, he seems to abase the authority of the law, when he calls it the letter that kills, the ministry of death, and the power of sin. These odious names he chooses on purpose to admonish us, that in the terrors of sin, wrath, and the judgment of God we trust not to our own righteousness or to the righteousness of the law, seeing that the law can do nothing but accuse us. Wherefore this diminishing of the law must be applied to the conflict of conscience, and not to the civil life, nor to careless minds.

He calls the law ''the elements of the world,'' that is, the outward laws and traditions written in a book. For although the law civilly bridles a man from evil, and constrains him to do well, yet, being kept after this sort, it does not deliver him from sin; it justifies him not, it prepares not a way for him to heaven, but leaves him in the world. I do not obtain righteousness because I break not the forbidding commandments, "Thou shalt do no murder," etc. Outward virtues and honest conversation are not the Kingdom of Christ nor the heavenly righteousness, but the righteousness of the flesh and of the world; which also the Gentiles had, and not only the meritmongers, as in the time of Christ, the Pharisees.

We see, then, that the law gives no lively, no healthful, no divine or heavenly thing, but only worldly things. Wherefore Paul very fitly calls the law the elements or rudiments of the world. Yet chiefly he speaks in contempt of the ceremonial laws; which though they profit ever so much, consist only in outward things, as meat, drink, apparel, places, times, the Temple, the feasts, washings, sacrifices, etc., which are but worldly things although ordained of God for the use of this present life, but not to justify or save before God. So the emperors' laws are rudiments of the world, for they deal with this present life, as of goods, possessions, inheritances, murders, adulteries, robberies, etc. As for canon laws and decretals, which are also rudiments of the world, they most wickedly bind men's consciences to the observation of outward things, contrary to the words of God and faith.

Wherefore the law of Moses gives nothing but worldly things; that is, it shows civilly and spiritually, the evils that are in the world. Yet, in its true use, it drives the conscience to seek after the promise of God and to look unto Christ. But that you may so do, you need the aid of the Holy Ghost who may say in your heart: It is not the will of God that you should only be terrified and killed, but that when you are brought by the law to the knowledge of your misery and damnation, you should not despair, but believe in Christ, "who is the end of the law for righteousness to every one that believeth" (Romans 10:4). Here all laws cease, and heavenly things begin now to appear. Indeed, the law says, "Thou shalt love the Lord thy God": but that I may be able to do so, or to apprehend Christ, this the law cannot give. I speak not this that the law should be despised, neither does Paul so mean. But because he was treating the matter of justification, it was necessary that he should so speak. We cannot speak basely enough of the law when on this matter. When the conscience is in this conflict she should think of nothing, know nothing, but Christ only and alone.

Learn here, then, to speak of the law as contemptuously as you can in the matter of justification, by the example of the Apostle, who called it the rudiments of the world, pernicious tradition, the strength of sin, the ministry of condemnation, etc. For if you allow the law to rule in your conscience when you stand before God, wrestling against sin and against death, then the law does nothing but set forth God as an angry Judge who rejects and condemns sinners. If you are wise, you will banish this stuttering, stammering Moses far from you.

Let the godly learn, therefore, that the law and Christ are two contrary things, whereof the one cannot abide the other. For when Christ is present, the law may in no case rule, but must depart out of the conscience, and leave the bed (which is so narrow that it cannot hold two, as Isaiah says, chapter 28:20), and give place only to Christ. Let Him reign alone in peace, and joy, and life, that the conscience may repose joyfully in Christ, without any feeling of the law, sin, and death.

Why does Paul give such odious terms to the law, which is a divine doctrine revealed from heaven? To this he answers that the law is holy and just and good, and that it is also the ministry of condemnation, sin, and death, but in different respects. Before Christ, it is holy; after Christ, it is death. Therefore, when Christ is come, we ought to know nothing at all of the law, unless it is in this respect, that it has power and dominion over the flesh to bridle it and to keep it under. Here is a conflict between the law and the flesh as long as we live.

Only Paul, of all the Apostles, calls the law "the rudiments of the world, weak and beggarly elements, the strength of sin, the letter that killeth," etc. (2 Corinthians 3:6). Whoever will be a right scholar in Christ's school, let him mark diligently this manner of speech used by the Apostle. Christ calls him an elect vessel, and therefore gave him an exquisite utterance, as a singular kind of speech above all the rest of the Apostles, that he, as an elect vessel, might faithfully lay the foundations of the article of justification and clearly set forth the same (Acts 9:15).

4—But when the fullness of the time was come, God sent forth his
Son, made of a woman, made under the law.

Mark here how carefully Paul defines Christ. Christ is the Son of God, and of a woman, who, for us sinners, was made under the law, to redeem us who were under the law. In these words he comprehends both the Person and the office of Christ. His Person consists of His divine and human nature. This he shows when he says: "God sent forth his Son, made of a woman." Christ, therefore, is very God, and very man. His office he shows in these words: "Being made under the law, to redeem them that were under the law."

And it seems that Paul here, as it were in reproach called the Virgin, the mother of the Son of God, but a woman; which was not well taken by some of the ancient doctors who would that he had called her a virgin rather than a woman. But Paul deals in this epistle with the most high and principal matter of all: to wit, of the gospel, of faith, of Christian righteousness; also, what the Person of Christ is, what is His office, what He has taken upon Him, and done for our cause, and what benefits He has brought to us wretched sinners. Wherefore the excellency of so high and so wonderful a matter was the cause that he had no regard of her virginity. It was enough for him to set forth and preach the inestimable mercy of God, who would that His Son should be born of that sex. Therefore, he mentions only the sex and not the dignity of the sex. He signifies that Christ was true and very man of womankind. John the evangelist when he sets forth the Word, says: "And was made flesh" (John 1:14), speaking not one word of His mother.

Furthermore, this verse also witnesses that Christ, when the time of the law was accomplished, abolished it, and so brought liberty to those who were oppressed therewith, but made no new law, after or besides that old law of Moses.

Christ came, then, not that He might make a new law, but (as Paul here says) He was sent by the Father into the world to redeem those who were kept in thraldom under the law. These words depict Christ lively and truly; they do not attribute to Him the office to make any new law, but to redeem them that were under the law. And Christ Himself says: "I judge no man," and, in another place: "I came not to judge the world, but to save the world" (John 8:15; 12:47). That is, I came not to bring any law, nor to judge men by the same, as Moses and other lawgivers; but I have a higher and better office. The law killed you, and I do judge, condemn, and kill the law, and so I deliver you from its tyranny.

It is very profitable for us to have always before our eyes this sweet and comfortable sentence, and such like, which sets out Christ truly and lively, that in our whole life, in all dangers, in the confession of our faith before tyrants, and in the hour of death, we may boldly and with all confidence say: O law, you have no power over me; therefore, you accuse and condemn me in vain. For I believe in Jesus Christ, the Son of God, whom the Father sent into the world to redeem us miserable sinners oppressed with the tyranny of the law. He gave His life, He shed His blood for me. Therefore, feeling your terrors and threatenings, O law, I plunge my conscience in the wounds, blood, death, resurrection and victory of my Savior, Christ. Besides Him I will see nothing, hear nothing.

This faith is our victory, whereby we overcome the terrors of the law, sin, death, and all evils, and yet not without great conflicts. And here do the children of God wrestle and sweat indeed. For often it comes into their minds that Christ will accuse them and plead against them, that He will require an account of their former life, and that He will condemn them. And why does this come? They have not yet fully put off the flesh, which rebels against the Spirit. Therefore, the terror of the law, the fear of death, and such heaviness often return to hinder our faith, that it cannot apprehend the benefits of Christ (who hath redeemed us from the curse of the law) with such assurance as it should do.

But how or by what means has Christ redeemed us? This was the manner: "He was made under the law." Christ, when He came, found us captives under tutors and governors, that is, shut up in prison under the law. What did He then? Although He was Lord of all, and therefore the law had no power of authority over Him (for He is the Son of God), yet, of His own accord He made Himself subject to the law. Here the law executed upon Him all the jurisdiction it had over us. It accuses and terrifies us; it makes us subject to sin, death, the wrath of God, and with His sentence condemns us. And this it does by good right: "For we are all sinners, and by nature the children of wrath" (Ephesians 2:3). Contrariwise: "Christ did no sin, neither was guile found in His mouth" (1 Peter 2:22). Therefore, He was not subject to the law. Yet the law was no less cruel against this innocent, righteous, and blessed lamb, than it was against us cursed sinners; indeed, it was much more rigorous. For it accused Him as a blasphemer and a seditious person; it made Him guilty before God of the sins of the whole world; it so terrified and oppressed Him with heaviness and anguish of spirit, that He sweat blood; and, briefly, it condemned Him to death, yes, even to the death of the Cross.

This was indeed an amazing combat, where the law, being a creature, gave such an assault to its Creator. Against all right, it practiced its whole tyranny upon the Son of God which it exercises upon us the children of wrath. Now, therefore, because the law so horribly sinned against God, it is accused and arraigned. There Christ said, "O law, thou cruel regent of all mankind, what have I done that thou hast accused Me, and condemned Me, who am innocent?" The law, which had before condemned and killed all men, is again so condemned and vanquished that it lost its whole right, not only over Christ, but also over all them that believe in Him; for to those Christ says, "Come unto me, all ye that labour" under the yoke of the law (Matthew 11:28). "I could have overcome the law by My absolute power, without Mine own hurt: for I am the Lord of the law, and therefore it has no right over Me. But I have made Myself subject to the law for your cause who were under the law, taking your flesh upon Me; and of My love for you I humbled and yielded Myself to the same prison, tyranny, and bondage of the law under the which you served as captives and bondslaves. Therefore, I have vanquished the law by double right and authority: first, as the Son of God, and Lord of the law; secondly, in your person—which is as if you had yourself overcome the law—for My victory is yours."

After this manner Paul speaks everywhere of this astonishing combat between Christ and the law; and to make the matter more apparent, he sets forth the law as a mighty person who had condemned and killed Christ: whom Christ, overcoming death, had conquered, condemned, and killed (Ephesians 2:15), killing enmity thereby: "Thou hast led captivity captive" (Psalms 68:18). He uses the same figure in his epistles to the Romans, Corinthians, and Colossians: "By sin He condemned sin" (Romans 8:3). Christ, therefore, by this victory banished the law out of our conscience, so that now it can no more confound us in the sight of God, drive us to desperation or condemn us, for the conscience, taking hold of this word, "Christ hath redeemed us from the law," is raised up by faith, and conceives great comfort. To those who abide in Christ, the law is dead forever. "Thanks be to God, which giveth us the victory through our Lord Jesus Christ" (1 Corinthians 15:57).

These things also confirm the doctrine that we are justified by faith only. For when this combat was fought between Christ and the law, none of our works came between, but only Christ was found who, putting upon Him our person, made Himself subject to the law, and in perfect innocence suffered all its tyranny. Therefore the law, as a thief and a cursed murderer of the Son of God, loses all its rights and deserves to be condemned. Wherever Christ is, or is once named, it is compelled to flee. If we believe, we are delivered from the law through Christ, who has triumphed over it by Himself (Colossians 2:15). Therefore, this glorious triumph, purchased for us by Christ, is not gotten by any works, but only by faith; therefore, faith alone justifies.

These words, Christ "made under the law," declare that the Son of God did not only perform one or two works of the law, that is, He was not only circumcised or presented in the Temple, or went up to Jerusalem at the appointed times, or lived civilly under the law, but he suffered all the tyranny of the law. For the law set upon Christ and so horribly assailed Him that He felt such anguish as no man on earth had ever felt the like. This His bloody sweat sufficiently witnesses, His comfort ministered by angels, that mighty prayer that He made in the garden, and that lamentable complaint upon the Cross. These things He suffered to redeem those that were under the law. For, as touching the flesh, we sin daily against the commandment of God. But Paul gives us good comfort when he says: "God sent forth His Son . . . to redeem them that were under the law." So Christ was not made a teacher of the law, but an obedient disciple to the law, that by His obedience He might redeem them that were under the law.

Paul teaches that God humbled His Son under the law, that is, constrained Him to bear the curse and judgment of the law, sin, death, etc. For Moses, the minister of the law, sin, wrath, death, apprehended, bound, condemned, and killed Christ; and all this He suffered. Therefore, Christ stands as a mere patient, and not as an agent, in respect of the law. He is not then a lawgiver, or a judge after the law; but in that He made Himself subject to the law, bearing the condemnation of the law, He delivered us from the curse thereby.

Now, whereas Christ, in the gospel, gives commandments, and teaches the law, or rather expounds it, this pertains not to the doctrine of justification, but to good works. Moreover, it is not the proper office of Christ (for which He came principally into the world) to teach the law, but an accidental or by-office; as it was to heal the sick, to raise up the dead, etc. These are indeed excellent and divine works, but yet not the very proper and principal works of Christ. For the prophets also taught the law and worked miracles. But Christ is God and man, who fighting against the law, suffered the utmost cruelty and tyranny thereof. And in that He suffered the tyranny of the law, He vanquished it in Himself; and afterwards, being raised again from the dead, He condemned and utterly abolished the law, which was our deadly enemy, so that it cannot condemn and kill the faithful anymore.

Seeing then that Christ has overcome the law in His own person, it follows that He is naturally God. For there is none else, whether man or angel, who is above the law, only God. But Christ is above the law for He has vanquished it; therefore, He is the Son of God, and naturally God. If you lay hold on Christ, as Paul here painted Him, you cannot err or be confounded. Moreover, you shall easily judge all kinds of life, of the religions and ceremonies of the whole world. But if this true picture of Christ be defaced, or in any way darkened, then follows a confusion of all things. For the natural man cannot judge the law of God. Here fails the cunning of the philosophers, of the canonists, and of all men. For the law has power and dominion over man. Therefore, the law judges man, and not man the law. Only a Christian has a true and certain judgment of the law. And how? That it does not justify. Wherefore then? Righteousness before God, which is received by faith alone, is not the final cause why the righteous do obey the law, but the peace of the world, thankfulness towards God, and good example of life, whereby others are provoked to believe the gospel.

5—To redeem them that were under the law, that we might receive the adoption of sons.

Earlier, Paul had called the blessing the blessing of the seed of Abraham, righteousness, life, the promise of the Spirit, deliverance from the law and the testament. Here he calls it the adoption and the inheritance of eternal life. All these are included in the word *blessing*. For when the curse is abolished, then succeeds the blessing, that is, righteousness, life, and all good things.

But by what merit have we received this blessing, this adoption, and inheritance? By none at all. For what can men deserve that are shut under sin, subject to the curse of the law, and worthy of everlasting death? We have then received this blessing freely, and being utterly unworthy of it, but yet not without merit. What merit is that? Not ours, but the merit of Jesus Christ, the Son of God, who being made under the law, not for Himself, but for us (as Paul said before: "He was made a curse for us"), redeemed us who were under the law. Wherefore, we have received this adoption by the redemption of Jesus Christ. And with this free adoption we have also received the Holy Ghost, whom God has sent into our hearts, crying, Abba, Father.

6—And because ye are sons, God hath sent forth the Spirit of His Son into your hearts, crying, Abba, Father.

The Holy Ghost is sent in two ways. In the primitive Church He was sent in a visible appearance. So He came upon Christ at Jordan in the likeness of a dove, and in the likeness of fire upon the Apostles and other believers. And this was the first sending of the Holy Ghost. It was necessary in the primitive Church, for it was expedient that it should be established by many miracles, because of the unbelievers, as Paul witnesses: "Wherefore tongues are for a sign, not to them that believe, but to them that believe not" (1 Corinthians 14:22). But after the Church was gathered together, and confirmed with these miracles, it was not necessary that this visible sending of the Holy Ghost should continue any longer.

Secondly, the Holy Ghost is sent by the Word into the hearts of the believers. Here it is said: "God sent the Spirit of His Son into your hearts." This sending is without any visible appearance. When by the hearing of the external Word we receive an inward fervency and light, we are changed and become new creatures; we also receive a new judgment, a new feeling, and a new moving. This change and this new judgment is no work of reason or of the power of man, but is the gift and operation of the Holy Ghost, who comes with the preached Word, purifying our hearts by faith and bringing forth in us spiritual motions. Therefore, there is a great difference between us and those who with force and subtlety persecute the doctrine of the gospel. For we by the grace of God can certainly judge by the Word, of the will of God towards us; but, without the Word, a man can give no certain judgment of anything.

Although it appear not before the world that we have been renewed in spirit and have the Holy Ghost, yet our judgment, our speech, and our confession declare sufficiently that the Holy Ghost with His gifts is in us. For before we could judge rightly of nothing. We spoke not as now we do. We confessed not that all our works were sin and damnable, that Christ is our only merit, both before grace and after, as now we do, in the true knowledge and light of the gospel. Wherefore, let this trouble us nothing at all, that the world (whose works we testify to be evil) judges us to be most pernicious persons, seditious, and heretical, destroyers of religion, and troublers of the common peace, possessed of the devil speaking in us and governing all our actions. Against this perverse and wicked judgment of the world, let the testimony of our conscience be sufficient, whereby we assuredly know that it is the gift of God that we not only believe in Jesus Christ, but that we also preach and confess Him before the world. As we believe with our heart, so do we speak with our mouth, according to that saying of the Psalmist: "I believed, therefore have I spoken" (Psalms 116:10).

Moreover, we exercise ourselves in the fear of God, and avoid sin as much as we may. If we sin, we sin not of purpose, but of ignorance, and we are sorry for it. We may slip, for the devil lies in wait for us day and night. The remnants of sin cleave fast in our flesh; therefore, concerning the flesh, yes, we are sinners, after we have received the Holy Ghost. And there is no great difference between a Christian and an honest civil man. For the works of a Christian in outward show are but base and simple. He does his duty according to his vocation, he guides his family, he tills the ground, he gives counsel, he aids and succors his neighbor. These works the carnal man does not much esteem, but thinks them to be common to all men, and such as the heathen may also do. For the world understands not the things which are of the Spirit of God, and therefore it judges perversely of the works of the godly. Not only do they not acknowledge them to be good works, but also they despise them and condemn them as most ungodly and unrighteous.

We ought not, therefore, to doubt whether the Holy Ghost dwells in us or not; but to be assuredly persuaded that we "are the temple of the Holy Ghost" as Paul says (1 Corinthians 3:16). For if any man feel in himself a love toward the Word of God, and willingly hears, talks, writes, and thinks of Christ, let that man know, that this is not the work of man's will or reason, but the gift of the Holy Ghost; for it is impossible that these things should be done without the Holy Ghost. Contrariwise, where hatred and contempt of the Word is, there the devil, the god of this world, reigns, "blinding men's hearts, and holding them captive, that the light of the glorious gospel of Christ, should not shine unto them" (2 Corinthians 4:4). We see this thing in most people, who have no love for the Word, but disregard it as though it pertained nothing at all to them. But whoever feels any love or desire for the Word, let them acknowledge with thankfulness that this affection is poured into them by the Holy

Ghost. For we bring not this desire and affection with us, neither can we be taught by any laws how to obtain it; this change is plainly and simply the work of the right hand of the Most High. Therefore, when we willingly and gladly hear the Word preached concerning Christ the Son of God, who was for us made man, and became subject to the law to deliver us from the malediction of the law, death, hell, and damnation; then let us assure ourselves that God, by and with this preaching, sends the Holy Ghost into our hearts. So it is very expedient for the godly to know that they have the Holy Ghost.

This I say, to confute that pernicious doctrine that no man can certainly know (although his life be ever so blameless) whether he be in the favor of God or no. Augustine said very well and godly, that "every man sees most certainly his own faith, if he have faith." We must be assured and without doubt that we are under grace, and that we have the Holy Ghost: "For if any man have not the Spirit of Christ, he is none of His" (Romans 8:9).

Wherefore, whether you are a minister of God's Word, or a magistrate in the commonwealth, you must assuredly think that your office pleases God; but this you can never do, unless you have the Holy Ghost. But you will say, I doubt not that my office pleases God, because it is God's ordinance, but I doubt of mine own person, whether it please God, or no. Here you must resort to the Word of God, which teaches us that not only the office of the person, but also the person pleases God. For the person is baptized, believes in Christ, is purged in His blood from all sin, lives in the communion and fellowship of His Church. He not only loves the pure doctrine of the Word, but rejoices greatly when he sees it advanced, and the number of the faithful increased.

Forasmuch, then, as Christ pleases God, and we are in Him, we also please God, and are holy. And although sin still remains in our flesh, and we daily fall and offend, yet grace is more abundant and stronger than sin. The mercy and truth of the Lord reigns over us forever. Wherefore sin cannot terrify us or make us doubtful of the grace of God, which is in us. So long as Christ, the vanquisher of sin, is at the right hand of God, making intercession for us, we cannot doubt the grace and favor of God towards us.

Moreover, God has sent the Spirit of His Son into our hearts, as Paul says here. But Christ is most certain that He pleases God; therefore we also, having the Spirit of Christ, must be assured that we are under grace for His sake who is most assured. This I have said concerning the inward testimony, whereby a Christian man's heart ought to be fully persuaded that he is under grace and has the Holy Ghost. Now, the outward signs (as I said before) are to gladly hear of Christ, to preach and teach Christ, to render thanks to Him, to praise Him, to confess Him, yes, if need be, with the loss of goods and life; also, to do our duty according to our vocation, as we are able—to do it in faith, joy, and cheerfulness. Not to thrust ourselves into another man's vocation, but to stand upon our own, to help our needy brother, to comfort the heavyhearted. By these signs, as by effects and consequences, we are fully assured and confirmed that we are in God's favor.

Here we may see what great infirmity is yet in the flesh of the godly. For if we could be fully persuaded that we are under grace, that our sins are forgiven, that we have the Spirit of Christ and are the children of God, then, doubtless, we should be joyful and thankful to God for this inestimable gift. But because we feel contrary emotions, that is, fear, doubt, anguish and heaviness of heart, we cannot assure ourselves hereof; indeed, our conscience judges it a great presumption and pride to challenge this glory. If we will understand this thing rightly, and as we should, we must put it in practice; for without experience and practice it can never be learned.

Let every man, then, so practice with himself, that his conscience may be fully assured that he is under grace, and that his person and his works do please God. And if he feel any wavering or doubting, let him exercise his faith, and wrestle against it, and labor to attain more strength and assurance of faith, and so be able to say: I know that I am accepted and have the Holy Ghost, not for my own worthiness, work, or merit, but for Christ's sake, who of His love towards us made Himself subject to the

law and took away the sin of the world. In Him do I believe. If I am a
sinner, and err, He is righteous and cannot err.

Moreover, I gladly hear, read, write, and sing of Him, and desire
nothing more than that His gospel may be known to the whole world, and
that many may be converted to Him. These things do plainly witness that
the Holy Ghost is present with us and in us. For such things are not
wrought in the heart by man's strength, nor gotten by man's industry or
travail, but are obtained by Christ alone, who first makes us righteous by
the knowledge of Himself in His holy gospel, and afterwards creates a
new heart in us, bringing forth new motions, and gives to us that
assurance whereby we are persuaded that we please the Father for His
sake. Also He gives us a true judgment, whereby we prove and try those
things which before we knew not, or else altogether despised. It behooves
us therefore to wrestle daily against this doubting that we may overcome
more and more and attain to a full persuasion and certainty of God's favor
towards us. For if we are not sure that we are in grace, we utterly deny
all His benefits.

Paul might have said: "God sent the Spirit of His Son into our hearts,"
calling, Abba, Father. But he says, "crying, Abba, Father," that he
might show and set forth the temptation of a Christian, who yet is but
weak, and weakly believes. In Romans 8 he calls this crying an
unspeakable groaning. Likewise he says: "The Spirit helpeth our
infirmities: for we know not what to pray for as we ought, but the Spirit
maketh intercession for us, with groanings which cannot be uttered."

This is a singular consolation when he says "that the Spirit of Christ is
sent into our hearts, crying, Abba, Father"; and again, "that He helpeth
our infirmities, making intercession for us." He who assuredly believes
this should never be overcome with any affliction, were it ever so great.
But there are many things which hinder this faith in us. First, our heart is
born in sin; and this evil is naturally grafted in us, that we doubt God's
good will towards us, and cannot assure ourselves that we please God.
Beside this, the devil our adversary ranges about with terrible roarings,
and says: "You are a sinner: therefore, God is angry with you, and will
destroy you forever." Against these roarings we have nothing to hold

onto, but only the Word, which sets Christ before us as a conqueror of sin and death and all evils. But to hold fast to the Word in this temptation is difficult, because we cannot sense the presence of Christ. We see Him not. Our heart does not feel His presence. Rather, it seems as if He is angry with us and that He has forsaken us. Moreover, when we are tempted, we feel the power of sin, the weakness of the flesh, and the wavering of the mind. We feel the fiery darts of the devil, the terrors of death, and the anger of God. All these things cry out horribly against us. And yet, when we are conscious of the terrors of the law, the thundering of sin, the assaults of death, the roarings of the devil, the Holy Ghost, says Paul, cries in our hearts: "Abba, Father." This cry pierces the clouds and the heaven, and ascends up into the ears of God.

These words signify that there is still infirmity in the godly; as Paul also says in Romans 8, "The Spirit helpeth our infirmities." Forasmuch, then, as the sense and feeling of the contrary is strong in us—that is, we feel more the displeasure of God than His good will and favor towards us—therefore the Holy Ghost is sent into our hearts, who not only sighs and makes request for us, but also cries mightily, "Abba, Father," and makes intercession for us according to the will of God. And thus, when we have taken hold of Christ by faith, we cry, through Him: "Abba, Father." And this our cry far surmounts the roaring of the law, sin, death and the devil.

Christ in the eighteenth chapter of Luke, in the parable of the wicked judge, calls this groaning of a faithful heart, a cry, and such a cry as ceasing not day and night, where He says: "Hear what the unjust judge saith. And shall not God avenge his own elect, which cry day and night unto him? Yea, I say unto you, he will avenge them speedily." We, at this day, can do nothing else but utter such groanings. And these are our guns and artillery, by which we have scattered the enterprises of our adversaries. They also shall provoke Christ to hasten the day of His glorious coming, whereby "He shall have put down all rule and all authority and power, and shall put all enemies under His feet" (1 Corinthians 15:24). Amen.

In the fourteenth chapter of Exodus, the Lord speaks to Moses at the

Red Sea: "Wherefore criest thou unto Me?" Yet Moses cried not, but trembled and almost despaired, for he was in great trouble. It seemed that infidelity reigned in him, and not faith. For he saw the people of Israel so compassed and enclosed with the Egyptian host and with the sea, that there was no way whereby they might escape. Here Moses dared not open his mouth. How then did he cry? We must not judge therefore, according to the feeling of our own heart, but according to the Word of God, which teaches us that the Holy Ghost is given to those that are afflicted, terrified, and ready to despair, to raise them up, and to comfort them, that they be not overcome of their temptations and afflictions, but may overcome them, and yet not without great terrors and troubles.

The schoolmen dreamed "that holy men had the Holy Ghost in such sort that they never had nor felt any temptation." They spoke of the Holy Ghost only by speculation and natural knowledge. But Paul says that "the strength of Christ is made perfect in weakness." Also that "the Spirit helpeth our infirmities." We have then most need of the help and comfort of the Holy Ghost; yes, and then is He most ready to help us, when we are most weak and nearest to desperation. If any man suffer affliction with a constant and joyful heart, then has the Holy Ghost done His office in him. And indeed He exercises His work specially and properly in those who have suffered great terrors and afflictions, and have approached, as the Psalm says, nigh to the gates of death. As I said of Moses, who saw death in the waters and on every side wherever he turned his face, he was in extreme anguish and desperation; and (no doubt) he felt in his heart a mighty cry of the devil against him, saying: All this people shall this day perish, for they can escape no way. Besides all this, the people cried out against him, saying: "Were there no graves in Egypt? Thou hast brought us out that we should die here in the wilderness. Had it not been better for us to have served the Egyptians than to die in the wilderness?" (Exodus 14:11ff.). The Holy Ghost was in Moses truly and effectually, and made intercession for him with unspeakable groaning, so that he sighed to the Lord and said: "O Lord, at Thy commandment have I led forth this people; help us therefore."

This matter I have the more largely prosecuted that I might plainly show what the office of the Holy Ghost is, and when He specially exercises it. In temptation, therefore, we must not judge according to our own sense and feeling, or by the crying of the law, sin, and the devil. If we follow our own sense and believe those cryings, we shall think ourselves to be destitute of all help and succor of the Holy Ghost and utterly cast away from the presence of God. No, rather let us then remember what Paul says, that the Spirit helps our infirmities, and also that He cries, "Abba, Father"; that is to say, He utters a certain sighing and groaning of the heart (as it seems to us), which before God is a loud cry and an unspeakable groaning. Wherefore, in the midst of your temptation and infirmity, cleave only to Christ, and groan to Him. He gives the Holy Ghost who cries, "Abba, Father." And this feeble groaning is a mighty cry in the ears of God, and so fills heaven and earth that God hears nothing else; and moreover, it stops the cries of all other things whatever.

You must note also that Paul says that the Spirit makes intercession for us in our temptation, not with many words or long prayer, but only with a groaning which cannot be expressed; and that He cries not aloud with tears, saying, "Have mercy on me, O God," etc., but only utters a little sound and a feeble groaning, as "Ah, Father!" This is but a little word, and yet it comprehends all things. The mouth speaks not, but the affection of the heart speaks after this manner: Although I am oppressed with anguish and terror on every side, and seem to be forsaken and utterly cast away from Your presence, yet am I Your child, and You are my Father for Christ's sake; I am beloved because of the Beloved. Wherefore, this little word "Father," conceived effectually in the heart, passes all the eloquence of Demosthenes, Cicero, and of the most eloquent rhetoricians that ever were in the world.

I have used many words to declare that a Christian must assure himself that he is in the favor of God, and that he has the crying of the Holy Ghost in his heart. This have I done, that we may learn to reject and utterly to abandon that devilish opinion which taught that a man ought to be uncertain of the grace of God towards him. If this opinion be received, then Christ profits nothing. For he that doubts of God's favor towards him must doubt also of the promises of God, and so consequently of the will of God, and of the benefits of Christ, namely that He was born, suffered, died, and rose again for us. There can be no greater blasphemy against God than to deny His promises, to deny God Himself, to deny Christ.

The whole Scripture teaches us above all things that we should not doubt, but assure ourselves and undoubtedly believe that God is merciful, loving, and patient; that He is neither dissembler nor deceiver, but that He is faithful and true, and keeps His promise. He has performed what He promised, in delivering His only begotten Son to death for our sins, that everyone who believes in Him might not perish, but have everlasting life. Here we cannot doubt but that God is favorable to us and loves us indeed, that the hatred and wrath of God is taken away, seeing He suffered His Son to die for us wretched sinners.

Let us give thanks to God that we are delivered from this monstrous doctrine of doubting, and can now assure ourselves that the Holy Ghost cries, and brings forth in our hearts unspeakable groanings; this is our anchor-hold foundation. The gospel commands us to behold not our own good works or perfection, but God the promiser, and Christ the mediator. Contrariwise, there are those who command us to look, not to God the promiser, nor unto Christ our high priest, but unto our own works and merits. Here, on the one side, doubting and desperation must follow; but on the other side, assurance of God's favor and joy of the Spirit. For we cleave unto God who cannot lie. For He says, Behold, I deliver My Son to death, that through His blood He may redeem you from your sins, and from eternal death. And this is the reason our doctrine is most sure and certain, because it carries us out of ourselves, that we should not lean upon our own strength, our own feeling, our own person, and our own works, but upon God, and upon His precious promise and truth, which cannot deceive us.

To establish their pernicious error, our foes point to the saying of Solomon, "The righteous, and the wise, and their works, are in the hands of God; and yet no man knoweth whether he be worthy of love or hatred" (Ecclesiastes 9:1).

This sentence of Solomon speaks nothing at all of the hatred or favor of God towards men, but is a moral sentence reproving the ingratitude of men. For such is the perverseness of the world that the better a man deserves, the less thanks he shall have, and oftentimes he who should be his best friend is found to be his worst enemy. Contrariwise, such as least deserve shall be most esteemed. So David, a holy man and a good king, was cast out of his kingdom. The prophets, Christ, and His Apostles, were slain. To conclude, the history of all countries witness that many well-deserving men were cast into banishment by their own citizens, and some miserably perished in prison. Wherefore, Solomon in this place speaks not of the conscience having to do with God, nor of the favor or judgment, the love or hatred of God; but of the judgments and affections of men among themselves. As though he would say, There are many just and wise men, by whom God works much good, and gives peace and quietness to men. But so far off are men from acknowledging the same that often they requite them most unkindly for their well-doings and deservings. Though a man do all things well, he knows not whether he shall have the favor or hate of other men.

So we, at this day, thought we should have found favor among our own countrymen, for we preached to them the gospel of peace, life, and eternal salvation; instead of favor, we have found bitter and cruel hatred. Indeed, at the first, many were greatly delighted with our doctrine, and received it gladly. We thought they would have been our friends and brethren, and that with one consent, together with us, they would have planted and preached this doctrine to others. But now we find that they are false brethren, and our deadly enemies, who sow and spread abroad false doctrine; and that which we preach well and godly, they wickedly pervert and overthrow, stirring up offenses in the churches. Whoever, therefore, does his duty godly and faithfully, and for his well-doing receives nothing but the unkindness and hatred of men, let him not vex himself, but let him say with Christ: "They hated me without a cause." And again with the Psalmist: "They compassed me about also with words of hatred; and fought against me without a cause. For my love they are my adversaries" (Psalms 109:3, 4).

No man can understand what God's will is and what pleases Him, but in His Word. This Word assures us that God cast away all the anger and displeasure which He had against us, when He gave His only begotten Son for our sins. Wherefore, let us be fully assured that God is merciful to us, that we please Him, that He has a care over us, that we have the Holy Ghost to make intercession for us with groanings that cannot be expressed.

7—Wherefore thou art no more a servant, but a son; and if a son, then an heir of God through Christ.

This is the summing up and conclusion of what Paul said before. As if he would say, This being true, that we have received the Spirit by the gospel, whereby we cry, Abba, Father, then is this decree pronounced in heaven, that there is now no bondage anymore, but only liberty, sonship, and adoption. And who brings this liberty? Verily, this groaning. By what means? The Father offers to me, by His promise, His grace and His fatherly favor. This remains then, that I should receive this grace. And this is done when I again with this groaning cry, and with a childlike heart assent to this name, Father. The Father and the Son meet, and are joined, and nothing at all comes between; no law or work is required. Here is the Father promising, and calling me His son, by Christ, "who was made under the law, to redeem them that were under the law, that we might receive the adoption of sons."

Paul here takes the word "servant" in a different sense than he did in the third chapter, where he says, "there is neither bond nor free," etc. Here he calls him a servant of the law who is subject to the law, as he did a little before. "We were in bondage under the elements of the world." To be a servant, in this place, is to be guilty and captive under the law, under the wrath of God and death, to behold God not as a merciful Father, but as a tormentor and an enemy. This is indeed to be in Babylonish captivity, and to be cruelly tormented therein. This bondage, says Paul (Acts 7:6) continues no longer, for "thou art no more a servant." When faith comes, bondage ceases, as he said in the third chapter.

Now, if we, by the Spirit of Christ, crying in our hearts, "Abba, Father," are no more servants, but sons, then it follows that we are not only delivered from all the abominations of men's traditions, but also from all the jurisdiction and power of the law of God. So Paul comforts us: "Thou art no more a servant, but a son." Let us therefore take hold of this consolation by faith, and say, "O law, your tyranny can have no place in the throne where Christ my Lord sits, for I am free, and a son, who must not be subject to any bondage, or any law." Let the servants abide with the ass in the valley; let none but Isaac ascend up into the mountain with his father Abraham.

Wherefore, the adoption brings with it the eternal kingdom, and the heavenly inheritance. Now, how inestimable the glory of this gift is, man's heart is not able to conceive, and much less to utter. In the meantime, we see this but darkly, and as it were afar off; we have this little groaning and feeble faith which only rests upon the hearing and the sound of the voice of Christ in giving the promise. Therefore, we must not measure it by reason, or by our own feelings, but by the promise of God. And because He is infinite, His promise is also infinite: "Wherefore thou art a son."

"Now if thou be a son, thou art also the heir of God through Christ." For by his birth the son is worthy to be an heir. There is no work or merit that brings him the inheritance, only his birth; and so in obtaining the inheritance he is simply a patient, and not an agent. No son had to work for it; in fact, he did not even need to worry about it; all he had to do to become an heir was to be born. So we obtain eternal gifts, namely, the forgiveness of sins, righteousness, the glory of the resurrection, and everlasting life, not as agents, but as patients: that is, not by doing, but by receiving. Nothing here comes between, but faith alone apprehends the promise offered. As a son, in the political or household government, is made an heir by his birth alone, so faith alone makes us sons of God, born of the Word, the Word of God, wherein we are conceived, carried, born and nourished up. By this birth, then, we are made new creatures: formed by faith in the Word, we are made Christians, children and heirs of God, through Jesus Christ. Now, being heirs, we are delivered from death, sin, and the devil, and we have righteousness and eternal life.

But this far passes man's capacity, that He calls us heirs; not of some rich and mighty prince, not of the emperor, not of the world, but of God, the Almighty Creator of all things. Our inheritance, then (as Paul says in Ephesians 2:7), is incalculable. And if a man could comprehend the great excellency of this matter, that he is the son and heir of God, and with a constant faith believe it, this man would esteem all the power and riches of all the kingdoms of the world but as dung, in comparison with his eternal inheritance. He would abhor whatever is high and glorious in the world; in fact, the greater the pomp and glory of the world, the more he would hate it. To conclude, whatever the world most highly esteems and magnifies, that should be, in his eyes, most vile and abominable. For what is all the world, with all its riches, power, and glory, in comparison with God, whose son he is? A man who could believe this would desire to be taken out of this life and to be with Christ (Philippians 1:23).

But the law of the members, striving against the law of the mind, hinders faith in us and suffers it not to be perfect. Therefore, we have need of the help and comfort of the Holy Ghost, who in our troubles and afflictions makes intercession for us. Sin yet remains in our flesh, which often oppresses the conscience, and so hinders faith, that we cannot with joy perfectly behold and desire those eternal riches which God has given to us through Christ. Paul himself feeling this battle of the flesh against the spirit, cries out, "O wretched man that I am! who shall deliver me from the body of this death?" (Romans 7:24). He accuses his body, calling it by an odious name, his death. It was as if he said, "My body afflicts me more than death itself." He had not always the sweet and joyful cogitations of the heavenly inheritance to come, but he felt often much heaviness of spirit, anguish, and fear.

Hereby we perceive how difficult a matter faith is. The great infirmity which is in the saints, and the striving of the flesh against the Spirit, sufficiently witness how feeble faith is in them. For a perfect faith would bring a contempt and loathing of this present life in the flesh. If we could fully assure ourselves and constantly believe that God is our Father and that we are His sons and heirs, we would not be so addicted to worldly things, trusting them when we have them, lamenting and despairing when we lose them. But we do the contrary, for the flesh is yet strong and faith is feeble. Therefore Paul says very well, that we have here, in this life, only the firstfruits of the Spirit, and that, in the world to come, we shall have the tenths also.

"Thou art an heir through Christ." Paul has Christ ever in his mouth: he cannot forget Him, for he well foresaw that nothing should be less known in the world (even among them who should profess themselves to be Christians) than Christ and His gospel. Therefore he talks of Him and sets Him before our eyes continually. And so often as he speaks of grace, righteousness, the promise, adoption, and the inheritance, he is accustomed to add, "in Christ," or "through Christ," covertly impugning the law. As if he would say, these things come to us neither by the law, nor by works, much less by our own strength, or by any of men's traditions, but only by Christ.

10

Again in Bondage

Galatians 4:8–21

8, 9—Howbeit, then, when ye knew not God, ye did service unto them which by nature are no gods. But now, after that ye have known God, or rather are known of God, how turn ye again to the weak and beggarly elements, whereunto ye desire again to be in bondage?

From this verse to the end of the epistle, Paul gives precepts regarding manners. But he first reproves the Galatians, because he is sore displeased that this divine and heavenly doctrine should be so suddenly and easily removed out of their hearts. As if he would say, "You have teachers who will bring you back to the bondage of the law. This I did not do: but by my doctrine I called you out of darkness into a wonderful light and clear knowledge of God. I brought you out of bondage, and set you in the freedom of the sons of God, by the grace and righteousness of God in the giving of heavenly and eternal blessing through Christ. Why, then, do you allow yourselves to be so easily brought from grace to the law and from freedom to bondage?"

But why does Paul say that the Galatians turned back to weak and beggarly elements, rudiments, or ceremonies: that is, to the law, since they never had the law, for they were Gentiles? Why didn't he say, "Once, when you knew not God, you did service to them which were no gods, but now seeing you know God, why do you turn back again, forsaking the true God, to worship idols?'' Does Paul take it to be all one thing to fall from the promise to the law, from faith to works, and to do service to them which by nature are no gods? I answer, whoever is fallen from the article of justification is ignorant of God, and is an idolater. Therefore, it is all one thing, whether he turns again to the law, or to the worshiping of idols; for when this article is taken away, there remains nothing but error, hypocrisy, impiety, and idolatry, no matter how in outward appearance it seems to be the very truth, the true service of God, and true holiness.

The reason is, because God will or can be known no other way than by Christ, according to John 1:18: ''The only begotten Son, which is in the bosom of the Father, He hath declared Him.'' He is the seed promised to Abraham, in whom God has established all His promises. Wherefore Christ is the only means, and, as we might say, the glass by which we see God and know His will. In Christ we see that God is not a cruel exactor or judge, but a most favorable, loving, and merciful Father who, to the end that He might bless us—that is, deliver us from the law, sin, death, and all evils, and might endue us with grace, righteousness, and everlasting life—''spared not his own Son, but delivered him up for us all'' (Romans 8:32). This is a true knowledge of God, and a divine persuasion, which deceives us not but depicts a living God.

He that is fallen from this knowledge conceives this fantasy in his heart: I will set up such a service of God, I will do this or that work, and I doubt not that God will accept my service and reward me with everlasting life for the same. For He is merciful and liberal, giving all good things even to the unworthy and the unthankful; much more then will He give to me grace and everlasting life for my good deeds and merits. This is the highest wisdom, righteousness, and religion that reason can judge of, and is common to all nations. They can go no higher than that Pharisee did, of whom it is said in the gospel he made profession: ''I fast twice in the week; I give tithes of all that I possess'' (Luke 18:12). They have no knowledge of Christian righteousness, or the righteousness of faith: ''For the natural man discerneth not the mysteries of God'' (1 Corinthians 2:14). There is therefore no difference except the difference of place, rites, religions, works, and worshipings, for there is one heart, opinion, and cogitation in them all.

Wherefore it is an extreme madness that they strive among themselves about the religion and service of God, contending that each of them have the true religion and proper worship of God. Though outward ceremonies may differ, yet in their hearts their opinion is alike, that one egg is not more like to another. For this is the thinking of them all: if I do this work and obey this rule, God will have mercy upon me; if I do it not, He will be angry. Therefore, every man that revolts from the knowledge of Christ falls into idolatry and conceives such a notion of God as is not agreeable to His nature.

Such a god, who in this way forgives sins and justifies sinners, can nowhere be found. Therefore, this is but a vain imagination, a dream, and an idol of the heart. For God has not promised that He will save and justify men for their religions, observations, ceremonies, and ordinances devised by men; God abhors nothing more (as the Scripture says) than such will-works, rites, and ceremonies, for which He overthrows kingdoms and empires. Therefore, as many as trust to their own strength and righteousness serve a god they themselves have devised, and not the true God. For the true God speaks thus: "No righteousness, wisdom, or religion pleases Me, but only that by which the Father is glorified through the Son. Whoever apprehends the Son and Me, and My promise in Him, by faith, to him I am God indeed, and a Father; him do I accept, justify and save." All others abide under wrath, because they worship that thing which by nature is no god.

Whoever forsakes this doctrine falls into ignorance of God; he understands not what the true Christian righteousness, wisdom, and service of God is: he is an idolater, abiding under the law, sin, death, and the power of the devil.

There are at this very day many who would be counted as the true professors of the gospel; and concerning words, they teach that men are delivered from their sins by the death of Christ. But because they attribute more to charity than to faith, they highly dishonor Christ and wickedly pervert His Word. For they dream that God regards and accepts us for our charities' sake. If this is true, then have we no need of Christ at all. Such men serve not the true God, but an idol of their own heart, which they themselves have devised. For the true God does not regard us or accept us for our charity, virtues, or newness of life, but for Christ's sake.

But they make this objection: the Scriptures command that we should love God with all our heart. It is true. But it follows not that because God commanded it, we do it. If we did love God with all our heart, then no doubt we should be justified, and live through our obedience, as it is written: "He that shall do these things shall live in them" (Leviticus 18:5; Romans 10:5). But the gospel says: You do not these things, therefore you shall not live in them. For this verse, "Thou shalt love the Lord thy God," requires a perfect obedience, a perfect fear, trust, and love towards God. These things men neither do nor can perform in this corrupt nature. Therefore this law, "Thou shalt love the Lord thy God," justifies not, but accuses, and condemns, according to that saying, the law causes wrath (Romans 4:15). Contrariwise, "Christ is the end of the law for righteousness to every one that believeth" (Romans 10:4). Of this we have spoken largely before.

How may these two contrary sayings, which the Apostle here sets down, be reconciled? "Ye knew not God, and ye worshiped God." I answer, All men naturally have this general knowledge, that there is a God, according to that saying: "Because as that which may be known of God is manifest in them" (Romans 1:19). For God was manifest in that the invisible things of Him did appear by the creation of the world. Moreover, the religions and ceremonies which were, and always remained among all nations, sufficiently witness that all men have had a certain general knowledge of God. But whether they had it by nature, or by the tradition of their forefathers, I will not here dispute.

But here some will object again: If all men knew God, why does Paul say that the Galatians knew not God before the preaching of the gospel? I answer, There is a double knowledge of God: general and particular. All men have the general knowledge, namely, that there is a God, that He created heaven and earth, that He is just, that He punishes the wicked. But what God thinks of us, what His will is towards us, what He will give, or what He will do so we may be delivered from sin and death, and be saved (which is the true knowledge of God indeed), this they know not. It may be that I know some man by sight, whom yet, I know not thoroughly, because I understand not what affection he bears towards me. So men naturally know that there is a God; but what His will is, or what is not His will, they do not know. For it is written: "There is none that understandeth, there is none that seeketh after God" (Romans 3:11). And in another place: "No man hath seen God at any time" (John 1:18). That is to say, no man has known what the will of God is. Now, what does it avail you, if you know that there is a God, and yet are ignorant of His will toward you? Here some think one thing, and some another. But all these are deceived, and become vain in their imaginations, as Paul says (Romans 1), not knowing what pleases or displeases God. Therefore, instead of the true God, they worship the dreams of their own hearts.

This is what Paul means when he says: "When ye knew not God"; that is, when you knew not the will of God, you served them which by nature were no gods. Upon this proposition, namely, that there is a God, has sprung all idolatry which, without the knowledge of the divinity, could never have come into the world. But because men had this natural knowledge of God, they conceived vain and wicked imaginations of God, without and against the Word, and so dreamed that God is such a one as by nature He is not. Now reason itself will enforce us to confess that man's opinion is no good. Therefore, whoever will worship God without His Word serves not the true God, as Paul says.

Whether we call the rudiments here the law of Moses, or else the traditions of the Gentiles (though Paul speaks chiefly of the law of Moses here), there is no great difference. For he that falls from grace to the law falls with no less danger than he that falls from grace to idolatry. For without Christ there is nothing else but mere idolatry.

Therefore, says Paul, with a certain admiration: "But now, seeing ye know God." As though he would say, This is a marvelous thing, that you, knowing God by the preaching of faith, so suddenly revolt from the true knowledge of His will, and do now again, at the instigation of the false apostles, return to the weak and beggarly elements and ceremonies, which you would serve again. You heard before, by my preaching, that it is the will of God to bless all nations: not by circumcision, or by the observation of the law, but by Christ promised to Abraham. They that believe in Him shall be blessed with faithful Abraham (Galatians 3:9). They are the sons and heirs of God. Thus (I say) have you known God.

Then he corrects the previous sentence, "seeing ye know God," and turns it after this manner, "yes, rather are known of God"; for he feared lest they had lost God utterly. As if he would say, "Alas! Are you come to this point that you know not God, but have departed from grace to be under the law? Even thus, God knows you." And indeed, our knowledge is rather passive than active; that is, it consists of this, that we are rather known of God than that we know Him. All our endeavor to know and to apprehend God is to allow God to work in us. He gives the Word, which when we have received by faith given from above, we are new-born, and made the sons of God. This then is the sense and meaning: "Ye are known of God"; that is, you are endued with faith and the Holy Ghost, whereby you are renewed and become new creatures. So, even by these words, he takes away all righteousness from the law, and denies that we attain the knowledge of God through the worthiness of our own works. "For no man knoweth the Father but the Son, and he to whom the Son will reveal him" (Luke 10:22). And also, "he by His knowledge shall justify many, for he shall bear their iniquities" (Isaiah 53:11). Wherefore our knowledge concerning God consists in suffering and not in doing.

He marvels that seeing they knew God truly by the gospel, they returned so suddenly to weak and beggarly elements, by the persuasion of the false apostles. As I myself should greatly marvel, if our Church (reformed in pure doctrine and faith) should be seduced by some fanatic, so that the members would own me as their pastor no more. That will yet someday come to pass, if not while we live, when we are dead and gone. For many shall then rise up who will be pastors and teachers, and shall spread abroad false and perverse doctrine, and shall quickly overthrow all that in so long a time we have built. Yet, notwithstanding, Christ shall remain and reign to the end of the world, and that marvelously.

Paul seems to speak very spitefully of the law when he calls it the rudiments, and weak and beggarly elements, and ceremonies. Is it not blasphemy to give such odious names to the law of God? The law ought to stand with the promises and grace. But, if it fights against them, it is no more the holy law of God but a false and devilish doctrine, and does nothing but drive men to desperation, and therefore must be rejected.

Wherefore when he calls the law weak and beggarly elements, he speaks of the law in respect of proud and presumptuous hypocrites who would be justified by it, and not of the law being spiritually understood. Paul here talks of hypocrites who are fallen from grace, or who have not attained to grace. These, abusing the law, seek to be justified by it. They exercise and tire themselves day and night in the works thereof, as Paul witnesses of the Jews: "For I bear record that they have the zeal of God, but not according to knowledge: for they being ignorant of the righteousness of God, go about to establish their own righteousness" (Romans 10:3). They hope to be enriched by the law and so to appease God and be saved. In this respect we may well say that the law is a weak and beggarly element which can neither give help nor counsel.

Paul therefore shows that they who seek to be justified by the law become daily more weak and beggarly. For of themselves they are weak and beggarly; that is, they are by nature the children of wrath, subject to death and condemnation; yet they seek to be strengthened by that which is weak. This thing the gospel witnesses in the case of the woman who was grieved with a bloody issue twelve years, and having spent her substance on many physicians, grew worse and worse (Mark 5:25). Even so as many as seek to be justified by works are not only not made righteous, but twice more unrighteous than they were before. This I have proved to be true in myself and in many others. I have known many who with great zeal have done great works, for the attaining of righteousness and salvation, yet were they more impatient, more weak, more miserable, faithless, more fearful, and more ready to despair than any other.

Whoever then seeketh righteousness by the law, imagining that God being angry and threatening must be pacified with works, can never find so many good works as are able to quiet his conscience, but still desires more. Yes, he finds sins in those works he has done already. Therefore, his conscience can never be certified, but he must always be in doubt and think to himself: You have not sacrificed as you should; you have not prayed properly; this you have left undone; this or that sin you have committed. Here the heart trembles and feels itself oppressed with innumerable sins, which still increase without end, so that he swerves from righteousness more and more, until at length he falls into desperation. At this point, many being at the point of death have uttered these desperate words: "O wretch that I am! I have not kept my order. Where shall I flee from the wrath of Christ, that angry judge? Would to God I had been made a swineherd, or the vilest wretch in the whole world."

Thus the monk at the end of his life is more weak, more beggarly, more faithless and fearful than he was at the beginning, when he first entered into his order. The reason is because he would strengthen himself through weakness, and enrich himself through poverty. The law, or men's traditions, or the rule of his order should have healed him when he was sick, and enriched him when he was poor; but he is become more feeble and more poor than the publicans and harlots. The publicans and harlots have not a heap of good works to trust unto, as the monks have; but although they feel their sins ever so much, yet they can say with the publican: "God, be merciful to me a sinner!" (Luke 18:13). But contrariwise the monk, regardless of all the works which he has done, be they ever so many and so great, thinks that he has never done enough, but has still an eye to more works; and so, by heaping up of works, he goes about to appease the wrath of God and to justify himself until he is driven to utter desperation. Wherefore, whoever falls from faith and follows the law is like Aesop's dog, which foregoes the flesh, and snatches at the shadow.

Wherefore, it is impossible that such as seek salvation by the law should ever find quietness and peace of conscience; yes, they do nothing else but heap laws upon laws, whereby they torment both themselves and others, and afflict men's consciences so miserably that through extreme anguish of heart, many die before their time. For one law always brings forth ten more, and so they increase without number and without end.

Now who would have thought that the Galatians, which had learned so sound and so pure a doctrine of such an excellent Apostle and teacher, could be so suddenly led away from the same, and utterly perverted by the false apostles? It is not without cause that I repeat this so often, that to fall away from the truth of the gospel is an easy matter. The reason is, because even godly men do not sufficiently consider what a precious and a necessary treasure the true knowledge of Christ is. Therefore, they do not labor as diligently and carefully as they should, to obtain and to retain the same. Moreover, the greater part of those that hear the Word are exercised with no cross; they wrestle not against sin, death, and the devil, but live in security without any conflict. Such men because they are not proved and tried with temptations, and therefore are not armed with the Word of God against the subtleties of the devil, never feel the use and power of the Word. Indeed, while they are among faithful ministers and preachers, they can follow their words, and say as they say, persuading themselves that they perfectly understand the matter of justification. But when they are gone, and wolves in sheep's clothing are come in their place, it happens to them as it did to the Galatians; that is to say, they are suddenly seduced and easily turned back to weak and beggarly elements.

The meaning therefore of Paul is this, that he would not have the conscience to serve under the law as a captive, but to be free and to have dominion over the law. For the conscience is dead to the law through Christ, and the law again unto the conscience.

10—Ye observe days, and months, and times, and years.

By these words he plainly declares what the false apostles taught, namely, the observation of days, months, times and years. Almost all the doctors have interpreted this verse as concerning the astrological days of the Chaldeans, saying that the Gentiles in doing business or awaiting the issues of life and affairs, did observe certain fixed days and months, and that the Galatians at the bidding of the false apostles did also the same. Augustine, whom others thereafter followed, expounded these words of

Paul as concerning that Gentile custom, although afterwards he interpreted them also of the days and months of the Jews.

But Paul here instructs the conscience; therefore, he speaks not of that
Gentile custom of observing days, which pertain only to the body, but he
speaks of the law of God, and of the observation of days and months
according to the law of Moses; that is to say, concerning religious days,
months, and seasons, which the Galatians taught by the false apostles
observed for justification. For Moses had commanded the Jews to keep
holy the Sabbath day, the new moons, the first and the seventh month, the
three appointed times or feasts (namely the Passover, the Feast of Weeks,
and of the Tabernacles) and the year of Jubilee. These ceremonies the
Galatians were constrained by the false apostles to keep as necessary to
righteousness. Therefore, he says that they, losing the grace and liberty
which they had in Christ, were turned back to the serving of weak and
beggarly elements. For they were persuaded by the false apostles that
these laws must be kept, and by keeping them they should obtain
righteousness; but if they kept them not, they should be damned.
Contrariwise, Paul can not allow men's consciences to be bound to the
law of Moses, but always delivers them from the law. ''Behold, I Paul,''
(says he, a little after in the fifth chapter), ''say unto you, that if ye be
circumcised, Christ shall profit you nothing''; and, ''Let no man
therefore judge you in meat, or in drink, or in respect of an holyday, or
of the new moon, or of the sabbath days'' (Colossians 2:16). So says our
Savior Christ: ''The kingdom of God cometh not with observation''
(Luke 17:20). Much less then are men's consciences to be burdened and
snared with human traditions.

Here some man may say: If the Galatians sinned in observing days and
seasons, how is it not sin when you do the same? I answer: We observe
the Lord's day, the day of His Nativity, Easter, and such feasts, with all
liberty. We burden not consciences with these ceremonies, neither teach
as the false apostles did that they are necessary to righteousness, or that
we can make satisfaction for sins by them; but we keep them to the end
that all may be done orderly and without tumult in the Church, and that
outward concord (for in spirit we have another concord) be not broken.

We chiefly observe such feasts to the end that the ministry of the Word may be preserved, that the people may assemble themselves at certain days and times to hear the Word, to come to the knowledge of God, to have communion, to pray together for all necessities, and to give thanks to God for all His benefits both bodily and spiritual. And it was for this cause above all, I believe, that the observation of the Lord's day, Easter, and Pentecost was instituted by the fathers.

11—I am afraid of you, lest I have bestowed upon you labour in vain.

Here Paul shows himself to be greatly troubled through the fall of the Galatians; he would more bitterly reprove them, but he fears that if he should deal with them more sharply, he should not only not make them better, but more offend them, and so utterly alienate their minds from him. Therefore, in writing he changes his words; and as though all the harm redounded unto himself, he says: "I am afraid of you, lest I have bestowed my labour upon you in vain"; that is to say, it grieves me that I have preached the gospel with so great diligence and faithfulness among you, and see no fruit come of it. Notwithstanding, although he shows a very loving and a fatherly affection towards them, yet he chides them somewhat sharply, but yet covertly. For when he says that he had labored in vain, that is to say, that he had preached the gospel among them without any fruit, he shows covertly that either they were obstinate unbelievers, or else were fallen from the doctrine of faith. Now both these, unbelievers as well as backsliders from the doctrine of faith, are sinners, wicked, unrighteous, and damned. Such therefore obey the law in vain; they observe days, months, and years in vain. And these words, "I am afraid of you, lest I have bestowed upon you labour in vain," contain a secret excommunication. For the apostle means that the Galatians were secluded and separate from Christ unless they speedily returned to sound and sincere doctrine again; yet he pronounced no open sentence against them. For he perceived that he could do no good with over-sharp dealing; wherefore he changes his style.

12—Be as I am; for I am as ye are.

Now the greater part of his epistle being finished, and the blame given, he begins to perceive that he had handled them too sharply. Therefore, being careful lest he should do more harm than good through his severity, he wishes to show that his chiding proceeds from a fatherly affection and a true apostolic heart; so he qualifies the matter with sweet and gentle words, to the end that those who were offended by correction might be won again by sweetness.

And here he shows to all pastors and ministers that they ought to bear a fatherly affection, not towards ravening wolves, but towards the poor sheep, miserably seduced and going astray, patiently bearing with their faults and infirmities, and restoring them with the spirit of meekness, for they cannot be brought into the right way by any other means. And here it is to be noted, by the way, that such is the nature and fruit of true and sound doctrine that when it is well taught and well understood, it joins men's hearts together with a singular concord; but when men reject godly and true doctrine, this unity and concord is soon broken. Therefore, as soon as you see your brethren seduced by false apostles from the article of justification, you shall perceive that they will pursue with bitter hatred those whom before they most tenderly loved.

This we find true at this day, in our false brethren, who at the beginning of the reformation of the gospel, were glad to hear us, and read our books with zeal and affection; they acknowledged the grace of the Holy Ghost in us, and reverenced us for the same as the ministers of God. Some of them also lived with us for a while and behaved themselves very modestly and soberly; but when they were departed from us and perverted by the wicked doctrine of the sectaries, they showed themselves more bitter enemies to our doctrine and our name than any other. I do much and often marvel why they should conceive such hatred against us, whom once they loved; for we offended them not, nor gave them any occasion to hate us. Verily, there is no other cause, but they have gotten to themselves new masters and teachers, whose poison has so infected them that now of very friends they are become mortal enemies. There were very few among the

Galatians who continued in the sound doctrine of the Apostles. All the rest, being seduced by the false apostles, did not acknowledge Paul for their pastor and teacher anymore. And I fear that this epistle brought very few of them back from their error.

Wherefore, to fall in faith is an easy matter, but most perilous, to wit, from high heaven into the deep pit of hell. For they who so fall cannot easily be recovered, but most commonly they remain perverse and obstinate in their error. Therefore, the latter end of these men is worse than the beginning, as our Savior Christ witnesses when He says: "When the unclean spirit is gone out of a man . . . when he returneth, he taketh with himself seven other spirits more wicked than himself, and they enter in and dwell there" (Matthew 12:43–45).

Paul therefore, perceiving through the revelation of the Holy Ghost that it was to be feared lest the minds of the Galatians, whom he had called foolish and bewitched, should rather be stirred up against him by his sharp chiding, is so troubled that he cannot tell what and how to write to them. So, being in this perplexity, he says: "I am troubled, I am at my wit's end for your sakes"; that is, I know not how to deal with you.

> *12—Brethren, I beseech you, be as I am; for I am as ye are: ye have not injured me at all.*

These words are to be understood, not of doctrine, but of affections. The meaning is not, "Be ye as I am, that is to say, think of doctrine as I do," but "Bear such an affection towards me as I do towards you." It is as though he would say, if I have sharply chided you, pardon my sharpness, and judge not my heart by my words, but my words by the affection of my heart. For my heart is loving and fatherly.

Even so, we may also say of ourselves: Our correction is severe, and our manner of writing vehement; but there is no bitterness in our heart, no envy, no desire of revenge; instead, there is in us a godly care and a sorrow of spirit.

The schoolmaster chastises the scholar, not to hurt him, but to reform him. The rod is sharp, but correction is necessary for the child, and the heart of him that corrects, loving and friendly. So the father chastises his son, not to destroy him but to reform and amend him. Stripes are sharp and grievous to the child, but the father's heart is loving and kind; and unless he loved his child, he would not chastise him, but cast him off, despair of his welfare, and suffer him to perish. This correction therefore which he gives his child is a token of fatherly affection, and is very profitable for the child. Even so, O my Galatians, think likewise of my dealing towards you: then you will not judge my chiding to be sharp and bitter, but profitable for you. "No chastening for the present seemeth to be joyous, but grievous: nevertheless afterward it yieldeth the peaceable fruit of righteousness" (Hebrews 12:11). Let the same affection therefore be in you towards me which I bear towards you. I bear a loving heart towards you; the same I desire again of you.

With this fair speech he still continues, that he might pacify their minds which were stirred up against him by his sharp chiding. Notwithstanding, he revokes not his severe words. Indeed, he confesses that they were sharp and bitter; but necessity (says he) compelled me to reprehend you somewhat sharply and severely. But that which I did proceeded from a sincere and loving heart towards you. The physician gives a bitter potion to his patient, not to hurt him, but to cure him. If then the bitterness of the medicine, which is given to the sick body, is not to be imputed to the physician, but to the medicine and the malady, consider my severe and sharp chiding in the same way.

Ye have not injured me at all. It is as much as if he said: I confess that I have chided you somewhat bitterly; but take it in good part, and then shall you find this my chiding to be no chiding, but a praying and a beseeching. If a father sharply corrects his son, it is as much as if he said: My son, I pray thee to be a good child. It seems to be a scolding; but if you consider the father's heart, it is a gentle and earnest beseeching.

You have not offended me, but yourselves, and therefore I am troubled, not for myself, but for the love I bear you. Think not therefore that my chiding did proceed out of malice or any evil affection. For I take God to witness, you have done me no wrong, but have bestowed great benefits upon me.

Thus he prepares their minds to suffer his fatherly chastisement with a childlike affection. And this is to temper wormwood or a bitter potion with honey and sugar, to make it sweet again. So parents speak gently to their children after they have well beaten them, giving them apples, pears, and other like things, whereby the children know that their parents love them and seek to do them good, however sharp their correction appears.

13, 14—Ye know how through infirmity of the flesh I preached the gospel unto you at the first. And my temptation which was in my flesh ye despised not, nor rejected, but received me as an angel of God, even as Jesus Christ.

Here he declares the benefits he had received of the Galatians. The first, which was the greatest of all, was this: When I first began to preach the gospel among you through infirmity of the flesh and great temptations, my cross did not offend you, but you showed yourselves loving and kind, and even received me as an angel of God, yes, rather, as Jesus Christ Himself. This is indeed a great commendation of the Galatians, that they received the gospel from a man so afflicted on every side as Paul was. For all the mighty, wise, religious, and learned men hated, persecuted, and slandered Paul. But with all this, the Galatians not only heard this poor, despised, afflicted Paul, but acknowledged themselves to be his disciples, and received the Word of God from him as though he had been an angel. Such a generous commendation he gives to no one else, besides these Galatians.

Jerome, and certain other of the ancient fathers, expound this infirmity of the flesh to be some disease of the body, or some temptation of lust. These men lived when the Church was outwardly in a peaceable and prosperous condition, without any cross or persecution. Then the bishops began to increase in riches, estimation, and glory in the world, and many even exercised tyranny over the people, as the ecclesiastical history witnesses. Few did their duty, and they that would seem to do it, forsaking the doctrine of the gospel, set forth their own decrees. Now, when bishops and pastors are not exercised in the Word of God, they fall into security; for they are not exercised with temptations, with crosses and persecutions, which usually always follow the pure preaching of the Word. Therefore, it was impossible that they should understand Paul. But we, by the grace of God, have sound and sincere doctrine, which also we preach freely, and therefore are compelled to suffer the hatred, afflictions, and persecutions of the devil and the world. And if we were not exercised outwardly by tyrants and sectaries, with force and subtlety, and inwardly with terrors and fiery darts of the devil, Paul should be as obscure and unknown to us as he was in times past to the whole world. Therefore, the gift of knowledge, interpretation of the Scriptures, and our study—together with our outward and inward temptations—open to us the meaning of Paul, and the sense of the Holy Scriptures.

Paul, therefore, calls the infirmity of the flesh no disease of the body, or temptation of lust, but his suffering and affliction, which he sustained in his body; which he sets against the virtue and power of the Spirit. But, lest we pervert Paul's words, let us hear him speaking in 2 Corinthians 12:9, 10: "Most gladly therefore will I rather glory in mine infirmities, that the power of Christ may rest upon me. Therefore, I take pleasure in infirmities, in reproaches, in necessities, in persecutions, in distresses for Christ's sake: for when I am weak, then am I strong." And in the eleventh chapter: "In labours more abundant, in stripes above measure, in prisons more frequent, in death oft. Of the Jews five times received I forty stripes save one. Thrice was I beaten with rods, once was I stoned, thrice I suffered shipwreck. . . ." These sufferings and afflictions which he experienced in his body he calls the infirmity of the flesh, and not any corporal disease. He makes mention of this his infirmity in many places, as in 1 Corinthians 4:12; 2 Corinthians 4:9, 11, 12, and in many others.

We see then that Paul calls afflictions the infirmities of the flesh, as the other Apostles, the prophets, and all godly men did; notwithstanding, he was mighty in spirit. For the power of Christ was in him, which always reigned and triumphed through him. He testifies in 2 Corinthians 12, "For when I am weak, then am I strong"; and again: "Thanks be to God, who always maketh us to triumph in Christ." As though he would say,

"Indeed our foes may rage cruelly against us, yet we continue constant and invincible against all their assaults, and our doctrine prevails." This was the strength and power of spirit in Paul, against which he sets here the infirmity and bondage of the flesh.

This infirmity of the flesh in the godly offends reason. Therefore, Paul highly commends the Galatians because they were not offended with his great infirmity, and with the contemptible forms of the cross which they saw in him; but they received him as an angel, yes, as Christ Jesus. And Christ Himself also arms the faithful against base and contemptible forms of the cross, in which He appears, when He says: "Blessed is he that shall not be offended in Me" (Matthew 11:6). Surely it is a great matter that they who believe in Him do acknowledge Him to be Lord of all and Savior of the world, even though they know that He has been a very scorn of men and a contempt to the world (Psalms 22:7). This is a great matter, I say, that believers are not moved with these great offenses; instead, they esteem this poor Christ, so spitefully used, spit upon, scourged, and crucified, more than the riches of the richest, the strength of the strongest, the wisdom of the wisest, the holiest of all the holy, with all the crowns the scepters of all the kings and princes of the whole world. They therefore are worthily called blessed of Christ, who are not offended in Him.

Now Paul had not only outward temptations, but also inward and spiritual temptations, as Christ had in the garden. He speaks of these in 2 Corinthians 12 where he writes of "the thorn in the flesh, the messenger of Satan to buffet me." It was a spiritual temptation. And herein is no repugnance, that he added the word *flesh*, "a thorn in the flesh." For the Galatians and others had seen him often in great heaviness, anguish, and terror. The spiritual temptations he confesses in 2 Corinthians 7:5: "Fightings without and fears within." And Luke says in the Acts that Paul "thanked God, and took courage" when he was welcomed by the brethren at Appii forum, after his depression in the tempest (Acts 28:15).

But why was Paul not despised by the Galatians? It seemed that they despised him when they fell away from his gospel. Yet he says, when I first preached to you, you did not do as others have done, who, offended

at my infirmity and temptation of the flesh, despised and rejected me. For
man's reason is soon offended with this contemptible form of the cross,
and judges them to be stark mad who, being so afflicted themselves, go
about to comfort, help, and succor others. Also, those who boast of their
riches in Christ, that is, righteousness, strength, victory over sin, and
death, and all evils; of joy, salvation, and everlasting life—and yet are
poor, needy, weak, heavyhearted and despised, evil-entreated, and slain
as noxious to civil government and religion, while they who kill them
think they do God service (John 16:2). These, I say, are scorned of men,
and compelled to hear: "Physician, heal thyself." And hereof come the
complaints of the Psalms: "I am a worm, and no man." "Trouble is near;
for there is none to help" (Psalms 22:6, 11).

It is a great commendation, therefore, that the Galatians did not so act,
but, on the contrary, received Paul as an angel, yes, as Christ Jesus. So
he commends them and tells them he will always remember it and will
greatly esteem them for it. By these words, he shows how entirely they
loved and trusted him before the coming of the false apostles, and he
moves them to return and embrace him with no less love than they did
before.

15a—Where is then the blessedness ye spake of?

As if he would say, How happy were you counted? How much were
you then praised and commended. The like manner of speech we have in
the song of the Virgin Mary: "All generations shall call me blessed."
These words, "Where is the blessedness ye spake of?" contain a
vehemence. Paul is saying, You were not only blessed, but in all things,
most blessed, and most commended. Thus he goes about to mitigate his
sharp chiding, fearing that the Galatians should be offended, especially
since the false apostles would take hold of his words and slander him; for
the nature of these vipers is to pervert words which proceed from a simple
and sincere heart and wrest them exactly contrary to their true meaning.
They are marvelously cunning workmen in this matter, far passing the wit
and eloquence of all the rhetoricians. For they are led by a wicked spirit,

which so bewitches them that they cannot do otherwise but maliciously pervert their words and writings. Therefore are they like the spider that sucks venom out of sweet and pleasant flowers, and this proceeds not of the flowers, but of his own venomous nature, which turns that into poison which is of itself good and wholesome. Paul therefore, by these mild words, goes about to prevent the false apostles, to the end that they should have no occasion to slander and pervert his words after this manner: Paul calls you foolish, bewitched, and disobedient to the truth, which is a sure token that he seeks not your salvation, but accounts you damned and rejected by Christ.

15—For I bear you record, that if it had been possible, ye would have plucked out your own eyes, and have given them to me.

He praises the Galatians above measure. You did not only treat me most courteously, says Paul, but you would have plucked out your eyes for me. Yes, you would have given your lives for me, for in that you received me, and maintained me (whom the world counted most execrable), you turned on your own heads the hatred and indignation of both the Jews and the Gentiles.

So also, at this day, the name of Luther is most odious to the world. He that praises me sins worse than any idolater, blasphemer, perjurer, whoremonger, adulterer, murderer, or thief. It must be, therefore, that the Galatians were well established in the doctrine and faith of Christ, seeing that they with so great danger to their lives received and maintained Paul, who was hated throughout the world. Otherwise, they would never have sustained the cruel hatred of the whole world.

16—Am I therefore become your enemy, because I tell you the truth?

Here he shows the reason why he speaks to them so gently; for he suspects that they took him for their enemy, because he had reproved them so sharply. I pray you, set apart these rebukes, and separate them from doctrine, and you shall find that my purpose was not to rebuke you, but to teach you the truth. I confess that my epistle is sharp and severe; but by this severity I go about to call you back again to the truth of the gospel, from which you are fallen; therefore apply this bitter medicine, not to your persons, but to your disease, and think of me not as an enemy, but as your father. Unless I loved you as my children, I would not have reproved you so sharply.

It is the part of a friend to admonish his friend when he does something wrong. And when the friend is admonished, he is not angry but gives thanks to his friend. In the world, truth causes hatred; he is accounted an enemy who speaks the truth. But among friends, this is not so; much less among Christians.

17—They zealously affect you, but not well; yea, they would exclude you, that ye might affect them.

Paul reproves here the flattery of the false apostles; for Satan aims, by his ministers, with subtlety and craft, to beguile the simple: as Paul says elsewhere, "by good words and fair speeches they deceive the hearts of the simple" (Romans 16:18). For first of all they make great protestations that they seek nothing else but the advancement of God's glory, and that they are moved by the Spirit to teach the infallible truth, that the elect may be delivered from error, and may come to the true light, and knowledge of the truth. Moreover, they promise undoubted salvation to those who receive their doctrine. The Galatians might say, why do you inveigh so much against our teachers, for that they be so zealous over us? that is for love and care of us; this ought not to offend thee. Indeed, says he, they are jealous over you, but their jealousy is not good or for your benefit. Here note that zeal or jealousy signifies angry love, or a godly envy. Elijah says, "I have been very jealous for the Lord God of hosts" (1 Kings 19:10). After this manner the husband is jealous towards his wife, the father towards his son, and the brother towards his brother, because they love them; yet so, they hate their vices, and go about to mend them. Such a zeal the false apostles pretended to bear towards the Galatians. Paul confesses that they were very zealous, but their zeal, says he, was not good. He therefore warns us to put a difference between a good zeal and an evil zeal. I am as zealous over you as they, Paul says; now judge which of our zeals is best, mine or theirs: which is good and which is evil. Wherefore let not their evil zeal seduce you.

"For they would exclude us, that ye might affect them." True, they are very zealous towards you, but they seek to make you zealous toward them and to reject me. They hate our doctrine, and desire that it be utterly abolished and their own preached among you. To this end, they go about by this jealousy to pluck your hearts from me, and to make me odious unto you; so that when you have conceived hatred of me and my doctrine, you should love them only, and receive no doctrine but theirs. Thus he brings suspicion upon the false apostles, showing the Galatians that they are being deceived by them. So our Savior Christ also warns us, "Beware of false prophets, which come to you in sheep's clothing" (Matthew 7:15).

Paul suffered the same temptation which we suffer at this day. He was greatly troubled that after the preaching of his doctrine, which was divine and holy, he saw so many sects, commotions, false teachers, and other like things, which were the cause of evils and offenses. He was accused by the Jews of being a pestilent fellow, a mover of sedition in his nation, and of being the leader of the sect of the Nazarenes (Acts 24:5). The Gentiles also cried out against him in Philippi that he was a troubler of the city, and preached customs which were not lawful for them to receive (Acts 16:20, 21).

Such other troubles, as famines, wars, dissensions, and sects, the Jews and Gentiles imputed to the doctrine of Paul and the other Apostles; therefore they persecuted them as common plagues, enemies of the public peace and of religion.

Yet the Apostles did not for this cease to do their office, but constantly preached and confessed Christ; for they would obey God rather than men (Acts 5:29), and reasoned it better that the whole world should be in an uproar than that Christ should not be preached. It was, no doubt, a heavy cross to the Apostles to see these offenses, for they were not made of iron. They grieved that the Jewish people, for whose sake Paul wished to be separate from Christ, should perish in their errors (Romans 9:3). It was heavy news to Paul when he heard that the Corinthians denied the resurrection of the dead, and that all Asia was revolted from his doctrine.

But he knew that his doctrine was not the cause of these offenses and divisions, and therefore was not discouraged, but went forward, knowing that the gospel which he preached was the power of God unto salvation to all that believe, though it seemed to Jews and Gentiles a foolish and offensive doctrine (Romans 1:16). Therefore, he says, as Christ did of those offended at His teaching: "Let them alone: they be blind leaders of the blind" (Matthew 15:14).

We are also constrained at this day to hear the same spoken of us which was said of Paul: that the doctrine of the gospel, which we profess, is the cause of great enormities, as wars, seditions, sects, and numerous offenses. Surely we preach no heresies, or wicked doctrine, but we preach the glad tidings concerning Christ, that He is our high priest and our Redeemer. At the beginning of the gospel, the more the priests and rulers forbade the Apostles to preach in the name of Christ, the more they gave witness that the same Jesus, whom they had crucified, is both Lord and Christ, that whoever should call on His Name should be saved, and that there is no other name under heaven given unto men, whereby they may be saved (Acts 2:21, 36). Even so we now preach Christ, not regarding the clamors of all our adversaries, who cry out that our doctrine is seditious, that it troubles commonwealths, overthrows religion, teaches heresies, and, in short, is the cause of all evils. The same was said when Christ and His Apostles preached.

We will continue to speak and set forth the wonderful works of the Lord as long as we have breath, and will endure the persecutions of our adversaries, until the time that Christ, our high priest and King, shall come from heaven, who, we hope, will come shortly, as a just judge, to take vengeance upon all those that obey not His gospel. So be it.

There are very many at this day who are possessed with the zeal of which the Apostle here speaks: who pretend great religion, modesty, doctrine, and patience, and yet, in very deed, are ravening wolves, seeking only to discredit us that the people may esteem, love, and reverence them only, and receive no doctrine but theirs. We cannot remedy this, as Paul could not in his time. Notwithstanding, he gained some by his admonitions; so I hope do we.

> *18—But it is good to be zealously affected always in a good thing, and not only when I am present with you.*

I commend you for this, Paul says, that you loved me so entirely when I preached the gospel among you in the infirmity of the flesh. You ought to bear the same affection towards me now, when I am absent, even as if I had never departed from you; for, although I am absent in body, yet you have my doctrine, which you ought to retain and maintain, seeing you received the Holy Ghost through it. I do not therefore reprehend your zeal, but I praise it, as far as it is a zeal of God or of the Spirit, and not of the flesh. Now the zeal of the Spirit is always good; for it is an earnest affection and motion of the heart to a good thing, and so is not the zeal of the flesh. He commends therefore the zeal of the Galatians that he may pacify their minds and that they may patiently suffer his correction. As if he would say: Take my correction in good part; for it proceeds of no anger or malice, but of a sorrowful heart and care for your salvation. This is a good example to teach all ministers how to be careful for their sheep, and to try every way, that by chiding, fair speaking, or entreating, they may keep them in sound doctrine, and turn them from subtle seducers and false teachers.

> *19—My little children, of whom I travail in birth again until Christ be formed in you.*

All his words are weighty and fitly framed to the purpose that they may move the hearts of the Galatians, and win their favor again. And these are sweet and loving words, when he calls them his little children. When he says: "Of whom I travail in birth," it is an allegory. For the Apostles are in the place of parents; as schoolmasters also are, in their place and calling. For as parents beget the bodily form, so they beget the form of the mind. Now, the form of a Christian mind is faith, or the confidence of the heart that lays hold on Christ and cleaves to Him alone, and to nothing else. The heart being furnished with this confidence, or assurance, that for Christ's sake we are righteous, has the true form of Christ. Now, this form is given by the ministry of the Word, as it is said, 1 Corinthians 4:15: "I have begotten you through the gospel," that is to say, in spirit, that ye might know Christ and believe in Him. Also 2 Corinthians 3: "Ye are the epistle of Christ ministered by us, written not with ink, but with the Spirit of the living God." For the Word comes from the mouth of the Apostle or of the minister, and enters into the heart of him who hears it. There the Holy Ghost is present, and imprints the Word in the heart, so that it consents to it. Thus every godly teacher is a father who engenders and forms the true shape of a Christian mind by the ministry of the Word.

Moreover, by these words, "Of whom I travail in birth," he touches the false apostles. As though he would say: I did beget you rightly through the gospel, but these corrupters have formed a new shape in your heart, not of Christ, but of Moses; so that now your faith is not grounded anymore upon Christ, but upon the works of the law. This is not the form of Christ, but it is altogether devilish. Paul says not: "Of whom I travail in birth until my form be fashioned in you," but "until Christ be formed in you"; that is to say, I travail that you may receive again the shape and similitude of Christ, and not of Paul. In these words he again reproves the false apostles, for they had abolished the form of Christ in the hearts of the believers, and had devised another form, that is to say, their own; as he says (6:13): "They would have you circumcised, that they might glory in your flesh."

Of this form of Christ he speaks also in Colossians 3: "Put ye on the new man which is renewed in knowledge after the image of him that created him." Paul therefore goes about to repair the form of Christ in the Galatians that was disfigured and corrupted by the false apostles; which is, that they should feel, think, and will, as God does, whose thought and will is that we should obtain remission of our sins and everlasting life by Jesus Christ His Son, whom He sent into the world to the end He might be the propitiation for our sins, yes, for the sins of the whole world, and that we through this His Son should know that He is appeased and become our loving Father. They that believe this are like unto God: that is to say, all their thoughts are of God, as the affection of their heart is; they have the same form in their mind which is in God or in Christ. This is to be renewed in the spirit of our mind, and the new man is to be put on, which after God is created in righteousness and true holiness, as Paul says (Ephesians 4:23 ff.).

He says then, that he travails again of the Galatians in birth, and yet so notwithstanding, that the form of the children should not be the form of the Apostle, so that the children should not resemble the form of Paul, or of Cephas (1 Corinthians 1:12), but of another father, that is to say, of Christ. I will fashion Him, says he, in you, that the same mind may be in you which was in Christ Himself (Philippians 2:5). To be brief: "I travail of you"; that is to say, I labor carefully to call you back to your former faith, which you have lost (being deceived by the subtlety of the false apostles) and are returned to the law and works. Therefore, I must now again carefully travail to bring you back from the law to the faith of Christ.

20a—I desire to be present with you now, and to change my voice.

These are the true cares of an Apostle. It is a common saying, that a letter is a dead messenger; for it can give no more than it has. And no epistle or letter is written so exactly, wherein there is not somewhat lacking. For the circumstances are varied; there is a diversity of times, places, persons, manners, and affections, all of which no epistle can express. Therefore, it moves the reader diversely, making him now sad, now merry, as he himself is disposed. But if anything is spoken sharply or out of time, the lively voice of a man may expound, mitigate, or correct it. Therefore, the Apostle wishes that he were with them, to the end he might temper and change his voice, as he should see it needful by the qualities of their affections. If he should see any of them very much troubled, he might so temper his words that they should not be oppressed with more heaviness; contrariwise, if he should see others highminded, he might more sharply reprehend them, lest they should be too secure and careless, and so at length treat God with contempt.

Wherefore he could not devise how he, being absent, should deal with them by letters. As if he should say: If my epistle is too sharp, I fear I shall more offend than amend some of you; and if it be too gentle, it will not profit those which are perverse and obstinate; for dead letters and words give no more than they have. Contrariwise, the lively voice of a man compared to an epistle, is a queen; for it can add and diminish, it can change itself into all manner of affections, times, places, and persons.

20b—For I stand in doubt of you.

I am so troubled in my spirit, that I know not how by letters to behave toward you. Here is a lively description of the true affection of an Apostle. He omits nothing, he chides the Galatians, he entreats them, he highly commends their faith, laboring by all means to bring them back again to the truth of the gospel, and to deliver them out of the snares of the false apostles. These vehement words, proceeding from a heart stirred up and inflamed with a hot burning zeal, ought diligently to be considered.

21—Tell me, ye that desire to be under the law, do ye not hear the law?

Here Paul would have closed his epistle, for he desired not to write any more, but rather to be present with the Galatians and to speak to them himself. But being in great perplexity and very careful for this matter, he uses this allegory which came into his mind. For people are greatly delighted with allegories, and Christ Himself used them. For they are often pictures which set forth things as if they were painted before the eyes of the simple, and therefore they move and persuade especially the simple and ignorant. First therefore, he stirs up the Galatians through their ears with words and writings. Secondly, he paints out the matter itself before their eyes with this allegory.

Paul was marvelously cunning in the handling of allegories, for he is wont to apply them to the doctrine of faith, to grace, and to Christ. To use allegories is sometimes very dangerous. Unless a man has perfect knowledge of Christian doctrine, he cannot use allegories rightly and as he should.

But why does Paul call the Book of Genesis, out of which he alleges the history of Ishmael and of Isaac, the law, seeing that book contains nothing at all concerning the law; and especially that place which he alleges, speaks not of any law, but only contains a plain history of Abraham's two children? Paul calls the first book of Moses the law after the manner of the Jews, although it contains no law besides the law of circumcision, but principally teaches faith, and witnesses that the patriarchs pleased God because of their faith; yet the Jews called the Book of Genesis, with the rest of the books of Moses, the law. So did Paul himself. And Christ under the name of the law included not only the books of Moses, but also the Psalms: "But this cometh to pass, that the word might be fulfilled that is written in their law: They hated me without a cause" (John 15:25; Psalms 35:19).

11

Isaac and Ishmael

Galatians 4:22–31

22, 23—For it is written, that Abraham had two sons, the one by a bondmaid, the other by a freewoman. But he who was of the bondwoman was born after the flesh; but he of the freewoman was by the promise.

Paul is saying here: so, you have forsaken grace, faith, and Christ, and have turned back again to the law. Since you wish to be under the law and learn from it, then allow me to talk with you of the law. Consider the law diligently. You shall find that Abraham had two sons, Ishmael by Hagar, and Isaac by Sarah. They were both the true sons of Abraham. Ishmael was as much the true son of Abraham as Isaac was, for both came of one father, of one flesh, and of one seed. What then was the difference? It is not that the mother of the one was free and the other bond, but that Ishmael was born after the flesh, that is to say, without the promise and the Word of God. Isaac was born according to the promise. What then? I grant that they were both the children of one father, and yet there is a difference.

Whereas, Hagar conceived and brought forth Ishmael, there was no word of God that foreshowed that this should come to pass; but, by the permission of Sarah, Abraham went in to her servant Hagar, whom Sarah, being barren, had given as wife to Abraham. Sarah had heard that

Abraham by the promise of God should have seed of his body, and she hoped that she should be the mother of this seed. But when she had waited now for the promise many years with great anguish of spirit, and saw that the matter was so long deferred, she was out of hope. This holy woman therefore gave place for the honor of her husband, and resigned her right to another, that is to say, to her maid (although she suffered not her husband to marry another wife out of his house, but gave unto him in marriage her own servant to the end that she might obtain children by her). For so says the history: "Now Sarai, Abram's wife, bare him no children; and she had an handmaid, an Egyptian, Hagar by name. And Sarai said to Abram: Behold now, the Lord hath restrained me from bearing. I pray thee go in to my maid; it may be that I may obtain children by her" (Genesis 16). This was a great humility of Sarah, who so abased herself, and took in good part this temptation and trial of her faith. For thus she thought: God is no liar; that which He has promised to my husband, He will surely perform. But perhaps God wills not that I should be the mother of that seed. It shall not grieve me that Hagar should have this honor, unto whom let my lord enter, for I may perhaps obtain children by her.

Ishmael therefore is born without the Word, at the request of Sarah. There is no word of God which commanded Abraham thus to do, or promised thus unto him a son.

In the ninth chapter of Romans, he sets forth the same argument which here he repeats and sets in an allegory, and concludes strongly that not all the sons of Abraham are the sons of God. Abraham has two sorts of children. Some are born of his flesh and blood, but the Word and promise of God goes before, as Isaac. Others are born without the promise, as Ishmael. Therefore, the children of the flesh are not the children of God, but the children of the promise are the children of God. And by this argument he stops the mouths of the Jews who gloried that they were the seed and children of Abraham.

Ishmael, because he was not promised by God to Abraham, is a son after the flesh only, and not after the promise, and therefore he was born at adventure, as other children are. For no mother knows whether she shall have a child or no, or if she perceive herself to be with child, yet she cannot tell whether it shall be a son or a daughter. But Isaac was expressly named (Genesis 17:19): "Sarah thy wife shall bear thee a son; and thou shalt call his name Isaac." Here the son and the mother are expressly named. Thus, for this humility of Sarah, because she gave up her right and suffered the contempt of Hagar, God requited her with this honor, that she should be the mother of the promised son.

24a—Which things are an allegory.

Allegories do not strongly persuade in theology, but as certain pictures they beautify and set out the matter. For if Paul had not proved the righteousness of faith against the righteousness of works by strong and pithy arguments, he should have little prevailed by this allegory. But because he had fortified his cause before with invincible arguments, taken from experience, from the example of Abraham, from the testimonies of the Scripture, and from similitudes, now in the end of his disputations he adds an allegory, to give a beauty to all the rest. For it is a seemly thing sometimes to add an allegory when the foundation is well laid and the matter thoroughly proved. For as painting is an ornament to set forth and garnish a house already built, so is an allegory the light of a matter which is already otherwise proved and confirmed.

24b, 25a—For these are the two covenants; the one from the mount Sinai, which gendereth to bondage, which is Agar. For this Agar is mount Sinai in Arabia.

As a figure of God, Abraham had two sons, that is to say, two sorts of people who are represented by Ishmael and Isaac. These two are born unto him by Hagar and Sarah, which signifies the two Testaments, the Old and the New. The Old is of Mount Sinai, begetting unto bondage, which is Hagar. For the Arabians in their language call Hagar the same mountain which the Jews call Sinai (which seems to have that name of brambles and thorns) which also Ptolemy and the Greek commentaries witness.

Now this serves very well to the purpose, that Mount Sinai in the Arabian language signifies as much as a handmaid; and I think the likeness of this name gave Paul light and occasion to seek out this allegory. As Hagar the bondmaid brought forth to Abraham a son, and yet not an heir but a servant: so Sinai, the allegorical Hagar, brought forth to God a son, that is to say, a carnal people. Again, as Ishmael was the true son of Abraham, so the people of Israel had the true God to be their Father, who gave them His law, His oracles, religion, and true service, and the Temple; as it is said in Psalms 147:19:"He showeth his word unto Jacob." But Ishmael was born of a bondmaid after the flesh, that is to say, without the promise, and could not therefore be the heir. So the mystical Hagar, that is to say, Mount Sinai, where the law was given and the Old Testament ordained, brought forth to God, the great Abraham, a people, but without the promise, that is to say a carnal and a servile people, and not the heir of God. For the promises as touching Christ the giver of all blessing, and as touching the deliverance from the curse of the law, from sin and death, also as touching the free remission of sins, of righteousness and everlasting life, are not added to the law, but the law says, "He that shall do these things shall live in them" (Leviticus 18:5; Romans 10:5).

Therefore, the promises of the law are conditional, promising life, not freely, but to such as fulfill the law, and therefore they leave men's consciences in doubt: for no man fulfills the law. But the promises of the New Testament have no such condition joined to them, nor require anything of us, nor depend upon any condition of our worthiness, but bring and give to us freely forgiveness of sins, grace, righteousness and life everlasting for Christ's sake.

Therefore, the law or the Old Testament contains only conditional promises; for it has always such conditions as these joined to it: If ye hearken to My voice, if ye keep My statutes, if ye walk in My ways, ye shall be My people, etc. The Jews, not considering this, laid hold of those conditional promises as if they had been absolute and without all conditions; they supposed that God could never revoke, but must keep them. So when they heard the prophets foreshow the destruction of the city of Jerusalem, of the Temple, of the kingdom and priesthood, they persecuted and killed them as heretics and blasphemers of God; for they saw not this condition that was annexed: If ye keep My commandments, it shall go well with you.

Therefore, Hagar the bondmaid brings forth but a bondservant. Ishmael then is not the heir, although he is the natural son of Abraham, but remains a bondman. What is lacking? The promise and the blessing of the Word. So the law given in Mount Sinai, which the Arabians call Hagar, begets none but servants. For the promise made concerning Christ was not annexed to the law. Wherefore, O ye Galatians, if you forsaking the promise and faith, fall back to the law and works, you shall always continue servants; that is, you shall never be delivered from sin and death, but you shall always abide under the curse of the law.

> *25b—And answereth to Jerusalem which now is, and is in bondage with her children.*

This a wonderful allegory. As Paul a little before made Hagar of Sinai, so now of Jerusalem he would gladly make Sarah, but he dares not, neither can he so do; but is compelled to join Jerusalem with Mount Sinai, for he says that the same pertains to Hagar, seeing Mount Hagar reaches even to Jerusalem. And it is true that there are continual mountains reaching from Arabia Petraea unto Kadesh-barnea of Jewry. He says then that this Jerusalem which now is, that is to say, this earthly and temporal Jerusalem, is not Sarah, but pertains to Hagar, for there Hagar reigns. For in it is the law begetting unto bondage: in it the worship and ceremonies, the Temple, the kingdom, the priesthood; and whatever was ordained in Sinai by the mother, which is the law, the same is done in Jerusalem. Therefore, I join her with Sinai, and I comprehend both in one word, to wit, Sinai or Hagar.

I would not have been so bold to handle this allegory after this manner, but would rather have called Jerusalem Sarah or the New Testament, especially seeing the preaching of the gospel began in it, the Holy Ghost was there given, and the people of the New Testament were there born; and I would have thought that I had found out a very fit allegory. Wherefore it is not for every man to use allegories at his pleasure: for a goodly outward show may soon deceive a man, and cause him to err. Who would not think it a very fit thing to call Jerusalem Sarah? Indeed Paul makes Jerusalem Sarah, but not this corporal Jerusalem which he simply joins unto Hagar; but that spiritual and heavenly Jerusalem, in which the law reigns not, nor the carnal people, as in that Jerusalem which is in bondage with her children, but wherein the promise reigns, wherein is also a spiritual and a free people.

To the end that the law should be quite abolished, the earthly Jerusalem was by the permission of God horribly destroyed with all her ornaments, the Temple, the ceremonies. Now although the New Testament began in it, and so was spread throughout the whole world, yet notwithstanding it is the city of the law, of the ceremonies and of the priesthood, all instituted by Moses.

26—But Jerusalem which is above is free, which is the mother of us all.

That earthly Jerusalem which is beneath, having the policy and ordinances of the law, is in bondage with her children; that is to say, she is not delivered from the law, sin, and death. But Jerusalem which is above, that is to say, the spiritual Jerusalem, is Sarah, engendering us into liberty and not into bondage. Now this heavenly Jerusalem which is above is the Church, that is to say, the faithful dispersed throughout the whole world, which have one and the same gospel, one and the same faith in Christ, the same Holy Ghost, and the same sacraments.

Therefore understand not this word ''above'' as the triumphant Church in heaven; but as the militant Church on earth. For the godly are said to have their conversation in heaven (Philippians 3): ''Our conversation is in heaven''; not locally, but in that a Christian believes, in that he lays hold of those inestimable, those heavenly and eternal gifts, he is in heaven.

Ephesians 1: "Who hath blessed us with all spiritual blessings in heavenly places in Christ." We must therefore distinguish the heavenly and spiritual blessing from the earthly. For the earthly blessing is to have a good civil government both in nations and families; to have children, peace, riches, fruits of the earth, and other corporal commodities. But the heavenly blessing is to be delivered from the law, sin, and death; to be justified and quickened to life; to have peace with God; to have a faithful heart, a joyful conscience and a spiritual consolation; to have the knowledge of Jesus Christ, the gift of prophecy, and the revelation of the Scriptures; to have the gifts of the Holy Ghost, and to rejoice in God. These are the heavenly blessings which Christ gives to His Church.

Wherefore Jerusalem which is above, that is to say, the heavenly Jerusalem, is the Church which is now in the world, and not the city of the life to come, or the Church triumphant. But Paul says here that the old and earthly Jerusalem belongs to Hagar, and that it is in bondage with her children, and is utterly abolished. But the new and heavenly Jerusalem which is a queen and a freewoman, is appointed of God in earth and not in heaven, to be the mother of us all, of whom we have been engendered, and yet daily are engendered. Therefore, it is necessary that this our mother should be in earth among men, as also her generation is. Notwithstanding she engenders by the Holy Ghost, by the ministry of the Word and sacraments, and not in the flesh.

This I say so that we should not be carried away with our cogitations into heaven, but that we should know that Paul sets the Jerusalem which is above against the earthly Jerusalem, not locally but spiritually. For there is a distinction between those things which are spiritual, and those which are corporal or earthly. The spiritual things are "above," the earthly are beneath; so Jerusalem which is above is distinguished from the carnal and temporal Jerusalem which is beneath, not locally (as I have said) but spiritually. For this spiritual Jerusalem, which took her beginning in the corporal Jerusalem, has not any certain place as has the other in Judea; but it is dispersed throughout the whole world, and may be in Babylon, in Turkey, in Tartary, in Scythia, in Judea, in Italy, in Germany, in the isles of the sea, in the mountains and valleys, and in all places of the world where men dwell which have the gospel and believe in Jesus Christ.

Wherefore Sarah or Jerusalem our free mother, is the Church itself, the spouse of Christ, of whom we all are born. This mother engenders free children without ceasing to the end of the world, as long as she exercises the ministry of the Word, that is to say, as long as she preaches and publishes the gospel. Now, she teaches the gospel after this manner: to wit, that we are delivered from the curse of the law, from sin, death and all other evils by Jesus Christ, and not by the law, neither by works. Therefore Jerusalem which is above, that is to say, the Church, is not subject to the law and works, but she is free and a mother without the law, sin, and death.

This allegory teaches very aptly that the Church should do nothing else but preach and teach the gospel truly and sincerely, and by this means should bring forth children. So we are all fathers and children, one to another, for we are begotten one of another. I, being begotten by another through the gospel, do now beget another, who shall also beget another hereafter, and so this begetting shall endure to the end of the world. Now I speak of the generation, not of Hagar the bondmaid, which engenders her bondservants by the law; but of Sarah the freewoman, who bears heirs without the law, and without man's works or endeavors. As Isaac has the inheritance of his father only by the promise and by his birth, without the law and without works, even so we are born through the gospel, of that freewoman Sarah, that is to say, the Church, true heirs of the promise. She instructs us, nourishes us, and carries us, in her womb, in her lap and in her arms; she forms and fashions us to the image of Christ, until we grow up to a perfect man. So all things are done by the ministry of the Word. Wherefore the office of the freewoman is to bear children to God her husband without ceasing and without end; that is to say, such children as know that they are justified by faith and not by the law.

27—For it is written, Rejoice, thou barren that bearest not; break forth and cry, thou that travailest not: for the desolate hath many more children than she which hath an husband.

This verse in Isaiah the prophet is altogether allegorical. It is written that the barren and she who has no children must have abundance of children. After the same manner Hannah signifies in her song, out of which Isaiah took this prophecy (1 Samuel 2:4 ff.): "The bows of the mighty men are broken, and they that stumbled are girded with strength. They that were full have hired out themselves for bread; and they that were hungry ceased: so that the barren hath born seven, and she that hath many children is waxed feeble." A marvelous matter (says he): she that was fruitful shall be made barren, and she that was barren fruitful.

The Apostle shows, by this allegory of Isaiah, the difference between Hagar and Sarah, that is to say, between the Synagogue and the Church, or between the law and the gospel. The law being the husband of the fruitful woman, that is to say, of the Synagogue, begets very many children. For men of all ages, not only idiots, but also the wisest and best do neither see nor know any other righteousness than the righteousness of the law; much less do they know any which is more excellent. They think themselves righteous if they follow the law and outwardly perform the works thereof. And in this word "law" I include all laws, human and divine.

These have many disciples and shine in the righteousness and glorious works of the law, yet they are not free, but bondservants; for they are the children of Hagar. Now if they are servants, they cannot be partakers of the inheritance, but shall be cast out of the house; for servants remain not in the house forever (John 8:35). Yes, they are already cast out of the kingdom of grace and liberty: "For he that believeth not is condemned already" (John 3:18). They remain therefore under the malediction of the law, under sin and death, under the power of the devil, and under the wrath and judgment of God.

Now, if the moral law itself, or the Ten Commandments of God, can do nothing else but engender servants, that is to say, cannot justify, but only terrify, accuse, condemn, and drive men's consciences to desperation, how then, I pray you, shall the traditions of men justify? They therefore that teach and set forth either the traditions of men or the law of God as necessary to obtain righteousness before God do nothing else but engender bondservants. Notwithstanding such teachers are counted the best men; they obtain the favor of the world, and are most fruitful mothers, for they have an infinite number of disciples. They who teach the righteousness of works by the law beget many children who outwardly seem to be free, but in conscience they are servants and bondslaves of sin; therefore, they are to be cast out of the house and condemned.

Contrariwise, Sarah the freewoman, that is to say, the true Church, seems to be barren. For the gospel, which is the Word of the Cross, shines not so brightly as the doctrine of the law and works, and therefore she has not as many disciples to cleave unto her. Moreover, she bears this title, that she forbids good works, makes men secure, idle, and negligent, raises up heresies and seditions, and is the cause of all mischief; and therefore she seems to bring no success or prosperity, but all things seem to be full of barrenness, desolation, desperation. Therefore, the wicked are certainly persuaded that the Church with her doctrine cannot long endure. The Jews assured themselves that the Church which was planted by the Apostles should be overthrown. Thus they speak to Paul in Acts 28:22: "As concerning this sect, we know that everywhere it is spoken against." Christ and His Apostles were oppressed; but after their death the doctrine of the gospel was further spread abroad than it was during their life. In like manner our adversaries may oppress us at this day, but the Word of God shall abide forever. The Church may seem to be barren and forsaken, weak and despised, and outwardly to suffer persecution, but she is fruitful before God, engendering by the ministry of the Word an infinite number of children, heirs of righteousness and everlasting life; although outwardly they suffer persecution, yet in spirit they are most free, and are most victorious conquerors against the gates of hell.

The prophet therefore confesses that the Church is in heaviness; or else he would not exhort her to rejoice. He grants that she is barren before the world; or else he would not call her barren and forsaken, having no children. But before God, says he, she is fruitful, and therefore he bids her to rejoice.

Paul therefore plainly shows by this allegory the difference between the law and the gospel: first, when he calls Hagar the Old Testament, and

Sarah the New; again, when he calls the one a bondmaid, the other a freewoman; moreover, when he says that the married and fruitful is become barren and cast out of the house with her children; contrariwise, when the barren and forsaken is become fruitful, and brings forth an infinite number of children, and those also inheritors. By these differences are compared the two sorts of people, of faith and of the law. The people of faith have not the law for their husband, they serve not in bondage, they are not born of that mother Jerusalem which now is; but they have the promise, they are free, and are born of free Sarah.

We therefore (following the example and diligence of Paul) do endeavor as much as possible, to set forth plainly the difference between the law and the gospel, which is very easy concerning the words. For who does not see that Hagar is not Sarah, and that Sarah is not Hagar? A man may easily discern these things. But when the conscience wrestles with the judgment of God, it is the hardest thing to say with a sure and steadfast hope: I am not the son of Hagar, but of Sarah.

Paul then by this testimony of Isaiah has proved that Sarah, that is to say, the Church, is the true mother who brings forth free children and heirs; contrariwise, that Hagar, that is to say, the Synagogue, engenders many children indeed, but they are servants and must be cast out. Moreover, because this place speaks also of the abolishing of the law, and of Christian liberty, it ought to be diligently considered. For as it is the most principal and special article of Christian doctrine, to know that we are justified and saved by Christ, so it is also very necessary to know and understand well the doctrine concerning the abolishment of the law. For it helps very much to confirm our doctrine about faith, and to attain sound and certain consolation of conscience, when we are assured that the law is abolished.

I have often said before that a Christian laying hold of the benefit of Christ through faith has no law, but all the law is to him abolished with all its terrors and torments. This place of Isaiah teaches the same thing, and therefore it is very notable and full of comfort, stirring up the barren and forsaken to rejoice. But the Holy Ghost turns this sentence, and pronounces the barren worthy of praise and blessing; contrariwise, the fruitful and such as bring forth children, accursed, when he says, "Rejoice thou barren, for the desolate hath many more children than the married wife."

Because therefore we are the children of the freewoman, the law our old husband is abolished (Romans 7). As long as he had dominion over us, it was impossible for us to bring forth children free in spirit, or knowing grace; but we remained with the other in bondage. True it is, that as long as the law reigns, men are not idle, but they labor, they bear the burden and the heat of the day, they bring forth many children; but the fathers as well as the children are bastards, and do not belong to the free mother. Therefore, they are at the length cast out of the house and inheritance with Ishmael; they die and are damned. It is impossible therefore that men should be justified and saved by the law, although they travail ever so much, and be ever so fruitful therein. Accursed therefore be that doctrine, life, and religion which endeavor to get righteousness before God by the law or the works thereof.

Thomas Aquinas and other school-doctors, speaking of the abolishment of the law, say that the judicial and the ceremonial laws are pernicious and deadly since the coming of Christ, and therefore they are abolished; but not so the moral law. These knew not what they said. But if you speak of the abolishment of the law, talk of the law as it is in its own proper use and office, and as it is spiritually taken; and include the whole law, making no distinction at all between the judicial, ceremonial, and moral law. For when Paul says that we are divorced from the curse of the law by Christ, he speaks of the whole law, and principally of the moral law, which only accuses, curses, and condemns the conscience, which the other two do not. Wherefore we say that the moral law, or the law of the Ten Commandments, has no power to accuse and terrify the conscience in which Christ reigns by His grace, for He has abolished the power thereof.

Not that the conscience does not at all feel the terrors of the law, but that they cannot condemn it, nor bring it to desperation: "For there is now no condemnation to them that are in Christ Jesus" (Romans 8:1). Also: "If the Son shall make you free, ye shall be free indeed" (John 8:36). However then a Christian man be terrified through the law showing him his sin, yet he despairs not, for he believes in Christ, and being baptized in Him and cleansed by His blood, he has remission of all his sins. Now, when our sin is pardoned through Christ (who is the Lord of the law), the law, being a servant, has no more power to accuse and condemn us for sin, seeing it is forgiven us and we are now made free. Wherefore the law is wholly abolished to them that believe in Christ.

But, you say, I do nothing. You can indeed do nothing to deliver yourself from the tyranny of the law. But hear this joyful tidings which the Holy Ghost brings to you out of the words of the prophet: "Rejoice, thou that art barren." As if he would say: "Why art thou so heavy, why dost thou so mourn, since there is no cause why thou shouldest so do?" But I am barren and forsaken, you say. Well, although you are barren and forsaken, not having the righteousness of the law, notwithstanding Christ is your righteousness: He was made a curse for you, to deliver you from the curse of the law. If you believe in Him, the law is dead unto you. And look how much Christ is greater than the law, so much you have a more excellent righteousness than the righteousness of the law. Moreover, you are fruitful and not barren; for you have many more children than she who has a husband.

Now, although the gospel does not make us subject to the judicial laws of Moses, yet it does not exempt us from the obedience of all political laws, but makes us subject in this corporal life, to the laws of that government wherein we live; that is to say, it commands everyone to obey his magistrate and laws, "not only for wrath, but also for conscience sake" (1 Peter 2; Romans 13). And the Emperor [or any other Prince] should not offend, if he used some of the judicial laws of Moses; in fact, he might use them freely and without offense.

Likewise, we are not bound to the ceremonies of Moses; much less to the ceremonies of the Pope. But because this bodily life cannot be altogether without ceremonies or rites (for there must be some instruction), therefore the gospel allows ordinances to be made in the Church regarding days, times, places, etc., that the people may know upon what day, in what hour, and in what place to assemble together to hear the Word of God. It permits also that lessons and readings should be

appointed, as in the schools, especially for the instruction of children and
such as are ignorant. These things it permits to the end that all may be
done comely and orderly in the Church (1 Corinthians 14). Not that they
which keep such ordinances do thereby merit remission of sins. Moreover, they may be omitted without sin, as long as it is done without
offense to the weak. Neither is it true that the ceremonies of Moses after
the revelation of Christ are deadly; else would the Christians have sinned
in observing the feasts of Passover and Pentecost, which the old Church
instituted by the example of the Mosaic law.

Paul speaks here especially of the abolishment of the moral law. If only
grace or faith in Christ justify, then the whole law is abolished without
any exception. And this he confirms by the testimony of Isaiah, whereby
he exhorts the barren and forsaken to rejoice.

He calls the Church barren because her children are not begotten by the
law, by works, by any industry or endeavor of man, but by the word of
faith in the Spirit of God. Here is nothing else but being born; no working
at all. Contrariwise, they that are fruitful, labor and exercise themselves
with great travail in bearing and bringing forth; and here is altogether
working, and no birth. But because they endeavor to get the rights of
children and heirs by the righteousness of the law or by their own
righteousness, they are servants and never receive the inheritance, though
they tire themselves to death with continual travail. For they go about to
obtain by their own works against the will of God, that which God of His
mere grace will give to all believers for Christ's sake. The faithful work
well also; but they are not thereby made sons and heirs, but this they do
to the end that they might glorify God by their good works, and help their
neighbors.

28—Now we, brethren, as Isaac was, are the children of promise.

That is to say, we are not children of the flesh, as Ishmael or as all the
fleshly Israel who gloried that they were the seed of Abraham and the
people of God. But Christ answered them, in John 8: "If ye were the sons
of Abraham, ye would not seek to kill Me which hath spoken the truth

unto you"; also: "If God were your father, then would ye love Me and receive My word." We are not such children, says Paul, as they are who remain servants, and at length shall be cast out of the house. But we are children of the promise, as Isaac was; that is to say, of grace and of faith, born only of the promise. Therefore we are pronounced righteous, not by the law, by works, or our own righteousness, but by the mere grace of God. Paul repeats very often, and diligently sets forth the promise which is received by faith alone; for he knew that it was very necessary so to do.

29—But as then he that was born after the flesh persecuted him that was born after the Spirit, even so it is now.

This verse contains a singular consolation. Whoever is born and lives in Christ, and rejoices in this birth and inheritance of God, has Ishmael for his enemy and his persecutor. This we learn by experience; for we see that all the world is full of tumults, persecutions, sects and offenses. Wherefore, if we did not arm ourselves with this consolation of Paul, we should never be able to withstand the violence and subtle sleights of Satan. For who should not be troubled with these cruel persecutions of our adversaries, and with these sects and infinite offenses which busy and fantastical spirits stir up at this day? Verily it is no small grief to us when we are constrained to hear that all things were in peace and tranquillity before the gospel came abroad; but since the preaching and publishing thereof, all things are unquiet, and the whole world is in an uproar, so that everyone arms himself against another. When a man that is not endued with the Spirit of God hears this, by and by he is offended, and judges that the disobedience of subjects against their magistrates, that seditions, wars, plagues and famine, that the overthrowing of commonwealths, kingdoms and countries, that sects, offenses, and such other infinite evils proceed from the teaching of the gospel.

Against this great offense we must comfort and arm ourselves with this sweet consolation, that the faithful must bear this name and this title in the world, that they are seditious and schismatics, and the authors of innumerable evils. And so our adversaries think they have a just cause against us, yes, that they do God high service when they hate, persecute, and kill us (John 16:2). It cannot be then but that Ishmael must persecute Isaac; but Isaac again persecutes not Ishmael. Whoso will not suffer the persecution of Ishmael, let him not profess himself to be a Christian.

But let our adversaries tell us what good things ensued the preaching of the gospel of Christ and His Apostles. Did not the destruction of the kingdom of the Jews follow? Was not the Roman empire overthrown? Was not the whole world in an uproar? And yet the gospel was not the cause, which Christ and His Apostles preached for the profit and salvation of men, and not for their destruction. But these things followed through the iniquity of the people, the nations, the kings and princes, who being possessed of the devil would not hearken to the Word of grace, life, and eternal salvation; but detested and condemned it as a doctrine most pernicious and hurtful to religion and nations. And that this should so come to pass, the Holy Ghost foretold by David when he says, in Psalms 2:1: "Why do the heathen rage?"

Such tumults and hurly-burlies we hear and see at this day. The adversaries lay the fault in our doctrine. But the doctrine of grace and peace stirs not up these troubles; but the people, nations, kings and princes of the earth (as the Psalmist says) rage and murmur, conspire and take counsel, not against us (as they think) nor against our doctrine, which they blaspheme as false and seditious; but against the Lord and His anointed. Therefore, all their counsels and practices are and shall be disappointed and brought to nought: "He that sitteth in the heavens shall laugh: the Lord shall have them in derision" (Psalms 2:4). Let them cry out therefore as long as they want that we raise up these tumults and seditions; notwithstanding this Psalm comforts us, and says that they themselves are the authors of these troubles. They cannot believe this, and much less can they believe that it is they which murmur, rise up, and take counsel against the Lord and His anointed; nay, rather they think that they maintain the Lord's cause, that they defend His glory, and do Him acceptable service in persecuting us. But the Psalm lies not, and that shall the end declare. Here we do nothing, but we only suffer, as our conscience bears us witness in the Holy Ghost. Moreover, the doctrine for which they raise up such tumults and offenses is not ours, but it is the doctrine of Christ. This doctrine we cannot deny, nor forsake the defense thereof, seeing Christ says: "Whosoever shall be ashamed of me and of my words in this adulterous and sinful generation, of him also shall the Son of man be ashamed" (Mark 8:38).

He therefore that will preach Christ truly and confess Him to be our righteousness must be content to hear that he is a pernicious fellow and that he troubles all things. "They which have turned the world upside down [said the Jews of Paul and Silas] are come unto us, and have done contrary to the decrees of Cæsar" (Acts 17). And in Acts 24: "We have found this pestilent fellow stirring up sedition among all the Jews throughout the whole world, and a ringleader of the sect of Nazarenes." In like manner also the Gentiles complain in Acts 16: "These men trouble our city." So at this day they accuse Luther of being a troubler of the Roman empire. If I would keep silence, then all things should be in peace which the strong man possesses (Luke 11:21). But by this means the gospel of Christ should be blemished and defaced.

Christ Himself, when He foresaw in spirit the great troubles which should follow His preaching, comforted Himself after this manner: "I am come to send fire upon the earth; and what will I, if it be already kindled?" (Luke 12:49). In like manner, we see at this day that great troubles follow the preaching of the gospel through the persecution and blasphemy of our adversaries, and the contempt and ingratitude of our own people. This matter so grieves us that often, after the flesh, we think it had been better that the doctrine of the gospel had not been published, than that after the preaching thereof, the public peace should be so troubled. But according to the Spirit, we say boldly with Christ: "I came to send fire upon the earth, and what will I but that it should now be kindled?" Now, after this fire is kindled, there follow great commotions. For it is not a king or an emperor that is thus provoked; but the god of this world, who is a most mighty spirit. This weak Word, preaching Christ crucified, sets upon this mighty and terrible adversary. Behemoth, feeling the divine power of this Word, stirs up all his members, shakes his tail, and makes the depth of the sea boil like a pot (Job 41:31).

Wherefore let it not trouble us that our adversaries are offended and cry out that there comes no good by the preaching of the gospel. They are infidels, they are blind and obstinate, and therefore it is impossible that they should see any fruit of the gospel. But contrariwise, we who believe see the inestimable profits and fruits thereof; although outwardly for a time we are oppressed with infinite evils, despised, spoiled, accused, condemned as the outcasts and filthy dung of the whole world, and put to death, and inwardly afflicted with the feeling of our sin, and vexed with devils. For we live in Christ, in whom and by whom we are kings and lords over sin, death, the flesh, the world, hell, and all evils. In whom and by whom also we tread under our feet that dragon which is the king of sin and death. How is this done? In faith. For the blessedness which we hope for is not yet revealed, which in the meantime we wait for in patience, and yet do now assuredly possess by faith.

We ought therefore diligently to learn the article of justification, for only that is able to support us against these infinite slanders and offenses and to comfort us in all our temptations and persecutions. For we see that it cannot otherwise be but that the world will be offended with the doctrine of godliness, and continually cry out that no good comes of it. For "the natural man receiveth not the things of the Spirit of God: for they are foolishness to him" (1 Corinthians 2:14). He only beholds the outward evils, troubles, rebellions, murders, sects, and other such-like things. With these sights he is offended and blinded, and finally falls into the contempt and blaspheming of God's Word.

On the contrary part, we ought to stay and comfort ourselves in this, that our adversaries do not accuse and condemn us for any manifest wickedness which we have committed, as adultery, murder, theft, and such like, but for our doctrine. And what do we teach? That Christ the Son of God, by the death of the Cross, has redeemed us from our sins and from everlasting death. Therefore, they do not impugn our life, but our doctrine; yes, the doctrine of Christ, and not ours. Therefore, if there be any offense, it is Christ's offense and not ours; and so the fault wherefore they persecute us, Christ has committed, and not we. Now whether they will condemn Christ, and pluck Him out of heaven as a heretic and seditious person for this fault, that He is our only justifier and Savior, let them look to that. Indeed, after the flesh, it grieves us that these Ishmaelites hate and persecute us so furiously; notwithstanding, according to the spirit, we glory in these afflictions, both because we know that we suffer them not for our sins, but for Christ's cause, whose benefit and whose glory we set forth, and also because Paul gives us warning beforehand that Ishmael must mock and persecute him. The Jews expound this verse in Genesis 21 by saying that Ishmael constrained Isaac to commit idolatry. If he did so, I believe not that it was any such gross idolatry as the Jews dream of, to wit, that Ishmael made images of clay, after the manner of the Gentiles, which he compelled Isaac to worship; for this Abraham would not have allowed. But I think that Ishmael was in outward show a holy man, outwardly a lover of religion; he sacrificed and exercised himself in well-doing. Therefore, he mocked his brother Isaac, and would be esteemed a better man than he for two causes: first, for his religion and service to God; secondly, for his inheritance. He thought that the kingdom and priesthood pertained to him by the right of God's law as the first-born, and therefore he persecuted Isaac spiritually because of religion, and corporally because of the inheritance.

This persecution always remains in the Church, especially when the doctrine of the gospel flourishes, to wit, that the children of the flesh mock the children of the promise, and persecute them. It vexes the children of the flesh that we do not set forth their righteousness, their works and worshipings, devised and ordained by men, as available to obtain grace and forgiveness of sins. And for this cause they go about to cast us out of the house, that is to say, they vaunt that they are the Church, the children and people of God, and that the inheritance belongs to them. Contrariwise, they excommunicate and banish us as heretics and seditious persons; and if they can, they kill us also; and in so doing they think they do God good service. So, as much as in them lies, they cast us out of this life and the life to come.

As soon therefore as the Word of God is brought to light, the devil is angry, and uses all his force and subtle sleights to persecute it, and utterly to abolish it. Therefore, he cannot do otherwise but raise up infinite sects, offenses, cruel persecutions, and murders. For he is the father of lying and of murder. He spreads his lies throughout the world by false teachers, and he kills men by tyrants. By these means he possesses both the spiritual and the corporal kingdom: the spiritual kingdom by the lying of false teachers; the corporal kingdom by the sword of tyrants. Thus this father of lying and of murder stirs up persecution on every side, both spiritual and corporal, against the children of the freewoman.

If we are the children of the promise, and born after the Spirit, we must surely look to be persecuted by our brother who is born after the flesh; that is to say, not only our enemies, which are manifestly wicked, shall persecute us, but also such as were at first our dear friends, with whom we were familiarly conversant in one house, who received from us the doctrine of the gospel, shall become our deadly enemies and persecute us extremely. For they are brethren after the flesh, and must persecute the brethren who are born after the Spirit. So Christ in Psalms 41:9 complains of Judas: "Mine own familiar friend, in whom I trusted, which did eat of my bread, hath lifted up his heel against me." But this is our consolation, that we have not given any occasion to our Ishmaelites to persecute us.

But not only Paul arms us against such persecutions and offenses, but Christ Himself also comforts us in the fifteenth chapter of John, saying: "If ye were of the world, the world would love his own: but because ye are not of the world, but I have chosen you out of the world, therefore the world hateth you." As if He would say: I am the cause of all these persecutions which you endure; and if you are killed, it is I for whose sake you are killed; for if you did not preach My word and confess Me, the world would not persecute you. If they have persecuted Me, they will also persecute you for My name's sake.

By these words Christ lays all the fault upon Himself, and delivers us from all fear. As if He would say: You are not the cause why the world hates and persecutes you, but My name which you preach and confess is the cause. But be of good comfort; I have overcome the world. This upholds us, so that we doubt nothing but that Christ is strong enough not only to bear, but also to vanquish all the cruelty of tyrants and the subtle sleights of heretics.

30—Nevertheless what saith the scripture? Cast out the bondwoman
and her son: for the son of the bondwoman shall not be heir with the
son of the freewoman.

This word of Sarah was very grievous to Abraham; and no doubt, when
he heard this sentence, he was moved with compassion towards his son
Ishmael, for he was born of his flesh. And this the Scripture plainly
witnesses when it says: "And this thing was very grievous in Abraham's
sight, because of his son." But God confirmed the sentence which Sarah
pronounced, saying to Abraham: "Let it not be grievous in thy sight
because of the lad, and because of thy bondwoman; in all that Sarah hath
said unto thee, hearken unto her voice; for in Isaac shall thy seed be
called" (Genesis 21:9–12).

The Ishmaelites hear in this place the sentence pronounced against
them, which overthrows the Jews, Grecians, Romans, and all others who
persecute the Church of Christ. The same sentence also shall overthrow
all who trust in their own works, who boast themselves to be the people
of God and the Church, who trust that they shall surely receive the
inheritance, and judge us who rest upon the promise of God not only to
be barren and forsaken, but also heretics cast out of the Church. But God
overthrows their judgment and pronounces this sentence against them,
that because they are the children of the bondwoman, and persecute the
children of the freewoman, therefore they shall be cast out of the house
and shall have no inheritance with the children of promise. This sentence
is ratified and can never be revoked, for the Scripture cannot be broken:
it shall assuredly come to pass that our Ishmaelites shall not only lose the
ecclesiastical and political government which they now have, but also
everlasting life.

Although you live a holy life, tiring and consuming your body with
continual travail, and walking in humility and the religion of angels, yet
are you servants of the law, of sin, and of the devil, and must be cast out
of the house; for you seek righteousness and salvation by your works, and
not by Christ. If you have nothing but this holiness and chastity of life to
set against the wrath and judgment of God, you are in very deed the son

of the bondwoman who must be cast out of the kingdom of heaven and
be damned. This we say is to labor in vain, except you take hold of that
"one thing" alone which Christ says is "necessary" and choose the good
part with Mary, which shall not be taken from you (Luke 10:42).

This did Bernard, a man so godly, so holy, and so chaste, that he is to
be commended and preferred above all. Being once grievously sick and
having no hope of life, he put not his trust in his single life wherein he had
lived most chastely, not in his many good works and deeds of charity, but
removed them far out of his sight, and laying hold on the benefit of Christ
by faith, he said: "I have lived wickedly, but thou Lord Jesus Christ by
double right dost possess the kingdom of heaven: first, because thou art
the Son of God; secondly, because thou hast purchased it by thy death and
passion. The first thou keepest for thyself by thy birthright. The second
thou givest to me, not by the right of my works, but by the right of
grace." He set not against the wrath and judgment of God his monkery
and his angelic life; but he took hold of that one thing which was
necessary, and so was saved. I think that Jerome, Gregory, and many
other of the fathers and hermits were saved in the same manner. And it
is not to be doubted but that also in the Old Testament many kings of
Israel and other idolaters were saved in like manner, who at the hour
of death casting away their vain trust which they had in idols, took hold of
the promise of God concerning the Seed of Abraham which should come,
that is to say, Christ, in whom all nations should be blessed. And if at this
day there be any which shall be saved, they must simply lean not to their
own good deeds and deserts, but to the mercy of God offered to us in
Christ only, and say with Paul: "I have not mine own righteousness,
which is of the law, but that which is through the faith of Christ"
(Philippians 3:9).

*31—So then, brethren, we are not children of the bondwoman, but
of the free.*

Paul here concludes his allegory of the barren Church and of the
fruitful people of the law. We are not, says he, the children of the

bondwoman; that is to say, we are not under the law which begets into bondage, that is, which terrifies, accuses, and brings to desperation. But we are delivered from it by Christ; therefore, it cannot terrify or condemn us. Of this we have spoken enough before. Moreover, although the sons of the bondwoman do persecute us ever so much for a time, yet this is our comfort, that they shall themselves at length be cast into outer darkness and be compelled to leave the inheritance to us, which belongs to us as the sons of the freewoman.

Paul therefore by these words, "bondwoman" and "freewoman," took occasion to reject the righteousness of the law and to confirm the doctrine of justification. And he takes hold of this word "freewoman," vehemently urging and amplifying the same, especially in the beginning of the following chapter. Whereupon he takes occasion to reason of Christian liberty, which is purchased by Christ, and is to us at this day a most strong fort. Now, Christian liberty is a very spiritual thing, which the carnal man does not understand. Yes, they who have the firstfruits of the Spirit, and can talk well thereof, do very hardly retain it in their heart. Therefore, if the Holy Ghost does not magnify it that it may be esteemed accordingly, it will be condemned.

12

Stand Fast

Galatians 5:1–12

Paul, now drawing towards the end of his epistle, defends the doctrine of faith and Christian liberty against the false apostles, against whom he casts out very thundering words to beat them down and utterly to vanquish them. And he exhorts the Galatians, intermingling threatenings and promises, trying every way to keep them in that liberty which Christ has purchased for them.

> *1a—Stand fast therefore in the liberty wherewith Christ hath made us free.*

That is to say: be you steadfast. So Peter says (1 Peter 5:8, 9): "Be sober, be vigilant; because your adversary the devil, as a roaring lion, walketh about, seeking whom he may devour: whom resist stedfast in the faith." Do not be careless, says he, but be steadfast and constant. Lie not down and sleep, but stand up. Be watchful and constant, that you may keep and hold fast that liberty with which Christ has made you free. They that are negligent cannot keep this liberty, for Satan hates the light of the gospel, that is to say, the doctrine of grace, liberty, consolation, and life. Therefore, when he sees that it begins to appear, he fights against it with all might and main, stirring up storms and tempests to utterly overthrow it. So Paul warns the faithful not to sleep, not to be negligent; but constantly and valiantly to resist Satan.

Every word has a certain vehemence. "Stand," says he; as if he should say: Here you have need of great diligence and vigilance. "In that liberty." In what liberty? Not in that wherewith the Emperor has made us free, but in that wherewith Christ has made us free. There is a civil liberty; there is also a fleshly, or rather a devilish, liberty, whereby the devil reigns throughout the whole world. For they that enjoy this liberty obey neither God nor laws, but do what they please. But we speak here not of this liberty, though the whole world seeks no other liberty. Neither do we speak of the civil liberty, but of a far different manner of liberty, which the devil hates and resists with all his power.

This is that liberty whereby Christ has made us free, not from an earthly bondage, from the Babylonical captivity, or from the tyranny of the Turks, but from God's everlasting wrath. And where is this done? In the conscience. There rests our liberty, and goes no farther. For Christ has made us free, not civilly, nor carnally, but divinely; that is to say, we are made free in that our conscience is now free and quiet, not fearing the wrath to come. This is that true and inestimable liberty; if we compare the other (the civil and the carnal), they are but as one drop of water compared to the whole sea. For who is able to express what a thing it is, when a man is assured in his heart that God neither is nor will be angry with him, but will be forever a merciful and a loving Father to him for Christ's sake? This is indeed a marvelous and incomprehensible liberty, to have the most high and sovereign Majesty so favorable to us that He does not only defend, maintain, and succor us in this life, but also will so deliver us that our bodies, which are sown in corruption, in dishonor and infirmity, shall rise again in incorruption, in glory and power (1 Corinthians 15:42 ff.). Wherefore, this is an inestimable liberty, that we are made free from the wrath of God forever; and is greater than heaven and earth and all other creatures.

Of this liberty there follows another, whereby through Christ we are made free from the law, sin, death, the power of the devil, and hell. For, as the wrath of God cannot terrify us, since Christ has delivered us from the same, so the law, sin, and death cannot accuse and condemn us. And although the law accuse us, and sin terrify us, they cannot drive us to desperation. For faith, which overcomes the world, eventually says: "These things do not belong to me; for Christ has made me free, and delivered me from them all." Likewise death, which is the most mighty and most dreadful thing in all the world, is utterly vanquished in the conscience by this liberty of the Spirit. So the majesty of this Christian liberty is highly to be esteemed and diligently considered. It is an easy matter for a man to speak these words: "Freedom from the wrath of God, from sin and from death"; but in the time of temptation, in the agony of conscience, in practice to apply them to himself, and to feel the excellence of this liberty and the fruit thereof, is a harder matter than can be expressed.

Therefore, our conscience must be instructed and prepared beforehand so when we feel the accusation of the law, the terrors of sin, the horror of death, and the wrath of God, we may remove these heavy sights and fearful fantasies out of our minds, and set in their place the freedom purchased by Christ, the forgiveness of sins, righteousness, life, and the everlasting mercy of God. And though the feeling of the contrary be very strong, let us assure ourselves that it shall not long endure, according to that saying of the prophet: "In a little wrath I hid my face from thee for a moment; but with everlasting kindness will I have mercy on thee" (Isaiah 54:8). But this is very hard to do. Wherefore, that liberty which Christ has purchased for us is not as soon believed as it is named. If it could be apprehended with a sure and steadfast faith, then no rage or terror of the world, of the law, sin, death, or the devil, could be so great, but by and by it should be swallowed up as a little drop of water is swallowed by the sea. And certainly this Christian liberty swallows up at once and takes quite away the whole heap of evils, the law, sin, death, God's wrath, and briefly the serpent himself, with his head [and whole power], and replaces them with righteousness, peace and everlasting life. But blessed is he that understands and believes.

Let us learn, therefore, to magnify this our liberty, which no emperor, no prophet or patriarch, no, nor any angel from heaven has obtained for us, but Jesus Christ the Son of God, by whom all things were created both in heaven and earth. Which liberty He has purchased with no other price than with His own blood, to deliver us, not from any bodily or temporal servitude, but from a spiritual and everlasting bondage under most cruel and invincible tyrants, to wit, the law, sin, death, and the devil, and so to reconcile us to God His Father. Now since these enemies are overcome, and we are reconciled to God by the death of His Son, it is certain that we are righteous before God, and that whatever we do pleases Him. And although there are certain remnants of sin still in us, they are not laid to our charge, but pardoned for Christ's sake.

Paul uses words of great force and vehemence, which ought to be diligently weighed. "Stand (says he) in that liberty wherewith Christ hath made us free." This liberty then is not given to us by the law, or for our righteousness, but freely for Christ's sake. Christ, in the eighth chapter of John, says: "If the Son shall make you free, ye shall be free indeed." He only is set between us and the evils which trouble and afflict us; He overcomes them and takes them away, so that they can no more oppress us nor condemn us. Instead of sin and death, He gives us righteousness and everlasting life; and by this means He changes the bondage and terrors of the law into liberty of conscience and consolation of the gospel, which says: "Be of good cheer, my son; thy sins be forgiven thee" (Matthew 9:2). Whoever believes in Christ has this liberty.

Reason cannot perceive the excellence of this matter but, when a man considers it in spirit, he shall see that it is inestimable. For who is able to conceive in his mind how great and unspeakable a gift it is to have the forgiveness of sins, righteousness, and everlasting life instead of the law, sin, death, and the wrath of God, and to have God Himself favorable and merciful forever?

Our liberty has for her foundation Christ Himself, who is our everlasting high priest, sitting at the right hand of God and making intercession for us. Wherefore the forgiveness of sins, righteousness, life, and liberty which we have through Him are sure, certain, and perpetual, as long as we believe in it. So, if we cleave to Christ with a steadfast faith, and stand fast in that liberty wherewith He has made us free, we shall obtain those inestimable gifts; but if we be careless and negligent, we shall lose them. It is not without cause that Paul bids us watch and stand fast; for he knew that the devil seeks nothing more than to rob us of this liberty which cost Christ so great a price, and to entangle us again by his ministers in the yoke of bondage.

1b—And be not entangled again with the yoke of bondage.

Paul has spoken most profoundly concerning grace and Christian liberty, and with high and mighty words has exhorted the Galatians to continue in the same; for it is easily lost. Therefore, he bids them stand fast, lest that, through negligence or security, they fall back again from grace and faith to the law and works. Now because reason (which far prefers the righteousness of the law before the righteousness of faith) perceives no danger herein, he inveighs against the law of God, and with great contempt he calls it a yoke, yes, a yoke of bondage. So Peter calls it also (Acts 15:10): "Why tempt ye God, to put a yoke upon the neck of the disciples?" The false apostles abased the promise and magnified the law and the works thereof. But Paul says the contrary. They that teach the law this way do not set men's consciences at liberty, but snare and entangle them with a yoke, yes, and that with a yoke of bondage.

He speaks therefore of the law very contemptuously, and calls it a hard bondage and a servile yoke. And this he does not without great cause. For this pernicious opinion that the law justifies is deeply rooted in man's reason, and all mankind is so wrapped in it that it can hardly get out. And Paul compares those that seek righteousness by the law to oxen that are tied to the yoke. As oxen drawing in the yoke with great toil receive nothing but forage and pasture, and when they are able to draw the yoke no more are appointed to the slaughter, even so they that seek righteousness by the law are captives and oppressed with the yoke of bondage, that is to say, with the law; and when they have tired themselves a long time in the works of the law with great and grievous toil, in the end this is their reward, that they are miserable and perpetual servants. And whereof? Even of sin, death, God's wrath and the devil. Wherefore there is no greater or harder bondage than the bondage of the law. It is not without cause then that Paul calls it the yoke of bondage.

He uses therefore very vehement words. For he would persuade them that they should not allow this intolerable burden to be laid upon their shoulders by the false apostles or be entangled again with the yoke of bondage. As if he should say: We stand not here upon a matter of small importance, but either of everlasting liberty or everlasting bondage. For as freedom from God's wrath and all evils is not temporal but everlasting; even so the bondage of sin, death, and the devil is not temporal but everlasting. For such workers as go about to accomplish all things precisely and exactly can never find quietness and peace of conscience. In this life they always doubt the good will of God towards them; and after this life they shall be punished for their unbelief with everlasting damnation.

Therefore the doers of the law are rightly called the devil's martyrs, who take more pains, and punish themselves more in purchasing hell, than the martyrs of Christ do in obtaining heaven. For they are tormented in two ways: first, they miserably afflict themselves while they live here, by doing many hard and great works, and all in vain; and afterwards, when they die, they reap eternal damnation. Thus are they most miserable martyrs, both in this life and in the life to come, and their bondage is everlasting. Contrariwise, the godly have troubles in the world, but in Christ they have peace, because they believe that He has overcome the world (John 16:33). Wherefore we must stand fast in that freedom which Christ has purchased for us by His death, and we must take good heed that we are not entangled again with the yoke of bondage.

2—Behold, I Paul say unto you, that if ye be circumcised, Christ shall profit you nothing.

Stirred up with zeal, Paul thunders against the law and circumcision. He says, ''I who know that I have not received the gospel by man, but by the revelation of Jesus Christ, and have commission and authority from above to publish and to preach it unto you, tell you this new but undoubted truth, that if you are circumcised, Christ shall profit you nothing at all.'' This is a very hard sentence which Paul declares, that to be circumcised is to make Christ utterly unprofitable; the Galatians, being deceived by the subtlety of the false apostles, believed that, besides faith in Christ, it was needful for the faithful to be circumcised, without which they could not obtain salvation.

This verse is a touchstone, whereby we may most certainly and freely judge all doctrines, works, religions, and ceremonies of all men. Whoever teach that there is anything necessary to salvation besides faith in Christ, or shall devise any work or religion, or observe any rule, tradition, or ceremony whatever, that by such things they shall obtain forgiveness of sins, righteousness, and everlasting life: they hear in this verse the sentence of the Holy Ghost pronounced against them by the Apostle, that Christ profits them nothing at all. If Paul dared to give this sentence against the law and circumcision, which were ordained of God Himself, what would he say against the chaff and dross of men's traditions?

For all those who have reposed their trust and confidence in their own works, righteousness, vows, and merits hear in this verse their judgment, that Christ profits them nothing. For if they can put away sins and deserve forgiveness of sins and everlasting life through their own righteousness, then to what purpose was Christ born? What profit have they by His passion and blood-shedding, by His resurrection, victory over sin, death and the devil, if they are able to overcome these monsters by their own strength? And what tongue can express [or what heart can conceive] how horrible a thing it is to make Christ unprofitable? Therefore, the Apostle utters these words with great displeasure and indignation: ''If ye be circumcised, Christ shall profit you nothing''; that is to say, no profits shall redound to you of all His benefits, but He has bestowed them all upon you in vain.

Nothing under the sun is more hurtful than the doctrine of men's traditions and works, for they utterly abolish and overthrow the truth of the gospel, faith, the true worshiping of God, and Christ Himself, in whom the Father has ordained all things. ''In Christ are hid all the treasures of wisdom and knowledge''; ''In him dwelleth all the fullness of the Godhead bodily'' (Colossians 2:3, 9). Wherefore all they who are either authors or maintainers of the doctrine of works are oppressors of the gospel, make the death and victory of Christ unprofitable, blemish and deface His sacraments, and utterly take away the true use thereof. Whoso is not moved with these words of Paul and cannot be driven from the law and circumcision, nor yet from the confidence which he has in his own righteousness and works, nor be stirred up to seek that liberty which is in Christ, his heart is harder than stone and iron.

This is therefore a most certain and clear verse, that Christ is unprofitable, that is to say, He is born, crucified, and risen again in vain to him that is circumcised, that is, who puts his trust in circumcision. For Paul speaks not here of the work of circumcision in itself, but of the use of the work, that is to say, of the confidence and righteousness that is annexed to the work. Therefore, whoso receives circumcision, with this opinion that it is necessary to justification, to him Christ avails nothing.

Let us bear this well in mind in our private temptations, when the devil accuses and terrifies our conscience to drive it to desperation. For he is the father of lying, and the enemy of Christian liberty; therefore he torments us every moment with false fears, that when our conscience has lost this Christian liberty, it should always be in dread, feeling itself accused and terrified. When that great dragon, that old serpent the devil comes and lays to your charge that you have not only done no good, but have also transgressed the law of God, say to him: You trouble me with the remembrance of my sins past; you also put me in mind that I have done no good; but this is nothing to me: for if either I trusted in mine own good deeds, or distrusted because I have done none, Christ should both ways profit me nothing at all. Therefore, whether you lay my sins before me, or my good works, I pass not; but removing both far out of my sight, I rest only in that liberty wherein Christ has made me free. I know Him to be profitable to me; therefore, I will not make Him unprofitable, which I should do, if either I should presume to purchase myself favor and everlasting life by my good deeds, or should despair of my salvation because of my sins.

Wherefore let us learn with all diligence to separate Christ far from all works, good as well as evil; from all laws both of God and man, and from all troubled consciences: for with all these Christ has nothing to do. He has to do, I grant, with afflicted consciences, but not to afflict them more; rather, to raise them up, and in their affliction to comfort them. Therefore, if Christ appear in the likeness of an angry judge or lawgiver that requires an account of our life past, then let us assure ourselves that it is not Christ, but a raging fiend. For the Scripture paints out Christ to be our reconciler, our advocate and our comforter. Such a one He is and ever shall be; he cannot be unlike Himself.

When the devil, transforming himself into the likeness of Christ, disputes with us in this way: "This you ought to have done and you have not done it, and this you ought not to have done and you have done it, therefore I will take vengeance upon you," do not be deceived but think to yourself, "Christ does not speak to poor afflicted and despairing consciences in that way; He does not break the bruised reed nor does He quench the smoking flax" (Matthew 12:20).

True it is that He speaks sharply to the hard-hearted; but those who are terrified and afflicted, He most lovingly and comfortably invites unto Himself, saying: "Come unto me, all ye that labour and are heavy laden, and I will give you rest" (Matthew 11:28); "I came not to call the righteous, but sinners" (9:13); "Be of good cheer, son; thy sins are forgiven thee" (9:2); "Be of good cheer; I have overcome the world" (John 16:33); "The Son of man is come to seek and to save that which was lost" (Luke 19:10). We must take good heed therefore lest that we, being deceived with the infinite subtleties of Satan, receive an accuser and condemner instead of a Comforter and Savior, and so lose the true Christ and make Him unprofitable unto us.

> *3—For I testify again to every man that is circumcised, that he is a debtor to do the whole law.*

The first inconvenience is indeed very great, where Paul says that Christ profits them nothing who are circumcised; and this that follows is nothing less, where he says that they who are circumcised are debtors to keep the whole law. He speaks these words with such earnestness and vehemence of spirit that he confirms them with an oath: "I testify," that is to say, I swear by all that is sacred. But these words may be expounded two ways, negatively and affirmatively. Negatively, after this manner: I testify to every man who is circumcised that he is a debtor to keep the whole law, that is to say, that he performs no piece of the law; yes, that in the very work of circumcision he is not circumcised, and even in the fulfilling of the law he fulfills it not, but transgresses it. And this seems to me to be the simple and true meaning of Paul in this place. Afterwards in the sixth chapter he expounds himself saying: "They themselves which are circumcised keep not the law." So he says also before in the third chapter: "Whosoever are of the works of the law are under the curse." As if he said: Although you are circumcised, yet are you not righteous and free from the law; but by this deed you are rather made debtors and bondservants of the law; and the more you go about to satisfy the law, and to be set free from it, the more you entangle and snare yourselves in the yoke thereof, so that it has more power to accuse and condemn you. This is to go backward like the crab and to wash away filth with filth.

And this which I say by occasion of Paul's words, I have learned by experience in the monastery, both in myself and others. I have seen many who have painfully travailed, and on mere conscience have done as much as was possible for them to do, in fasting, in prayer, in wearing of hair, in punishing and tormenting their bodies with sundry exercises (whereby at length they would have utterly consumed them, yes, although they had been made of iron), and all to this end that they might obtain quietness and peace of conscience; notwithstanding, the more they travailed, the more they were stricken down with fear, and especially when the hour of death approached, they were so fearful that I have seen many murderers [and other malefactors], condemned to death, dying more courageously than they did who had lived very holily.

Therefore it is most true, that they who do the law, do it not. For the more men go about to satisfy the law, the more they trangress it. The more a man strives to pacify his conscience, the more he troubles and torments it. When I was a monk, I endeavored as much as was possible to live after the straight rule of my Order: I tried to reckon up all my sins (yet being always very contrite before), and I returned to confession very often, and thoroughly performed the penance that was enjoined to me; yet for all this my conscience was always in doubt, and said: This or that you have not done rightly; you were not contrite enough; this sin you did omit in your confession. Therefore, the more I went about to help my weak, wavering, and afflicted conscience by men's traditions, the more weak and doubtful and the more afflicted I was. And thus, the more I observed men's traditions, the more I transgressed them, and in seeking after righteousness through my Order, I could never attain it: for it is impossible (as Paul says) that the conscience should be pacified by the works of the law.

Wherefore they who seek to be justified and quickened by the law are much further off from righteousness and life than the publicans, sinners, and harlots. For these cannot trust to their own works to obtain grace and forgiveness of sins.

In the *Lives of the Fathers* we read of Arsenius (of whom I made mention before). Although he had lived a long time in the highest holiness and abstinence, yet when he felt that death was not far off, he began to grieve and fear exceedingly. Being asked why he feared death, seeing he had lived holily all his days and had served God without ceasing, he answered that he had indeed lived blamelessly according to the judgment of men, but the judgments of God were other than those of men. So he by the holiness and austerity of his life had attained to nothing else but the fear and horror of death. If he was saved, he must have cast away all his own righteousness and rested only on the mercy of God, saying: I believe in Jesus Christ the Son of God, our Lord, who suffered, was crucified, and died for my sins.

The other exposition is affirmative. He that is circumcised is also a debtor to do the whole law. For he that receives Moses in one point must of necessity receive him in all. He that of necessity observes one part of the law has a duty to observe all other parts. And it helps nothing to say that circumcision is necessary, and not the rest of Moses' laws. For by the same reason that you are bound to keep circumcision, you are also bound to keep the whole law. Now to be bound to keep the whole law is nothing else but to show, in effect, that Christ is not yet come. If this is true, then we are bound to keep all the Jewish ceremonies and laws touching meats, places, and times; and Christ must be looked for as yet to come, that He may abolish the Jewish kingdom and priesthood, and set up a new kingdom throughout the whole world. But the whole Scripture witnesses that Christ is already come, that by His death He has redeemed the human race, that He abolished the law, and that He has fulfilled all things which all the prophets have foretold of Him. Therefore, the law being abolished and taken away, He has given unto us grace and truth. It is not then the law nor the works thereof, but it is faith in the Christ which has come that makes a man righteous.

Some would bind us at this day to certain of Moses' laws as the false apostles would have done at that time. But this is not to be allowed. For if we give Moses leave to rule over us in anything, we are bound to obey him in all things. Wherefore we will not be burdened with any law of Moses. We grant that he is to be read among us and to be heard as a prophet and a witness-bearer of Christ, and moreover, that out of him we may take good examples of good laws and holy life. But we will not allow him in any way to have dominion over our conscience. In this case, let him be dead and buried, and let no man know where his grave is (Deuteronomy 34:6).

The former exposition, that is to say, the negative, seems to me to be more apt and more spiritual; notwithstanding, both are good, and both do condemn the righteousness of the law. The first is, that we are so far from obtaining righteousness by the law that the more we go about to accomplish the law, the more we transgress the law. The second is, that he who will perform any piece of the law, is bound to keep the whole law. And to conclude, that Christ profits them nothing at all who will be justified by the law.

Hereby it appears that Paul means nothing else but that the law is a plain denial of Christ. Why then did God give it? Before the coming of Christ, and before His manifestation in the flesh, the law was necessary:

"For the law is our schoolmaster to bring us unto Christ." But now that Christ is revealed, we are no longer under the schoolmaster. Whoever teaches that the law is necessary to righteousness teaches a plain denial of Christ and of all His benefits; he makes God a liar, yes, he makes the law also a liar, for the law itself bears witness of Christ and of the promises made concerning Christ, and has foretold that He should be a king of grace, and not of the law.

> *4—Christ is become of no effect unto you, whosoever of you are justified by the law; ye are fallen from grace.*

Here Paul expounds himself and shows that he speaks not simply of the law, or of the works of circumcision, but of the confidence and opinion that men have to be justified thereby. As if he would say: I do not utterly condemn the law or circumcision (for it is lawful for me to drink, to eat, and to keep company with the Jews, according to the law; it is lawful for me to circumcise Timothy); but to seek to be justified by the law, as if Christ were not yet come, or, being now present, He alone were not able to justify, this is what I condemn: for this is to be separated from Christ. Therefore he says: "You are abolished," that is, you are utterly void of Christ, Christ is not in you, He works not in you anymore; you are not partakers of the knowledge, the spirit, the fellowship, the favor, the liberty, the life, or the doings of Christ, but you are utterly separate from Him, so that He has no more to do with you, or you with Him.

These words of Paul are to be noted, that to seek to be justified by the law is nothing else but to be separated from Christ, and to make Him utterly unprofitable. What can be spoken more mightily against the law? What can be set up against this thunderbolt? Wherefore it is impossible that Christ and the law should dwell together in one heart; either the law or Christ must give place. But if you think that Christ and trust in the law can dwell together, then be sure that Christ dwells not in your heart, but the devil in the likeness of Christ, accusing and terrifying you, and exacting of you the law and the works thereof unto righteousness. For the true Christ neither calls you to a reckoning for your sins, nor bids you to trust your own good works. And the true knowledge of Christ disputes not whether you have done good works to righteousness or evil works to condemnation, but simply concludes after this sort: if you have done good works, you are not therefore justified; or if you have done evil works, you are not therefore condemned. I neither take from good works their praise nor commend evil works. For it is Christ alone who justifies me, both against my evil deeds and without my good deeds. If I have this persuasion of Christ, I lay hold of the true Christ. But if I think that He exacts the law and works of me to salvation, then He becomes unprofitable unto me, and I am utterly separated from Him.

This is then the final conclusion: either you must forego Christ or the righteousness of the law. If you retain Christ, you are righteous before God; but if you stick to the law, Christ avails you nothing: you are bound to keep the whole law, and you have a death sentence already pronounced against you: "Cursed is every one that fulfilleth not" (Deuteronomy 27:26).

4b—Ye are fallen from grace.

That is to say, you are no longer in the Kingdom of Grace. For as he that is in a ship drowns if he falls into the sea, even so he which is fallen away from grace must perish. He therefore that will be justified by the law has made shipwreck and has cast himself into the danger of eternal death. Now, if they fall from grace, whither shall they fall, I pray you, who will be justified by the moral law, their own traditions, and vows? Even to the bottom of hell.

Christ Himself teaches us: "He that believeth on the Son hath everlasting life: and he that believeth not the Son shall not see life; but the wrath of God abideth on him" (John 3:36); and again: "He that believeth not is condemned already" (John 3:18).

These words, "ye are fallen from grace," must not be coldly or slenderly considered; for they are weighty and of great importance. He who falls from grace utterly loses the atonement, the forgiveness of sins, the righteousness, liberty and life that Jesus Christ has merited for us by

His death and resurrection; instead, he purchases for himself the wrath and judgment of God, sin, death, the bondage of the devil and everlasting damnation. And this verse strongly confirms and fortifies our doctrine concerning faith. Indeed, this verse ought to frighten the enemies of faith and grace, that is to say, all who seek righteousness by works, from persecuting and blaspheming the Word of grace, life, and everlasting salvation. But they are so hard-hearted and obstinate that seeing they see not and hearing they hear not (Matthew 13:13) this dreadful sentence of the Apostle pronounced against them.

> 5—*For we through the Spirit wait for the hope of righteousness by faith.*

Paul here knits up the matter with a notable conclusion, saying: You will be justified by the law, by circumcision and by works, but we seek not to be justified by this means, lest Christ should be made unprofitable unto us, and we become debtors to perform the whole law, and so finally fall away from grace; we wait through the Spirit by faith for the hope of righteousness. Every word is to be noted, for they are pithy and full of power. He not only says, "We are justified by faith," or "through the Spirit by faith," but adds: "we wait for the hope of righteousness," including hope also, that he may include the whole matter of faith.

Hope, after the manner of the Scripture, is taken two ways, namely, for the thing that is hoped for, and for the affection of him who hopes. For the thing that is hoped for, it is taken in the first chapter of the Colossians: "For the hope which is laid up for you in heaven," that is to say, the thing which you hope for. For the affection of him who hopes it is taken in the eighth chapter to the Romans: "For we are saved by hope." So hope in this place also may be taken two ways, and so it yields a double sense. The first is: We wait through the Spirit by faith for the hope of righteousness, that is to say, the righteousness hoped for, which shall certainly be revealed in the time appointed. The second: We wait through the Spirit by faith for righteousness with hope and desire; that is to say, we are righteous, although our righteousness is not yet revealed, but hangs yet in hope (Romans 8:24). For as long as we live here, sin remains in our flesh; there is also a law in our flesh and members, rebelling against the law of our mind, and leading us captives to the service of sin (Romans 7:13). Now when these affections of the flesh do rage and reign, and we on the other side do through the Spirit wrestle against the same, then is there a place for hope. Indeed we have begun to be justified through faith: whereby also we have received the firstfruits of the Spirit, and the mortification of the flesh is also begun in us; but we are not yet perfectly righteous. It remains then that we are to be perfectly justified, and this is what we hope for. So our righteousness is not yet in actual possession, but lies under hope.

This is a sweet and a sound consolation, whereby afflicted and troubled consciences, feeling their sin, and terrified with every fiery dart of the devil, may be marvelously comforted. For the feeling of sin, the wrath of God, death, hell, and all other terrors, is intensely strong in the conflict of conscience; as I myself being taught by experience do know. Then counsel must be given to the tempted in this manner: Brother, you desire to have a sensible feeling of your justification—that is, you would have such a feeling of righteousness as you have of sin; but that will not be. But your righteousness ought to surmount the feeling of sin, and hope that you are righteous before God. That is to say, your righteousness stands not on your own feeling, but on your hoping that it shall be revealed in due time. Wherefore, you must not judge according to the feeling of sin which troubles and terrifies you, but according to the promise and doctrine of faith, whereby Christ is promised to you, who is your perfect and everlasting righteousness. Thus my hope, consisting in the inward affection, is stirred up by faith (in the midst of all terrors and feeling of sin) to hope that I am righteous. Moreover, if hope is here taken for the thing which is hoped for, it is thus to be understood that that which a man now does not see he hopes in time shall be made perfect and clearly revealed.

Either sense may stand; but the first, touching the affection of hoping, brings more consolation. For my righteousness is not yet perfect, it cannot yet be felt; yet I do not despair: for faith shows me Christ in whom

I trust, and when I have laid hold of Him by faith, I wrestle against the fiery darts of the devil, and I take a good heart through hope against the feeling of sin, assuring myself that I have a perfect righteousness prepared for me in heaven. So both these sayings are true: that I am righteous already by that righteousness which is begun in me, and also that I am raised up in the same hope against sin, and wait for the full consummation of perfect righteousness in heaven. These things are not rightly understood until they are put into practice.

Here rises a question: What difference is there between faith and hope? Even to those of us who travail in the Holy Scriptures with much diligence, it is hard to find any difference. For there is so great affinity between faith and hope, that the one cannot be separated from the other. Notwithstanding, there is a difference between them.

First, they differ in their subject: for faith rests in the understanding, and hope rests in the will. But in very deed they cannot be separated, the one having respect to the other, as the two cherubims of the mercy-seat (Exodus 25:20).

Secondly, they differ in their office. For faith tells what is to be done, it teaches, prescribes, and directs. Hope is an exhortation which stirs up the mind that it may be strong, bold, and courageous; that it may suffer and endure in adversity, and in the midst thereof wait for better things.

Thirdly, they differ in their object. For faith has for her object the truth, teaching us to cleave surely thereto, and looks upon the Word and promise of the thing that is promised. Hope has for her object the goodness of God, and looks upon the thing which is promised in the Word, that is, upon such matters as faith teaches us to be hoped for.

Fourthly, they differ in order: for faith is the beginning of life before all tribulation (Hebrews 11), but hope comes afterwards, proceeding from tribulation (Romans 5).

Fifthly, they differ by the diversity of working: for faith is a teacher and a judge, fighting against errors and heresies, judging spirits and doctrines; but hope is the general or captain of the field, fighting against tribulation, the cross, impatience, heaviness of spirit, weakness, desperation and blasphemy, and it waits for good things even in the midst of all evils.

Therefore, when I am instructed by faith in the Word of God, and lay hold of Christ, believing in Him with my whole heart, then am I righteous by this knowledge; soon, however, the devil comes and labors to extinguish my faith by wiles and subtleties, that is to say, by lies, errors, and heresies. Moreover, because he is a murderer, he goes about also to oppress it by violence. Here hope lays hold on the thing revealed by faith, and overcomes the devil who wars against faith; and after this victory follows peace and joy in the Holy Ghost. So that in very deed, faith and hope can scarcely be discerned from each other, and yet there is a certain difference between them.

In civil government, prudence and fortitude differ, and yet these two virtues are so joined together that they cannot easily be severed. Now, fortitude is a constancy of mind which is not discouraged in adversity, but endures valiantly, and waits for better things. But if fortitude is not guided by prudence, it is but temerity and rashness. On the other side, if fortitude is not joined with prudence, that prudence is but vain and unprofitable. Therefore as in policy, prudence is vain without fortitude, even so in divinity, faith without hope is nothing: for hope endures adversity and is constant therein, and in the end overcomes all evils. And on the other side, as fortitude without prudence is rashness, even so hope without faith is a presumption in spirit, and a tempting of God; for it has no knowledge of Christ and of the truth which faith teaches, and therefore it is but a blind rashness and arrogance. Wherefore a godly man must first have a right understanding instructed by faith, according to which the mind may be guided in afflictions that it may hope for those good things which faith has revealed and taught.

Faith is the dialectic, which conceives the idea of whatever is to be believed. Hope is the rhetoric, which amplifies, urges, persuades, and exhorts to constancy, to the end that faith should not fail in time of temptation, but should keep hold of the Word and firmly cleave to it.

In short, faith is conceived by teaching; by teaching the mind is instructed what the truth is. Hope is conceived by exhortation; by exhortation hope is stirred up in afflictions, which confirm him that is already justified by faith, that he be not overcome by adversities, but that he may be able more strongly to resist them. Notwithstanding if the spark of faith should not give light to the will, it could not be persuaded to lay hold upon hope. We have faith then, whereby we understand and know the heavenly wisdom, apprehend Christ, and continue in His grace. But as soon as we lay hold upon Christ by faith and confess Him, our enemies, the world, the flesh and the devil, rise up against us, hating and persecuting us most cruelly both in body and spirit. Wherefore we thus believing and justified through the Spirit by faith do wait for the hope of our righteousness. And we wait through patience; for we see and feel the opposite. For the world with his prince the devil assails us mightily both within and without. Moreover, sin still remains in us, which drives us into heaviness. Notwithstanding we give not over for all this, but raise up our mind strongly through faith, which lightens, teaches, and guides the same. And thus we abide firm and constant, and overcome all adversities through Him who has loved us, until our righteousness which we believe and wait for is revealed.

By faith therefore we began, by hope we continue, and by revelation we shall obtain the whole. In the meantime, while we live here, because we believe, we teach the Word and publish the knowledge of Christ unto others. Thus doing we suffer persecution with patience, being strengthened and encouraged through hope; whereunto the Scripture exhorts us with most sweet and comfortable promises taught and revealed to us by faith. And thus does hope spring up and increase in us (Romans 15:4): ''That through patience and comfort of the scriptures we might have hope.''

Paul therefore, not without cause joins patience in tribulation, and hope together, in the fifth and eighth chapters to the Romans, and in other places also, for by them hope is stirred up. But faith goes before hope; for it is the beginning of life, and begins before all tribulation: it learns Christ, and apprehends Him. Notwithstanding, the knowledge of Christ cannot be long without troubles and conflicts. In this case, the mind must be stirred up to a fortitude of Spirit (for hope is nothing else but a spiritual fortitude, as faith is nothing else but a spiritual prudence) which consists in suffering. These three things then do abide: Faith, which teaches the truth, and defends from errors; Hope, which endures and overcomes all adversities; and Charity, which works all good things as it follows in the text. And so is a man entire and perfect in this life, until the righteousness be revealed which he waits for; and this shall be a perfect and everlasting righteousness.

Moreover, this verse contains both a singular doctrine and consolation. As touching the doctrine, it shows that we are made righteous, not by works, sacrifices or all the ceremonies of Moses' law, much less by the works and traditions of men, but by Christ alone. Whatever is in us besides Him, whether it is law, work, suffering, or understanding, it is flesh and not spirit. Whatever then the world counts to be good and holy without Christ is nothing else but sin, error, and flesh. But we, Paul says, are far above all these things in the Spirit; for we possess Christ by faith, and in the midst of our afflictions we wait with hope for that righteousness which we possess already by faith.

The comfort is this: that in serious conflicts and terrors, wherein the feeling of sin, heaviness of spirit, desperation and such like, are very strong (for they enter deeply into the heart and mightily assail it), you must not follow your own feeling. For if you do, you will say: ''I feel the horrible terrors of the law and the tyranny of sin, not only rebelling against me, but also subduing and leading me captive, and I feel no comfort or righteousness at all. Therefore, I am a sinner and not righteous. If I am a sinner, then am I guilty of everlasting death.'' But against this feeling you must wrestle, and say: ''Although I feel myself utterly overwhelmed and swallowed up with sin, and my heart tells me that God is offended and angry with me, yet in very deed it is not true. The Word of God teaches a far different thing: namely, that 'God is near unto them that are of a broken heart; and saveth such as be of a contrite spirit' (Psalms 34:18); also 'He despiseth not a broken and a contrite heart' '' (Psalms 51:17). Moreover, Paul shows here that they who are justified through the Spirit by faith do not yet feel the hope of righteousness, but wait still for it.

Wherefore when the law accuses and sin terrifies you, and you feel nothing but the wrath and judgment of God, despair not for all that, but take unto you the armor of God, the shield of faith, the helmet of hope, and the sword of the Spirit (Ephesians 6:16 ff.), and see how good and how valiant a warrior you are. Lay hold of Christ by faith, who is the Lord of the law and sin, and of all things which accompany them. Believing in Him you are justified. Moreover, in the midst of these conflicts and terrors which often return and exercise you, wait patiently through hope for righteousness, which you have now by faith, although it is yet imperfect, until it is revealed perfect and eternal in the time appointed.

But you say: "I feel not to have any righteousness, or at the least, I feel it but very little." You must not feel, but believe that you have righteousness. And except you believe that you are righteous, you do great injury to Christ, who has cleansed you by the washing of water through the Word; who also died upon the Cross, condemned sin and killed death, that through Him you might obtain righteousness and everlasting life. These things you cannot deny (unless you will openly show yourself to be wicked and blasphemous against God).

Let us learn, therefore, in great and horrible terrors, when our conscience feels nothing but sin and judges that God is angry with us, and that Christ has turned His face from us, not to follow the sense and feeling of our own heart, but to stick to the Word of God. This verse therefore teaches plainly that the law and works bring us no righteousness or comfort at all: but the Holy Ghost does, who raises up hope even in terrors and tribulations. Very few know how weak and feeble faith and hope are under the cross, and in the conflict. For it seems they are but a smoking flax, which is ready to be put out with a vehement wind. But the faithful, who believe in the midst of these assaults and terrors, afterwards find by experience that the spark of faith, being very little is as an elemental fire which fills the whole heaven, and swallows up all our sins and all our terrors.

There is nothing more dear or precious in all the world, to the true children of God, than this doctrine. For they that understand this doctrine know that miseries, afflictions and calamities turn to the benefit and profit of the elect. Moreover, they know that God is most dear to them when He seems to be farthest off, and that He is then a most merciful and loving Savior when He seems to be most angry, to afflict, and to destroy. Also they know that they have an everlasting righteousness, which they wait for through hope, as a certain and sure possession laid up for them in heaven, even when they feel the horrible terrors of sin and death; moreover, that they are then lords of all things when they are most destitute of all things, according to that saying: "Having nothing, and yet possessing all things" (2 Corinthians 6:10). This, says the Scripture, is to conceive comfort through hope.

6—For in Jesus Christ neither circumcision availeth any thing, nor uncircumcision; but faith which worketh by love.

From this verse the schoolmen teach that we are justified by charity or works. For they say that faith, even though it is infused from above, justifies not, except it be formed by charity. And then they say that charity is gotten by our merit of congruence. And moreover, they affirm that even faith infused can stand together with mortal sin. Thus entirely do they take justification away from faith and attribute it to charity alone.

If they spoke of faith gotten by our own industry, or historical faith and a natural opinion conceived out of history, they might have a good case. But when they think thus of infused faith, they plainly confess that they are utterly devoid of all right understanding of faith. Moreover, they read this verse of Paul through colored glass and pervert the text after their own dreams. For Paul says not: Faith which justifies by love, or Faith made acceptable by love. But he says, "Faith which worketh by love." He says that works are done by faith through love, and not that a man is justified by love. It is therefore certain that great injury is done, not only to Paul, but also to faith and charity themselves, when this verse is wrested against faith on behalf of charity.

But so it happens to careless readers and such as bring their own cogitations to the reading of Holy Scripture, whereas they ought to come bringing nothing, but seeking to carry away thoughts from the Scriptures; and moreover, they ought diligently to consider the words, comparing those going before with those following after, and endeavor to grasp the complete sense of each verse, not picking out words and phrases to suit their own dreams. For in this verse Paul is not declaring what faith is nor what justification is, but what the Christian life itself is.

When Paul speaks here of faith working through love, he means a faith which is not feigned or hypocritical, but true and lively. That is that faith which exercises good works through love. It is as much to say as: He that will be a true Christian indeed must be a true believer. Now he believes not truly if works of charity follow not his faith. So on both hands, on the right hand as well as on the left, he shuts hypocrites out of Christ's kingdom. On the left hand he shuts out the Jews, and all such as will work their own salvation, saying: "In Christ neither circumcision," that is to say, no works, no worshiping, no kind of life in the world, but faith alone without any trust in works avails. On the right hand he shuts out all slothful and idle persons who say: Let us only believe and do what we please. Not so, you enemies of grace, says Paul. It is true that only faith justifies, but I speak here of faith which, after it has justified, is not idle, but occupied and exercised in working through love.

Paul therefore in this verse sets forth the whole life of a Christian, namely, that inwardly it consists in faith towards God, and outwardly in charity and good works towards our neighbor. A man is a perfect Christian inwardly through faith before God, who has no need of our works, and outwardly before men, whom our faith profits nothing, except by our charity or our works.

7—Ye did run well; who did hinder you that ye should not obey the truth?

These are plain words. Paul affirms that he is teaching them the same thing that he taught them before, and that they ran well so long as they obeyed the truth; but now they did not so, since they were misled by the false apostles. Moreover, he uses here a new figure of speech in calling the Christian life a course or a race. For among the Hebrews, to run or to walk signifies as much as to live or to be conversant. The teachers run when they teach purely, and the hearers or learners run when they receive the Word with joy. This was done as long as Paul was present, as he witnessed before in the third and fourth chapters. And here he says: "Ye did run well," that is to say, all things went forward well and happily among you, you lived very well, you went on the right way to everlasting life.

These words, "Ye did run well," contain in them a singular comfort. The temptation often exercises the godly that their life seems to them to be more a certain slow creeping than a running. But if they abide in sound doctrine, and walk in the Spirit, they should not be troubled that their doings seem to go slowly forward, or rather creep. God judges far differently. For that which seems to us to be very slow and scarcely to creep, runs swiftly in God's sight. Again, that which is to us nothing else but sorrow, mourning, and death, is before God, joy, mirth, and true happiness. Therefore Christ says: "Blessed are they that mourn: for they shall be comforted" (Matthew 5:4). All things shall turn to the best for them who believe in the Son of God, be it sorrow, or be it death itself. Therefore they are true runners indeed.

7b—Who did hinder you that ye should not obey the truth?

In like manner he said before in the third chapter: "Who hath bewitched you that you should not obey the truth?" And here Paul shows that men are so strongly bewitched with false doctrine that they embrace lies and heresies instead of the truth and spiritual doctrine. And on the other side, they say and swear that the sound doctrine which they loved before is erroneous; and that their error is sound doctrine, maintaining and defending the same with all their power. The same happens in this day. Therefore, I say that falling in doctrine comes not from man, but from the devil, and is most perilous, from the high heaven to the bottom of hell.

8—This persuasion cometh not of him that calleth you.

The devil is a malevolent persuader, and knows how to amplify the least sin in such a way that he who is tempted shall think it to be a most heinous and horrible crime and worthy of eternal damnation. Here the troubled conscience must be comforted and raised up as Paul raised up the Galatians, to wit, that this persuasion comes not of Christ.

Satan is a cunning workman and will lay against you words like these: "True it is that Christ is meek, gentle, and merciful, but to sinners He threatens wrath and destruction; your life is neither according to Christ's Word nor His example: for you are a sinner, and there is no faith in you; indeed, you have done no good at all, and therefore those verses which set forth Christ as a severe judge belong to you, and not those comfortable verses that show Him to be a loving and a merciful Savior."

Here is the answer that you must give Satan: The Scripture depicts Christ to us in two ways. First, as a gift: if I take hold of Him in this way, I can want nothing. For "in Christ are hid all the treasures of wisdom and knowledge" (Colossians 2:3). He, with all that is in Him, "is made unto me of God, wisdom, and righteousness, and sanctification, and redemption"(1 Corinthians 1:30). Therefore, although I have committed both many and grievous sins, yet if I believe in Him, they shall all be swallowed up by His righteousness. Secondly, the Scripture depicts Him as an example to be followed, as a mirror to behold and view how much is yet wanting in me, that I become not secure and careless. But in the time of tribulation I must see Christ as a gift, who dying for my sins has bestowed upon me His righteousness, and has done and accomplished that for me which was wanting in my life: "For he is the end of the law for righteousness to every one that believeth" (Romans 10:4).

It is good to know these things, not only to the end that every one of us may have a sure and a certain remedy in the time of temptation, but also to the end we may be able to resist the furious heresies of our time. Christ must be set forth to those who are cast down and bruised through the heavy burden and weight of their sins as a Savior and a gift, and not as an example and a lawgiver. But to those who are secure and obstinate, He must be set forth as an example; also the hard verses of the Scripture must be laid before them, that they may repent. Let every Christian therefore when he is terrified and afflicted learn to say: "O cursed Satan, why do you now dispute with me of doing and working, seeing I am terrified and afflicted for my sins already? Rather, seeing I now labor and am heavy laden, I will not hearken to you who are an accuser and a destroyer, but to Christ the Savior of mankind, who says that He came into the world to save sinners, to comfort such as are in terror, anguish, and desperation, and to preach deliverance to the captives. This is the true Christ, and there is none other but He. I can seek examples of holy life in Abraham, Isaiah, John the Baptist, Paul, and other saints; but they cannot forgive my sins, they cannot deliver me from the power of the devil and from death, they cannot save me and give me everlasting life. For these things belong to Christ alone, whom God the Father has sealed; therefore, I will not hear you, nor acknowledge you for my teacher, O Satan, but Christ, of whom the Father hath said: 'This is my beloved Son, in whom I am well pleased; hear Him.' "

9—A little leaven leaveneth the whole lump.

This whole epistle witnesses how Paul was grieved with the fall of the Galatians, and how often he beat into their heads (sometimes chiding and sometimes entreating them) the exceeding great and horrible enormities that should ensue, unless they repented. This fatherly and apostolic admonition of Paul moved some of them nothing at all; for many of them acknowledged Paul no more for their teacher, but preferred the false apostles far above him: of whom they thought themselves to have received the true doctrine, and not of Paul. Moreover, the false apostles no doubt slandered Paul among the Galatians and made him very odious to many.

Some others which had not yet utterly forsaken his doctrine thought that there was no danger in dissenting a little from him in the doctrine of justification and faith. Wherefore, when they heard that Paul made so heinous a matter of that which seemed to them to be but light and of small importance, they marveled. In response, Paul gives this proverbial sentence: "A little leaven leaveneth the whole lump [of dough]."

In philosophy, a small fault in the beginning is a great fault in the end. So in theology, one little error overthrows the whole doctrine. Wherefore we must separate life and doctrine far asunder. The doctrine is not ours, but God's whose ministers only we are called; therefore, we may not change or diminish one tittle thereof. The life is ours: therefore, as touching that, we are ready to do, to suffer and to forgive whatever our adversaries require of us. Doctrine is like a mathematical point, which can suffer neither addition nor subtraction. Contrariwise, life, which is like a physical point, can always yield somewhat.

Some charge that we break charity to the great hurt and damage of the churches. We protest that we desire nothing more than to be at unity with all men; but accursed be that charity which is preserved through the loss of the doctrine of faith. Therefore, when they make this matter of so little account, they do sufficiently witness what store they set by the Word of God. Which if they did believe to be the Word of God, they would not so trifle with it, but would hold it in high honor, and without any disputing or doubting would put their faith in it.

Let us allow them therefore to extol charity and concord as much as they want; but on the other side, let us magnify the majesty of the Word and faith. Charity may be neglected in time and place without any danger; but the Word and faith cannot be. Charity suffers all things, gives place to all men. Contrariwise, faith suffers nothing, gives place to no man. Charity in giving place, in believing, in giving and forgiving, is oftentimes deceived, and yet notwithstanding being so deceived, it suffers no loss which is to be called true loss indeed, that is to say, it loses not Christ; therefore, it is not offended, but continues still constant in well doing, yes, even towards the unthankful and unworthy. Contrariwise, in the matter of faith and salvation, when men teach lies and errors under the color of the truth, and seduce many, here has charity no place: for here we lose not any benefit bestowed upon the unthankful, but we lose the Word, faith, Christ, and everlasting life.

Paul therefore by this verse admonishes teachers as well as hearers to take heed that they esteem not the doctrine of faith as a light matter. It is a bright sunbeam coming down from heaven, which enlightens, directs, and guides us. As the world with all its wisdom and power is not able to stop or turn away the beams of the sun coming down from heaven unto the earth: even so can there be nothing added to the doctrine of faith, or taken from it; for that is an utter defacing and overthrowing of the whole.

10a—I have confidence in you through the Lord.

As if he would say: I have taught, admonished, and reproved you enough, so that you would hearken unto me. Notwithstanding, I hope well of you in the Lord. Here rises a question, whether Paul was right when he said he had a good hope or trust in the Galatians, seeing the Scripture forbids any trust to be put in men. Both faith and charity have their trust and belief. Faith trusts in God, and therefore it cannot be deceived; charity believes man, and therefore it is often deceived. Now, this faith that springs from charity is so necessary to this present life, that without it life cannot continue in the world. For if one man should not believe and trust another, what life should we live upon earth? The true Christians sooner believe and give credit through charity, than the children of this world do. For faith towards men is a fruit of the Spirit, or of Christian faith in the godly. Hereupon Paul had a trust in the Galatians, even though they were fallen from his doctrine; but yet in the Lord. As if he should say: I have confidence in you as long as the Lord is in you, and you in Him; that is to say, as long as you abide in the truth. Thus it is lawful for the godly to trust and believe men.

10b—That ye will be none otherwise minded.

In other words, Paul is saying, I have hope that you will not receive any other doctrine which shall be contrary to mine.

*10c—But he that troubleth you shall bear his judgment, whosoever
he be.*

By this sentence Paul, as a judge sitting upon the judgment seat,
condemns the false apostles, calling them by a very odious name,
troublers of the Galatians. He boldly condemns the false apostles in order
that the Galatians might flee from their doctrine and regard it as a most
dangerous plague. As if he should say: How dare you give ear to those
pestilent fellows, which teach you not, but only trouble you? The doctrine
that they deliver to you is nothing else but a troubling of consciences.
Wherefore they shall bear their judgment.

Now, a man may understand by these words: "Whosoever he be," that
the false apostles in outward appearance were very good and holy men.
And perhaps among them was some notable disciple of the Apostles, of
great name and authority. For it is not without cause that he uses such
vehement and pithy words. Why is Paul so obstinate in so small a matter?
Why does he so rashly pronounce sentence of eternal damnation against
those that are ministers of Christ as well as he? Because it is a perversion
of the doctrine of faith.

One little point of doctrine is of more value than heaven and earth; and
therefore we cannot abide to have the least jot thereof corrupted. We can
very well wink at the offenses and errors of life. For we also do daily err
in life and conversation; yes, all the saints err: and this they earnestly
confess in the Lord's Prayer. But our doctrine, by the grace of God, is
pure: we have all the articles of our faith grounded upon the Holy
Scripture.

*11—And I, brethren, if I yet preach circumcision, why do I yet suffer
persecution? then is the offense of the cross ceased.*

Paul, laboring by all means possible to call the Galatians back again,
reasons now by his own example. I have procured to myself (says he) the
hatred and persecution of the priests, the elders of the people, and my
whole nation, because I take away righteousness from circumcision.

Contrariwise, the false apostles preach circumcision and by this means they obtain and retain the favor of the Jews. Moreover, they would gladly bring to pass, that there should be no dissension, but peace and concord between the Gentiles and the Jews. But that is impossible without the loss of the doctrine of faith. Wherefore when he says: "If I yet preach circumcision, why do I yet suffer persecution? Then is the slander of the cross abolished," he means that it were a great absurdity, if the offense of the cross should cease. After the same manner he speaks in 1 Corinthians 1: "Christ sent me to preach the gospel: not with wisdom of words, lest the cross of Christ should be made of none effect."

Here some man may say: The Christians then are mad men, to cast themselves into danger of their own accord; for they, by preaching and confessing the truth, procure the hatred and enmity of the whole world. This, says Paul, does not trouble me; instead it makes me more bold, and causes me to hope well of the happy success and increase of the Church, which flourishes and grows under the cross. On the other hand, when the cross is abolished, and the rage of tyrants and heretics ceases on the one side, and all things are in peace, this is a sure token that the pure doctrine of God's Word is taken away.

Bernard says that the Church is in best state when Satan assails it on every side, by subtle sleights as well as by violence; and contrariwise, that it is in worst case when it is most at ease; and he refers to that sentence of Hezekiah in his song: "Behold, for peace I had great bitterness" (Isaiah 38:17), applying it to the Church living in ease and quietness. Wherefore Paul takes it for a most certain sign that it is not the gospel if it is preached in peace. Contrariwise, the world takes it for a most certain sign that the gospel is heretical and a seditious doctrine, because it sees great uproars, tumults, offenses and sects following the preaching of the gospel. Thus God sometimes shows Himself in the likeness of the devil and the devil in the likeness of God.

The cross immediately follows the doctrine of the Word. Now the cross of Christians is persecution with reproach and ignominy, and therefore it is very offensive. First they suffer as the vilest criminals in the world; and so did Christ Himself: "He was reputed amongst the wicked" (Isaiah

53). Moreover, murderers and thieves have their punishments qualified, and men have compassion on them. Contrariwise, as the world judges Christians to be the most pestilent and pernicious people, so does it think that no torments are sufficient to punish them for their heinous offenses. Neither is it moved with any compassion towards them. But let not this reproachful dealing, says Paul, move you, but rather let it confirm you. As long as the cross endures, it shall go well with the Christian cause.

In like manner Christ comforts His disciples in the fifth chapter of Matthew: "Blessed are ye, when men shall revile you, and persecute you, and shall say all manner of evil against you falsely, for my sake. Rejoice, and be exceeding glad: for great is your reward in heaven: for so persecuted they the prophets which were before you." As long as the Church teaches the gospel purely, it must suffer persecution. For the gospel sets forth the mercy and glory of God, and it discloses the trickery of the devil, painting him in his right colors. Nothing so stirs up the devil than the preaching of the gospel, for it strips away his disguise and shows him to be the devil and not God. Wherefore as long as the gospel flourishes, the cross and the offense thereof must follow it, or else truly the devil is not rightly touched, but slenderly tickled. If he is rightly hit, he begins to rage and to raise up troubles everywhere.

If Christians then will hold the Word of life, let them not be afraid or offended when they see that the devil is broken loose, that all the world is in an uproar, that tyrants exercise their cruelty, and heresies spring up; but let them assure themselves that these are signs, not of terror, but of joy. God forbid therefore that the offense of the cross should be taken away. If we should preach that which the prince of this world and his members would gladly hear, that is to say, the righteousness of works, then should we have a gentle devil, a favorable world, and merciful princes. But because we set forth the benefits and glory of Christ, they persecute and spoil us both of our goods and lives.

12—I would to God they were even cut off which trouble you.

Is this the part of an Apostle, not only to denounce the false apostles to be troublers of the Church, to condemn them, and to deliver them to

Satan, but also to wish that they might be utterly rooted out and perish? And what is this else but plain cursing? Paul alludes here to circumcision, as if he would say: They compel you to cut off the foreskin of your flesh; but I would that they themselves might be utterly cut off at the root.

Here rises a question, whether it is lawful for Christians to curse? When the matter is come to this point, that God's Word is evil spoken of and His doctrine blasphemed, then must we turn to this verse and say: Blessed be God and His Word, and whatever is without God and His Word, accursed be it; even though it be an Apostle or an angel from heaven. So he said before in the first chapter: "Though we, or an angel from heaven, preach any other gospel unto you than that which we have preached unto you, let him be accursed."

Hereby, we see how great a matter Paul made of a little leaven. A little leaven, although it be ever so little, yet if it be neglected, will be the cause that the truth and salvation shall be lost, and God Himself be denied. For when the Word is corrupted, and God denied and blasphemed, there remains no hope of salvation. Wherefore let us learn to extol the majesty and authority of God's Word.

Paul therefore does well in cursing those troublers of the Galatians, and in pronouncing sentence against them, to wit, that they are accursed with all that they teach and do, and in wishing that they might be cut off, especially that they might be rooted out of the Church of God, that is, that God should not govern or prosper their doctrine or their doings. And this cursing proceeds from the Holy Ghost. As Peter also in the eighth chapter of the Acts curses Simon the sorcerer: "Thy money perish with thee." And the Holy Scripture often uses cursing against such troublers of men's consciences, and chiefly in the Psalms, as: "Let death seize upon them, and let them go down quick into hell" (Psalms 55:15); also: "Let the wicked be turned into hell, and all the nations that forget God" (Psalms 9:17).

The Doctrine of Good Works

Now follow exhortations and precepts of life and good works. For it is the custom of the Apostles, after they have taught faith and instructed men's consciences, to add precepts of good works, whereby they exhort the faithful to exercise the duties of charity one toward another. And reason itself, after a sort, teaches and understands this part of doctrine; but as touching the doctrine of faith, it knows nothing at all. In order that it might appear that Christian doctrine does not destroy good works, or fight against civil ordinances, the Apostle also exhorts us to exercise ourselves in good works and in an honest outward behavior, and to keep charity and concord one with another.

13

Called Unto Liberty

Galatians 5:13–26

13—For, brethren, ye have been called unto liberty; only use not liberty for an occasion to the flesh, but by love serve one another.

As if he would say: You have now obtained liberty through Christ. Therefore, although the law, sin, and death trouble and terrify you, yet they cannot hurt you or drive you to despair. Now take heed that you use not that liberty as an occasion to the flesh.

This evil is common and the most pernicious of all others that Satan stirs up in the doctrine of faith. In many he turns this liberty, wherewith Christ has made us free, into the liberty of the flesh. Of this, Jude also complains in his epistle: "There are wicked men crept in unawares, turning the grace of our God into lasciviousness" (Jude 4). For the flesh is utterly ignorant of the doctrine of grace. Therefore, when it hears the doctrine of faith, it abuses and turns it into wantonness. If we are not under the law, it says, then let us live as we please, let us do no good, let us give nothing to the needy, and let us not suffer any evil, for there is no law to constrain us.

Wherefore there is danger on either side. If grace or faith is not preached, no man can be saved; for it is faith alone that justifies and saves. On the other side, if faith is preached, some will understand the doctrine of faith carnally and draw the liberty of the spirit into the liberty of the flesh. This may we see in all kinds of life. All boast themselves to be professors of the gospel, and all brag of Christian liberty, and yet serving their own lusts they give themselves to covetousness, pleasures, pride, envy, and such other vices. The grief hereof makes me sometimes so impatient that at times I wish such swine which tread precious pearls under their feet still remained under the tyranny of their former tradition; for it is impossible that this people of Gomorrah should be governed by the gospel of peace.

Moreover, even we who teach the Word do not do our duty with so great zeal and diligence in the light of the gospel as we did before in the darkness of ignorance. For the more certain we are of the freedom purchased for us by Christ, so much the more cold and negligent we are in handling the Word, in prayer, in well-doing, and in suffering adversities. And if Satan did not vex us inwardly with spiritual temptations, and outwardly with the persecutions of our adversaries, and moreover with the contempt and ingratitude of our own fellows, we should become utterly negligent of all good works; and so in time we should lose the knowledge and faith of Christ, forsake the ministry of the Word, and seek an easier kind of life for the flesh.

We know that the devil lays wait most of all for us that have the Word (for the rest he holds in captivity and slavery at his pleasure), and labors with might and main to take from us the liberty of the Spirit, or at least to turn the same into the liberty of the flesh. We teach our brethren with singular care and diligence by the example of Paul, that they think not this liberty of the Spirit, purchased by the death of Christ, is given to them that they should make it an occasion of carnal liberty, but that they should serve one another through love.

To the end therefore that Christians should not abuse this liberty, the Apostle lays a yoke upon their flesh by the law of mutual love. Wherefore let the godly remember, that in conscience before God, they are free from the curse of the law, from sin and from death, for Christ's sake; but as touching the body they are servants, and must serve one another through charity, according to this commandment of Paul. Let every man therefore endeavor to do his duty diligently in his calling, and to help his neighbor to the utmost of his power. This what Paul requires of us: "Serve ye one another through love."

Moreover, this doctrine concerning mutual love cannot be beaten into the heads of carnal men nor sink into their hearts. Christians gladly receive and obey it. Others, as soon as liberty is preached, infer: If I am free, then I may do what I please; this thing is my own, why then should I not sell it for as much as I may get? Moreover, seeing we obtain not salvation by our good works, why should we give anything to the poor? Thus do they most carelessly shake off the yoke of the flesh, and turn the liberty of the Spirit into wantonness and fleshly liberty. But we will tell such careless scorners that if they use their bodies and their goods after their own lust, they are not free, but have lost Christ and Christian liberty, are become bondslaves of the devil, and are seven times worse under the name of Christian liberty than they were previously. For the devil which was driven out of them has taken unto him seven other fiends worse than himself, and is returned into them again (Matthew 12:43).

We have a commandment from God to preach the gospel, which offers to all men liberty from the law, sin, death and God's wrath, freely for Christ's sake, if they believe. It is not in our power to conceal or revoke this liberty now published by the gospel, for Christ has given it to us freely and purchased it by His death. Neither can we constrain those swine who run headlong into all licentiousness and dissoluteness of the flesh. Therefore we do what we can, and we diligently admonish them. If we prevail nothing by these admonitions, we commit the matter to God, and He will recompense these scorners with just punishment in His good time. Meanwhile, this is our comfort, that as touching the godly our labor is not lost, many of whom no doubt by our ministry are delivered out of the bondage of the devil, and translated into the liberty of the Spirit.

Paul uses very apt and plain words when he says: "Brethren, ye are called into liberty." And because no man should dream that he speaks of

the liberty of the flesh, he says, ''Only use not your liberty as an occasion
to the flesh, but serve one another through love.''

*14—For all the law is fulfilled in one word, even in this: Thou shalt
love thy neighbour as thyself.*

After he has laid the foundation of Christian doctrine, Paul desires to
build gold, silver, and precious stones upon it. Now there is no other
foundation, as he himself says to the Corinthians, than Jesus Christ
(1 Corinthians 3:11). Upon this foundation he builds good works, all of
which he includes in one precept: ''Thou shalt love thy neighbour as
thyself.'' As if he should say, When I say that you must serve one another
through love, I mean the same thing that the law says in another place:
''Thou shalt love thy neighbour as thyself'' (Leviticus 19:18). And this is
truly to interpret the Scripture and God's commandments.

Now, in giving precepts of love, he touches the false teachers. As if
he said: O Galatians, I have taught you the true and spiritual life, and
now also I will teach you what good works really are. And this I will do
so that you may know that the vain and foolish works of ceremonies
which the false apostles urge are far inferior to works of charity. For
such is the foolishness and madness of all wicked teachers and
fantastical spirits that they not only leave the true foundation and pure
doctrine, but they also never attain to true good works. Therefore, they
build nothing but wood, hay and stubble upon the foundation (1
Corinthians 3:12). So the false apostles, who were the most earnest
defenders of works, did not teach or require the works of charity, such
as that Christians should love one another, and that they should be ready
to help their neighbors in all necessities, not only with their goods, but
also with their body, that is to say, with tongue, hand, heart, and with
their whole strength; but they only required that circumcision should
be kept and that days, months, years and times should be observed.
After they had destroyed the foundation, which is Christ, and darkened
the doctrine of faith, it was impossible that there should remain any

true use for good works. Take away the tree and the fruit must perish.

The Apostle therefore earnestly exhorts Christians to exercise themselves in good works, after they have received the pure doctrine of faith. The remnants of sin still remain in those that are justified, which hinder us from doing good works. Wherefore godly preachers should diligently teach and urge the true doctrine of good works. Let no man think therefore that he thoroughly knows this commandment: ''Thou shalt love thy neighbour as thyself.'' Indeed, it is very short and easy as far as the words; but show me the teachers and hearers, that in teaching, learning, and living, exercise and accomplish it rightly. If the faithful omit a minor religious obligation, they soon are troubled in their conscience, but if they neglect charity or bear not a sincere and brotherly love for their neighbor, they are not so troubled. For they do not regard the commandment of charity as seriously as they do their various religious acts.

Paul therefore reprehends the Galatians in these words: ''For all the law is fulfilled in one word.'' As if he said: You are drowned in your superstitions and ceremonies concerning places and times, which profit neither yourselves, nor others; and in the meanwhile, you neglect charity which you ought to have kept. What madness is this? So says Jerome: We wear and consume our bodies with watching, fasting, labor, etc., but we neglect charity, which is the only lady and mistress of works. And this may be well seen in the monks, who strictly observe the traditions concerning their ceremonies. If they omit anything, be it ever so little, they sin deadly. But when they not only neglect charity, but also hate one another to the death, they think they sin not, nor offend God at all.

Therefore by this commandment Paul not only teaches good works, but also condemns superstitious works. He not only builds gold, silver, and precious stones upon the foundation, but also throws down the wood, and burns up the hay and stubble.

14a—For all the law is fulfilled in one word.

As if he said: Why do you burden yourselves with the law? Why do you turmoil yourselves about the ceremonies of the law, about meats, days, places, and such other things? Leave off these follies, and hearken to what I say: All the law is fully comprehended in this one saying: "Thou shalt love thy neighbour as thyself." God delights not in the observation of the ceremonies of the law, neither has He any need of them. The only thing that He requires at your hands is this, that you believe in Christ whom He has sent. But if to faith, which is the most acceptable service of God, you will also add laws, then assure yourselves that all laws are included in this short commandment: "Thou shalt love thy neighbour as thyself." Endeavor to keep this commandment, which being kept, you have fulfilled all laws.

Paul is a very good expounder of God's commandments: for he sums up all of Moses in this short sentence: "Thou shalt love thy neighbour as thyself." Reason is offended with this baseness and shortness of words. To serve one another through love, that is, to instruct him who goes astray, to comfort him that is afflicted, to raise up him that is weak, to help your neighbor by all means possible, to bear with his infirmities, to endure troubles, labors, ingratitude and contempt in the Church and in civil life, to obey the magistrate, to give due honor to your parents, to be patient at home with a froward wife and an unruly family: these are works which reason judges to be of no importance. But indeed they are such works that the whole world is not able to comprehend the excellence and worthiness thereof.

Therefore, when men dream that they know well enough the commandment of charity, they are utterly deceived. Indeed, they have it written in their heart; for they naturally judge that a man ought to do unto another as he would another should do unto him. But it follows not therefore that they understand it; for if they did, they would also perform it indeed, and would prefer charity before all works. They would not so highly esteem their own superstitious toys, which they have devised and chosen unto themselves, God neither commanding nor approving them. They esteem them to be so holy and so excellent that they surmount and darken charity which is, as it were, the sun of all good works.

Indeed this is briefly spoken: "Love thy neighbour as thyself"; but yet very aptly and to the purpose. No man can give a more certain, a better or a nearer example than a man's own self. Therefore, if you would know how your neighbor ought to be loved, and would have a plain example thereof, consider well how you love yourself. If you are in need or in danger, you would be glad to have love and be helped by others. So you have no need of any book to instruct you how you ought to love your neighbor, for you have an excellent book of all laws, even in your heart. You need no schoolmaster in this matter. Ask counsel only of your own heart, and that shall teach you sufficiently that you ought to love your neighbor as yourself. Moreover, love or charity is an excellent virtue, which not only makes a man willing and ready to serve his neighbor with tongue, with hand, with money and worldly goods; but with his body and even with his life also.

Now, my neighbor is every man, especially he who needs my help, as Christ expounds it in the tenth chapter of Luke. Although he may have done me some wrong, or hurt me by any manner of way: yet he has not put off the nature of man, or ceased to be flesh and blood, and the creature of God most like myself; briefly, he ceases not to be my neighbor. As long then as the nature of man remains in him, so long also remains the commandment of love which requires at my hand that I should not despise my own flesh, nor render evil for evil, but overcome evil with good.

Paul therefore commends charity to the Galatians and to all the faithful, and exhorts them that through charity one of them should serve another. As if he would say: You need not burden yourselves with circumcision, and with the ceremonies of Moses' law; but before all things continue in the doctrine of faith which you have received of me. Afterwards, if you will do good works, I will in one word show you the chief and greatest works, and how you shall fulfill all laws: ''Serve you one another through love.'' You shall not lack them to whom you may do good, for the world is full of such as need the help of others. This is a perfect and a sound doctrine of faith and love; and also the shortest and the longest theology. The shortest as far as the words and sentences; but as far as the use and

practice, it is more large, more long, more profound, and more high than
all the world.

> *15—But ye bite and devour one another, take heed that ye be not*
> *consumed one of another.*

By these words Paul witnesses that if the foundation, that is to say, if
faith in Christ is overthrown by wicked teachers, no peace or concord can
remain in the Church, either in doctrine or life. When once the concord
of the Church is broken, there is no measure nor end of that evil; for the
authors of schisms, dissenting among themselves, teach, one that this
work, another that another work is necessary to righteousness. Each
approves his own opinion and superstition, and reprehends that of
another. Whereby it comes to pass that one bites and devours another;
that is to say, one judges and condemns another, until at length they are
consumed. Hereof not only the Scripture, but also the examples of all
times bear witness.

But they who hold the doctrine of faith, and love one another
according to this precept of Paul, censure not the life and works one of
another, but each approves the other's manner of life and his duty which
he does in his vocation. No godly man thinks the office of a magistrate
to be better in the sight of God than the office of a subject; for he knows
that both are ordained by God and have the commandment of God. He
distinguishes not between the office or work of a father and of a son, a
schoolmaster and a scholar, a master and a servant, but he confidently
declares that both are pleasing to God, if they are fulfilled in faith and
obedience towards God. In the sight of the world, no doubt, these kinds
of life and their duties are unequal; but this external inequality does not
hinder the unity of the Spirit, whereby all think and believe the same
concerning Christ, namely, that through Him alone we obtain remission
of sins and righteousness. Moreover, in respect of external behavior and
duty, one judges not another, nor censures his work, neither praises he
his own, but with one mouth and spirit they confess that they have one

and the same Savior Christ, with whom there is no respect of persons or of work.

This it is impossible for them to do which neglect the doctrine of faith and love, and teach superstitious works. The monk grants not that the works of the layman, which he does in his vocation, are as good and acceptable to God as his own. The nun far prefers her own kind of life and works before the life and works of a matron that has a husband, for she judges that hers are able to deserve grace and everlasting life, while the matron's are not able. No monk will be persuaded that the works of a common Christian, which are done in faith and obedience towards God, are better and more acceptable to God than those superstitious works which they themselves have chosen.

Paul therefore teaches that such occasions of discord are to be avoided, and he shows how they may be avoided. This, says he, is the way to unity and concord: Let every man do his duty in that kind of life which God has called him to; let him not lift up himself above others, nor find fault at other men's works and commend his own, but let everyone serve another through love. This is a true and simple doctrine touching good works.

It is a hard and a dangerous matter to teach that we are made righteous by faith without works, and yet to require works. Here unless the ministers of Christ are faithful and wise disposers of the mysteries of God, rightly dividing the Word of truth, faith and works are soon confounded. Both these doctrines, faith as well as works, must be diligently taught and urged; and yet so that both may remain within their bounds. Otherwise, if they teach works only then faith is lost. If only faith is taught, then carnal men soon dream that works are not needful.

The Apostle began a little before to exhort men to do good works, and to teach that the whole law was fulfilled in one word, namely: "Thou shalt love thy neighbour as thyself." Here will some man say: Paul throughout his whole epistle takes away righteousness from the law, for he says: "By the works of the law shall no flesh be justified" (Galatians

2:16). But now when he says that the whole law is fulfilled in one word, he seems to have forgotten the matter, and to be of a quite contrary opinion: to wit, that they who do the works of charity fulfill the law and are righteous. To this objection he answers in the following verse:

16—This I say then, Walk in the Spirit, and ye shall not fulfil the lust of the flesh.

As if he should have said: I have not forgotten my former discourse concerning faith, neither do I now revoke it in that I exhort you to mutual love, saying that the whole law is fulfilled through love, but I am still of the same mind and opinion that I was before. So that you may rightly understand me, I add this: "Walk in the Spirit."

Although Paul speaks plainly enough, yet he is still misunderstood, for the schoolmen argue, "If love is the fulfilling of the law, it follows then that love is righteousness: therefore, if we love, we are righteous." These men argue from the Word to the work thusly: The law has commanded love; therefore, the work of love follows naturally. But this is a foolish consequence, to draw an argument from precepts.

True it is that we ought to fulfill the law, but sin hinders us. Indeed, the law prescribes and commands that we should love God with all our heart, and that we should love our neighbor as ourselves; but there is not one man to be found upon the whole earth who so loves God and his neighbor as the law requires. But in the life to come, where we shall be thoroughly cleansed from all vices and sins and shall be made as pure and as clear as the sun, we shall love perfectly and shall be righteous through perfect love. But in this life that purity is hindered by the flesh; for as long as we live, sin remains in our flesh. Why? Because the corrupt love of ourselves is so mighty that it far surmounts the love of God and of our neighbor. In the meantime, that we may be righteous in this life also, we have Christ the mercy-seat and throne of grace, and because we believe in Him, sin is not imputed to us. Faith therefore is our righteousness in this life. But in the life to come, when we shall be thoroughly cleansed and delivered from all sins and concupiscences, we shall have no more need of faith and hope, but we shall then love perfectly.

It is a great error therefore to attribute justification to love, which cannot pacify God: for love even in the faithful is imperfect and impure. But no unclean thing shall enter into the kingdom of God (Ephesians 5:5). In the meanwhile, this confidence sustains us, that Christ, who alone committed no sin, and in whose mouth was never found any guile, overshadows us with His righteousness (1 Peter 2:22). Being covered with this cloud, we begin to love and to fulfill the law. Yet for this fulfilling we are not justified or accepted by God while we live here. But when Christ has delivered up the kingdom to God His Father, and abolished all principality, and God shall be all in all, then shall faith and hope cease, and love shall be perfect and everlasting (1 Corinthians 13). This thing the schoolmen understand not; therefore, when they hear that love is the sum of the whole law, they infer: the law justifies. But that is not the meaning of Paul.

If we were pure from all sin, and were inflamed with perfect love both towards God and our neighbor, then should we indeed be righteous and holy through love, and God could require no more of us. This is not done in this present life, but is deferred until the life to come. Indeed, we receive here the gift and firstfruits of the Spirit, so that we begin to love, though very slenderly. But if we loved God truly and perfectly as the law of God requires, then should we be as well contented with poverty as with wealth, with pain as with pleasure, and with death as with life.

But now man's nature is so corrupt and drowned in sin that it cannot have any right sense of God. It loves not God, but hates Him. Wherefore as John says: "We loved not God, but He loved us, and sent his Son to be the propitiation for our sins" (1 John 4:10). And as Paul says in the second chapter: "Christ hath loved me and given Himself for me"; and in the fourth chapter: "God sent forth His Son, made of a woman, and made under the law, that He might redeem them which were under the law." We, being redeemed and justified by this Son, begin to love, according to that saying of Paul in the eighth chapter to the Romans: "That which was impossible to the law . . . God sending his own Son . . . condemned sin in the flesh: that the righteousness of the law might be fulfilled in us''; that is, might begin to be fulfilled.

So Paul shows by these words: "Walk in the Spirit," how he would have that verse to be understood where he said: "Serve ye one another through love," and again: "Love is the fulfilling of the law." As if he should say: When I bid you love one another, this is what I require of you, that you walk in the Spirit. For I know that you shall not fulfill the law, because sin dwells in you as long as you live; therefore, it is impossible that you should fulfill the law. In the meanwhile, walk in the Spirit, that is, wrestle in the Spirit against the flesh.

It appears then that he has not forgotten the matter of justification. For when he bids them to walk in the Spirit, he plainly denies that works justify. As if he would say: When I speak of the fulfilling of the law, I mean not that you are justified by the law; but this I mean, that there are two contrary captains in you, the Spirit and the flesh. God has stirred up in your body a strife and a battle: for the Spirit wrestles against the flesh, and the flesh against the Spirit. Here I require nothing else of you but that you follow the Spirit as your captain and guide, and that you resist that captain the flesh; for that is all that you are able to do. Obey the Spirit and fight against the flesh. Therefore, when I teach you to observe the law, and exhort you to love one another, think not that I go about to revoke that which I have taught concerning the doctrine of faith, and that I now attribute justification to the law or to charity; but my meaning is that you should walk in the Spirit and that you should not fulfill the lusts of the flesh.

16b—And ye shall not fulfil the lust of the flesh.

As if he would say: The desires or lusts of the flesh are not yet dead in us, but spring up again and fight against the Spirit. The flesh of no faithful man is so good, which being offended would not bite and devour. Yet even at the first brunt he cannot refrain himself, but is angry with his neighbor, desires to be revenged, and hates him as an enemy, or at the least loves him not so much as he should.

Therefore, the Apostle has given this rule for the faithful that they should serve one another through love, that they should bear the burdens and infirmities one of another, and that they should forgive one another. And without this bearing and forbearing through love, it is impossible that peace and concord should continue among Christians. You see many things in me which offend you, and I see many things in you which I do not like. If we bear not with one another through love, there shall be no end of dissension, discord, envy, hatred and malice.

So Paul would have us to walk in the Spirit, lest we fulfill the lust of the flesh. As if he should say: Although you are moved with wrath and displeasure against your brother, offending you or doing anything heinously against you, yet resist and repress these emotions through the Spirit; bear with his weakness, and love him. For your brother does not cease to be your neighbor because he slips or offends you; but then has he most need that you should show your charity toward him. And this commandment: "Thou shalt love thy neighbour as thyself," requires the same thing: that you should not obey the flesh. But wrestle against it in the Spirit, and continue in the Spirit to love your neighbor, although you find nothing in him worthy of love.

The schoolmen take the concupiscence of the flesh for carnal lust. Indeed, it is true that even the godly, especially adolescents, are tempted with fleshly lust. Indeed, those who are married (so corrupt and pestilent is the flesh) are not without such carnal lust. Here let everyone (I speak now to the godly being married, both man and wife) diligently examine himself, and no doubt, many shall find this in themselves, that the beauty or manners of another man's wife pleases him more than his own, and so contrariwise his own lawful wife he loathes or dislikes, and loves her which is unlawful. And this commonly happens, not in marriage only, but in all other matters. Men set light by that which they have, and are in love with that which they have not. As the poet says:

> *Of things most forbidden we always are fain:*
> *And things most denied we seek to obtain.*

I do not deny therefore but that the concupiscence of the flesh includes carnal lust, but not that only. For concupiscence includes all other corrupt affections, wherewith the very faithful are infected, some more, some less: as pride, hatred, covetousness, impatience, and such like. Indeed, Paul includes afterwards among the works of the flesh not only these gross vices, but also idolatry, heresies, and such other. It is plain therefore that he speaks of the whole concupiscence of the flesh, and of the whole dominion of sin. He speaks therefore not only of carnal lust, pride and covetousness, but also of incredulity, distrust, despair, hatred, and contempt of God, idolatry, heresies and such other when he says: ''And ye shall not fulfill the lust of the flesh.'' As if he should say: I write to you that you should love one another. If you had perfect charity, no adversity could be so great, which should be able to hurt and hinder that charity. There should be no wife, were she ever so ugly, whom her husband would not love entirely, loathing all other women, though they were ever so fair and beautiful. But this is not done, therefore it is impossible for you to be made righteous through love.

When I exhort you to walk in the Spirit, that you obey not the flesh, or fulfill not the concupiscence of the flesh, I do not require of you that you should utterly put off the flesh or kill it, but that you should bridle and subdue it. For God will have mankind endure even to the last day. And this cannot be done without parents, which beget and bring up children. So the flesh must continue, and consequently sin, for flesh is not without sin. Therefore, in respect of the flesh we are sinners; but in respect of the Spirit, we are righteous: and so we are partly sinners and partly righteous. Notwithstanding, our righteousness is much more plentiful than our sin, because the holiness and righteousness of Christ our mediator far exceeds the sin of the whole world; and the forgiveness of sins which we have through Him is so great, so large, and so infinite, that it easily swallows up all sins.

The schoolmen imply that the whole concupiscence of the flesh is overcome when fleshly lust is subdued, although they were never able to suppress and keep it under with any yoke that they could lay upon the flesh. Jerome was a marvelous defender of chastity, but he confesses: ''I, who for fear of hell had condemned myself to such a prison, thought myself oftentimes to be dancing among young women, when I had no other company but scorpions and wild beasts. My face was pale with fasting, but my mind was inflamed with desires in my cold body, and although my flesh was half dead already, yet the flames of fleshly lust boiled within me.''

If Jerome felt in himself such flames of fleshly lust, who lived in the barren wilderness with bread and water, what do our clergymen feel who so stuff and stretch out themselves with all kinds of dainty fare that it is a marvel their bellies burst not? Wherefore these things are written, not to hermits and monks, nor to sinners in the world only, but to the universal Church of Christ and to all the faithful: whom Paul exhorts to walk in the Spirit, that they fulfill not the lust of the flesh; that is to say, not only to bridle the gross emotions of the flesh, as carnal lust, wrath, impatience, and such like, but also the spiritual emotions, as doubting, blasphemy, idolatry, contempt and hatred of God.

Paul, as I have said, does not require of the godly that they should utterly put off or destroy the flesh; but that they should bridle it, that it might be subject to the Spirit. In the thirteenth chapter to the Romans, he bids us ''cherish the flesh.'' For as we may not be cruel to other men's bodies, nor vex them with unreasonable labor, even so we may not be cruel to our own bodies. Wherefore, according to Paul's precept, we must cherish our flesh, that it may be able to endure the labors both of the mind and of the body; but yet only for necessity's sake, and ''not to nourish the lust thereof.'' Therefore, if the flesh begin to wax wanton, repress it and bridle it by the Spirit.

17a—For the flesh lusteth against the Spirit, and the Spirit against the flesh.

When Paul says that the flesh lusts against the Spirit, and the Spirit against the flesh, he warns us that we shall feel the concupiscence of the flesh, that is to say, not only carnal lust, but also pride, wrath, heaviness, impatience, incredulity, and such like. Notwithstanding, he would have us so to feel them that we consent not to them, nor accomplish them; that is, that we neither think, speak, nor do those things which the flesh provokes us to. Paul says: I know that the flesh will provoke you to wrath, envy, doubting and incredulity; but resist it by the Spirit, that you sin not.

17b—And these are contrary the one to the other: so that ye cannot do the things that ye would.

These two captains or leaders, the flesh and the Spirit, are one against another in your body, so that you cannot do what you would. And this verse says plainly that Paul is writing these things to the saints, that is, to the Church believing in Christ, baptized, justified, renewed, and having full forgiveness of sins. Yet he says that she has flesh rebelling against the Spirit. After the same manner he speaks of himself in the seventh chapter to the Romans: "I am carnal, sold under sin"; and again: "I see another law in my members, warring against the law of my mind," also: "O wretched man that I am!"

Here, not only the schoolmen, but also some of the old fathers are much troubled, seeking how they may excuse Paul. For it seems to them unseemly to say that that elect vessel of Christ should have sin. But we credit Paul's own words, wherein he plainly confesses that he is sold under sin, that he is led captive of sin, that he has a law in his members rebelling against him, and that in the flesh he served the law of sin. Here again they answer, that the Apostle speaks in the person of the ungodly. But the ungodly do not complain of the rebellion of their flesh, of any battle or conflict, or of the capacity and bondage of sin; for sin reigns in them. This is the complaint of Paul and of all the saints. They who have claimed that Paul and other saints had no sin have done very wickedly. For they have robbed the Church of a singular consolation; they have abolished the forgiveness of sins and made Christ of no effect.

When Paul says: "I see another law in my members," he does not deny that he has flesh, and the vices of the flesh in him. It is likely that he felt sometimes the emotions of carnal lust. But yet these emotions no doubt were well suppressed in him, and if he felt the lust of the flesh, wrath, impatience, and such like, he resisted them by the Spirit, and suffered not those emotions to bear rule in him. Therefore, let us not allow such comforting verses (wherein Paul describes the battle of the flesh against the Spirit in his own body) to be corrupted with such foolish glosses.

But this must be our ground and anchor-hold, that Christ is our perfect righteousness. If we have nothing we may trust, yet these three things (as Paul says), faith, hope, and love, remain. Therefore, we must always believe and always hope; we must always take hold of Christ as the head and fountain of our righteousness. He that believes in Him shall not be ashamed. Moreover, we must labor to be outwardly righteous also: that is to say, not to consent to the flesh, which always entices us to some evil; but to resist it by the Spirit.

Let no man therefore despair if he feels the flesh stirring up new battles against the Spirit, or if he cannot subdue the flesh and make it obedient to the Spirit. I also wish myself to have a more valiant and constant heart which might be able not only boldly to condemn the threatenings of tyrants, the heresies, offenses and tumults which the fantastical spirits stir up; but also might shake off the vexations and anguish of spirit, and briefly, might not fear the sharpness of death, but receive and embrace it as a most friendly guest. But I find another law in my members, rebelling against the law of my mind.

Let no man marvel therefore or be dismayed when he feels in his body this battle of the flesh against the Spirit; but let him pluck up his heart and comfort himself with these words of Paul: "The flesh lusteth against the Spirit," and "These are contrary one to another, so that ye do not those things that ye would." For by these verses he comforts those who are tempted. As if he should say: It is impossible for you to follow the guiding of the Spirit in all things without any feeling or hindrance of the flesh; nay, the flesh will resist and hinder you, that you cannot do those things that gladly you would. Therefore, when a man feels this battle of the flesh, let him not be discouraged, but let him resist in the Spirit, and say: I am a sinner, and I feel sin in me, for I have not yet put off the flesh, in which sin dwells so long as it lives; but I will obey the Spirit and not the flesh: that is, I will by faith and hope lay hold upon Christ, and by His Word I will raise up myself, and being so raised up, I will not fulfill the lust of the flesh.

It is very profitable for the godly to know this, and to bear it well in mind; for it wonderfully comforts them when they are tempted. When I was a monk I thought that I was utterly cast away whenever I felt the concupiscence of the flesh; that is to say, if I felt any evil emotion, fleshly lust, wrath, hatred, or envy against any brother. I tried many ways, I went to confession daily, but it profited me not; for the concupiscence of my flesh did always return, so that I could not rest, but was continually vexed with these thoughts: "This or that sin you have committed; you are infected with envy, with impatience, and such other sins; therefore, you are entered into this holy order in vain, and all your good works are unprofitable." If then I had rightly understood these sentences of Paul: "The flesh lusteth contrary to the Spirit, and the Spirit contrary to the flesh," and "these two are one against another, so that ye cannot do the things that ye would do," I should not have so miserably tormented myself, but should have thought and said to myself, as now commonly I do: "Martin, you shall not utterly be without sin, for you still have the flesh; you shall therefore feel the battle thereof, according to that saying of Paul, 'The flesh resisteth the Spirit.' Despair not therefore, but resist it strongly, and fulfill not the lust thereof."

I remember that Staupitius said: "I have vowed unto God above a thousand times that I would become a better man; but I never performed that which I vowed. Hereafter I will make no such vow: for I have now learned by experience, that I am not able to perform it. Unless therefore God is favorable and merciful unto me for Christ's sake, and grant unto me a blessed and a happy hour when I shall depart out of this miserable life, I shall not be able with all my vows and all my good deeds to stand before Him." This was not only a true, but also a godly and a holy desperation: and this must they all who will be saved confess both with mouth and heart. For the godly trust not to their own righteousness, but say with David: "Enter not into judgment with thy servant: for in thy sight shall no man living be justified" (Psalms 143:2), and: "If Thou, Lord, shouldst mark iniquities, O Lord, who shall stand?" (Psalms 130:3). They look to Christ their reconciler, who gave His life for their sins. Moreover, they know that the remnant of sin which is in their flesh is not laid to their charge, but freely pardoned. Meanwhile, they fight in the Spirit against the flesh, lest they should fulfill the lust thereof. And although they feel the flesh to rage and rebel against the Spirit, and they themselves also fall sometimes into sin through infirmity, yet are they not discouraged, nor think therefore that their state and kind of life, and the works which are done according to their calling, displease God; but they raise up themselves by faith.

The faithful therefore receive great consolation by this doctrine of Paul. He who knows not this doctrine, and thinks that the faithful ought to be without fault, and yet sees the contrary in himself, must at length be swallowed up by the spirit of heaviness and fall into desperation. But whoso knows this doctrine well and uses it rightly, to him the things that are evil turn into good. For when the flesh provokes him to sin, he is stirred up and forced to seek forgiveness of sins by Christ, and to embrace the righteousness of faith which otherwise he would not so greatly esteem. Therefore, it profits us very much to feel sometimes the wickedness of our nature and corruption of our flesh, that even by this means we may be waked and stirred up to faith and to call upon Christ. And by this occasion a Christian becomes a mighty workman and a wonderful re-creator, who of heaviness can make joy, of terror comfort, of sin righteousness, and of death life, when he by this means of repressing and bridling the flesh makes it subject to the Spirit.

Wherefore let not them who feel the concupiscence of the flesh despair of their salvation. Yes, the more godly a man is, the more does he feel that battle.

But here may some man say that it is dangerous to teach that a man is not condemned, if eventually he overcome not the emotions and passions of the flesh which he feels. For when this doctrine is taught among the common people, it makes them careless, negligent and slothful.

This battle of the flesh against the Spirit, all the saints have had and felt. He who searches his own conscience, if he is not a hypocrite, shall well perceive that to be true in himself. All the faithful confess that their flesh and the Spirit are so contrary the one to the other that they are not able to perform that which they would do. Therefore, the flesh hinders us so that we cannot keep the commandments of God, nor love our neighbors as ourselves, much less can we love God with all our heart. Therefore, it is impossible for us to become righteous by the works of the law. Indeed, there is a good will in us, and so must there be (for it is the Spirit itself which resists the flesh), which would gladly do good, fulfill the law, love God and his neighbor, and such like, but the flesh obeys not this good will, but resists it; and yet God imputes not to us this sin, for He is merciful to those that believe, for Christ's sake.

But it follows not therefore that you should make a light matter of sin, because God does not impute it. True it is that He does not impute it; but to whom, and for what cause? Not to them that are hardhearted and secure, but to such as repent and lay hold by faith upon Christ the mercy-seat, for whose sake, as all their sins are forgiven them, even so the remnants of sin which are in them are not imputed to them. They make not their sin less than it is, but amplify it and set it out as it is indeed; for they know that it cannot be put away by satisfactions, works, or righteousness, but only by the death of Christ. And yet the greatness and enormity of their sin does not cause them to despair, but they assure themselves that it shall not be imputed to them, for Christ's sake.

This I say, lest any man should think that after faith is received, there is little account to be made of sin. Sin is truly sin, whether a man commit it before he has received the knowledge of Christ or after. And God always hates sin: indeed, all sin is damnable. But to him who believes not in Christ, not only all his sins are damnable, but even his good works also are sin; according to that saying: "Whatsoever is not of faith is sin" (Romans 14:23). Therefore, the error of the schoolmen is most pernicious, which distinguishes sins according to the fact, and not according to the person. He who believes has as great sin as the unbeliever. But to him who believes, it is forgiven and not imputed; to the unbeliever, it is not pardoned but imputed. To the believer it is venial; to the unbeliever it is mortal, not for any difference of sins, or because the sin of the believer is less, but for the difference of the persons. For the believer assures himself by faith that his sin is forgiven him, since Christ has given Himself for it. Therefore, although he has sin in him and daily sins, yet he continues godly; but contrariwise, the unbeliever continues wicked. And this is the true wisdom and consolation of the godly, that although they have and commit sins, yet they know that for Christ's sake they are not imputed unto them.

This I say for the comfort of the godly. For they feel they do not love God so fervently as they should do, that they do not trust Him so heartily as they would, but rather they oftentimes doubt whether God has a care for them or not; they are impatient, and are angry with God in adversity. Hereof proceed the sorrowful complaints of the saints in the Scriptures, and especially in the Psalms. And Paul himself complains that he is "sold under sin" (Romans 7:14); and here he says that the flesh resists the Spirit.

Hereby we may see who are very saints indeed. They are not sticks and stones so that they are never moved with anything, never feel any lust or desires of the flesh. The thirty-second Psalm witnesses that the saints do confess their unrighteousness, and pray that the wickedness of their sin may be forgiven, where it says: "I said, I will confess my transgressions unto the Lord; and thou forgavest the iniquity of my sin." And in Psalms 143, David prays: "O Lord, enter not into judgment with Thy servant: for in thy sight shall no man living be justified." All the faithful therefore speak and pray the same thing, and with the same Spirit.

18—But if ye be led by the Spirit, ye are not under the law.

Paul cannot forget his doctrine of faith, but still repeats it and beats it into their heads even when he deals with good works. Here some man may object: How can it be that we should not be under the law? We have flesh which lusts against the Spirit, and fights against us, torments and brings us into bondage. Indeed we feel sin, and cannot be delivered from the feeling thereof. And what is this but to be under the law? But says he: Let this not trouble you; only be led by the Spirit, that is to say, show yourselves willing to follow and obey that will which resists the flesh, and does not accomplish the lusts thereof. Then are you not under the law. So Paul speaks of himself (Romans 7:25): "In my mind I serve the law of God," that is to say, in the Spirit I am not subject to any sin; but yet in my flesh I serve the law of sin. The faithful then are not under the law, that is to say, in the Spirit, for the law cannot accuse them, nor pronounce sentence of death against them, although they feel sin, and confess themselves to be sinners; for the power and strength of the law is taken from it by Christ, "who was made under the law, to redeem them that were under the law" (Galatians 4:4).

So great is the power of the dominion of the Spirit, that the law cannot accuse the godly, though they commit that which is sin indeed. For Christ is our righteousness, whom we apprehend by faith: He is without sin, and therefore, the law cannot accuse Him. As long as we cleave unto Him, we are led by the Spirit and are free from the law. And so the Apostle, even when he teaches good works, forgets not his doctrine concerning justification; but always shows that it is impossible for us to be justified by works.

And with these words: "If ye be led by the Spirit, ye are not under the law," you may greatly comfort yourself and others that are grievously tempted. For it often comes to pass that a man is so vehemently assailed with wrath, hatred, impatience, carnal desire, heaviness of spirit, or some other lust of the flesh, that he cannot it shake off. What should he do in this case? Should he despair? No, but let him say to himself: "Your flesh fights and rages against the Spirit. Let it rage as long as it wants. Only see that in any case you consent not to it, to fulfill the lust thereof, but walk wisely and follow the leading of the Spirit. In so doing you are free from the law. It accuses you, and terrifies you, but altogether in vain. In this conflict therefore of the flesh against the Spirit, there is nothing better than to have the Word of God before your eyes, and therein to seek the comfort of the Spirit.''

And let not him that suffers this temptation be dismayed, in that the devil can so aggravate sin, that during the conflict he thinks himself to be utterly overthrown, and feels nothing else but the wrath of God and desperation. Let him not follow his own feeling, but let him take hold of this saying of Paul: ''If ye be led by the Spirit,'' that is, if you raise up and comfort yourselves through faith in Christ, ''ye be not under the law.'' So shall he have a strong buckler wherewith he may beat back all the fiery darts with which the wicked fiend assails him. Therefore, when the emotions of the flesh rage, the only remedy is to take the sword of the Spirit, that is, the Word of salvation, and to fight against them. If we do this, we shall obtain the victory. But if we do not use the Word, there is no counsel or help remaining. I myself have good experience. I have suffered many and various passions, and the same also very vehement and great. But as soon as I have laid hold of any place of Scripture, and stayed myself upon it as upon my chief anchor-hold, immediately temptations vanished away; without the Word it would have been impossible to overcome them.

The sum of all that Paul has taught in this discourse concerning the conflict between the flesh and the Spirit is this: that the saints or believers cannot perform that which the Spirit desires. For the Spirit would gladly that we be altogether pure, but the flesh will not allow it. Notwithstanding they are saved by the remission of sins, which is in Christ Jesus. Moreover, because they walk in the Spirit and are led by the Spirit, they are not under the law, that is to say, the law cannot accuse and terrify them, nor shall it ever be able to drive them to desperation.

19a—Now the works of the flesh are manifest.

This verse is not unlike this sentence of Christ: "By their fruits ye shall know them. Do men gather grapes of thorns, or figs of thistles? Even so every good tree bringeth forth good fruit; but a corrupt tree bringeth forth evil fruit" (Matthew 7:16). Paul teaches the same thing Christ taught, that works and fruit sufficiently testify whether the trees be good or evil, whether men follow the guiding of the flesh or of the Spirit. As if he should say: Lest some of you might say for himself, that he understands me not now when I deal with the battle between the flesh and the Spirit, I will set before your eyes first the works of the flesh, and then also the fruit of the Spirit.

And this Paul does because there were many hypocrites among the Galatians (as there are also at this day among us), who outwardly pretended to be godly men, and boasted much of the Spirit, but they walked not according to the Spirit, but according to the flesh. So Paul tells them that they aren't what they boasted themselves to be. And lest they should despise this admonition, he pronounces against them this dreadful sentence, that they should not be inheritors of the kingdom of heaven.

Every age, even in the faithful, has its peculiar temptations: in his youth a man is assailed most of all by fleshly lusts; in his middle age by ambition and vain glory; and in his old age by covetousness. There was never yet any of the saints whom the flesh has not often in his lifetime provoked. Therefore, they shall never be without the desires and battle of the flesh. But it is one thing to be provoked by the flesh, and another thing to assent to the flesh, and without fear or remorse to perform and fulfill the works thereof, and to continue therein, and yet to counterfeit holiness.

Sometimes it happens that the saints fall and perform the desires of the flesh, as David fell horribly into adultery. Also he was the cause of the slaughter of many men when he caused Uriah to be slain in the forefront of the battle, and thereby also he gave occasion to the enemies to glory and triumph over the people of God, to worship their idol, and

to blaspheme the God of Israel. Peter also fell most grievously and horribly when he denied Christ. But although these sins were great and
heinous, yet they were not committed because of any contempt of God
or of a willful and obstinate mind, but through infirmity and weakness.
Again, when they were admonished, they did not obstinately continue in
their sins, but repented. To those therefore who sin and fall through
infirmity, pardon is not denied, so that they rise again and continue not
in their sin; of all things, continuance in sin is the worst. But if they
repent not, but still obstinately continue in their wickedness and perform
the desires of the flesh, it is a certain token that there is deceit in their
spirit.

No man therefore shall be without desires so long as he lives in the
flesh; therefore no man shall be free from temptations. Some are tempted
one way and some another, according to the difference of the persons.
One man is assailed with more vehement and grievous emotions, as with
bitterness and anguish of spirit, blasphemy, distrust, and desperation;
another with more gross temptations, as with fleshly lusts, wrath, envy,
hatred and such like. But in this case Paul requires that we walk in the
Spirit and resist the flesh. But whoso obeys the flesh, and continues
without fear or remorse in accomplishing the desires and lusts thereof, let
him know that he pertains not unto Christ; and although he brag of the
name of a Christian ever so much, yet does he but deceive himself. For
they which are of Christ crucify their flesh with the affections and lusts
thereof.

This verse contains in it a singular consolation: for it teaches us that
the saints live not without concupiscence and temptations of the flesh,
nor yet without sins. It warns us therefore to take heed that we do not as
some did, who labored to be without all feeling of temptations or sins,
as though they had been very senseless blocks and without all affections.
Assuredly Mary felt great grief and sorrow of heart when she missed her
son (Luke 2). David in the Psalms complains that he is almost
swallowed up with excessive sorrow for the greatness of his temptations
and sins. Paul also complains that he has battles without and terrors
within (2 Corinthians 7:5), and that in his flesh he serves the law of sin.

Therefore, the saints of the schoolmen are like the Stoics, who imagined such wise men as in the world were never yet to be found. And by this foolish persuasion, which proceeds from the ignorance of this doctrine of Paul, the schoolmen brought both themselves and others into horrible desperation.

When I was a monk I often wished that I might once see the life of some saint or holy man. In the meantime, I imagined such a saint living in the wilderness abstaining from meat and drink, and living only with roots of herbs and cold water. For thus writes St. Jerome in a certain place: "As touching meats and drinks I say nothing, forasmuch as it is excess, that even such as are weak and feeble should use cold water, or eat any sodden thing." But now in the light of the gospel we plainly see who they are whom Christ and His Apostles call saints: not they who live a single life, or observe days, meats, apparel, and such other things, or in outward appearance do other great works, but they which believe that they are sanctified and cleansed by the death and blood of Christ. So Paul everywhere calls them holy, the children and heirs of God. Whosoever then believes in Christ, whether he or she is man or woman, bond or free, is a saint; not by his own works, but by the works of God.

With great rejoicing I give thanks to God that He has abundantly and above measure granted unto me that which I so earnestly desired of Him when I was a monk: for He has given me the grace to see not one but many saints, yes, an infinite number of true saints, not such as the schoolmen have devised, but such as Christ Himself and His Apostles describe; of which number I also, by the grace of God, am one. For I am baptized, and I do believe that Christ my Lord by His death has redeemed and delivered me from all my sins, and has given to me eternal righteousness and holiness.

Let us now learn by the Holy Scriptures that all they who faithfully believe in Christ are saints. The world has in great admiration the holiness of Benedict, Gregory, Bernard, Francis, and such like, because it hears that they have done certain rare and excellent works. Doubtless Hilary, Cyril, Athanasius, Ambrose, Augustine and others were saints also, who lived not so severe a life as they did, but were conversant among men, and did eat common meats, drank wine, and used clean and comely apparel, so that in a manner there was no difference between them and other honest men as touching the common custom, and the use of things necessary for this life. These men taught the faith of Christ sincerely and purely, without any superstition; they resisted heretics, they purged the Church from innumerable errors; their company and familiarity was comforting to many, and especially to those which were afflicted and heavyhearted, whom they raised up and comforted by the Word of God. For they did not withdraw themselves from the company of men, but they executed their offices where most people were.

These things declare who are the true saints indeed, and which is to be called a holy life: not the life of those who lurk in caves and dens, who make their bodies lean with fasting, who wear hair, and do other like things with this persuasion and trust, that they shall have singular reward in heaven above all other Christians; but of those who are baptized and believe in Christ, which put off the old man with his works—but not at once, for concupiscence remains in them so long as they live.

Therefore, we rightly confess in the articles of our belief that we believe there is a holy Church. It is invisible, and therefore her holiness cannot be seen; for God hides her and covers her with infirmities, with sins, with errors, with various forms of the cross and offenses, that according to the judgment of reason it is nowhere to be seen. They who are ignorant of this, when they see the infirmities and sins of those who are baptized, have the Word and believe it, are offended, and judge them not to pertain to the Church. Meanwhile, they dream that the hermits and monks are the Church because they do certain superstitious works which reason magnifies and highly esteems. Therefore, they judge them to be saints and to be the Church. In so doing they change the article of faith from ''I believe that there is a holy Church'' to ''I see that there is a holy Church.'' Such is not true holiness.

But thus teach we, that the Church has no spot nor wrinkle, but is holy, and yet through faith only in Christ Jesus. She is holy in life by abstaining from the lusts of the flesh, but yet not in such sort that she is delivered from all evil desires, or purged from all wicked opinions and errors. For the Church always confesses her sins, and prays that her faults may be pardoned (Matthew 6:12); also, she believes in the forgiveness of sins. Let Christians then endeavor to avoid the works of the flesh; but the desires they cannot avoid.

It is very profitable therefore for the godly to feel the uncleanness of their flesh, lest they should be puffed up with some vain opinion of the righteousness of their own works, as though they were accepted before God for the same. This feeling humbles them, that they are constrained to fly unto Christ their mercy-seat. In Him they find a sound and perfect righteousness. Thus they continue in humility because of the uncleanness which yet remains in their flesh, for which if God would judge them, they should be found guilty of eternal death. But because they lift not up themselves proudly against God, they come forth into the Presence of God, and pray that for His sake their sins may be forgiven them; God spreads over them an infinite heaven of grace, and does not impute to them their sins, for Christ's sake.

> *19, 20a—The works of the flesh are manifest, which are these;*
> *Adultery, fornication, uncleanness, lasciviousness, idolatry, witch-*
> *craft.*

Paul does not recite all the works of the flesh, but uses only a representative number. First, he reckons up the kinds of lusts, as adultery, fornication, uncleanness, lasciviousness. Now, not only carnal lust is a work of the flesh, but he numbers also among the works of the flesh idolatry and witchcraft.

Idolatry

All religion whereby God is worshiped without His Word and commandment is idolatry. And the more holy and spiritual it seems to be in outward show, so much the more dangerous and pernicious it is. For it turns men away from faith in Christ, and causes them to trust to their own strength, works and righteousness. In Christ alone the Father is well pleased: whoso hears Him and does that which He has commanded, the same is beloved because of the Beloved. He commands us to believe His Word, and to be baptized, and not to devise any new worshiping or service of God.

I have said before that the works of the flesh are known to all men. But idolatry has such a goodly show and is so spiritual, that it is known but to very few, that is, only to them who believe in Christ.

Hereby it is plain that Paul calls flesh whatever is in man, comprehending all the three powers of the soul, that is, the will that lusts, the will that is inclined to anger, and the understanding. The works of the will that lusts are adultery, fornication, uncleanness, and such like. The works of the will inclined to wrath are quarrelings, contentions, murder, and such other. The works of understanding or reason are errors, false religions, superstitions, idolatry, heresies, and such like. It is very necessary for us to know these things, for this word "flesh" has been so darkened that it is understood to be nothing else but the accomplishing of fleshly lust. But here we see that Paul reckons idolatry and heresy among the works of the flesh. Although religion may seem to be ever so holy and spiritual, yet it is nothing else but a work of the flesh, an abomination and idolatry against the gospel, against faith, and against the true service of God. This do the faithful see, for they have spiritual eyes.

Witchcraft

Of witchcraft I have spoken before in the third chapter. This vice was very common before the light and truth of the gospel was revealed. When I was a child, there were many witches who bewitched both cattle and men, but especially children, and did great harm also to the crops by tempests and hailstorms which they caused by their enchantments. But now in the light of the gospel these things are not so commonly heard of, for the gospel thrusts the devil out of his seat with all his illusions. But now he bewitches men much more horribly, namely, with spiritual sorcery and witchcraft.

Paul reckons witchcraft among the works of the flesh, which is not a work of fleshly lust but a kind of idolatry. For witchcraft covenants with the devils; superstition or idolatry covenants with God, though not with the true God, but with a counterfeit God. So idolatry is indeed a spiritual witchcraft. As witches enchant cattle and men, so idolaters go about to bewitch God, and to make Him as they imagine Him. Now they imagine Him to be such a one as will justify them, not of His mere grace and through faith in Christ, but because of their works of their own choosing, and in recompense thereof will give them righteousness and life everlasting. But while they go about to bewitch God, they bewitch themselves. For if they continue in this wicked opinion which they conceive of God, they shall die in their idolatry and be damned.

Sects

By the name of *sects* Paul means here not those divisions or contentions which rise sometimes in the government of households or of nations for worldly and earthly matters, but those which rise in the Church about doctrine, faith, and works. Heresies, that is to say, sects, have always been in the Church. Among Christians, the Word, faith, worship, religion, sacraments, Christ, God, heart, soul, mind, and will are all one and common to all; and as touching outward behavior, although there are various conditions of life and differing vocations, the spiritual unity is not hindered. And they which have this unity of the Spirit can certainly judge all sects, which otherwise no man could understand.

Drunkenness, Gluttony

Paul does not say that to eat and drink are works of the flesh, but to be drunken and to overeat, which of all other vices are most common at this day. Whoever is given to this more than beastly excess, let him know that he is not spiritual, no matter how much he boasts himself so to be, for he follows the flesh and performs the works thereof. Paul would therefore that Christians should flee drunkenness and overeating, living soberly and moderately without all excess, lest by pampering the flesh they should be provoked to wantonness. But it is not sufficient only to restrain this outrageous wantonness and lust of the flesh which follows drunkenness and overeating; but also the flesh when it is most sober and in his best temperance must be subdued and repressed, lest it fulfill his lusts and desires. For it often comes to pass that even they who are most sober are tempted most of all; as Jerome writes of himself: "My face was pale with fasting, and my mind was inflamed with fleshly desires in my cold body, and although my flesh was half dead already, yet the flames of carnal lusts boiled within me." Hereof I myself also had experience when I was a monk. The heat therefore of carnal lust is not quenched by fasting only, but we must be aided also by the Spirit, that is, by meditation of God's Word, faith, and prayer. Indeed, fasting represses the gross assaults of fleshly lust; but the desires of the flesh are overcome not by abstinence from meat and drink, but only by earnest meditation on the Word of God and invocation of Christ.

And Such Like

For it is impossible to reckon up all the works of the flesh.

21b—Of the which I tell you before, as I have also told you in time past, that they which do such things shall not inherit the kingdom of God.

This is a very hard and a terrible saying, but yet very necessary against false Christians and careless hypocrites who brag of the gospel, of faith and of the Spirit, and yet in all security they perform the works of the flesh. But chiefly the heretics, being puffed up with opinions of spiritual matters are altogether carnal; therefore, they perform and fulfill the desires of the flesh, even with all the powers of the soul. Therefore most necessary it was that so horrible and terrible a sentence should be pronounced by the Apostle against such obstinate hypocrites, that some of them being terrified by this severe sentence may begin to fight against the works of the flesh, by the Spirit.

22, 23—But the fruit of the Spirit is love, joy, peace, longsuffering, gentleness, goodness, faith, meekness, temperance.

The Apostle says not, the works of the Spirit, as he said the works of the flesh, but he adorns these Christian virtues with a more honorable name, calling them the fruit of the Spirit. For they bring with them most excellent fruits and maximum usefulness, for they that have them give glory to God, and with the same do allure and provoke others to embrace the doctrine and faith of Christ.

Love

It might have been enough to have said "love," and no more; for love extends itself into all the fruits of the Spirit. And in 1 Corinthians 13, Paul attributes to love all the fruits which are done in the Spirit, when he says: "Love is patient, courteous," etc. Notwithstanding, he would set it here by itself among the rest of the fruits of the Spirit, and in the first place, thereby to admonish the Christians that before all things they should love one another, giving honor one to another through love, every man esteeming better of another than of himself, because they have Christ and the Holy Ghost dwelling in them, and because of the Word, baptism, and other gifts of God which Christians have.

Joy

This is the voice of the bridegroom and of the bride, that is to say, sweet cogitations of Christ, wholesome exhortations, pleasant songs or psalms, praises and thanksgiving, whereby the godly do instruct, stir up, and refresh one another. Therefore, God loves not heaviness of spirit; He hates comfortless doctrine, heavy and sorrowful cogitations, and loves cheerful hearts. For therefore has He sent His Son, not to oppress us with heaviness and sorrow, but to cheer up our souls in Him. For this cause the prophets, the Apostles, and Christ Himself exhort us, yes, they command us to rejoice and be glad: "Rejoice greatly, O daughter of Zion; shout, O daughter of Jerusalem: behold, thy King cometh unto thee" (Zechariah 9:9). And in the Psalms it is often said: "Be joyful in the Lord." Paul says: "Rejoice in the Lord always." And Christ says: "Rejoice because your names are written in heaven." Where this joy of the Spirit is, there the heart inwardly rejoices through faith in Christ, with full assurance that

He is our Savior and our Bishop, and outwardly it expresses this joy with words and gestures. Also, the faithful rejoice when they see that the gospel spreads abroad, that many are won to the faith, and that the kingdom of Christ is enlarged.

Peace

Both towards God and men Christians are to be peaceable and quiet; not contentious, nor hating one another, but bearing one another's burden through longsuffering or perseverance, without which peace cannot continue. Therefore, Paul puts it next after peace.

Longsuffering or Perseverance

A man not only bears adversities, injuries, reproaches, and such like, but also with patience waits for the amendment of those who have done him any wrong. When the devil cannot by force overcome those which are tempted, then he seeks to overcome them by stretching their patience. For he knows that we are earthen vessels, which cannot long endure and hold many knocks and violent strokes; therefore, with long continuance of temptations he overcomes many. To vanquish his continual assaults we must use longsuffering, which patiently looks not only for the amendment of those which do us wrong, but also for the end of those temptations which the devil raises up against us.

Gentleness

Christians must not be sharp and bitter, but gentle, mild, courteous and fair spoken, and such as make others to delight in their company. They can wink at other men's faults, and will be well contented to yield and give place to others, contented to bear with those who are froward and intractable, as someone said: "Thou must know the manners of thy friend, but thou must not hate them." Such a one was our Savior Christ. It is said of Peter that he wept often as he remembered the sweet mildness of Christ. It is an excellent virtue and most necessary in every kind of life.

Goodness

This is when a man willingly helps others in their necessity by giving, lending, and such other means.

Faith

When Paul reckons faith among the fruit of the Spirit, he speaks not of faith in Christ, but of the sincerity of one man towards another. He says in 1 Corinthians 13 that charity "believeth all things." Therefore, he that has this faith is not suspicious, but of a sincere and single heart. Although he is deceived, and finds himself to be mocked, yet such is his mildness that he lets it pass. Briefly, he gives credit to all men, but he puts not his trust in any man. On the contrary, where this virtue is lacking, men are suspicious, froward, wayward, dogged; they give place to nobody, give credit to nobody, they can suffer nothing. Whatever is well said or done by another, they cavil and slander it, and whoso will not laud and magnify them, is hateful to them. Therefore, it is impossible for them to keep charity, friendship, concord, and peace with men. But if these virtues are taken away, what is this life, but biting and devouring each another? Faith therefore in this verse is when one man gives credit to another. For what manner of life should we lead in this world, if one man should not credit another?

Meekness

This is when a man is not lightly moved or provoked to anger. There are infinite occasions in this life which provoke men to anger, but the godly overcome them by meekness.

Temperance

This is a sobriety or modesty in the whole life of man, which virtue Paul sets against the works of flesh. He would therefore that Christians should live soberly and chastely, that they should not be adulterers, fornicators, nor wantons; and if they cannot live chastely, he would have them marry: also, that they should not be contentious or quarrelers, that they should not be given to drunkenness or gluttony, but that they should abstain from all these things.

23b—Against such there is no law.

The righteous has no need of any law to admonish or to constrain him; without constraint of the law, he willingly does those things which the law requires. Therefore, the law cannot accuse and condemn those who believe in Christ. Indeed, the law accuses and terrifies their consciences, but Christ vanquishes it with all its terrors and threatenings. To them therefore the law is utterly abolished, and has no right to accuse them. They have received the Holy Ghost by faith, who will not suffer them to be idle. Although the flesh resist, yet they walk after the Spirit. So a Christian accomplishes the law inwardly by faith and outwardly by works.

24—And they that are Christ's have crucified the flesh with the affection and lusts.

True believers are no hypocrites. Therefore, let no man deceive himself; for whoever belongs to Christ has crucified the flesh with all the vices and lusts thereof. For the saints are inclined to sin, and do neither fear nor love God so perfectly as they ought to do. They are provoked to anger, to envy, to impatience, to carnal lust, and such emotions, but they do not yield to them because they crucify the flesh with all the passions and vices thereof. They do this not only when they repress the wantonness of the flesh with fasting and other exercises, but also when they walk according to the Spirit; that is, when they, being armed with the Word of God, with faith and with prayer, do not obey the lusts of the flesh.

When they resist the flesh, they nail it to the Cross with the affections and desires thereof, so that although the flesh is yet alive, yet can it not perform that which it would do, forasmuch as it is bound both hand and foot, and fast nailed to the Cross. The faithful then so long as they live here crucify the flesh; that is to say, they feel the lusts thereof, but they obey them not.

25—If we live in the Spirit, let us also walk in the Spirit.

The Apostle reckoned heresy and envy among the works of the flesh, and pronounced sentence against those who are envious, and who are authors of sects, that they should not inherit the kingdom of God. Now, as if he had forgotten that which he said a little before, he again reproves those who provoke and envy one another. Why? Was it not sufficient to have done it once? Indeed, he does it purposely: for he takes occasion here to inveigh against that execrable vice of vainglory, which was the cause of the troubles that were in all the churches of Galatia, and has been always most pernicious to the Church of Christ. Therefore in his Epistle to Titus, he would not that a proud man should be ordained a bishop. For pride (as Augustine truly said) is the mother of all heresies, or rather the headspring of all sin and confusion.

Now, vainglory or arrogance has always been a common poison in the world. There is no village in which someone or other would not be counted wiser and be more esteemed than all the rest. But they are chiefly infected with this disease who stand upon their reputation for learning and wisdom. In this case no man will yield to another, according to this saying: You shall not easily find a man who will yield to others the praise of wit and skill. But this vice is not so hurtful in private persons as it is in them that have any charge in the Church. In civil government it is not only a cause of troubles and ruins of states, but also the troubles and alterations of kingdoms and empires.

But when this poison creeps into the Church, it cannot be expressed how hurtful it is. Therefore, Paul earnestly exhorts the ministers of the Word to flee this vice, saying: "If we live in the Spirit." For where the Spirit is, it renews men and works in them new emotions: that is to say, whereas they were before vainglorious, wrathful and envious, it makes them now humble, gentle, and patient. Such men seek not their own glory, but the glory of God; they do not provoke one another, or envy one another, but give place one to another.

Now, as nothing is more dangerous to the Church than this execrable vice, so is there nothing more common: for when God sends forth laborers into His harvest, sooner or later Satan raises up his ministers also, who will in no wise be counted inferior to those that are rightly called. Here rises dissension. The wicked will not yield one hair's breadth to the godly; for they dream that they far surpass them in wit, in learning, in godliness, in spirit and other virtues. Much less ought the godly to yield to the wicked, lest the doctrine of faith come in danger. Moreover, such is the nature of the ministers of Satan that they can make a goodly show that they are very charitable, humble, lovers of concord, and are endued with other fruits of the Spirit; also, they protest that they seek nothing else but the glory of God and the salvation of men's souls, and yet are they full of vainglory, doing all things for no other end but to get praise and estimation among men. To be short, they think that godliness is gain, and that the ministry of the Word is delivered unto them that they may get fame and esteem. Wherefore they cannot but be authors of dissensions and sects.

Since the vainglory of the false apostles was the cause that the churches of Galatia were troubled and forsook Paul, this mischief gave the Apostle occasion to write this whole epistle. And if he had not so done, all his travail bestowed in preaching the gospel among the Galatians would have been spent in vain.

Not only does the Apostle Paul inveigh against the false apostles, which in his time troubled the churches of Galatia, but also he foresaw in spirit that there should be an infinite number of such, even to the world's end, who being infected with this pernicious vice should thrust themselves uncalled into the Church, boasting of the Spirit and heavenly doctrine, and under this pretense should quite overthrow the true doctrine and faith. Many such have we also seen in these days who, not being called, have thrust themselves into the Kingdom of the Spirit, that is to say, into the ministry of the Word; and by this hypocrisy they have purchased themselves fame and esteem, that they are great teachers of the gospel, and such as live in the Spirit and walk according to the same. But because the glory of these false teachers consisted in men's mouths and not in God, it could not be firm and stable; but, according to Paul's prophecy, it turned to their own confusion, and their end was destruction. For "the ungodly shall not stand in the judgment, but are like the chaff, which the wind driveth away" (Psalms 1:4).

The same judgment remains for all who in preaching the gospel seek their own things and not the things of Jesus Christ. For the gospel is not delivered to us that we should seek our own praise and glory thereby, or that the people should honor and magnify us who are its ministers, but to the end that the benefit and glory of Christ might be preached and published, and that the Father might be glorified in His mercy offered to us in Christ His Son, whom He delivered for us all, and with Him has given us all things. The gospel sets forth unto us heavenly and eternal things, which are not our own, which we have neither done nor deserved; but it offers these things to us who are unworthy. Why should we then seek praise and glory thereby? He therefore who seeks his own glory in the gospel speaks of himself; and he that speaks of himself is a liar, and there is unrighteousness in him. Contrariwise, he that seeks the glory of Him that sent him is true, and there is no unrighteousness in him (John 7:18).

Paul therefore gives earnest charge to all the ministers of the Word, saying, "If we live in the Spirit, let us also walk in the Spirit," that is to say: let us abide in the doctrine of truth which has been taught to us, in brotherly love and spiritual concord; let us preach Christ and the glory of God in simplicity of heart, and let us confess that we have received all things of Him; let us not think more of ourselves than of others; let us raise up no sects. For this is not to walk rightly, but rather to range out of the way, and to set up a new and perverse way of walking.

Hereby we may understand that God, of His special grace, makes the teachers of the gospel subject to the cross and to all kinds of afflictions, for the salvation of themselves and of the people; for otherwise they could by no means suppress and beat down this beast which is called

` vainglory. For if no persecution, no cross or reproach followed the doctrine of the gospel, but only praise, reputation, and glory among men, then would all the professors thereof be infected and perish through the poison of vainglory. Jerome said that he had seen many who could suffer great inconveniences in their body and goods, but none who could despise their own praises. For it is almost impossible for a man not to be puffed up when he hears anything spoken in the praise of his own virtues. Paul, although he had the Spirit of Christ, said that there was given to him the messenger of Satan to buffet him, so he would not be exalted out of measure through the greatness of his revelations. Therefore Augustine said very well: If a minister of the Word be praised, he is in danger; if a brother despise or dispraise him, he is also in danger. He that hears me preach the Word ought to honor me for the Word's sake; if he honors me, he does well, but if I am proud thereof, I am in danger. Contrariwise, if he despise me, I am out of danger; but he is not.

Wherefore we must by all means honor the ministry of the Word. We must also reverence one another, according to that saying: "in honour preferring one another" (Romans 12:10). But wherever this is done, sooner or later the flesh is tickled with these praises and waxes proud. For there is none who would not rather be praised than dispraised, except perhaps someone who is so well established that he will be moved neither by praises nor reproaches. A woman said of David (2 Samuel 14): "My lord the king is like an angel of God, which will neither be moved with blessing nor cursing." Likewise Paul said: "By honour and dishonour, by evil report and good report" (2 Corinthians 6:8). Such men are neither puffed up with praise, nor thrown down with dispraise, but endeavor simply to set forth the benefit and glory of Christ, and walk orderly in order to seek the salvation of souls. Contrariwise, they who wax proud in hearing of their own praises, not seeking the glory of Christ but their own, walk not orderly.

If you are praised, know that it is not you but Christ to whom all praise is due. For in that you teach the Word purely and live godly, these are not your own gifts, but the gifts of God; therefore, you are not praised, but God in you. When you acknowledge this, you walk orderly, and are not puffed up with vainglory: "For what hast thou that thou didst not receive?" (1 Corinthians 4:7).

If we far surpass others in spiritual gifts, we acknowledge these to be the gifts of God, given for the edifying of the Body of Christ; therefore, we are not proud of them. For we know that more is required of them to whom much is committed than of them who have received but little. Moreover, we know that there is no respect of persons before God. A poor artificer faithfully using the gift which God has given him pleases God no less than a preacher of the Word; for he serves God in the same faith and with the same Spirit. Wherefore we ought to regard the lowliest Christians no less than they regard us.

26a—Let us not be desirous of vain glory.

He who praises a man as a man, is a liar; for there is nothing praiseworthy in him, but all things are worthy of condemnation. Therefore, as touching our person, this is our glory, that all men have sinned and are guilty of everlasting death before God. But the case is otherwise when our ministry is praised. Wherefore we must not only wish, but also to the uttermost of our power endeavor, that men may magnify it and have it in due reverence; for this shall turn to their salvation. Therefore, when our ministry is praised, we are not praised for our own sakes, but we are praised in God and in His holy name (Psalms 89:17).

26b—Provoking one another, envying one another.

Here he describes the effect and fruit of vainglory. He who teaches any error, or is an author of any new doctrine, provokes others; and when they do not approve and receive his doctrine, he begins to hate them most bitterly. Indeed, there are some teachers who are inflamed against us because we will not give place to them and approve their errors. We did not first provoke them but, rebuking certain abuses in the Church, and faithfully teaching the article of justification, have walked in good order. But they have taught many things contrary to the Word of God. Because we would not lose the truth of the gospel, we have set ourselves against them and have condemned their errors.

14

Burden-Bearing

Galatians 6:1–18

1a—Brethren, if a man be overtaken in a fault, ye which are spiritual, restore such an one in the spirit of meekness.

This is another goodly moral precept, and very necessary in this day. The Sacramentarians seize upon this place and infer from it that we ought in patience to yield somewhat unto fallen brethren, and to conceal their error through love, which "believeth all things, hopeth all things, endureth all things" (1 Corinthians 13:7), especially seeing that Paul plainly teaches that they who are spiritual should restore them that err with a spirit of meekness.

Nothing has so grievously troubled me these many years as that discord in doctrine, whereof even the Sacramentarians themselves know very well that I was not the author, if they will but confess the truth. For that which I did believe and teach in the beginning concerning justification, the sacraments, and all other articles of Christian doctrine, that do I yet at this day believe and profess; and I do daily pray to Christ that He will preserve and strengthen me in that faith and confession unto the day of His coming in glory.

With such as love Christ and faithfully teach and believe His Word, we offer not only to keep peace and concord, but also to bear their infirmities and sins, and to restore them when they are fallen in a spirit of meekness.

So Paul did bear the infirmity and fall of the Galatians and others when they heartily repented. So he received into grace that unchaste Corinthian (2 Corinthians 2:7); also he reconciled Onesimus the runaway slave, whom he had begotten at Rome in his bonds, to his master (Philemon 17). Therefore, that which he teaches here concerning the duty of supporting the weak and restoring the fallen, that did he also himself perform, but towards such only as could be healed: that is to say, such as heartily confessed their sin, their fall, their error, and returned to the right way. Contrariwise, towards the false apostles, which were obstinate and defended their doctrine, saying that it was not error, but the very truth, he showed himself very hard and severe: "I would," said he, "they were even cut off which trouble you"; and "He that troubleth you shall bear his judgment, whosoever he be" (Galatians 5:10, 12). Again: "Though we or an angel from heaven . . . let him be accursed" (Galatians 1:8).

So neither can we allow this cause to be made of small account, because He whose cause it is, is great. In the articles of faith nothing ought to seem little or of small account to us, and such as we could forego. Wherefore let them first be at one with us in Christ, that is, let them confess their sin and correct their error; and if then we should be lacking in the spirit of meekness, they might justly accuse us.

He who diligently weighs the words of the Apostle may plainly perceive that he speaks not of heresies or sins against doctrine, but of sins into which a man falls not wilfully, but of infirmity. And so Paul uses gentle and fatherly words, not calling it error or sin, but a "fault." Again, to the intent to diminish the fault, he adds: "If any man be overtaken," that is to say, be beguiled by the devil or the flesh. This term of "man" also helps to diminish and qualify the matter. As if he should say: What is so proper to man as to fall, to be deceived, and to err? So says Moses in Leviticus 6:3: "They are wont to sin like men." Wherefore this is a sentence full of comfort, which once in a terrible conflict delivered me from death. As saints in this life do not only live in the flesh, but now and then also fulfill the lust of the flesh, Paul teaches how such men that are fallen should be dealt with, namely, that they which are strong should raise up and restore them again with the spirit of meekness.

Those who are in the ministry of the Word should not forget the fatherly and motherly affection which Paul here requires of them. And of this precept he has set forth an example (2 Corinthians 2:6), where he said that it was sufficient that he who was excommunicated was rebuked by many, and that they ought now to forgive him and comfort him, lest he should be swallowed up with overmuch sorrow. Wherefore I beseech you (says he) use charity towards him. Therefore, pastors and ministers must indeed sharply rebuke those which are fallen, but when they see that they are sorrowful for their offenses, then let them begin to raise them up again, to comfort them, and to diminish and qualify their faults as much as they can, lest they that be fallen be swallowed up with overmuch heaviness. As the Holy Ghost is precise in maintaining and defending the doctrine of faith, so is He mild and pitiful in forbearing and qualifying men's sins, if they which have committed them are sorrowful for the same.

Let them therefore to whom the charge of men's consciences is committed learn by this commandment of Paul how they ought to handle those who have offended. Brethren (says he), if any man be overtaken, do not trouble him or make him more sorrowful; be not bitter toward him; do not reject or condemn him, but amend him and raise him up again; and by the Spirit of mildness restore that which in him is decayed by the deceit of the devil or by the weakness of the flesh. For the kingdom whereunto you are called is a kingdom not of terror or heaviness, but of boldness, joy, and gladness. Therefore, if you see any brother cast down and afflicted by occasion of sin which he has committed, run to him and, reaching out your hand, raise him up again, comfort him with sweet words, and embrace him with motherly arms. A brother ought to comfort his fallen brother with a loving and meek spirit. For God would not have those that are bruised to be cast away, but to be raised up, as the Psalm says (145:14). For God has bestowed more upon them than we have done, that is to say, the life and blood of His own Son. Wherefore we ought also to receive, to aid and comfort such with all mildness and gentleness.

1b—Considering thyself, lest thou also be tempted.

This is a very necessary admonition to beat down the sharp dealings of pastors who show no pity in raising up and restoring again them who are fallen. "There is no sin (says Augustine) which any man has done, but another man may do the same." We stand on slippery ground; therefore, if we grow proud, there is nothing so easy to us as falling. It was well said therefore of one in the book called *The Lives of the Fathers,* when it was told him that one of his brethren was fallen into whoredom: "He fell yesterday (said he), and I may fall today." Paul therefore adds this earnest admonition, that pastors should not be rigorous and unmerciful towards the offenders or measure their own holiness by other men's sins; but they should bear a motherly affection towards them, and think thus with themselves: This man is fallen; it may be that I also shall fall more dangerously and more shamefully than he did. If they who are so ready to judge and condemn others would consider their own sins, they should find the sins of others who are fallen to be but motes and their own sins to be great beams (Matthew 7:3).

"Let him that thinketh he standeth take heed lest he fall" (1 Corinthians 10:12). If David, who was so holy a man, full of faith and the Spirit of God, did fall so grievously, and stricken in years, was overthrown with youthful lusts, why should we presume of our own constancy? God by such examples shows to us, first our own weakness, that we should not wax proud; then He shows us His judgments, that He cannot bear pride. Paul therefore says, "Considering thyself, lest thou also be tempted."

2—Bear ye one another's burdens, and so fulfil the law of Christ.

This is a gentle commandment, to which he joins a great commendation. The law of Christ is the law of love. Christ, after He had redeemed us, renewed us, and made us His Church, gave us no other law but the law of mutual love: "A new commandment I give unto you, That ye love one another, as I have loved you," and: "By this shall all men know that ye are my disciples'' (John 13:34). And to love is not to wish well one to another, but to bear one another's burdens, that is, to bear those things which are grievous unto you, and which you would not willingly bear. Therefore, Christians must have strong shoulders and mighty bones, that they may bear flesh, that is, the weakness of their brethren. Love therefore is mild, courteous, patient, not in receiving, but in giving; for it is constrained to wink at many things, and to bear them. Faithful teachers see in the Church many errors and offenses which they are compelled to bear. In household affairs there are many things done which displease the master of the house. But if we bear and wink at our own vices and offenses which we daily commit, let us also bear other men's faults, according to this saying: ''Bear ye one another's burdens,'' and: ''Thou shalt love thy neighbour as thyself.''

Seeing then there are vices in every state of life and in all men, Paul sets forth the law of Christ to the faithful, whereby he exhorts them to bear one another's burdens. They who do not, plainly witness that they understand not one jot of the law of Christ, the law of love, which, as Paul says (1 Corinthians 13) believes all things, hopes all things, and bears all the burdens of the brethren. This commandment then of bearing one another's burdens belongs not to them who deny Christ; neither does it belong to those who continue in their sins. On the contrary, it belongs to those who hear the Word of God and believe, and yet fall into sin, and after they are admonished, not only receive such admonition gladly, but also detest their sin and endeavor to amend; these, I say, are they who are overtaken with sin, and have the burdens that Paul commands us to bear. In this case, let us not be rigorous and merciless; but after the example of Christ, who bears and forbears such, let us bear and forbear them also; for if He punish not such (which He might justly do), much less ought we so to do.

3—For if a man think himself to be something, when he is nothing, he deceiveth himself.

Here again he reprehends the authors of sects, and paints them out in their right colors. Of all men they are the proudest, and dare take upon them all things. And this is what Paul says here: they think themselves to be something, that is, that they have the Holy Ghost, that they understand all the mysteries of the Scriptures, that they cannot err and fall, and need not the remission of sins.

So Paul adds very well, that they are nothing; but that they deceive themselves with the foolish persuasions of their own wisdom and holiness. They understand nothing therefore either of Christ or of the law of Christ; if they did, they would say: Brother, you are infected with such a vice, and I am infected with another. God has forgiven me ten thousand talents, and I will forgive you a hundred pence (Matthew 18:23). But when they require all things so exactly and will in no wise bear the burdens of the weak, they offend many with their severity, who begin to shun them and seek not counsel at their hands, nor regard what they teach. Pastors ought to behave toward those over whom they have taken charge, that they might love and reverence them, not for their person, but for their office and Christian virtues which ought to shine in them. Paul therefore in this verse rightly paints out such severe and merciless saints when he says: "They think themselves to be something," that is to say, being puffed up with their own foolish opinions and vain dreams, they have a marvelous persuasion of their own knowledge and holiness, and yet in very deed they are nothing and deceive themselves. Such men are well described in the third chapter of the Apocalypse in these words: "Thou sayest, I am rich, and increased with goods, and have need of nothing; and knowest not that thou art wretched, and miserable, and poor, and blind, and naked."

4—But let every man prove his own work, and then shall he have rejoicing in himself alone, and not in another.

He goes forward in rebuking those proud and vainglorious fellows. For the desire of vainglory is the occasion of all evils.

And this is the property of those who are infected with this poison of vainglory, that they have no regard whether their ministry is pure or not;

this only they seek, that they may have the praise of the people. So the false apostles, when they saw that Paul preached the gospel purely to the Galatians, and that they could not bring any better doctrine, began to find fault at those things which he had faithfully taught, and to prefer their own doctrine before the doctrine of Paul; and by this subtlety they won the favor of the Galatians, and brought Paul into hatred among them. There the proud and vainglorious do join these three vices together: first, they are greedy of glory; secondly, they are marvelous witty and wily in finding fault with other men's doings and sayings; and thirdly, when they have once gotten a name, they dare venture upon all things. Therefore, they are pernicious and pestilent fellows, for they seek their own, and not that which is of Jesus Christ (Philippians 2:21).

Against such Paul speaks here. As if he should say: Such vainglorious spirits do their work, that is to say, they teach the gospel to this end that they may win praise and esteem among men. When they have gotten this esteem, they begin to reprehend the sayings and doings of other men, and highly commend their own. By this subtlety they bewitch the minds of the people, who, because they have itching ears, are not only delighted with new opinions, but also rejoice to see those teachers which they had before abased and defaced by these new upstarts and glorious heads.

Let every man be faithful in his office; let him not seek his own glory, nor depend upon the praise and commendation of the people, but let his only care be to do his work truly, that is, let him teach the gospel purely. And if his work is sincere and sound, let him assure himself that he shall lack no praise either before God or among the godly. Wherefore, being furnished with the armor of righteousness on the right hand and on the left (2 Corinthians 6:7), let him say with a constant mind: I began not to teach the gospel to the end that the world should magnify me, and therefore I will not shrink from that which I have begun, if the world hate, slander, or persecute me. Such a one teaches the Word and attends his office faithfully, without any worldly respect, that is, without regard of glory or gain, without the strength, wisdom, or authority of any man. He leans not to the praise of other men.

Wherefore he who truly and faithfully executes his office cares not what the world speaks of him; he cares not whether the world praises or dispraises him, but he has praise in himself, which is the testimony of his conscience and glory in God. He may therefore say with Paul: This is our rejoicing, even the testimony of our conscience, that in simplicity and sincerity before God, and not in fleshly wisdom, but in the grace of God, we have conducted ourselves in the world and especially in our relations with you in the holiness and sincerity that are from God (2 Corinthians 1:12). This glory is uncorrupt and steadfast; for it depends not on other men's judgments, but on our own conscience, which bears us witness that we have taught the Word purely, ministered the sacraments rightly, and have done all things well. Therefore, it cannot be taken from us.

The other glory which the vainglorious seek is uncertain and most perilous, for it consists in the mouth and opinion of the people. Therefore can they not have the testimony of their own conscience, that they have done all things with simplicity and sincerity for the advancing of the glory of God only and the salvation of souls. For they seek to be counted famous through the work and labor of their preaching, and be praised of men. They have therefore a glory, a trust, and a testimony; but before men, not in themselves nor before God. The godly do not desire glory after this manner.

If Paul had had his praise before men, and not in himself, he should have been compelled to despair when he saw many cities, countries, and all Asia fall from him; when he saw so many offenses and slanders, and so many heresies follow his preaching.

So at this day, if our trust, our glory and rejoicing depended upon the judgment and favor of men, we should die with very anguish and sorrow of heart. We have nothing before men but reproach. But we rejoice and we glory in the Lord; and therefore we cheerfully and faithfully attend upon our office which He hath given us and which we know is acceptable to Him. Thus doing, we care not whether our work pleases or displeases the devil, whether the world love or hate us. For we, knowing our work to be well done, and having a good conscience before God, go forward

by honor and dishonor, by evil report and good report (2 Corinthians 6:8).
This, says Paul, is to have glory in yourself.

This admonition is very necessary against that vice of vainglory. The
gospel is a doctrine which brings with it the cross and persecution.
Therefore, Paul calls it the Word of the cross and of offense (1
Corinthians 1:18). It has not always steadfast and constant disciples.
Many there be that make profession thereof and embrace it, which
tomorrow, being offended with the cross, will fall from it and deny it.
They therefore that teach the gospel to the end that they may obtain the
favor and praise of men, must needs perish, and their glory be turned to
shame when the people cease to reverence and applaud them. Wherefore
let all pastors and ministers of the Word learn to have glory in
themselves, and not in the mouth of other men. If there are any that praise
them, as the godly are inclined to do, let them receive this glory but as a
shadow of true glory; and let them think the substance of glory to be
indeed the testimony of their own conscience. He that does so regards not
his own glory, but his only care is to do his office faithfully. When he thus
proves his own work, he has glory and rejoicing in himself, which no
man can take from him; for he has it surely planted and grounded in his
own heart, and not in other men's mouths, whom Satan can very easily
turn away, and can make that mouth and tongue now full of cursing,
which a little before was full of blessing.

Therefore, says Paul, if you are desirous of glory, seek it where it
should be sought, not in the mouths of other men, but in your own heart.
But if you glory in other men, and not in yourselves, that shame and
confusion which you have inwardly in yourselves shall not be without
reproach and confusion outwardly before men. This have we seen in
certain fantastical spirits who misused the gospel to gain praise among
men, contrary to the second commandment. Therefore, after their inward
confusion, there followed also an outward confusion and shame among
men, according to that saying: "They which despise Me, shall be
despised" (1 Samuel 2:30). Contrariwise, if we seek first the glory of
God by the ministry of the Word, then surely our glory will follow,
according to that saying: "Him that honoreth Me, I will glorify." To

conclude, let every man endeavor purely and faithfully to teach the Word, and let him have an eye to nothing else but the glory of God and the salvation of souls: then shall his work be faithful and sound; then shall he have glory and rejoicing in his own conscience, so that he may boldly say, this my doctrine and ministry pleases God. And this is indeed an excellent glory.

This verse may also be well applied to those works which are done of the faithful in every state of life. If a magistrate, a householder, a servant, a schoolmaster, a scholar abide in his vocation, and do his duty therein faithfully, not troubling himself with those works which pertain not to his vocation, he may glory and rejoice in himself; for he may say: I have done the works of my vocation appointed to me by God with such faithfulness and diligence as I was able. Therefore, I know that this work, being done in faith and obedience to God, pleases God.

This clause, "in himself" must so be understood that God is not excluded: that is, that every man may know, in what godly state of life soever he be, that his work is a divine work; for it is the work of his vocation having the commandment of God.

5—For every man shall bear his own burden.

It is extreme madness for you to seek glory in another, and not in yourself. For in the agony of death and the last judgment, it shall not profit you that other men have praised you; for other men shall not bear your burden, but you shall stand before the judgment seat of Christ, and shall bear your burden alone. There your praisers shall not help you. For when we die, these voices of praise shall cease. And in that day, when the Lord shall judge the secrets of all hearts, the witness of your own shall judge the secrets of all hearts, the witness of your own conscience shall stand either with you or against you (Romans 2:15). Against you, if you have your glory in other men; with you, if you have it in yourself, that is to say, if your conscience bears witness that you have fulfilled the ministry of the Word sincerely and faithfully, having respect to the glory of God only and the salvation of souls, or have otherwise done your duty according to your calling. And these words: "Every man shall bear his own judgment," are very vehement, and ought so to terrify us that we should not be desirous of vainglory.

This moreover is to be noted, that we are not discussing the matter of justification, where nothing avails but mere grace and forgiveness of sins, which is received by faith alone; where all our works, even our best works, have need of forgiveness of sins, because we do them not perfectly. But this is another case. He treats not here of the remission of sins, but compares true works and hypocritical works. Although the work or ministry of a godly pastor is not so perfect but that he has need of forgiveness of sins, yet in itself it is good and perfect in comparison to the ministry of the vainglorious man.

So our ministry is good and sound, because we seek the glory of God and the salvation of souls. No works can quiet the conscience before God; yet is it necessary that we should persuade ourselves that we have done our work uprightly, truly, and according to God's calling, that is, that we have not corrupted the Word of God, but have taught it purely. This testimony of conscience we have need of, that we have done our duty uprightly in our function and calling, and led our life accordingly. So far ought we then to glory as touching our works as we know them to be commanded of God, and that they please Him. For everyone in the last judgment shall bear his own burden, and therefore other men's praises shall not help or profit him.

6—Let him that is taught in the word communicate unto him that teacheth in all good things.

Here he preaches to the hearers of the Word, commanding them to bestow all good things upon those who have instructed them in the Word. I have sometimes marveled why the Apostles commanded the churches so diligently to nourish their teachers. For when I was a monk I saw that all men gave abundantly to the building and maintaining of goodly temples, to the increasing of the revenues and livings of those which were appointed to their service. The riches of the bishops and the rest of the clergy so increased that they had in possession the best and most fruitful grounds. Therefore, I thought that Paul had commanded this in vain, seeing that all manner of good things were not only abundantly given to the clergy, but also they overflowed in wealth and riches. I thought that men ought rather to be exhorted to withhold their hands from giving, than encouraged to give any more.

But now, since the gospel has been preached and published, we find by experience how poorly this commandment of nourishing and maintaining the pastors and ministers of God's Word is observed, which Paul here and in other places so diligently repeats and beats into the heads of his hearers.

And as often as I read the exhortations of Paul, whereby he persuades the churches either that they should nourish their pastors, or should give somewhat to the relief of the poor saints in Jewry, I do greatly marvel, and am ashamed that so great an Apostle should be constrained to use so many words for the obtaining of this benefit of the congregations. Writing to the Corinthians, he treats of this matter in two whole chapters (2 Corinthians 8 and 9). I would be loath to defame Wittenberg as he defamed the Corinthians in begging so carefully for the relief and succor of the poor. But this is the lot of the gospel when it is preached, that not only is no man willing to give anything for the finding of ministers and maintaining of scholars, but men begin to spoil, to rob, and to steal, and with diverse crafty means to beguile one another.

Now therefore we begin to understand how necessary this commandment of Paul is as touching the maintenance of the ministers of the Church. For Satan can abide nothing less than the light of the gospel. Therefore, when he sees that it begins to shine, then does he rage, and goes about with all main and might to quench it. And this he attempts in two ways: first, by lying spirits and force of tyrants, and then by poverty and famine. Because he could not oppress the gospel in this country by heretics and tyrants, he attempted to bring it to pass the other way, that is, by withdrawing the living of the ministers of the Word, to the end that they, being oppressed with poverty and necessity, should forsake their ministry, and so the miserable people being destitute of the Word of God, should become in time as savage as wild beasts. And Satan helps forward this horrible enormity by ungodly magistrates in the cities, and also by noblemen in the country, who take away the Church goods whereby the ministers of the gospel should live, and turn them to wicked uses.

Moreover, Satan turns men from the gospel by overmuch fullness. For when the gospel is diligently and daily preached, many being glutted therewith begin to loathe it, and little by little become negligent and untoward to all godly exercises. Again, there is no man that will now bring up his children in good learning and much less in the study of the Holy Scripture, but they employ them wholly to gainful arts or occupations. All these are Satan's practices, to no other end but that he may oppress the gospel in this our country without any violence of tyrants or subtle devices of heretics.

It is not without cause therefore that Paul warns the hearers of the gospel to make their pastors and teachers partakers with them in all good things. "If we (says he to the Corinthians) have sown unto you spiritual things, is it a great thing if we shall reap your carnal things?" (1 Corinthians 9:11). The hearers therefore ought to minister carnal things to them of whom they have received spiritual things. But both husbandmen, citizens and gentlemen at this day abuse our doctrine, that under the color thereof they may enrich themselves. They are not only prodigal givers; they are now become stark thieves and robbers and will not bestow one farthing upon the gospel or the ministers thereof, nor give anything for the relief and succor of the poor saints; which is a certain token that they have lost both the Word and faith, and that they have no spiritual goodness in them. For it is impossible that such as are godly indeed should suffer their pastors to live in necessity and penury. Whoso will not serve God in a little, and that to his own inestimable benefit, let him serve the devil in much to his extreme and utter confusion.

In that he says "in all his goods," it is not to be taken that all men are bound to give all that they have to their ministers, but that they should maintain them liberally, and give them that whereby they may be well able to live.

7a—Be not deceived; God is not mocked.

Some of our countrymen despise our ministry. They think it to be but
a sport and a game; therefore, they go about to make their pastors subject
to them like servants and slaves. And if we had not so godly a prince,
they would have driven us out of the country.

Paul threatens such tyrants and mockers of God, who so carelessly and
proudly scorn preachers, and yet pretend to be evangelicals and to
worship Him very devoutly. "Be not deceived," says he, "God is not
mocked," that is to say, He does not suffer Himself to be mocked in His
ministers. For He says: "He that despiseth you despiseth me" (Luke
10:16). Also He said unto Samuel: "They have not rejected thee, but
me" (1 Samuel 8:7). Therefore, although God defers His punishment for
a season, yet He will some day punish this contempt of His Word.
Moreover, God will not suffer His ministers to starve for hunger, but even
when the rich men suffer scarcity and hunger, He will feed them, and in
the days of famine they shall have enough.

7b—For whatsoever a man soweth, that shall he reap.

All these verses emphasize the same thing: that ministers should be
nourished and maintained. For my part, I do not gladly interpret such
verses: for they seem to commend us, and so they do indeed. Moreover,
if a man stand much in repeating such things to his hearers, it seems like
covetousness. Notwithstanding, men must be admonished, that they may
know that they ought to yield to their pastors both reverence and a
necessary living. Our Savior Christ teaches the same thing in the tenth
chapter of Luke: "Eating and drinking such things as they give: for the
labourer is worthy of his hire." And Paul says in another place: "Do ye
not know that they which minister about holy things live of the things of
the temple? and they which wait at the altar are partakers with the altar?
Even so hath the Lord ordained that they which preach the gospel should
live of the gospel" (1 Corinthians 9:13, 14).

8—For he that soweth to his flesh shall of the flesh reap corruption;
but he that soweth to the Spirit shall of the Spirit reap life
everlasting.

This metaphor of sowing he applies to the particular matter of nourishing and maintaining the ministers of the Word, saying: "He that soweth to the Spirit," that is to say, he that cherishes the teachers of God's Word, does a spiritual work, and "shall reap everlasting life."

Here rises a question, whether we deserve eternal life by good works? We have treated this matter very largely before in the fifth chapter. And very necessary it is, after the example of Paul, to exhort the faithful to exercise their faith by good works. For if works follow not faith, their faith is no true faith. Therefore, the Apostle says: "He that soweth to his flesh," that is to say, he that gives nothing to the ministers of God's Word, that man shall of the flesh reap corruption, not only in the life to come, but also in this present life. For the goods of the wicked shall waste away, and they themselves also at length shall shamefully perish. The Apostle seeks to stir up his hearers to be liberal and beneficial toward their pastors and preachers. But what a misery is it, that the perverseness and ingratitude of men should be so great, that the churches should need this admonition?

9—And let us not be weary in well doing: for in due season we shall
reap, if we faint not.

The Apostle passes from the particular to the general and exhorts to all good works. As if he should say: Let us be liberal and bountiful not only towards the ministers of the Word, but also towards all other men, and that without weariness. For it is an easy matter for a man to do good once or twice; but to continue, and not to be discouraged through the ingratitude and perverseness of those to whom he has done good, that is very hard. Therefore, he not only exhorts us to do good, but also not to be weary in doing good. And to persuade us, he adds: "For in due time we shall reap without weariness." As if he said: Wait and look for the perpetual harvest that is to come and then shall no ingratitude or perverse dealing of men be able to pluck you away from well-doing; for in the harvesttime you shall receive most plentiful increase and fruit of your seed.

10—As we have therefore opportunity, let us do good unto all men, especially unto them who are of the household of faith.

As if he had said: Let us do good while it is day; for when night comes we can no longer work (John 9:4). Indeed, men work many things when the light of truth is taken away, but all in vain; for they walk in darkness, and know not whither they go, and therefore all their life, works, sufferings and death are in vain. And by these words he touches the Galatians. As if he should say: Except you continue in the sound doctrine which you have received of me, your working of much good, your suffering of many troubles, and such other things profit you nothing. As he said before in the third chapter: "Have ye suffered so many things in vain?" And by a new figure of speech he terms those the household of faith, who are joined with us in the fellowship of faith, among whom the ministers of the Word are the chiefest, and then all the rest of the faithful.

11—Ye see how large a letter I have written unto you with mine own hand.

He closes his epistle with an exhortation to the faithful, and with a sharp rebuke or invective against the false apostles. Before, he cursed the false apostles. Now, he accuses them very sharply in order to turn away the Galatians from their doctrine. The teachers which you have (says he) are such as first regard not the glory of Christ and the salvation of your souls, but only seek their own glory. Secondly, they avoid the Cross. Thirdly, they understand not those things which they teach, much less do they perform them.

These false teachers, being accused of the Apostle for three such enormities, were to be avoided of all men. But yet all the Galatians obeyed not this warning of Paul.

"Behold," says he, "what a letter I have written unto you with mine own hand." This he says to move them, and to show his motherly affection towards them. As if he should say: I never wrote so long an epistle with my own hand to any other church as I have done to you. For as for his other epistles, as he spoke, others wrote them, and afterwards he subscribed his salutation and name with his own hand, as it is to be seen in the end of his epistles.

12—As many as desire to make a fair show in the flesh, they constrain you to be circumcised; only lest they should suffer persecution for the cross of Christ.

Your teachers (says Paul) do not regard the glory of Christ and your salvation, but seek only their own glory. Because they are afraid of the Cross, they preach circumcision and the righteousness of the flesh. Here is to be noted a certain vehemence in the word *constrain*. For circumcision is nothing of itself: but to be compelled to circumcision, and when a man has received it, to put righteousness and satisfaction therein—and if it is not received, to make it a sin—that is an injury to Christ.

13—For neither they themselves who are circumcised keep the law; but desire to have you circumcised, that they may glory in your flesh.

Although they keep the law outwardly in their actions; yet in keeping it, they keep it not. For without the Holy Ghost the law cannot be kept. But the Holy Ghost cannot be received without Christ; and where the Holy Ghost dwells not, there dwells an unclean spirit. Therefore, all that he does regarding the law is mere hypocrisy and double sin. For an unclean heart does not fulfill the law, but only makes an outward show thereof, and so is it more confirmed in wickedness and hypocrisy.

And this may also be applied to other works. He that works, prays, or suffers without Christ, works, prays and suffers in vain; for all that is not of faith is sin (Romans 14:23). It profits a man therefore nothing at all to be outwardly circumcised, to fast, to pray, or to do any other work, if he is a despiser of grace and is puffed up with the presumption of his own righteousness, which are horrible sins against the First Table; and afterward follow also other sins against the Second Table, as disobedience, carnal lust, furiousness, wrath, hatred, and such other. Therefore, he says very well that they who are circumcised keep not the law, but only pretend that they keep it.

What do the false apostles mean when they would have you to be circumcised? Not that you might become righteous, but that they may glory in your flesh. They are (says he) deceitful, shameless and vain spirits, who serve their own belly and hate the Cross.

These words, "That they may glory in your flesh," are very effective. As if he should say: They have not the Word of the Spirit; therefore, it is impossible for you to receive the Spirit by their preaching. Outwardly they observe days, times, sacrifices, and such other things according to the law, whereby you reap nothing else but unprofitable labor and damnation. Contrariwise, we glory not in your flesh, but glory as touching your spirit, because you have received the Spirit by our preaching (Galatians 3:2).

14a—But God forbid that I should glory, save in the cross of our Lord Jesus Christ.

The Apostle closes up the matter with great vehemence of spirit. As if he should say: This carnal ambition of the false apostles is so dangerous a poison that I wish it were buried in hell, for it is the cause of the destruction of many. But let them glory in the flesh, and let them perish with their cursed glory. As for me, I desire no other glory but that whereby I glory and rejoice in the Cross of Christ. After the same manner speaks he also in Romans 5: "We glory in tribulations"; also in 2 Corinthians 12: "I will glory in mine infirmities." Here Paul shows what is the glory and rejoicing of the Christians, namely, to glory and to be proud in tribulation, reproaches, infirmities.

The world not only thinks that Christians are wretched and miserable men, but also with a misguided zeal hates, persecutes, condemns and kills them as heretics and rebels. But because they do not suffer these things for murder, theft, and such other wickedness, but for the love of Christ, therefore they glory in tribulation and in the Cross of Christ, and are glad with the Apostles that they are counted worthy to suffer rebuke for the name of Christ (Acts 5:41). So must we glory at this day, because we suffer for Christ's sake, our Lord and Savior, whose gospel we truly preach.

Now our glorying is increased by these two things: first, because we are certain that our doctrine is sound and perfect: secondly, because our cross and suffering is the suffering of Christ. Therefore, when the world persecutes and kills us, we have no cause to complain or lament, but we ought rather to rejoice and be glad. Indeed, the world judges us to be unhappy and accursed; but on the other side, Christ, who is greater than the world, and for whom we suffer, pronounces us to be blessed, and wills us to rejoice: "Blessed are ye (says He), when men revile you, and persecute you, and say all manner of evil against you falsely for my sake. Rejoice, and be exceeding glad" (Matthew 5:11).

Moreover, the Cross of Christ does not signify that piece of wood which Christ did bear upon His shoulders, and to which He was afterwards nailed, but generally it signifies all the afflictions of the faithful, whose sufferings are Christ's sufferings (2 Corinthians 1:5): "The sufferings of Christ abound in us"; again: "Now rejoice I in my sufferings for you, and fill up that which is behind the afflictions of Christ in my flesh for his body's sake, which is the church" (Colossians 1:24). The Cross of Christ therefore generally signifies all the afflictions of the Church which it suffers for Christ; which He Himself witnessed when He said: "Saul, Saul, why persecutest thou me?" (Acts 9:4). Saul did no violence to Christ, but to His Church. But he that touches it, touches the apple of His eye. There is a more lively feeling in the head than in the other members of the body. And this we know by experience; for the little toe or the least part of a man's body being hurt, the head forthwith feels the grief thereof. So Christ our head makes all our afflictions His own, and suffers also when we, who are His Body, suffer.

It is profitable for us to know these things, lest we should be swallowed up with sorrow when we see that our adversaries cruelly persecute, excommunicate, and kill us. But let us think with ourselves, after the example of Paul, that we must glory in the cross which we bear, not for our sins, but for Christ's sake. If we consider only the sufferings which we endure, they are not only grievous but intolerable; but when we may say: Thy sufferings, O Christ, abound in us; or, as it is said in Psalms 44:22: "For thy sake we are killed all the day," then these sufferings are not only easy, but also sweet, according to this saying: "My yoke is easy, and my burden is light" (Matthew 11:30).

It is well known that we at this day suffer the hatred and persecution of our adversaries for none other cause, but because we preach Christ faithfully and purely. If we would deny Him, and approve their pernicious errors and wicked religion, they would not only cease to hate and persecute us, but would also offer us honor, riches, and many goodly things. Because therefore we suffer these things for Christ's sake, we may truly rejoice and glory with Paul in the Cross of our Lord Jesus Christ, that is to say, not in riches, in power, and in the favor of men, but in afflictions, weakness, sorrow, fightings in the body, terrors in the spirit, persecutions, and all other evils. Wherefore we trust it will shortly come to pass that Christ will say to us, "He that toucheth you toucheth the apple of mine eye" (Zechariah 2:8). As if He had said: He that hurteth you, hurteth Me; for if you did not preach My Word and confess Me, you should not suffer these things. So says He also in John: "If ye were of the world, the world would love his own: but because I have chosen you out of the world, therefore the world hateth you" (John 15:19).

14b—By whom the world is crucified unto me, and I unto the world.

This is Paul's manner of speaking: "The world is crucified to me," that is, I judge the world to be damned; "and I am crucified to the world,'' that is, the world again judges me to be damned. Thus we crucify and condemn one another. I abhor all the doctrine, righteousness, and works of the world as the poison of the devil. The world again detests my doctrine and deeds, and judges me to be seditious, a pernicious, a pestilent fellow, and a heretic. So at this day the world is crucified to us, and we to the world.

The Apostle speaks here of a matter of great importance: every faithful man judges that to be the wisdom, righteousness, and power of God which the world condemns as the greatest folly, wickedness, and weakness. And contrariwise, that which the world judges to be the highest religion and service of God, the faithful know to be nothing else but blasphemy against God. So the godly condemn the world, and again the world condemns the godly. But the godly have the right judgment on their side, for the spiritual man judges all things (1 Corinthians 2:15).

Wherefore the judgment of the world is as contrary to the judgment of the godly as God and the devil are contrary the one to the other. For as God condemns the doctrine and works of the devil, and contrariwise, as the devil condemns and overthrows the Word and the works of God, so the world condemns the doctrine and life of the godly, calling them most pernicious heretics and troublers of the public peace; and again, the godly call the world the son of the devil. This is Paul's meaning when he says, ''Whereby the world is crucified to me, and I unto the world.'' Now the world does not only signify in the Scriptures ungodly and wicked men, but the very best, the wisest, and holiest men that are of the world.

And here, by the way, he covertly touches the false apostles. As if he should say: I utterly hate and detest all glory which is without the Cross of Christ, as a cursed thing. For the world, with all the glory thereof, is crucified to me, and I to the world. Wherefore accursed be all they who glory in your flesh, and not in the Cross of Christ. Paul therefore witnesses by these words that he hates the world with a perfect hatred of the Holy Ghost; and again, the world hates him with a perfect hatred of a wicked spirit. As if he should say: It is impossible that there should be any agreement between me and the world. What shall I then do? Shall I give place and teach those things which please the world? No; but with a stout courage I will set myself against it, and will as much despise and crucify it as it despises and crucifies me.

To conclude, Paul here teaches how we should fight against Satan. As we see Paul himself to have stoutly despised the world, so we also should despise the devil the prince thereof, with all his forces, deceits, and hellish furies. O Satan, the more you hurt me, the more proud and stout I am against you, and laugh you to scorn. The more you terrify me and seek to bring me to desperation, so much the more confidence and boldness I take, not by my own power, but by the power of Christ my Lord, whose strength is made perfect in my weakness. Therefore, when I am weak, then I am strong (2 Corinthians 12:9).

15—For in Christ Jesus neither circumcision availeth any thing, nor uncircumcision, but a new creature.

It may seem that he should rather have said: Either circumcision or uncircumcision avails somewhat, seeing these are two contrary things. But now he denies that either the one or the other avails. As if he should have said: We must mount up higher; for circumcision and uncircumcision are things of no such importance that they are able to obtain righteousness before God. True it is, that they are contrary the one to the other; but this is nothing as touching Christian righteousness, which is not earthly, but heavenly, and therefore it consists not in corporal things. Therefore, whether you are circumcised or uncircumcised, it is all one thing: for in Christ Jesus neither the one nor the other avails anything at all.

The Jews were greatly offended when they heard that circumcision availed nothing. They easily granted that uncircumcision availed nothing; but they could not abide to hear that so much should be said of the law and circumcision, for they fought even unto blood for the defense of the law and circumcision. But Paul says another thing is much more excellent and precious than circumcision or uncircumcision. In Christ Jesus, says he, neither circumcision nor uncircumcision, neither single life nor marriage, neither meat nor fasting avail. All these things, yes, the whole world with all its laws and righteousness avail nothing for justification.

The wisdom of the flesh does not understand this, ''for it receiveth not the things of the Spirit of God'' (1 Corinthians 2:14). Therefore, it must have righteousness to stand in outward things. But we are taught out of the Word of God that there is nothing under the sun which avails unto righteousness before God, but Christ only. Whatever the Gentiles can do with all their wisdom, righteousness, laws, power, kingdoms and empires, it avails nothing in Christ Jesus. Also, whatever the Jews are able to do with their Moses, their law, their circumcision, their worshipings, their Temple, their kingdom and priesthood, it avails nothing. Wherefore in Christ Jesus we must not dispute of the laws, either of the Gentiles or of the Jews; we must simply pronounce that neither circumcision nor uncircumcision avails anything.

Are the laws then evil? Not so. They are good and profitable in their place and time. Moreover, we use also in the churches certain ceremonies and laws; not that the keeping of them avails unto righteousness, but for good order, example, quietness, and concord, according to that saying: ''Let all things be done decently and in order'' (1 Corinthians 14:40). But if laws are set forth and urged as though the keeping of them did justify a man, or the breaking thereof did condemn him, they ought to be taken away and abolished.

Now, a new creature, whereby the image of God is renewed, is not made by any counterfeiting of good works, but it is created by Christ after the image of God in righteousness and true holiness. When works are done, they bring indeed a new outward appearance with which the world and the flesh are delighted, but not a new creature: for the heart remains wicked as it was before. Therefore, a new creature is the work of the Holy Ghost, who cleanses our heart by faith and works the fear of God, love, chastity, and other Christian virtues, and gives power to bridle the flesh and to reject the righteousness and wisdom of the world. Here is created another sense and another judgment, that is to say, altogether spiritual, which abhors those things that before it greatly esteemed.

Wherefore the changing of garments and other outward things is not a new creature; rather, it is the renewing of the mind by the Holy Ghost. When the heart has conceived a new light, a new judgment, and new motions through the gospel, the outward senses are also renewed. For the ears desire to hear the Word of God and not the traditions and dreams of men; the mouth and tongue do not vaunt of their own works, righteousness and rules, but they set forth with joy the singular mercy of God offered to us in Christ. These changes bring a new spirit, a new will, new senses, and new operations of the flesh, so that not only do the eyes, ears, mouth, and tongue see, hear and speak otherwise than they did before, but the mind also approves differently than it did before. For before, being blinded with errors and darkness, it imagined God to be a merchant who would sell us His grace for our works and merits. But now, in the light of the gospel, it assures us that we are counted righteous by faith only in Christ.

16a—And as many as walk according to this rule, peace be on them, and mercy.

This he adds as a conclusion. This is the only and true rule wherein we ought to walk, namely, the new creature, which is neither circumcision nor uncircumcision, but the new man created after the image of God in righteousness and true holiness which inwardly is righteous in the spirit, and outwardly is holy and clean in the flesh. Blessed be that rule whereof Paul speaks in this verse; by which we live in the faith of Christ and are made new creatures, without any coloring or counterfeiting. To them who walk after this rule belongs peace, that is, the favor of God, forgiveness of sins, quietness of conscience, and mercy, that is to say, help in afflictions and pardon for the remnants of sin which remain in our flesh. Yes, although they who walk after this rule may be overtaken with any fault or fall, yet they are the children of grace and peace, and mercy upholds them so that their sin and fall shall not be laid to their charge.

16b—And upon the Israel of God.

As if he said: They are the Israel of God who with faithful Abraham believe the promises of God offered already in Christ, whether they be Jews or Gentiles, and not they who are begotten of Abraham, Isaac, and Jacob after the flesh. This matter is largely handled before in the third chapter.

17a—From henceforth let no man trouble me.

He concludes his epistle with a certain indignation. As if he said: I have faithfully taught the gospel as I have received it by the revelation of Jesus Christ; whoso will not follow it, let him follow what he will, so that hereafter he trouble me no more. At a word, this is my sentence, that Christ which I have preached is the only High Priest and Savior of the world. Therefore, either let the world walk according to this rule, of which I have spoken here and throughout all this epistle, or else let it perish forever.

17b—For I bear in my body the marks of the Lord Jesus.

This is the true meaning of Paul in this place: the marks that are in my body show well enough whose servant I am. If I sought to please men, requiring circumcision and the keeping of the law as necessary to salvation, I needed not to bear these marks in my body. But because I am the servant of Jesus Christ and walk after a true rule, that is, I openly teach and confess that no man can obtain the favor of God, righteousness, and salvation but by Christ alone, therefore I must bear the badges of Christ my Lord. These are not marks of mine own procuring, but are laid upon me against my will by the world and the devil, for no other cause but that I preach Jesus to be Christ.

The stripes and sufferings therefore which he bore in his body, he calls marks; the anguish and terror of spirit he calls the fiery darts of the devil. Of these sufferings he makes mention everywhere in his epistles, as Luke also does in the Acts. "I think," says he, "that God hath set forth us the apostles last, as it were appointed to death: for we are made a spectacle unto the world, and to angels, and to men'' (1 Corinthians 4:9). Again: ''Unto this hour we both hunger, and thirst, and are naked, and are buffeted, and have no certain dwellingplace, and labour, working with our own hands: we are reviled, we are persecuted, we are defamed, we are made as the filth of the world, and are the offscouring of all things'' (1 Corinthians 4:11). Also in another place: ''In much patience, in afflictions, in necessities, in distresses, in stripes, in imprisonments, in tumults, in labours, in watchings, in fastings'' (2 Corinthians 6:4). And again: ''In labors more abundant, in stripes above measure, in prison more frequent, in deaths oft. Of the Jews five times received I forty stripes save one. Thrice was I beaten with rods, once was I stoned, suffered shipwreck, a night and a day I have been in the deep; In journeyings often, in perils of waters, in perils of robbers, in perils of mine own countrymen, in perils by the heathen, in perils in the city, in perils in the wilderness, in perils in the sea, in perils among false brethren'' (2 Corinthians 11:23 ff.).

These are the true marks of which the Apostle speaks in this verse; which we also at this day, by the grace of God, bear in our bodies for Christ's cause. For the world persecutes and kills us, false brethren deadly hate us, Satan inwardly in our heart with his fiery darts terrifies us, and for no other cause, but because we teach Christ to be our righteousness and life. These marks we choose not of any sweet devotion, neither do we gladly suffer them, but because the world and the devil do lay them upon us for Christ's cause, we are compelled to suffer them, and we rejoice with Paul in the Spirit that we bear them in our body; for they are a seal and most sure testimony of true doctrine and faith.

18—Brethren, the grace of our Lord Jesus Christ be with your spirit. Amen.

This is his last farewell. He ends the epistle with the same words with which he began it. As if he said: I have taught you Christ purely, I have entreated you, I have chided you, and I have let pass nothing which I thought profitable for you. I can say no more, but that I heartily pray that